'This book offers many ideas in restructuring residential and community-based care. Gerontologists representing different countries share their care perspectives, giving us fresh ideas to develop better programs for our elders and persons with dementia. I would highly recommend this book.'

Christopher J. Johnson, *PhD., Clinical Professor, Dementia and Aging Studies Program, Department of Sociology, Texas State University, U.S.A.*

'This book is timely and important. Due to an ageing population worldwide, there is an increasing need to provide insight into different perspectives of what constitutes good care for older people. Whether this is within families, communities or in long-term care facilities. Especially people with dementia, a disease which has high human and economic costs due to increasing care needs, need care which is characterised by good theoretical frameworks, is evidence-based and has the correct person-centred perspective. The goal of all care should be to provide the necessary support, but also to be mindful of older people's dignity and promote their independence and self-efficacy as much as possible. This book brings together expertise around the world to discuss examples of care for older people and as such fills an important area in the literature.'

Eef Hogervorst, *Professor of Biological Psychology, Director of Dementia Research at Loughborough University, UK, and Visiting Professor at Respati University Indonesia.*

'The book, *Care of Older Persons*, edited by Dr. Mala Kapur Shankardass, an expert on ageing issues, is a worthy and valuable resource covering a cross-section of ageing populations in ageing societies. The book highlights many care dimensions from varied perspectives in a meaningful way, providing great insights into concerns of care in different countries. It is a very significant and beneficial collection of chapters for scholars and researchers in the area.'

Lucy W. Maina, *Associate Professor of Sociology, Kenyatta University, Nairobi, Kenya; Chair, Kenya Association of Gerontology and Geriatrics; Former Secretary, IAGG-Africa Region.*

CARE OF OLDER PERSONS

This book explores the implications and significant ethical, social, economic and health challenges that an ageing world population presents. It provides valuable insights on concerns related to providing, organizing, planning and managing care for older persons in both formal and informal settings.

As the number of older persons increases rapidly around the globe, caring for them is a very important aspect of all ageing and aged societies. While in most countries the care of older persons is provided informally by family members, the changing social scene, family structures and work and employment patterns are leading many nations to create provisions for formal care through institutions or paid services of caregivers. This book offers perspectives on formal and informal care from countries such as Japan, the Netherlands, the USA, India, South Africa and Poland, among others. The essays in this book underline a rights-based approach and focus on ethical, social, economic, health and legal aspects of care as they pertain to the universal phenomena of ageing as well as the specific demographic and epidemiological realities of the selected countries. They discuss concerns such as long-term care provisions, catering to the needs of people affected by dementia, providing residential care, taking the needs of family care providers into account, the growing requirement for paid care workers and channelizing training of both skilled and semi-skilled care providers to suit the needs of older people.

This volume would be of interest to scholars and those working in the fields of sociology, health studies, age and ageing, psychology, social work, medical sciences, nursing and public policy. It will also be useful to NGO sector workers, administrators, as well as grassroots workers involved with the care of older persons.

Mala Kapur Shankardass, an international consultant, is an academician, researcher, writer and an activist with higher educational qualifications inclusive of doctoral and post-doctoral specialization in sociology, health social sciences, and gerontology. Now retired, she has 38 years of teaching experience and has held important positions as a senior faculty member at the University of Delhi, India. She continues to lecture at different academic departments in both Indian and foreign universities and is also involved with prestigious assignments with various institutions, including the United Nations.

CARE OF OLDER PERSONS

Emerging International Perspectives

Edited by Mala Kapur Shankardass

LONDON AND NEW YORK

Designed cover image: Getty Images

First published 2025
by Routledge
4 Park Square, Milton Park, Abingdon, Oxon OX14 4RN

and by Routledge
605 Third Avenue, New York, NY 10158

Routledge is an imprint of the Taylor & Francis Group, an informa business

© 2025 selection and editorial matter, Mala Kapur Shankardass; individual chapters, the contributors

The right of Mala Kapur Shankardass to be identified as the authors of the editorial material, and of the authors for their individual chapters, has been asserted in accordance with sections 77 and 78 of the Copyright, Designs and Patents Act 1988.

All rights reserved. No part of this book may be reprinted or reproduced or utilised in any form or by any electronic, mechanical, or other means, now known or hereafter invented, including photocopying and recording, or in any information storage or retrieval system, without permission in writing from the publishers.

Trademark notice: Product or corporate names may be trademarks or registered trademarks, and are used only for identification and explanation without intent to infringe.

British Library Cataloguing-in-Publication Data
A catalogue record for this book is available from the British Library

ISBN: 978-1-032-34566-6 (hbk)
ISBN: 978-1-032-86639-0 (pbk)
ISBN: 978-1-003-52843-2 (ebk)

DOI: 10.4324/9781003528432

Typeset in Sabon
by Deanta Global Publishing Services, Chennai, India

CONTENTS

List of Figures   *x*
List of Tables   *xiv*
Contributors   *xvi*
Foreword   *xxiii*
Acknowledgements   *xxvi*

PART I
Care perspectives   **1**

1   Care of older persons: A discourse analysis   3
    Mala Kapur Shankardass

2   Ethical challenges in the care of aging population:
    Experience from the United States of America   17
    Letha M. Joseph

3   Seniors' poverty in British Columbia, Canada: A social
    justice issue   32
    Karen Lok Yi Wong

4   End of life care and the ageing population: Asian perspectives   44
    Jagriti Gangopadhyay

viii Contents

5 Why restructuring residential care matters: A global perspective 59
   Sumana Das

6 Developing a model for caregiver's training and support 73
   Ruchika Kuba and G. Mythili

7 Emerging challenges of care of elderly: Need for newer strategies for nurses in India 93
   Sandhya Gupta

PART II
Family care, community care and long-term care **109**

8 Sense of belonging in community-based care among South African older persons: A rapid review 111
   Keshenaa Fakir, Erika Hitge, and Jaco Hoffman

9 Population ageing and care arrangements in later life in the Netherlands 140
   Louise Meijering and Tobias Vogt

10 Aged people care in Poland 157
    Artur Fabiś and Joanna K. Wawrzyniak

11 Care for the elderly in Singapore: Policies, delivery systems, and paradigms 173
    Ho Mun Wai

12 From policy to practice: A comparative Anglo-German view of long-term care provision for older people 201
    Ingrid Eyers, Kimberly Stoeckel, and Laura Allen

13 Canadian experience in providing care in long-term care homes 218
    Suraj Laxman Gopinathbirla and Kanwal Shankardass

14 Expanding policies for hiring foreign long-term care workers in Japan: Current status, challenges, and responses 230
    Noriko Tsukada

PART III
Dementia care   **263**

15 Formal community-based care: Older adults' experiences of home-based and day care services in South Africa   265
Maryna Rankin and Jaco R Hoffman

16 Caring for older people with dementia: A global perspective   280
Frances J. Morris

17 Caring for people with dementia in Australia   299
Claire Morrisby and Barbara Blundell

18 Care services for older adults with dementia in Türkiye   325
Isil Kalayci

19 Dementia care: Management and challenges in India   337
Esha Arora, Rhea Wason, and Ashish Goel

20 The San Lawrenz Dementia Friendly Community Pilot Project   347
Pauline Refalo and Maria Aurora Fenech

21 Epilogue on Care of Older Persons: What the future holds   374
Mala Kapur Shankardass

Index   377

LIST OF FIGURES

6.1	Model for caregiver portal	82
8.1	PRISMA flow diagram of search strategy and appraisal process	120
9.1	Median age of populations in Europe in 2020	141
9.2	Median age of Dutch provinces in 2019	142
9.3	Remaining life expectancy at age 65 for women (left) and men (right) in Dutch provinces 2019	144
11.1	Age distribution of resident population (Department of Statistics, 2020)	174
11.2	Age pyramid of resident population (Department of Statistics, 2020)	175
11.3	Resident old-age support ratio (Department of Statistics, 2020)	175
11.4	Framework of analysis	177
11.5	Healthcare industry transformation map (Ng, 2018)	180
11.6	Comparison of Eldershield and Careshield Life	183
11.7	Public housing development by the Housing and Development Board (HDB) in Singapore (HDB, 2020)	184
11.8	Layout of a 3Gen flat (HDB, 2020)	185
11.9	Ang Mo Kio Thye Hua Kwan Hospital located at the Yio Chu Kang Constituency is a community hospital (AMKH, 2020). It provides a comprehensive range of services including residential step-down care, palliative care, day care, dialysis services, etc.	190
11.10	Participation rates of residents in the workforce (Department of Statistics, 2020). Residents refer to Singapore citizens and permanent residents	192

List of Figures **xi**

11.11	Integrated model for policy development for the care of the elderly	198
12.1	Caregiving framework	205
13.1	Resident profile of long-term care homes in Ontario A) shows the split of male to female residents, B) shows the age distribution of residents, and C) shows selected medical conditions present in residents	220
14.1	Working age population (15–64), workforce, and number of care workers needed, 2007 and 2025 (tentative calculation)	231
14.2	Reasons for why certified care workers experienced changing jobs	232
14.3	JLPT levels required by administrators and LTC workers	247
14.4	Perceptions to accept foreign LTC workers	247
14.5	Perceptions toward three policy options (a). Increasing EPA Certified Care Worker Candidates. (b). Creating a New Status of Residence, "Nursing Care". (c). Adding a "Nursing Care" Job Category to the "*Ginou-jissyu*"(Technical Intern Training) Program	252
14.6	Reasons for why respondents agreed with adding a "Nursing Care" job category to the "*Ginou-Jissyu*" (Technical Intern Training) Program (MA)	253
14.7	Reasons for why respondents did not agree with adding a "Nursing Care" job	254
14.8	Reasons for why care workers chose their jobs (M.A.)	255
14.9	Reasons for why care workers quit their previous care-related jobs (M.A.)	256
19.1	Management of dementia	340
20.1	Changes in population structures in Malta by age groups and selected years (2013–2019)	348
20.2	Changes in population structures in Gozo and Comino by age groups and selected years (2013–2019)	348
20.3	Thematic data analysis was employed (Braun and Clarke, 2006; Jeong and Othman, 2016; Smith, Flower and Larkin, 2009; Noon, 2018; Smith and Osborn, 2007)	354
20.4	The ramp leading up to the church of San Lawrenz. As can be observed, there is no pavement leading to the ramp, which is positive especially for persons with mobility issues. However, the gradient of the ramp stood at 15.5%. According to the Global Designing Cities Initiative (n.d.), pedestrian ramps should have a gradient of not more than 1:10 (10%) or ideally 1:12 (8%). The ramp leading to the	

	Church was calculated as 1.4m:9m, leading to a gradient of 15.5%, affectively rendering the ramp to be steep	358
20.5	The Village Square with different shaded cobblestones, which potentially could have confused the older persons living with dementia when walking. There are no pavements, reducing the chances of falling incidents for older persons with mobility issues	359
20.6	Benches installed in the middle of the pavement, obstructing the sidewalk. Adequate height of the pavement which stood at 14 cm	359
20.7	Planters on the pavements	360
20.8	A discontinued pavement can be particularly dangerous considering the bend in this part of the road	360
20.9	A stone in the midst of the discontinued pavement. Vehicles are also parked against the wall, forcing pedestrians to walk straight on the road. Moreover, on the other side of the road, the pavement was discontinued through the installation of a ramp by a tenant with more planters on the other side of the pavement	361
20.10	Another example from a part of the village where the pavement is non-existent. A temporary outer wall built in front of a construction site. Construction objects were placed against the outer side of the wall, serving as an obstruction for pedestrians walking on that side of the road	362
20.11	Signage leading to the church of San Lawrenz. Signage is about 1.85 m from the pavement. The yellow colour of the sign blends with the stone colour of the houses in the background, possibly posing a challenge for older persons living with dementia to notice the sign. Signs should stand on their own on poles without other objects such as, in this case, mirrors. Mirrors can cause confusion to older persons living with dementia (Conners et al., 2014; Breen et al., 2001; Bartolotti et al., 2012). The planters on the pavement are obstructive to older persons living with dementia who might have mobility issues as well as visuospatial or depth perceptual issues	365
20.12	Signage with opposing directions to two separate locations within the village of San Lawrenz. The obstructive material on the pavement together with the building machinery, which the researchers noted at the time of the study	366

20.13 Sign at the entry of the village. The sign is too small to be noticed instantly, personifying the lack of awareness of the project amongst its own residents. A close-up image is provided in Figure 20.14   367
20.14 Close up of the entry sign to the village   367

LIST OF TABLES

4.1	Socio-demographic information of the respondents	47
6.1	Competencies for cognitive domain	77
6.2	Competencies for the Affective domain	77
6.3	Competencies for the psychomotor domain	78
6.4	Instructional strategies and delivery mechanisms of the three domains	80
7.1	Example of identified frailty risk factors (functional declines) and recommendations	100
9.1	Share of Dutch population aged 65 with difficulties with Activities of Daily Living and contribution of selected diseases and health conditions to years lived with disability	145
9.2	Care and support paid from the different provisions (Zorgwijzer, 2020)	148
11.1	Life expectancy of Singapore residents (Department of Statistics, 2020)	174
11.2	Singapore's total fertility rate (Department of Statistics, 2020)	174
11.3	Healthcare personnel in Singapore in 2009 and 2019 (Department of Statistics, 2020)	179
11.4	Indicative cost (for Singapore citizen after subsidies) of staying at public acute hospitals subsidised by the government (Evlanova, 2020)	187
11.5	Indicative cost of staying at private acute hospitals (Evlanova, 2020)	188
11.6	Healthcare establishments in Singapore (MOH, 2020)	189

11.7	Indicative cost of nursing homes in Singapore (Moneysmart, 2019)	190
11.8	Subsidy for staying in nursing home (Moneysmart, 2019)	191
11.9	Government expenditure on healthcare in Singapore (Department of Statistics, 2020)	197
13.1	Direct care staffing mix within St. Peter's Residence	225
14.1	List of status of residence categories (as of March 2023)	234
14.2	Pass rates of national examination for EPA-Certified Care Worker candidates (%)	236
14.3	Major responses to the four types of concerns	241
14.4	Characteristics of responding institutions for the elderly (N=722)	243
14.5	Characteristics of the respondents (administrators) (N=722)	245
14.6	Characteristics of the respondents (LTC workers) (N=586)	246
14.7	Averaged scores for factors relating to security and retention rates of LTC workers	248
14.8	Averaged scores for challenges to accept EPA/foreign LTC workers	250
20.1	Prevalence data of older persons living with dementia in Malta and Gozo	348
20.2	Profile characteristics of the older persons living with dementia and the informal carers (names are fictious)	356

CONTRIBUTORS

Laura D. Allen is a Post-Doctoral Researcher at the Erickson School of Aging Studies at the University of Maryland, Baltimore County. While completing her PhD at Bar-Ilan University in Israel, she was a grant recipient within the EU Horizon 2020 Marie Skłodowska-Curie Network EuroAgeism. She was also a Fulbright scholar in the Netherlands and has a BS in healthcare administration.

Esha Arora is a medical specialist at District Hospital, Mohali, Punjab. She has a particular interest in geriatrics and elderly care. She has completed an observership in geriatric medicine from the Royal Perth Hospital, Australia, and is an active member of ACAP (Asia Pacific Consortium of Active Ageing).

Barbara Blundell is a Senior Lecturer in Social Work at the Curtin School of Allied Health and a member of the dementia and ageing domain of the enAble Institute. Barbara's teaching and research focus on ageing and disability issues (including aged and disability care and caregiving), elder abuse, and advocacy and service and social policy responses to these issues.

Sumana Das is a State-Aided College Teacher in the Sociology Department at Jogamaya Devi College, which is affiliated with the University of Kolkata. She obtained first-class grades in MA Applied Sociology, and MPhil. She is currently pursuing a PhD at the University of Burdwan. Sumana has expertise in women's studies, Medical Sociology, Gerontology, and Research Methodology. She has participated in both major and minor ESRC-ICSSR projects as a Project Assistant. She has joined many National and International

Seminars and Webinar as a speaker. Additionally, she serves as a visiting faculty member in various medical and nursing colleges run by the West Bengal University of Health and Science. Sumana carries out duties as a moderator, Head Examiner, and in other administrative capacities. She has authored numerous book chapters, journal papers, and pieces covering various facets of her specialization.

Ingrid Eyers is an Anglo-German gerontologist who has worked extensively in the care sector and academia of England and Germany. Currently, Ingrid is an Adjunct Professor at the Global Center on Ageing at the Erickson School of Aging Studies at the University of Maryland, Baltimore County, USA.

Artur Fabiś has Habilitation in social sciences and a Doctorate of Humanities in the field of pedagogy. He is an andragogue and gerontologist. He serves as the coordinator of statutory research at the Pedagogical University of Cracow and is the author of reports on social research on learning in adulthood and old age. Currently, he is a professor in the Institute of Educational Sciences at the WSB University in Dąbrowa Górnicza. Fabiś is the author of two monographs, co-author of three monographs, and editor and co-editor of 18 multi-author monographs and issues of scientific journals. He is also the author and co-author of over 50 texts in multi-author monographs and scientific journals in Poland and abroad in the fields of andragogy and gerontology.

Keshenaa Fakir is a registered Clinical Psychologist with the Health Professions Council of South Africa (HPCSA) and the Health and Care Professions Council (HCPC) in the United Kingdom. She completed her Master's in Clinical Psychology at North West University (NWU). Keshenaa was a presenter at the 24th Association of Medical Councils of Africa (AMCOA) International Conference and 2nd runner-up in the three-minute thesis competition at NWU.

Maria Aurora Fenech graduated from the University of Nottingham with a PhD in Rehabilitation and Ageing, with the dissertation "Physical Restraint Use within Long Term Care Settings in Malta". She is a Senior Lecturer within the Department of Gerontology and Dementia Studies at the University of Malta, researching areas of elder abuse, care homes, and social aspects of dementia care.

Jagriti Gangopadhyay is currently an Assistant Professor at the Manipal Centre for Humanities, Manipal Academy of Higher Education (MAHE). She was awarded the Shastri Publication Grant by the Shastri Indo-Canadian Institute for her monograph, "Culture, Context and Aging of Older Indians:

Narratives from India and Beyond" (Springer). She has also co-edited the book "Eldercare Issues in China and India" (Routledge).

Ashish Goel is a Professor and the Head of the Department of Medicine at Dr. B.R. Ambedkar State Institute of Medical Sciences (AIMS Mohali). He is involved in the provision of geriatric services in the hospital. In his current institution, he is involved in teaching undergraduate medical students and has previously trained and guided several postgraduate students in Medicine. He is also the President of the Indian Academy of Geriatrics.

Suraj Laxman Gopinathbirla is a second-year internal medicine resident at McMaster University. He completed both his undergraduate studies within the Biomedical Discovery and Commercialization and subsequent medical education at McMaster University.

Sandhya Gupta, PhD (Geriatric Care) and MSc (Psychiatric Nursing), is a retired Associate Professor, Department of Mental Health Nursing, and was also formerly acting Principal, College of Nursing, AIIMS, New Delhi. She has been working in the field of Mental Health for the last 41 years and has been decorated with many prestigious awards. She is a member of various expert advisory committees, a reviewer for journals, and has over 135 publications in scientific journals.

Erika Hitge is a mental health practitioner in private practice in Johannesburg, South Africa. She completed a BA, Psychology Honours, MDIAC (Play Therapy), and PhD in Psychology. Erika is a research consultant and supervisor for North-West University. She contributes to public awareness about various psychology topics in social media, publications, and on radio and television.

Jaco R. Hoffman is Professor of Social Gerontology at Ageing and Generational Dynamics (AGenDA), Optentia Research Unit, North-West University, South Africa. He is also a Professorial Fellow at the Oxford Institute of Population Ageing, University of Oxford, UK, besides being Co-Director at the International Longevity Centre (ILC) South Africa and Honorary Professor at the IAA, Department of Medicine, Faculty of Health Sciences, University of Cape Town, Cape Town, South Africa.

Letha M. Joseph, Doctorate in Nursing Practice, University of North Carolina is an adult and gerontology certified nurse practitioner in the post-acute and long-term care unit of Veterans Affairs Healthcare System, Durham, North Carolina, USA. Also a consulting associate/ clinical instructor at the Duke University School of Nursing, earlier was an Adjunct Nursing Faculty at

Simmons University, Boston, full-time faculty at Holy Family Hospital, New Delhi, and at King Faisal Hospital, Taif, KSA, and Al Maktoum Hospital, DOHMS-Dubai.

Isil Kalayci works as an Associate Professor in the Faculty of Health Sciences, Department of Gerontology at Suleyman Demirel University, Isparta, Türkiye.

Ruchika Kuba, MD in PSM, is presently the Director of the School of Health Sciences at IGNOU, India. She has coordinated the development and implementation of many open and distance learning programmes for health professionals and para-professionals in geriatrics, MCH, hospital waste management, patient safety, etc. She has coordinated national and international projects and adopted innovative models like the flipped classroom, three-tier, and blended teaching.

Louise B. Meijering is a full professor in Health Geography at the Population Research Centre, Faculty of Spatial Sciences at the University of Groningen, the Netherlands. Her research is centred around well-being and mobility in relation to the socio-spatial environment. Louise has led several externally funded research projects, including Meaningful Mobility (2019–2024), which is funded through a prestigious ERC Starting Grant. In the project, she and her team study the indoor and outdoor mobility of older adults in the Netherlands, the UK, and India.

Frances J. Morris, granddaughter, daughter, and sister of PWD, researches the many aspects of dementia. Using neuroplastic excitation of healthy sensory neurones, she repairs/assists memory of PWDs to return. She is an international speaker and teacher. She has been known to have several memory repair groups at once. Also an author, her book covering the multitudinous aspects of dementia will be published in late 2023 or early 2024. She earned her PhD from the University of Kentucky, USA.

Claire Morrisby is an Occupational Therapist and Lecturer in the School of Allied Health at Curtin University. Claire has extensive clinical experience in aged care and dementia and teaches and researches in these areas. Claire's PhD investigated the experiences of people with dementia and their spousal carers and developed effective dementia communication skills training for professional care workers.

G. Mythili, Additional Director at the Staff Training and Research Institute, Indira Gandhi National Open University, India. She has conducted various workshops and training programmes on ODL/Online. Her areas of interest are: Massive Open Online Course (MOOC); E-Learning; Online Training;

Training and Development; Multimedia Design and Development; Web Design and Development; OER & Open Source Tools; Staff Development; and Programme Evaluation.

Maryna Rankin is a Researcher at the Ageing and Generational Dynamics (AGenDA), Optentia Research Unit, North-West University, South Africa. She obtained her BSocSci (Hons) from the University of South Africa. In 2019, she completed the MHSc in Gerontology at North-West University in Potchefstroom.

Pauline Refalo is an Occupational Therapist with 7 years of experience in mental health. She holds a BSc (Hons) in Occupational Therapy from the University of Malta and an MA in Ageing and Dementia. Her research focused on a dementia-friendly community project in Gozo. She advocates for dementia awareness and serves as the secretary of the Mental Health Association Gozo.

Kanwal Shankardass is a family physician practising in Dundas, Ontario, Canada. He is an Associate Clinical Professor in the Department of Family Medicine at McMaster University. He is the medical director at St. Peter's Residence at Chedoke Long Term Care Home in Hamilton, Ontario. He is the Physician Lead of the Greater Hamilton Health Network Long Term Care Advisory and the Medical Lead, Thrive Group Centre of Excellence, Hamilton, Ontario.

Mala Kapur Shankardass is an international consultant, academician, researcher, writer, and activist with higher educational qualifications, including doctoral and post-doctoral specialization in sociology, health social sciences, and gerontology. She retired in March 2021 after 38 years of teaching experience and holding important positions as a Senior Faculty Member at the University of Delhi, India. She continues to lecture at different academic departments in both Indian and foreign universities and is also involved with prestigious assignments with various institutions, including the United Nations. She is a member of different committees constituted by various ministries and departments under the Government of India. She holds honorary positions with a few international and national organizations and is an Editorial Advisor to scientific journals. She has been involved with examining research projects and reviewing manuscripts for publishing houses and universities based in India and abroad. She has published 12 books with reputable world publishers, has 3 forthcoming books in the next few months, many chapters, and over 100 articles in specialized journals, magazines, and newspapers. She is the recipient of fellowships and awards for her professional work. She is a life member of various professional bodies.

Kimberly J. Stoeckel, PhD, is a gerontologist with experience in clinical social work and academic research. Currently, she is an Adjunct Professor at the Erickson School of Aging at the University of Maryland, Baltimore County. She has worked internationally as a researcher at Hebrew University, Jerusalem, and as a consultant and trainer with the WHO and HelpAge International Jordan.

Noriko Tsukada, PhD, is a full Professor at the Nihon University College of Commerce, Tokyo, Japan. She received a BA and MA in Education from Fukuoka University of Education in Japan. She also earned an MGS from Miami University in 1993 and a PhD from UCLA in 1997 in the USA. Dr. Tsukada researches policies for foreign care workers and elder abuse.

Ho Mun Wai received his undergraduate and postgraduate education at the National University of Singapore (NUS), Lancaster University (UK), and the University of South Australia. He has served as Vice-Dean (Admin) in the School of Medicine at NUS, as well as in various leadership and academic roles in the Vocational and Technical Education sectors.

Rhea Wason has completed her MBBS and medical internship at Maulana Azad Medical College and its affiliated hospitals. She has a particular interest in medical research and geriatric medicine, which led her to be associated with the student chapter of the Indian Academy of Geriatrics. She has served as the General Secretary and was one of the founding members of the organization.

Joanna K. Wawrzyniak is a doctor in pedagogy, a graduate of the University of Opole, and a gerontologist specializing in sociological and psychological issues related to old age. She focuses in particular on the lifestyles and activities of pensioners and biographical studies. She is the author and co-author of monographs, academic and methodology textbooks, among them: „Autobiografia jako twórcze wyzwanie. Scenariusze warsztatów biograficznych" (*Autobiography as a creative challenge. Biographical workshop scenarios*) (2013), „Starość człowieka – szanse i zagrożenia. Implikacje pedagogiczne" (*Old age – opportunities and threats. Pedagogical implications*) (2017), author of many scientific papers in andragogy and gerontology, and co-author of numerous activation and education projects addressed to adults and seniors (for example, „Szkoły Dorosłego Człowieka" (*School for Adults*) (2018); „Życie bez płciowego bagażu" (*Diversity – life without the gender luggage*) (2018). He is an Assistant Professor at WSB University in Wrocław.

Karen Lok Yi Wong is a PhD student at the University of British Columbia, Canada. She is a registered social worker and researcher and has been practising and researching in diverse settings related to older adults, such as community senior services centres, long-term care, and geriatric acute care.

Tobias C. Vogt is an Assistant Professor for Healthy Ageing at the Population Research at the University of Groningen, the Netherlands. He is also leading the health demography centre at the Prasanna School of Public Health, Manipal Academy for Higher Education, Manipal University, India. His work is centred around behavioural and contextual determinants of life course health in developing and developed countries.

FOREWORD

In graduate school in the 1970s, I was fortunate to work with Honolulu's first task force on long-term care. Older adults, family caregivers, and individuals working in a variety of health and social services came together to assess our state's current and future needs for elder care. Our mission was to understand all the things an elder might need as he or she progressed from independence to dependence to frailty to death, as well as the available programs to meet these needs. From here, we would make recommendations to improve our system of care.

First, our group heard presentations from members about local care needs and services. Then we studied aging policy to see how our eligibility and payment systems influenced care. We learned that few programs were available to all elders. Rather, most were means-tested or targeted to elders in the greatest social and economic need or were available to purchase if elders were wealthy enough to afford them. We learned that different administrative departments within state government had responsibility for different funding streams. For example, the Department of Human Services administered Medicaid, which funded custodial care for frail elders in nursing homes, while the Department of Health oversaw home-care agencies, nursing homes, and hospice, which were more likely funded by Medicare to provide skilled medical and nursing services. Meanwhile, our Executive Office on Aging received and distributed federal funds to support congregate and home-delivered meals, as well as an array of services to help elders needing extra help with chores to remain in their homes. Clearly, there was no single agency in charge of "aging!"

When we had covered programs available locally, we researched programs in other parts of the country, looking for new and innovative approaches to care. We learned that other states struggled with the same issues. But we also learned about creative approaches to the system. For example, some states and programs were supporting "case managers," who were individuals that could assess an elder's needs and link him/her to the most appropriate services and funding streams. Massachusetts's addressed their nursing home shortage by training and supervising families to "adopt" and care for unrelated frail elders. They envisioned a "geriatric foster family" system akin to the child foster care system.

New York State was experimenting with a program called "Nursing Home Without Walls." In this program, Medicaid funds could be used to support home and community-based care for elders who would otherwise be institutionalized at Medicaid's expense, as long as the home and community-based services package was a third less costly. San Francisco had developed a program called On Lok. This program creatively tapped Medicare, Medicaid, and Administration on Aging funds to provide comprehensive care for older adults in Chinatown, making sure that elders received the best care in the least restrictive environment.

Even with the innovations, we came to understand the complexity of and gaps in the US system of care for older adults. Since then, some changes have been made locally and nationally to begin to address care options and quality. But at the same time, our older adult population has continued to expand, as have educational and employment opportunities for women, who have long provided the bulk of (free) home-based care to dependent family members. Thus, demand for services has continued to increase, and we have even more questions today than we had in the 1970s. For example:

- How should responsibility for eldercare be shared between the elder, him/herself, the family, the community, and the government?
- What societal changes are needed to ensure that all people can age healthily so that disability (and subsequent need for services) can be delayed?
- What programs are needed to keep older adults in their homes, where care should be least expensive, while concurrently assuring that they do not suffer from social isolation, abuse, or neglect?
- How can families be equipped to best support older family members, especially now that societies need more women in the workforce and women themselves enjoy working and/or must work to support themselves and their families?
- How will the increasing prevalence of dementia impact demand for long-term care services?

- How can we recruit and retain staff members who are humane in their approach, as well as skilled in their care delivery?
- What are the advantages and disadvantages of bringing in long-term care workers from other countries?
- How are we dealing with end-of-life?
- What are the underlying social justice and equity issues in eldercare?

These questions and more are addressed in this wonderful book by Dr. Kapur Shankardass. It is helpfully organized into sections, and each section includes informative and thought-provoking chapters. Dr. Kapur Shankardass masterfully sets the stage in her introduction. The next section explores ethical challenges, senior poverty, and local and global perspectives on care and carers. The following section includes chapters on family, community, and long-term care, with examples from Canada, Japan, the Netherlands, Poland, Singapore, and South Africa. The book then includes several chapters focused on dementia care, with examples from Australia, India, Malta, and Turkey. Each chapter is fascinating, and the entire book makes a significant contribution to the literature.

Clearly, we have not solved the problems of eldercare. But this book, and others like it, helps us continue to explore the challenges associated with the rapid aging of the human race on a global scale and to learn about ways other communities are addressing these challenges.

Kathryn L Braun, DrPH
Professor of Public Health and Social Work
Barbara Cox Anthony Endowed Chair on Aging
University of Hawai'i at Mānoa, Hawaii

ACKNOWLEDGEMENTS

This edited volume is the outcome of the dedication and scholarly discourse of many professionals and experts in their respective fields, to whom I express my sincere gratitude for their continuous support and cooperation. It has been a while since I reached out to the contributing authors to express their thoughts on care aspects related to older people, and their encouragement and patience with my ideas to shape this book have been overwhelming. Without naming them individually here, as their names are listed in the contents and also in each of their chapters, I collectively thank each one of them for their confidence in my ability to join their views in a systematic manner. This way, researchers, academicians, and various stakeholders involved with the significant aspect of care of older persons can learn, discuss, and take the important task of caring for older people forward in terms of policy development, initiation of programmes, or work at grassroots levels in communities. In families, in institutions, experts can influence thinking by bringing a change in attitude and images of older persons. My special thanks to all of them, each representing a country, a region, or a specific discipline, for sharing their thoughts and experiences to make this book a very meaningful addition in the field of ageing studies.

This book would not have been completed without the support of Ms Shoma Choudhary and Ms Shloka Chauhan from Routledge, whose guidance helped me in editing the book for publication purposes. I would like to express my sincere thanks to them.

I would like to express my appreciation to my husband Suman Shankardass, who supported me in countless ways through many months required to complete this work. His continuous guidance with appropriate vocabulary was always welcome throughout this journey. His enduring partnership is remarkable. I also want to thank my son Varun, daughter-in-law Trisha, and my family members, including my siblings, for encouraging me in my literary pursuits. I am grateful to the distractions by my grandson Kirat and granddaughter Sirat, which provided the necessary stress busters.

Finally, special thanks to the professionals from across the globe who endorsed this book with their complimentary words and belief in my ability to handle this exciting project.

PART I
Care perspectives

1
CARE OF OLDER PERSONS
A discourse analysis

Mala Kapur Shankardass

As the author of the first chapter of the book 'Care of Older Persons' which is the prerogative of the Editor I bring the advantage of gerontological discourse on age care, surpassing purely medical, legal, social or economic aspects of care as applied to ageing populations. It serves as an introduction to the following chapters, which deal with specific dimensions of care, bringing in theoretical and empirical perspectives which are meaningful globally and from respective country's point of view. The editor of this volume doesn't claim for this collection to be exhaustive or all-inclusive of the developments on the topic as they have emerged over time and specifically in this century. However, an attempt for this project was to bring together certain reflections over recent times, which give a flavour of diversity in the thoughts on care aspects, bringing attention to a few aspects as seen relevant from each author's perspective. The contents of the book indicate certain selected dimensions of care aspects as seen emerging globally and in different countries. The discourses in chapters show that care needs of ageing populations are changing, and they can turn around with various emerging demands based on emerging societal circumstances, as seen during the COVID-19 pandemic (Shankardass, 2023) and while respective authors indicate the development of some responses globally, as well as in various nations, to cater towards the growing care requirements influenced by demographic, epidemiological and technological transitions taking place, they also point to existent gaps and what can be done to overcome these. The care of older persons is a broad concept, encompassing many elements related to medical and nursing care, assisted living, adult day care activities as part of home care, hospital care, hospice care, long-term care and so on. It can be looked at from practitioners' perspectives, care receivers' and givers' viewpoints,

DOI: 10.4324/9781003528432-2

administrative and policy/programme dimensions, ideological and legal concerns, etc. In my opinion, it is not possible to do justice in covering every aspect related to care for ageing populations in any one book, as there are many correlated factors influencing and shaping it through various phases and determining circumstances, inclusive of communications, awareness, scientific developments, relationships, cultural and social expectations, economic considerations and other global currents. Hopefully, a sequel to this publication, again edited by me, will highlight the missed discourses and upcoming issues, which I do plan for in the next couple of years.

In many ways the current volume is different from earlier book publications which were specific to only one approach, namely highlighting care from a nursing or medical perspective. Moving away from the past trend of a one-dimensional focus on nursing or medical care, this collection brings narrations on different care perspectives and approaches from experts with various disciplinary specializations on care issues. For instance, most books in the past emphasize specifically the practitioner's viewpoint, more so from a nursing management perspective (Anderson & Anderson, 2003; Hindle & Coates, 2011; Barker, 2013; Moyle, Parker & Bramble, 2014; Geirsdóttir & Bell, 2021; Santy-Tomlinson, Falaschi, & Hertz, 2018–2021), or pointedly dealt with specific health and therapeutic problems (Ryan, 2020; Hertz & Santy-Tomlinson, 2018; Pickering, Zwakhalen & Kaasalainen, 2018), or discussed pathological, clinical and neuroscience aspects (Martin & Preedy, 2020a & b), or bring focus only on long-term care provisions (Capitman et al, 2005; Stephenson, 2018) or discussed selectively home care aspects (Ceci, Björnsdóttir & Purkis, 2013). Furthermore, a few earlier books on the subject of care of older persons are textbooks for medical and nursing students (Kaur, Kishore & Singh, 2014). Pertinently, this book, being different from existing publications, takes the reader in one volume towards multiple emerging aspects related to ethical challenges in providing care, social justice and equity issues, end-of-life care, provisions in residential institutions, the development and emphasis on training caregivers, as well as focusing on newer strategies required for nursing older people. In addition this book through narratives on various countries focuses on issues of care arrangements as they emerge with upcoming requirements, the development of policies and programmes catering to the current and growing needs of older people, the delivery of care services at the family, community and institutional levels, paradigm changes in thought processes on meeting care needs of older people, especially in terms of responses towards long-term care provisions, discussing challenges in the availability of adequate and appropriate staff for providing care in institutional, family and community settings, the feasibility of having care staff from foreign countries, options at the local level of caregivers being able to cater to existing needs and an analysis of people's experiences of receiving care in particular conditions or circumstances, for instance when affected by dementia. The challenges in providing dementia care are many, which certain countries are preparing to face in innovative and practical directions from both health and social care perspectives (Shankardass, 2021a). A section of the book on dementia care through specific chapters makes important contributions towards advancing knowledge in this direction while two other sections of the book elaborate on different care perspectives and on issues related to care provided at family and community levels as well as discuss different dimensions related to long-term care. All these chapters highlight some newer developments related to age care concerns, which require both academic and practical discourses on the suitability of these aspects for present and future ageing needs.

The preparedness of societies in meeting age care provisions is a critical dimension that requires urgent attention from a holistic approach, which in contemporary ageing societies is essential. The chapters bring to life the evolving narrations from different countries, providing multiple perspectives on many relevant aspects pivotal to family, community and long-term care. The attraction of this volume lies in the fact that it collectively focuses on many issues, making the reader avoid searching for them as individual articles in various journals. However, since it is difficult for any book to be exhaustive, the chapters are selective but nonetheless represent concerns from Africa, America, Asia, Canada and Europe. Though not all countries are covered, those randomly selected with voluntary authors bring attention to emerging issues and the shaping of responses which are meaningful for all ageing societies within the national, regional and global contexts. The ethnographic evidence with theoretical overtones provided in the chapters of this volume makes for a descriptive, narrative, expository and argumentative discourse on the care of older people. With these intentions this is a valuable contribution to the growing literature on the subject. The presentations of concerns related to diverse issues, as referred to above, bring forth the criticality of the preparedness of societies to absorb the growing demands for both social and health care, notwithstanding the heterogeneity seen among older people in terms of gender, socio-economic and geographical differences, along with issues of frailty as well as impacts of age-related diseases and ailments, especially with regard to long-term provisions and dementia care. The latter has emerged as a serious concern, especially since there is at present no cure for the disease, and with increases in longevity, the number of people being affected by it is growing. Patients affected by it need relief from symptoms, delay in its progression and management of the treatment, along with reducing the burden of care on caregivers who are mostly from the family. Thus, many countries have an interest in dealing with dementia care and have adopted various non-conservative approaches to provide care (Shankardass, 2021a). Health ministries and departments in various countries have taken particular steps through policy and program developments to incorporate a public health approach for addressing dementia care concerns based on recommendations of WHO (2015). Systematic strategies are developing across the world to include not only dementia-affected patients but also families in care planning. Based on upcoming research on dementia care issues Europe is making steady progress, followed by America and the Asia Pacific regions (Sun, et al, 2020).

The topic of care of older persons can be dealt with and understood in varied ways. It is a vast subject bringing in multiple discourses in which it can be viewed, discussed and practised. There is available literature, mostly articles in journals, presenting particular views and practices related to the care of older persons in different settings and at micro as well as macro levels. The concern for the care of older people brought in a lot of interest, especially in the last two years when the world was hit by the COVID-19 pandemic, and the resultant publications, based on highlighting various dimensions related to the coronavirus, elaborated on many care aspects and initiatives taken or overlooked by families, communities, governments and older people too. Many publications are available as articles and chapters in books or journals. The fact that a forthcoming volume has been compiled by me (Shankardass, 2023) and one of my articles published recently touches on many dimensions (Shankardass, 2021b) has led to avoiding a greater focus on that subject in the present collection of contributions to prevent duplication. Thus, taking into account the available book publications and a number of articles in journals, I, as the editor of this collection of chapters, humbly submit that this author, with whatever expertise can be credited to her, is aware of the happenings around the world regarding how care aspects affecting the lives of older people are changing from the perspective of caregivers and care receivers as ageing of societies takes place along with various demographic, epidemiological and environmental changes, and more stakeholders get involved in organizing, planning and delivery of aged care in developing and developed nations. However, keeping an open mind and taking forward thoughts on care aspects pertaining to ageing populations, she doesn't attempt in this volume to be critical or competitive in her approach to what exists academically and as a practical guide and what could be the future. The editor simply brings together various authors working in the field of ageing to voluntarily present their perspectives, experiences and challenges which they see related to care issues and responses that they capture from their professional standing. This free approach, reflected in chapters based on individual analytical research outputs, presents an interesting and unique open way to voice and share various dimensions, though not all on care for older persons as it unfolds at various levels in different societies, providing a national, regional and global understanding of an important issue affecting ageing societies.

Care of older persons reflects the growth of perspectives that recognize their specific needs, provisions from a rights-based approach and making them an integral part of society. Providing care that isolates older people, increases the risk of abuse or overlooks their autonomy is now being questioned by experts and advocates, as it is seen to exist in some forms in certain countries. This is despite that literature on age care over the last 50 years increasingly is reflecting a philosophy of person-centred dignified care, with stress on developing policies and practices that incorporate aspects of safety, compassion, appropriateness and bring in the human element, especially when care is provided in institutional settings (Gold & Kaufman, 1970). In addition, there is a growing perception of not viewing older people as expendable and taking into account their social and physical needs. Gradually but encouragingly, attempts are being made in countries to have informed carers at the family and community levels who would be equipped to provide medical, functional and emotional care. Home care, which is preferred by ageing individuals and governments, is now being patterned to be of high quality (Ceci, Björnsdóttir & Purkis, 2013) by taking into account the challenges in caregiving, especially with regard to problems in providing for frail older people and for those in difficult, complex social and healthcare contexts. The thinking of many experts in recent times is for encouraging independence in older people, voicing against the medicalization of care and bringing in the use of assistive technologies which support providing quality care, thus emphasizing on the reconfiguration of home care practices. A crucial issue in countries is how governments are developing institutional care provisions – geriatric hospitals, clinics, senior residential care set-ups/senior care facilities and old age homes/hospices along with supporting home care provisions, especially when it comes to training caregivers, hiring paid care providers and addressing certain specificities such as end-of-life care or dealing with dementia or long-term care. Besides, concern with reducing elder abuse in formal and informal settings is a paramount aspect of providing quality age care. Pertinent in this context are discourses in many countries on how care provided at different levels and in multiple settings can be designed to meet the needs and requirements of senior citizens at various stages by taking into account gender considerations, requirements for primary healthcare, acute or tertiary care or mental healthcare, or just keeping focus on active ageing mechanisms which may delay the need for care from families, communities or institutions. Along with this perspective on care over the years has emerged the need to promote healthy ageing, to bring focus on age-friendly cities, enabling environments for older people, and to develop empowering strategies such as providing for health and social security and having adequate insurance and pension policies (Shankardass, 2010). Within this wider understanding of care for older persons, the critical analysis of government policies and programmes towards the well-being of ageing populations can't be undermined.

In the broader context is the need to encourage the growth of geriatrics in countries inclusive of geriatric medical education, geriatric health and social care, geriatric nursing, geriatric social workers, geriatric counselling, geriatric therapists and geriatric care awareness. Overriding global concerns for the care of older persons are national policies that recognize the ageing needs of their populations and plan for these by taking into account health and social aspects. There is no doubt that the care of older persons is a very important aspect of all ageing and aged societies across countries, and much progress has been made on many dimensions over the years, especially with directions given by gerontologists and various United Nations agencies, to name a few, such as UN Program on Ageing, UNFPA, ESCAP and WHO. The major developments based on initiatives taken by UN organizations led to compelling documents beginning with the Vienna Plan of Action on Ageing in 1982, which set the tone for raising awareness and policy action for the care of older persons by paying attention to various facets (UN, 1983). The Madrid International Plan of Action on Ageing (MIPAA), which had approval of all UN Member countries, superseded the Vienna Plan in 2002 as the ageing scenario had drastically changed in societies calling for new direction to absorb the growing needs of older people, encompassing development issues, paying attention to health and well-being into old age, as well as ensuring enabling and supportive environments (UN, 2002). The integration of these directions is relevant for the care of all cohorts and segments of older people since they merge along with identifying individual care needs based on gender, disabilities, social and economic status, and the geographical distribution of older persons (Lewis, Purser & Mackie, 2020). This thus creates awareness and responses to age care in terms of equity and reduces the pressure on health and social care systems in societies. While these are promising initiatives, nonetheless there exist many challenges that are significant and extensive from a public policy perspective, namely prevailing ageism (WHO, 2021). Quite significantly, the Madrid Plan in the last 20 years has provided directions to nations, accepted by some governments more than others, but definitely contributed towards mainstreaming social and healthcare strategies and programmes, although disparately.

While in most countries, especially in the Asian region, the popular practice for care of older persons is through informal means provided by family members, both immediate and extended, the changing social scene, family structures, work and employment patterns, demographics and epidemiological transitions are leading certain nations to have provisions for formal care through institutions or paid services of caregivers at home. Such practices are not only to reduce the burden of care on women carers from the family but also to find substitutes for them and emphasize quality and appropriately defined care. In many countries there is reduced availability of women as carers given certain family composition patterns and greater participation of women in the labour force with longer working hours. This socio-economic reality has facilitated a concept of 'reciprocal care' whereby grandparents provide child care and families adopt varied forms of care-delivery mechanisms. This, in several countries, has led to incentivizing informal care where cash payments are given to hired carers providing care in home and community settings. In some parts of the world, especially in European countries, multi-generational family structures are involved in caregiving, but interestingly some non-siblings and non-affines across generations are involved in care relationships, especially where marriage bonds have weakened. We also see situations where even if co-residence is not there between family members, support remains for older relatives, and geographical non-proximity does not hinder care, which can take many forms: financial, psychological/emotional, social or health related. Interestingly a trend that has evolved and is seen by many developed countries as a viable option is to tax the adult generation to fund the care needs of older people (CPA, 2014). Glendinning et al. (2004) note that in all countries where age care is funded by taxation or insurance, intergenerational conflicts are less or non-existent. However, increasingly such options are being critically reviewed as creating an economic crisis in rapidly ageing societies, whether it is the Nordic welfare model considered to have the best social policy towards the care of older persons, or the liberal model characteristic of Anglophone democracies where lower-income groups are supported by governments for their care needs and other economic groups buy care services, or the Asian countries model which through familistic legislation continues the tradition of family care for older persons. However, it seems to be decreasing in practice, and pressure is on countries to bring in alternatives or support to family caregiving. Some countries are showing positive outcomes in this regard, namely, China, Korea, Japan, Malaysia, Singapore and Thailand (Shankardass, 2014). These countries, the more developed Asian nations, in recent times, have launched universal long-term care provisions with support in the form of health insurance (Kröger and Yeandle, 2013). Quite rightly pointed out by Hope et al. (2012) families in most societies have been the backbone for acceptance and prevalence of LTC, but many social currents, such as changes in family structures, migration and failing support ratios, are affecting its functioning.

Available practices and reviews on the dynamics of informal and formal care in later years, as Formosa indicates (2021), have opened up a Pandora's box. As also chapters of this book reflect, there are various issues with the delivery of health and social care, whether it is done through informal or formal means. Families, communities and institutions are not always able to cope in an appropriate, adequate and efficient manner in providing quality care from a rights-based approach. There are concerns related to accessibility, equity, delivery mechanisms, availability of care resources and above all, providing care in ethically sound, abuse-free and enabling environments. For many governments it is hurricane task to cope with age care needs as not only is the population of older people growing rapidly in most countries, but also medical and technological developments are shaping varied and new age care requirements. Integrated health and social care are gaining popularity (Goodwin, et al., 2014) in this century as an approach to improve care for older people. It puts pressure on not adopting any single organizational model of age care, rather stressing on it as a means to an end for a holistic delivery of care with an emphasis on self-management and bringing in a team of different professional care providers as well as informal carers and by using technology as a supportive tool for the delivery of care.

Recent research suggests that in some countries in the last few years, greater use of technology is enhancing caregiving, especially for older people in their homes (Tao & McRoy, 2015). The affordability and accessibility of new care mechanisms available and needed is a matter that requires attention as well as planning in all nations. Furthermore, the heterogeneity of older people demands need-specific responses in policies, services and provisions. How much available care facilities cater to providing satisfaction to older people is a major research question that should be addressed by taking in an analysis of multiple care parameters. In addition, experts from different disciplinary backgrounds must be together in guiding for better available care mechanisms providing an integrated and holistic approach from a life course perspective. WHO (2018) recommends realigning primary health care (PHC) to population ageing for developing integrated care for older people. The PHC approach can play a key role in providing holistic care to older adults, as it incorporates responding to growing health needs by planning supportive policies and regulatory frameworks based on person-centred integrated care, starting at the primary level by assessing health and social needs. It is also inclusive of empowering older people and their families to manage health systems and make decisions about health care.

Despite such guidelines many countries lack a visionary outlook in providing safe, robust, need-sensitive care facilities and have also not been able to put into practice active ageing policies and programmes that can reduce the burden of care. While the importance of physical health care is recognized by families, communities and societies in general, the mental well-being of older persons is a largely ignored aspect. Psychological ailments are undermined by health and social care professionals as well as by families mainly because older people and ageing issues have not yet been mainstreamed despite various advocacy attempts to do so from many quarters, and also due to prevailing ageism in societies. Besides, older people on their own give limited importance to these aspects, often viewing decline in their health, including mental health issues, as part of ageing and end-of-life pattern. Anecdotal evidence from many countries indicates that voicing need for mental health care is still a stigma in many communities. A welcome development is that later-life care in these dimensions is recently gradually gaining ground, more so after the COVID-19 pandemic (Shankardass, 2021b). Later life mental health well-being, though much needed, is easily compromised due to many age-related ailments and circumstances. Chronic diseases and frailty among older people deserve a special, urgent response from both the health and social care sectors.

An encouraging development seen across the world, though at different paces, is growing emphasis on the provision for long-term care which over the years is being understood in a wider and more comprehensive context. Earlier it was looked at in the last century as a burden on societies brought in by ageing populations; however, its meaning has now positively shifted since the last couple of decades from comprising mainly mere residential care services towards the entire gambit of provisions for the care of older persons. As Phillips (2000) suggested at the beginning of the 21st century when demographic changes started getting recognition and the understanding of ageing issues got importance and inclusion in policies and programmes, adopting a broader view of LTC was essential. LTC, as was beginning to be understood from the turn of the century, incorporates care and social support needs of currently active older persons. This outline provides an inclusive approach, especially covering those living in the community, alone, with family members or in some other group settings. LTC encompasses a range of support services which work towards helping older people live independently or with their families.

Institutional and residential long-term care has received favour as a policy response in many countries, and over the last two decades, considerable improvements have taken place in organizing and delivering long-term care (LTC) in different settings (Phillips & Chan, 2002). Yet there are still many deficiencies seen in the way these provisions are structured, monitored and regulated. Experts have been reviewing these care services critically and have made certain valuable suggestions for upgrading these provisions. A few chapters in this book also analyse the LTC facilities available in certain countries, and while some of these narrations depict faults in how these care services have evolved over the years, the authors do discuss the strengths of LTC and its ability to meet the emerging health as well as social care needs of older people. Much like the deliberations in the book, the discourses on this topic are generally both captious and commendatory. Moving ahead from what was historically the trend in terms of workhouses and storehouses to keep ailing older people, considered quite dreadful (Gold & Kaufman, 1970) the modifications in care provisions in the last few decades are laudatory, which has encouraged building dignified care for older people, setting professional standards, putting in place regulatory and accountable mechanisms for improved care in all kinds of settings, along with an emphasis on age care literacy and training. Yet, in some of the Asian countries, much more needs to be done in this direction, and many socio-cultural barriers need to be broken to bring in quality care for older people, particularly in rural and remote areas where people are living alone in later years due to both out and in migration patterns. Nonetheless, research indicates progress with regard to the shift from curative operations as part of health care towards health promotion. In many Asian countries, strategies have been adopted which facilitate illness prevention from an early age and this gets support from family-based services and community rehabilitation care (Shankardass, 2011). Further in the last few years, various care giving mechanisms have been established within and beyond the family in some countries, which can serve as an example for others to follow (Shankardass, 2014). Due to prevailing economic and development disparity between nations in Asia and elsewhere, a number of nations reflect different paths of responding to ageing, even though few have developed effective care policies based on a coherent conceptual framework shaping care practices to be suitable to individual needs of older people (Shankardass, 2011). Despite cultural and development commonality, countries in Asia and even in other regions vary in the details of care and services.

One important component in ageing societies is community care, which has undergone changes from traditional means of providing it to moving towards a 'top-bottom' framework, which over time was niggling many gerontologists, and consequently in more recent times, it has led to recognizing and protecting the care rights of older people through changes in societal attitudes and professional understandings. Along with the movement to advocate for providing quality care to older people in homes, communities and institutions there is also a call for securing the rights of caregivers, whether they provide informal or formal care along with putting in place educational opportunities for the geriatric care workforce, upgradation of skills of various levels of semi-professional and professional care providers, including administrators/managers, nursing and auxiliary staff, medical practitioners and other professionals involved with various aspects of care. Interestingly, ageing societies are deliberately and consciously professionalizing social services for home care and institutional care for older people. Much more attention is being given in countries to supporting family caregivers by providing various incentives and training and facilitating the availability of assistive technologies, though these are dependent on each nation's demographic reality, economic resources and political will. State's role in gearing up home-based supportive care and services, especially for frail older people, has emerged as an urgent need (Ceci, Björnsdóttir &

Purkis, 2013). Significantly there is increasing focus on the living surroundings for older people and the safety of private and public spaces, which affect aspects of care. Governments are becoming conscious of setting up quality assurance committees and legislations to protect care rights of providers and receivers, raising awareness on care needs and promote care-related products that can enhance the paraphernalia required to deliver care in a systematic, appropriate, affordable and easy way. Indeed, there are strong global recommendations for making later-life care sensitive and providing an acceptable pleasant experience for older people. In treating certain ailments, evidence-based care strongly supports increasing longevity, often overlooking the need to preserve functional capacities, maintain independence, improve quality of life with a focus on pain reduction, manage costs and decrease visits to hospitals and the rate of hospitalization. In other words the concerns being raised are to bring in patient's perspective in age care (Bell, et al., 2016). The voices against care increasingly becoming medicalized or institutionalized are growing, with demand for focusing on 'homeward bound' care. What is observed in societies based on global initiatives is that there are processes being adopted to encourage de-institutionalization and concept of 'ageing-in-place' as being promoted by the World Health Organization. To strengthen these practices, there is invariably a need to develop and expand community care, which many countries are strategically planning, though certain nations still need to work on it.

Of course, there are various ongoing challenges, and among them, an important one is that there is, to large extent, limited data in respective countries. In many developing regions, especially in Asia, some residential care homes are not registered with the government or any other recognized authorized body, thus lacking age care standards and accountability. Similarly, there is no count of a large majority of informal care workers, whether paid or unpaid, and there is no regulation of work hours or care responsibilities and duties. Also, disturbingly, many parts of the world have no specific age care policies and, in addition have either small or no social security benefits that can facilitate age care mechanisms in families, communities or in institutions. An important aspect of care which has been successfully launched in many countries is bringing into the fold primary healthcare setups for older people. On the other hand, there has also been a keen focus on developing LTC and palliative care, though certain nations face various constraints in delivering these.

As concluding comments, I would state that care of older persons has always been an important function of societies. However, in this century with rapid increase in the number of older people, it has become extremely significant that due attention be paid to various aspects and dimensions of care for older persons (Chang, 2010). Providing care to older people has become a challenging task requiring various considerations in terms of the types of care to be given – simple, specialized, pertaining to certain specificities of disease, long-term, palliative, end of life; where to be provided – home, community or institution; how to be trained for delivering care or equipped to do so; and how to incorporate gender concerns as well as relate it to the needs of emerging age-connected ailments and diseases such as dementia. Surpassing these concerns are certain considerations that draw on basic human principles, namely for age care to be person-centred with a focus on maintaining the dignity of older person by keeping their privacy intact, striving to improve the lot of carers, minimize aspects of abuse and neglect, and enhancing the reliability of carers and their credentials. A task at hand for all involved in the ageing field, in whatever capacity, is a common goal – to aim for uncovering and sharing all kinds of knowledge on the care of older persons that informs care providers, professionals, skilled, semi-skilled or unskilled, policy makers, administrators and civil society members and takes them to work towards explicating the basis of that knowledge with the overall purpose of improving age care as well as constructing a meaningful discourse on it. Discourses on age care must be considerate towards the creation of an appropriate, efficient, adequately trained and prepared carers/workforce, public health contributions, developing new approaches towards care delivery and receiving along the continuum, with a focus on allocation of resources to support fresh or redesigning initiatives. It is an arduous task, but dialogue has to carry on with vigorous support from all stakeholders.

I am happy to state that the collection of chapters in this volume deliberates on pertinent age care aspects that pertain to some of the present discourses central to advancing gerontological thoughts and vital to influence further research in this field, with the aim of engineering effective policies and programmes to cater to the needs of older people. However, there is still not enough evidence to suggest which countries have been able to provide better care to their ageing populations, nor any consensus has developed on whether older people can derive better care living in families, through community resources, or in institutions and if the private sector can deliver better care or governments can fully support age care aspects. A middle-range theory is that it be the prerogative of governments, non-governmental organizations as well as private institutions (UK Essays, 2018), but where such partnerships have resulted in good practices and easy solutions for comprehensive care of older persons has yet to be identified. At present, many of the care-related queries touch on several wider social, cultural, economic, medical, political, technological and personal issues for which there are no concrete answers. Hopefully, this publication will generate further intensive critical thinking on the care of older persons and take forward discourses on the subject, along with providing enriching perspectives on it.

References

Anderson & Anderson M. (2003). *Caring for Older Adults Holistically,* 3rd Edition, F.A. DAVIS, MeriPustak.

Barker, S. (Ed). (2013). *Caring for Older People in Nursing,* Sage Publishing House.

Bell, S., Patel, N., Patel, N., Sonani, R., Badheka, A. & Forman, D. (2016). Care of older adults. *Journal of Geriatric Cardiology,* 13, 1–7. 10.11909/j.issn.1671-5411.2016.01.019

Capitman, J., Leutz, W., Bishop, C. & Casler, R. (2005). Long-Term Care Quality: Historical Overview and Current Initiatives. Report for the National Commission for Quality Long Term Care, US.

Ceci, C., Björnsdóttir, K. & Purkis, M. E. (2013). *Perspectives on Care at Home for Older People,* Routledge.

Chang, R. (2010). Eldercare services to grow as life expectancy rises, *The Straits Times,* March 10.

CPA. (2014). The care and support of older people – An international perspective, Centre for Policy on Ageing (CPA), Rapid review, July.

Formosa, M. (2021). Building evidence for the impact of older adult learning on active ageing: A quantitative study. *Studies in Adult Education and Learning,* 27(2), 53–74. https://doi.org/10.4312/as/9934

Geirsdóttir, O. G. & Bell, J. J. (Eds). (2021). *Interdisciplinary Nutritional Management and Care for Older Adults: An Evidence Based Practical Guide for Nurses,* Springer Nature.

Glendinning, C., Davies, B., Pickard, L. & ComasHerrera, A. (2004). Funding long-term care for older people: Lessons from other countries, York: Joseph Rowntree.

Gold, J. G. & Kaufman, S. M. (1970). Development of care of elderly: Tracing the history of institutional facilities. *The Gerontologist,* 10(4), Winter, 262–274. https://doi.org/10.1093/geront/10.4_Part_1.262

Goodwin, N., Dixon, A., Anderson, G. & Wodchis, W. (2014). Providing integrated care for older people with complex needs: Lessons from seven international case studies, Kings Fund.

Hertz, K. & Santy-Tomlinson, J. (Eds). (2018). *Fragility Fracture Nursing: Holistic Care and Management of Orthogeriatric Patients,* Springer Nature.

Hindle, A. & Coates, A. (2011). *Nursing Care of Older People,* Oxford University Press.

Hope, P., Bamford, S-M, Beales, S., Brett, K., Kneale, D., Macdonnell, M. & McKeon, A. (2012). Creating Sustainable Health and Care Systems in Ageing Societies, Report of the Ageing Societies Working Group 2012, Imperial College.

Kaur, S., Kishore, J. & Singh, A. (2014). *Comprehensive Textbook of Elderly Care,* Century Publications.

Kröger, T. & Yeandle, S. (Eds). (2013). *Combining Paid Work and Family Care: Policies and Experiences in International Perspective,* Bristol: Policy Press.

Lewis, B., Purser, K. & Mackie, K. (2020). *The Human Rights of Older Persons: A Human Rights-based Approach to Elder Law,* Springer.

Martin, C. R. & Preedy, V. R. (Eds). (2020a). *Diagnosis and Management in Dementia: The Neuroscience of Dementia,* Vol 1, Academic Press: An imprint of Elsevier.

Martin, C. R. & Preedy, V. R. (Eds). (2020b). *Genetics, Neurology, Behaviour, and Diet in Dementia: The Neuroscience of Dementia,* Vol 2, Academic Press: An imprint of Elsevier.

Moyle, W., Parker, D. & Bramble, M. (2014). *Care of Older Adults,* Cambridge University Press.

Phillips, D. R. (2000). Long-term Care. In E. F. Borgatta and R. J. V. Montgomery (Eds) *Encyclopedia of Sociology*, Second edition, 1652–63. New York: Macmillan Reference.

Phillips, D. R. & Chan, A. C. M. (Eds). (2002). *Ageing and Long-Term Care National Policies in the Asia-Pacific*, Singapore: Institute for Southeast Asian Studies & IDRC.

Pickering, G., Zwakhalen, S. & Kaasalainen, S. (Eds). (2018). *Pain Management in Older Adults: A Nursing Perspective*, Springer.

Ryan, S. (2020). *Nursing Older People with Arthritis and Other Rheumatological Conditions*, Springer.

Santy-Tomlinson, J., Falaschi, P. & Hertz, K. (Series Eds). (2018-2021). *Perspectives in Nursing Management and Care for Older Adults*, Springer Book Series.

Shankardass, M. K. (2010). Care Concerns, Enabling Environmental Challenges and Policy Responses in Asia, with special reference to India, *Issues of Ageing and Disability: International Perspectives*, (1), NGO Committee on Ageing, New York, December.

Shankardass, M. K. (2011). Policy Initiatives on Population Ageing in Select Asian Countries. Working Paper Series on Ageing. United Nations Population Fund, December.

Shankardass, M. K. (2014). Policy Initiatives on Population Ageing in Select Asian Countries and Their Relevance to the Indian Context. In G. Giridhar, K. M. Sathyanarayana, S. Kumar, K. S. James & M. Alam (Eds) *Population Ageing in India*, Cambridge University Press.

Shankardass, M. K. (2021a). *Dementia Care: Issues, Responses and International Perspectives*, Springer Nature.

Shankardass, M. K. (2021b). Home, the Vulnerable and the Pandemic. In G. D Tripathy, A. Jalan, & M. K. Shankardass (Eds) *Sociological Reflections on the COVID 19 Pandemic: Redefining the Normal*, Springer Nature.

Shankardass, M. K. (Ed). (2023). *Handbook on COVID 19 Pandemic and Older Persons: Narratives and Issues from India and Beyond*, Springer Nature.

Stephenson, K. (2018). *History of Long-Term Care*, Self-published https://saaha-care.co.za/wp-content/uploads/2018/09/HISTORY-OF-ELDER-CARE.pdf

Sun, F., Chima, E., Wharton, T. & Iyengar, V. (2020). National policy actions on dementia on the Americas and Asia – Pacific consensus and challenges. *Revista Panamericana de Pública*, 44, e2., Published online January 22. doi: 10.26633/RPSP.2020.2 PMCID: PMC6971847

Tao, H. & McRoy, S. (2015). Caring for and keeping the elderly in their homes, *Chinese Nursing Research* 2, 31–34.

UK Essays, (2018). Caring for the Elderly Essay. Retrieved from https://www.ukessays.com/essays/social-work/caring-for-the-elderly-analysis-social-work-essay.php?vref=1

United Nations, (1983). *Vienna International Plan of Action on Ageing*, New York: United Nations.

United Nations, (2002). *Madrid International Plan of Action on Ageing*, New York: United Nations.

WHO, (2015). Dementia a public health priority, World Health Organization, Geneva.

World Health Organization, (2018). Integrated Care for Older People: Realigning Primary Health Care to Population Ageing. WHO/HIS/SDS/2018.44.

World Health Organization, (2021). *Global Report in Ageism*. https://www.who.int/teams/social-determinants-of-health/demographic-change-and-healthy-ageing/combatting-ageism/global-report-on-ageism

2
ETHICAL CHALLENGES IN THE CARE OF AGING POPULATION

Experience from the United States of America

Letha M. Joseph

Introduction

Ethical principles govern the morally accepted practices in healthcare. Ethical principles serve as the core values for healthcare professionals. Healthcare professionals working with the aging population often face ethical questions related to many aspects of care. Unfortunately, ethical questions are often hard to address. To address ethical questions appropriately, healthcare professionals need a broader understanding of ethical principles and their applications to healthcare. Prevailing ethical principles in healthcare are autonomy, beneficence, non-maleficence, and justice.

Autonomy

The principle of autonomy underlines the aging individual's right to act on their will and take part in their care decisions. The principle of autonomy reminds healthcare professionals of the individual's right to receive accurate and complete information that enables them to make informed choices. The United Nations Madrid International Plan of Action on Ageing emphasized the autonomy of older adults in healthcare decision-making. The concept of autonomy is complex, and it goes beyond freedom and self-determination in decision-making. Decision-making depends on older adults' values, culture, motives, and cognitive, emotional, and physical status. The principle of autonomy requires healthcare professionals to respect older adults' needs, plans, culture, and beliefs that impact their healthcare decisions. However, changes in older adults' physical and cognitive capacity can impair their decision-making ability. For example, a sensory deficit may affect an older adult's ability to receive information and, in turn, their ability to make an informed decision. Additionally, cognitive decline may impair their decision-making capacity. In some instances, family involvement with competing interests can create challenges to a patient's autonomy in decision-making.

An older adult's refusal of treatment is a common challenge while caring for the aging population. Such refusals bring questions about the individual's autonomy. When the patient has the cognitive ability to make such a decision, refusal of treatment expresses the patient's sense of autonomy. However, healthcare professionals may experience ethical dilemmas when a patient's treatment refusal raises questions about the healthcare professional's duty to 'do good' and 'avoid harm' for this patient.

Beneficence

The principle of beneficence underlines the healthcare professionals' duty to act for the patient's benefit. The term 'benefit' is broad, and it covers the overall well-being of the patient, including the patient's quality of life and comfort. However, several factors, including concerns about treatment benefits, treatment-related pain, discomfort, and suffering, end-of-life care decisions, and cost of care, can challenge the ethical principle of beneficence (Podgorica et al., 2020). Furthermore, on certain occasions, when healthcare professionals act in the best interest of the patient, there is a possibility that healthcare professionals may start to think for patients and make decisions for patients, leading to a paternalistic approach where the healthcare professional accidentally overlooks patients' autonomy.

Non-maleficence

The principle of non-maleficence implicates the healthcare professional's duty to prevent any harm to patients. Older adults are prone to healthcare-related injuries and adverse events. Age-related physiological changes increase older adults' vulnerability to medication side effects and treatment complications. Multiple comorbidities further increase their risk for complications. Therefore, healthcare professionals in geriatrics need the expertise to identify potentially harmful practices and provide specialized, high-quality care to older adults. When healthcare professionals act in their patients' best interests and to prevent harm, their actions may interfere with patients' right to autonomy. For example, oral feeds may be dangerous for an older adult with dysphagia with aspiration risk and its life-threatening complications. However, enteral feeding recommendations lead to ethical questions of autonomy vs. beneficence/non-maleficence if the patient wants regular food and not tube feeds.

Justice

Justice is the ethical principle that necessitates the equitable distribution of healthcare services (Daher, 2013), being fair to patients, and providing their dues (Podgorica et al., 2020). When the healthcare community works for the equitable distribution of available resources, older adults may get marginalized, raising ethical questions about justice. For example, during the COVID-19 pandemic, inadequate resources such as hospital beds, ventilators, and healthcare workforce imposed selective hospitalization of patients with COVID-19, where some older adults were denied hospital care (Giwa & Teaster, 2021). Denial of healthcare resources based exclusively on age is against the principle of justice. In addition, older adults can be victims of stereotyping and discrimination from ageism, racism, limited technological skills, and low socioeconomic status. The high prevalence of various forms of elder abuse and exploitation also alerts healthcare professionals to be vigilant about such problems and bring justice to older adults.

Many factors, including healthcare professionals' culture, beliefs, and values, impact the way they approach ethical concerns. Healthcare professionals' awareness of the potential impact of personal culture, beliefs, and values on a patient's value system assists them in separating personal beliefs and values from those of the patient. In the context of the principles of autonomy, beneficence, non-maleficence, and justice, let us examine some everyday situations in the United States that create ethical dilemmas in older adults' care.

Informed consent and decision-making

The principle of autonomy gives older adults the right to self-determination and decision-making. While caring for older adults with cognitive decline, healthcare professionals may question these patients' decision-making capacity. However, cognitive decline does not exclude older adults from all decision-making. Older adults' ability to articulate and communicate the proposed treatment plan's purpose, benefits, risks, and alternatives determines their decision-making capacity (Mueller et al., 2004). When older adults have significant cognitive decline, their surrogates speak for the patient and make the potential choices the older adults would have made if they could reasonably make their care decisions. Surrogates' role is not to make decisions for their older adult but to assist them in shared decision-making. Unfortunately, sometimes the surrogates may act on their motives, which may not be in the patient's best interest. As a healthcare provider working with older adults, this author had a similar concern and approached the hospital ethics committee on a few occasions to protect patient rights and quality of life. Timely goals of care conversations and documentation of patient preferences give aging people an opportunity to make informed decisions and communicate their wishes to significant people for healthcare decisions when they have the cognitive abilities.

Moreover, healthcare professionals have the moral responsibility to provide comprehensive information to patients and surrogates for informed decision-making. This information includes the benefits and risks of the proposed treatment, safety plans for minimizing the risk, and alternative treatments. However, under circumstances where patients lack decision-making capacity and in the absence of surrogates, if a delay in decision-making negatively impacts healthcare outcomes, healthcare professionals make healthcare decisions considering the patients' best interests. In such situations, healthcare providers have the ethical responsibility to act on the ethical principles of beneficence and non-maleficence. For such emergency decision-making, U.S. laws protect and safeguard healthcare providers.

Patient confidentiality

Patients have a right to privacy and confidentiality, and healthcare professionals need patient permission to share a patient's health-related information with someone. However, in certain situations, keeping the patient information confidential may be harmful to the patient, someone around the patient, or both. For example, consider a situation where Mrs. R, a 70-year-old female, shows signs of physical abuse and does not want to report the abuse to the authorities. Mrs. R has the right to confidentiality. Although Mrs. R intends to keep the abuse confidential, the healthcare professional has to 'do good' (beneficence) and 'avoid harm' (non-maleficence) for Mrs. R. The perpetrator may continue the abuse, and Mrs. R's life may be in danger. In this case, the healthcare professional has the ethical responsibility to report the suspected abuse to the legal authorities.

Now, consider Mr. A, a 74-year-old male with significant cognitive decline who lives alone and continues to drive. Mr. A refuses to disclose this information to his son, who lives out of state. At the same time, the healthcare professional is concerned about Mr. A's safety and public safety. Mr. A acknowledges the safety concerns but does not want to bother his son, who lives several hundred miles away. The desire to respect Mr. A's autonomy and independence and the implications of his driving creates an ethical dilemma for the healthcare professional. In the United States, many aging people live by themselves with minimal or no family or social support, and situations such as Mr. A's are common. Here, the healthcare provider can connect Mr. A with a clinical social worker, who can work with Mr. A and identify alternatives to approaching his son. Or, even with his son's input, Mr. A can locate community resources for a safer ride to meet his transportation needs.

Additionally, after communicating with Mr. A, the healthcare professional may inform the driving license authority in the interest of public safety. Taking someone's driving privileges away can be perceived as a considerable threat to their autonomy. However, healthcare professionals have ethical obligations to work for their patients' benefit, and breaching confidentiality to address genuine concerns about patient safety or public safety is ethically acceptable.

Care of older adults with dementia

The number of people living with dementia is increasing. Healthcare professionals frequently encounter ethical challenges while caring for older adults with dementia. The diagnosis of dementia itself brings ethical questions. While timely diagnosis is essential, an early diagnosis with a label of dementia sometimes brings restrictions and associated emotional problems for older adults (Hughes & Common, 2015). For example, Mr. B, a 56-year-old office manager with early signs of cognitive decline, wants to keep his early dementia confidential and continue his job and other routine activities. Ethical concerns arise when Mr. B's cognitive decline affects his work performance. For example, when he forgot about a few workplace meetings, coworkers became concerned. Mr. B may experience discrimination due to his cognitive decline.

Additionally, Mr. B's cognitive decline can even create serious workplace problems. While Mr. B has the autonomy to make decisions, the healthcare professional has the ethical responsibility to explore the nature of his job and suggest modifications or assistive technology to manage his job-related responsibilities. Additionally, the healthcare professional has the ethical and legal obligation to monitor the disease progression and identify any safety concerns related to the disease. Down the road, the healthcare professional may encounter a situation where the duty to 'do good' (beneficence) and 'avoid harm' (non-maleficence) outweighs the autonomy of Mr. B in making his decisions and his right to confidentiality.

Years later, Mr. B shows signs of significant cognitive decline, and the family thinks he needs to spend the rest of his life in a care facility. However, Mr. B is not in agreement with the care facility plans. The healthcare professional is concerned about Mr. B's safety and wants to respect Mr. B's autonomy while upholding the principle of non-maleficence. Such conflicts bring ethical dilemmas. The healthcare professional needs to consider Mr. B's safety and well-being along with the safety and well-being of his family and the people around him. Furthermore, a broader approach with social, cultural, economic, and legal implications will help create an appropriate strategy to support Mr. B and his family in making decisions about Mr. B's placement in a care home.

Common misconceptions about older adults' decision-making capacity when they have dementia can impact their care. Early signs of cognitive decline can be an alert to ensure advanced care planning. Discussion of patients' values and goals of care at the early appearance of cognitive decline allows the patient to contribute to the decision-making (Perin et al., 2021). On the other hand, people with dementia may refuse care, creating ethical dilemmas for healthcare professionals focused on 'doing good' and 'avoiding harm' to the patient. For example, if a patient does not allow vital signs or blood glucose monitoring or refuses to take medications for chronic medical conditions such as hypertension or diabetes, the patient can experience complications.

Similarly, patients wandering in the unit can create safety concerns for themselves and others. On such occasions, ethical choices should reflect the balance between autonomy and beneficence/non-maleficence. A modified care environment and specially trained professionals can improve the care of people with dementia.

For people with dementia, healthcare activities such as pain management and advance care planning have additional ethical implications compared to people without dementia. Other sections of this chapter outline these implications and strategies to address the associated ethical concerns. In brief, the care of older adults with dementia brings several ethical questions for healthcare professionals. As Nuffield Council on Bioethics (Hope, 2009) recommends in the comprehensive framework for ethical approaches in caring for people with dementia, 'the person should come first.' However, a broad approach to personhood involving biological, social, psychological, and spiritual dimensions will reduce ethical concerns when working with older adults with dementia (Hughes & Common, 2015).

Advance care planning and goals of care conversation

'Dying in America: Improving quality and honoring individual preferences near the end of life,' the consensus report from the National Academy of Medicine (Institute of Medicine), claimed that in the United States, patients receive more intensive health care at the end of their lives than required or desired by patients (Institute of Medicine, 2015). Timely 'goals of care' discussions can lead to goal-aligned advanced care planning that reduces non-beneficial aggressive medical care, improves the quality of life and patient satisfaction, and lowers healthcare costs. A timely 'goals of care' conversation focuses on the patient's overall well-being and ensures the patient's autonomy in healthcare-related decisions. Healthcare professionals can provide accurate information on the disease, treatments and prognosis, complications, and alternatives to treatment to prepare older adults for care decisions. Ethical principles of beneficence and non-maleficence dominate such conversations.

To be fair to older adults, age alone does not govern the prognosis or care decisions. Timeliness of the goals of care discussion is vital to ensure patient autonomy because delay can limit the patient's ability to make such decisions. During times of critical illness or at stages closer to the end of life, patients may not be able to identify and communicate healthcare decisions and their care preferences. Advance Care Planning refers to shared decision-making between a person and caregivers anticipating the deterioration in the person's decision-making capacity (Knight, 2019). During advance care planning, individuals communicate their healthcare goals and preferences, such as the procedures they would like to receive and the procedures they do not want to receive as part of end-of-life care (Bailoor et al., 2018).

Additionally, advance care planning is the opportunity to name a surrogate who can execute healthcare-related decisions when the individual can no longer do so. Advance care plans documented in an official format become advance directives or living wills (Harrison & Smith, 2021). A legally binding document termed 'Advanced Decision to Refuse Treatment' serves a similar purpose in certain countries (Dempsey, 2014). The process of advance care planning handles several ethical questions. Advance care planning gives older adults a form of 'extended autonomy.' Older adults need adequate information on healthcare options to execute this extended autonomy. At the same time, healthcare professionals can remind older adults of their rights to information and self-determination. Historically, advance care planning was wrongly attributed as the occasion to decide on matters related to 'to resuscitate' or 'not to resuscitate.' Healthcare professionals educate older adults and their families that advance care planning is the time to discuss and decide on care choices such as artificial nutrition and hydration, hospitalization, care in the intensive care unit, and procedures. Procedures could be as simple as blood draws to complicated surgeries or cardiopulmonary resuscitation. In brief, advance care planning is the opportunity for older adults to discuss what matters to them in their care and identify the care they would like to receive which aligns with their life goals. A collaborative effort of healthcare professionals makes successful goals of care conversations and advance care planning.

End-of-life care

End-of-life care aims to provide comfort, alleviate suffering, and support the patient's dignified death. Patients have the right to receive end-of-life care based on their and families' ethical, cultural, spiritual, and religious preferences. In the United States, a country with cultural diversity, healthcare professionals may not know patients' culture-specific practices. Learning about different cultures may not be practical. Additionally, culture constantly evolves. The right step is to ask the patient and family about their preferences. Moreover, the patient's values and priorities will inform the patient's care while supporting the patient's autonomy.

However, the incongruity in care goals and treatment choices that patients or their surrogates expect during end-of-life care can create ethical concerns for healthcare professionals. Requiring futile interventions to prolong life that increases the patient's suffering and discomfort brings concerns to the clinician's practice rooted in beneficence and non-maleficence. For example, when a patient stops eating and drinking, the family may ask for artificial nutrition and hydration. If the patient can decide on nutrition, the healthcare professional supports the patient's decision-making autonomy. However, artificial nutrition and hydration may not align with comfort-focused end-of-life care. Therefore, healthcare professionals can remind the family about the patient's care goals and the artificial nutrition and hydration's negative impact on patients' goals. Ethical concerns arise when the family insists on artificial nutrition or hydration. Unfortunately, the healthcare provider has to consider the surrogates' decisions when patients cannot make and communicate their own choices.

Addressing ethical dilemma in end-of-life care – theoretical framework

End-of-life care for the aging population can be ethically challenging for healthcare professionals. The social process of 'reframing the meaning of life and professional values' may serve as the theoretical underpinning for healthcare professionals' approaches to ethical dilemmas in end-of-life care (Pan et al., 2021). According to this framework, the initial step is recognizing the healthcare professional's emotions while managing older adults dealing with emotionally challenging situations such as the end of life. Healthcare professionals who are vigilant to older adults' physical, emotional, spiritual, and psychological aspects of healthcare needs will be sensitive to their patients' suffering. In situations where the healthcare professionals realize their helplessness in curing the illness or solving their patients' problems, uncertainty in dealing with the patients' loved ones, and lack of confidence in managing emotionally challenging situations can be traumatizing.

Additionally, healthcare professionals realize the influence of their culture and values in their approach to caring for patients in such emotionally challenging conditions. The impact of personal values and beliefs can create ethical dilemmas. Healthcare professionals try to apply practical strategies to cope with such difficulties. They may draw strength from external support and try to reframe values associated with their professional roles. They realize the need to fulfill responsibilities related to their professional roles. Ultimately, they recognize their role in providing end-of-life care and facilitating comfort during the most challenging times for a patient and their family, which helps healthcare professionals identify new meaning for their lives.

Pain management in older adults

Adequate pain management is an ethical responsibility in healthcare. Pain assessment and management in older adults have additional challenges compared to pain management in young adults. Pain is not a normal part of aging. Older adults' response to pain is different from young adults' pain response. Older adults may consider pain an expected part of aging and may not report pain due to social and cultural reasons. Furthermore, healthcare professionals may underestimate older adults' pain, limiting access to adequate pain management.

Individuals with cognitive decline or communication deficits may experience additional challenges in reporting pain. Relying on standardized pain assessment tools may not identify the pain severity in individuals with communication challenges. Healthcare professionals have an ethical responsibility to be vigilant to subtle changes in behavior and consider unidentified pain as a potential etiology for the new behavior. The lack of standardized pain assessment tools for older adults with dementia or sensory deficits is another challenge. Failure to identify pain and suffering in patients with cognitive decline or communication challenges can be observed as a healthcare professional's negligence (Denny & Guido, 2012). While older adults' pain assessment can be challenging, pain management also brings additional challenges.

Older adults' high vulnerability to opioid-related complications makes pain management highly challenging. Though older adults may experience acute pain, chronic pain is more prevalent in older adults. The effectiveness of opioids in chronic pain management is questionable. Several non-pharmacological approaches are safe and effective in managing chronic pain and the physical, psychological, and social impact of pain (US Department of Health and Human Services, 2019). Healthcare professionals have an ethical responsibility to offer or direct patients to other professionals for non-pharmacological interventions commonly known as complementary and alternative treatment modalities. Withholding information on complementary modalities based on healthcare professionals' personal preferences or limited skills is unethical. Multimodal pain management can decrease pain severity and improve the health-related quality of life in older adults with chronic pain (Institute of Medicine, 2011). Older adults will benefit from healthcare professionals' open-minded approach to embracing multimodal interventions with traditional pharmacological pain treatment. Moreover, healthcare professionals need to engage in ongoing education and training to deliver patient-centered comprehensive pain management interventions for older adults (Jukić & Puljak, 2018). Furthermore, for a patient with pain, bringing the pain to zero (the commonly used numeric pain scale identifies zero as the absence of pain) or becoming pain-free is an unrealistic goal.

Adequate pain control reduces pain severity, improves emotional well-being, promotes rest and sleep, and improves functional status.

The concept of pain relief as a human right may bring additional ethical questions. Autonomy and the principle of beneficence govern the patient's right to adequate pain relief. However, side effects and complications of commonly used pain management agents alert the healthcare professional to the principle of non-maleficence. For example, during end-of-life care, a patient may be on higher doses of narcotic pain medications, leaving the patient sedated most of the time. The balance in pain control and the patient's need to have meaningful interaction with family members can be a challenge. Furthermore, questions about euthanasia and physician-assisted death arise with higher doses of narcotics during end-of-life care. Finding the balance between beneficence and non-maleficence in older adults' pain management is challenging. Furthermore, healthcare providers can face legal challenges, as in the case of the Ohio physician accused of killing 14 patients (Meyer, 2022). Veracity in discussing the potential side effects of pain medications and the side effects patients and their significant people are willing to accept can bring patient autonomy in pain management decisions during end-of-life care.

Abuse and neglect

Abuse and neglect of older adults are social problem. Abuse can manifest in several forms, such as physical, emotional, or sexual. Financial exploitation, caregiver neglect, and abandonment are additional forms of abuse. Health care professionals have an ethical responsibility to identify any signs of abuse and ensure older adults' safety. In the United States, if the healthcare professional notices any evidence of mistreatment, when the patient reports mistreatment, or if the healthcare professional suspects an increased risk for probable abuse, neglect, exploitation, or abandonment, the healthcare professional has the ethical responsibility to report the concern to Adult Protective Services (APS). Victims of abuse may be scared of the perpetrator and may not want the healthcare professional to report the abuse. However, safety concerns outweigh the client's autonomy, and healthcare professionals need to uphold the principles of beneficence and non-maleficence and ensure justice for the client.

Older adults and clinical research

Older adults' participation in clinical research and lack of research participation can raise ethical concerns. Older adults' vulnerability to adverse reactions and side effects and additional steps in enrolling older adults may limit their chances of participating in clinical research studies. Additionally, potential ethical concerns related to the capacity for voluntary participation and consent may favor excluding older adults from clinical research (Shepherd, 2016). Multimorbidity also can exclude older adults from research studies. On the other hand, a lack of trust may limit older adults' intent to participate. Finally, challenges in using technology may limit older adults' participation unless the research team makes additional efforts to get older adults' participation. Due to older adults' limited participation in clinical research, studies may find inadequate evidence to support specific clinical interventions for older adults. Fortunately, there have been efforts to create guidelines that improve older adults' participation in clinical research (Diener et al., 2013).

When older adults participate in clinical research, researchers have the ethical responsibility to ensure older adults' capacity to make an informed decision to participate. Additionally, healthcare professionals need to advocate for older adults' right to information and self-determination while making research participation decisions. The principle of justice reminds the healthcare professional to explore whether the older adult's enrollment is by manipulation. Additionally, when surrogates consent to the older adult's participation, the researcher must ensure the decision is made in the participant's best interest and not for the surrogate's benefit.

Cultural diversity and older adults in the United States

Ethical concerns related to older adults' care in the United States are similar to those in other countries in several aspects. However, there are some unique challenges associated with the multicultural nature of the population. In 2018, 15.8% of the United States population was 65 or older, and by 2030, all the baby boomers will join the age group of 65 or older (Census Bureau, 2018). Many older adults continue to live in communities with support from family, community resources, and home health services. However, a good portion of older adults may not have adequate support to stay in the community, or they may need care in settings such as assisted living facilities or skilled nursing facilities to meet their complex care needs. Skilled care in these facilities may not be affordable for all older adults who may need residential care to manage their care needs. The inability to provide the most appropriate care and support for such older adults creates ethical questions of beneficence, non-maleficence, and justice.

Care settings

On the other hand, some older adults prefer to continue living in their community to preserve their independence as they choose their familiar surroundings. Nevertheless, the community or home care may not provide the necessary care for these older adults, eventually leading to placement in care facilities. Provision to support those older adults who prefer to 'age in place' by creating support services for in-home care will preserve their independence and autonomy. Such ethical concerns highlight healthcare professionals' responsibility for advocacy to influence healthcare policies and regulations related to older adults.

Care facilities can bring additional ethical concerns. For example, older adults in assisted living and skilled nursing facilities may receive care from foreign-educated healthcare professionals. Older adults' sensory impairments can add to their difficulty in understanding and communicating meaningfully with foreign-educated healthcare professionals. Moreover, some foreign-educated professionals may not have experience working with older adults in their countries and may work in care homes as part of their emigration contract. In addition, foreign-educated healthcare professionals unfamiliar with the cultural practices of older adults may require training and support to deliver culturally appropriate care to older adults in these facilities. Thus, enhancing a healthcare workforce with expertise in caring for the aging population becomes a national priority.

In the United States, care in skilled nursing facilities, aka nursing homes, is highly regulated. However, COVID-19 disproportionately affected nursing home residents, leading to questions about the safety and quality of care provided in nursing homes. Staffing challenges, infection control practices, physical layout, and other care-related factors in nursing homes need to improve so that older adults can receive quality healthcare in a safe environment.

Community-dwelling older adults require support and oversight based on their cognitive status and physical and mental capacity. They need proper housing, food security, transportation support, and provisions to avoid social isolation. In the United States, the individualistic culture creates a social system where older adults may need to live by themselves, increasing exploitation vulnerability. Older adults living alone can become targets for scammers, resulting in economic loss. Older adults living in solitude have the right to socialization, safe living conditions, and ongoing support to meet instrumental activities of life.

Access to care

Poor access to care is another ethical concern in the United States. Racial and ethnic minorities, in general, continue to experience inadequate access to healthcare. Older adults belonging to racial and ethnic minorities suffer from inequities originating from double oppression. There is a gap in timely advance care planning, utilization of palliative care, and end-of-life care among ethnic and racial minorities (Chen et al., 2021).

The recent surge in telehealth for routine healthcare has also brought ethical concerns for older adults. In addition, the COVID-19 pandemic created broader applications for telehealth services. Lack of access to technology can limit older adults' utilization of telehealth services. Additionally, sensory deficits and dementia-related challenges may necessitate technology modifications for older adults for successful telehealth utilization. This digital divide can limit older adults' ability to use telehealth services and receive healthcare from the comfort of their homes.

Ageism

Older adults in the United States experience the effects of ageism. The COVID-19 pandemic exposed ageism and its impact on older adults. As the pandemic emerged, older adults' increased risk of contracting the disease and their fatal outcomes received propaganda. Social media even portrayed the Coronavirus disease as the 'boomer remover syndrome.' As a result, older adults experienced increased social isolation and anxiety. Some of the older adults lacked a backup plan to arrange the necessities of life. Generalizing older adults' risk based on chronological age is a form of ageism that raises ethical questions. General fear and concerns about the scarcity of resources led to selective delivery of healthcare services such as hospitalization, intensive care unit, and ventilator care for patients with COVID-19. Unofficial reports of denying care for older adults and open remarks from people in power about the rationing of care were unfair. Situations such as the pandemic may call for selective use of healthcare resources. However, triaging and rationing based merely on chronological age is against the principle of justice (Previtali et al., 2020).

Moving Forward

Literature is limited on ethical concerns stemming from older adults' family dynamics and relationship issues. However, clinicians frequently experience ethical problems arising from the incongruity in care recommendations from different family members, power struggles between children from other relationships, and demands to prolong the family member's life. Additionally, the U.S. immigrant population is aging. With cultural diversity and varying rates of acculturation, migrant populations face unique ethical challenges as they age. The impact of migrant status and the associated ethical implications in migrant older adults' lives and healthcare are worth exploring.

Conclusion

Healthcare professionals working with older adults face ethical dilemmas. Since culture plays a significant role in ethical approaches, the ethical concerns in U.S. older adults' care may be slightly different from those in some other countries. However, ethical questions are not simple enough for a straightforward right or wrong answer. The complexity of ethical questions reminds healthcare professionals of their vulnerability. Addressing each ethical question in its unique context using the ethical principles of autonomy, beneficence, non-maleficence, and justice will empower healthcare professionals to overcome ethical dilemmas.

References

Bailoor, K., Kamil, L. H., Goldman, E., Napiewocki, L. M., Winiarski, D., Vercler, C. J., & Shuman, A. G. (2018). The voice is as mighty as the pen: Integrating conversations into advance care planning. *Journal of Bioethical Inquiry*, 15(2), 185–191. https://doi10.1007/s11673-018-9848-7-

Census Bureau Washington (D.C.). (2018). Older people projected to outnumber children for first time in U.S. history. Census Bureau. Press release. Available from: https://www.census.gov/newsroom/press-releases/2018/cb18-41-population-projections.html

Chen, G., Hong, Y.-R., Wilkie, D. J., Kittleson, S., Huo, J., & Bian, J. (2021). Geographic variation in knowledge of palliative care among U.S. adults: Findings from 2018 health information national trends survey. *The American Journal of Hospice & Palliative Care*, 38(3), 291–299. https://doi.org/10.1177/1049909120946266

Daher, M. (2013). Ethical issues in the geriatric patient with advanced cancer 'living to the end'. *Annals of Oncology: Official Journal of the European Society for Medical Oncology*, 24(Suppl 7), vii55–vii58. https://doi.org/10.1093/annonc/mdt262

Dempsey, D. (2014). Refusing treatment: Practical, legal and ethical issues. *Nursing & Residential Care*, 16(8), 454–458. https://doi-org/10.12968/nrec.2014.16.8.454

Denny, D. L., & Guido, G. W. (2012). Undertreatment of pain in older adults: An application of beneficence. *Nursing Ethics*, 19(6), 800–809. https://doi.org/10.1177/0969733012447015

Diener, L., Hugonot-Diener, L., Alvino, S., Baeyens, J. P., Bone, M. F., Chirita, D., Husson, J. M., Maman, M., Piette, F., Tinker, A., von Raison, F., & European Forum for Good Clinical Practice Geriatric Medicine Working Party. (2013). Guidance synthesis. Medical research for and with older people in Europe: Proposed ethical guidance for good clinical practice: Ethical considerations. *The Journal of Nutrition, Health & Aging*, 17(7), 625–627. https://doi.org/10.1007/s12603-013-0340-0

Giwa, A. O., & Teaster, P. B. (2021). Facing the COVID-19 winter: Ethical lessons for treating older adults. *Journal of the American Geriatrics Society*, 69(3), 604–605. https://doi.org/10.1111/jgs.16983

Harrison, K. L., & Smith, A. K. (2021). Ethics & informed decision making. Walter, L. C., Chang, A., Chen, P., Harper, G., Rivera, J., Conant, R., Lo, D., & Yukawa, M. (Eds.), *Current Diagnosis & Treatment Geriatrics*, 3e. McGraw Hill.

Hope, T. (2009). Ethical dilemmas in the care of people with dementia. *British Journal of Community Nursing*, 14(12), 548–550. https://doi.org/10.12968/bjcn.2009.14.12.45532

Hughes, J., & Common, J. (2015). Ethical issues in caring for patients with dementia. *Nursing Standard (Royal College of Nursing (Great Britain): (1987)*, 29(49), 42–47. https://doi.org/10.7748/ns.29.49.42.e9206

Institute of Medicine. (2015). *Dying in America: Improving Quality and Honoring Individual Preferences Near the End of Life*. Washington, D.C.: The National Academies Press. https://doi.org/10.17226/18748

Institute of Medicine (U.S.) Committee on Advancing Pain Research, Care, and Education. (2011). *Relieving Pain in America: A Blueprint for Transforming Prevention, Care, Education, and Research*. National Academies Press (U.S.).

Jukić, M., & Puljak, L. (2018). Legal and ethical aspects of pain management. *Acta Medica Academica*, 47(1), 18–26. https://doi.org/10.5644/ama2006-124.2111

Knight, K. (2019). Who is the patient? Tensions between advance care planning and shared decision-making. *Journal of Evaluation in Clinical Practice*, 25(6), 1217–1225. https://doi-org/10.1111/jep.13149

Meyer, H. (2022). Doc Accused of Killing 14 Patients Found Not Guilty – Medscape. Doc Accused of Killing 14 Patients Found Not Guilty (medscape.com)

Mueller, P. S., Hook, C. C., & Fleming, K. C. (2004). Ethical issues in geriatrics: A guide for clinicians. *Mayo Clinic Proceedings*, 79(4), 554–562. https://doi.org/10.4065/79.4.554

Pan, S., Li, X., Shen, Y., Chen, J., & Koniak-Griffin, D. (2021). Reframing the meaning of life and professional values: A theoretical framework of facilitating professional care for terminally ill patients. *Nursing & Health Sciences*, 23(1), 167–175. https://doi.org/10.1111/nhs.12792

Perin, M., Ghirotto, L., & De Panfilis, L. (2021). 'Too late or too soon': The ethics of advance care planning in dementia setting. *Bioethics*, 35(2), 178–186. https://doi-org/10.1111/bioe.12814

Podgorica, N., Flatscher-Thöni, M., Deufert, D., Siebert, U., & Ganner, M. (2020). A systematic review of ethical and legal issues in elder care. *Nursing Ethics*, 28(6), 895–910. Advance online publication. https://doi.org/10.1177/0969733020921488

Previtali, F., Allen, L. D., & Varlamova, M. (2020). Not only virus spread: The diffusion of ageism during the outbreak of COVID-19. *Journal of Aging & Social Policy*, 32(4–5), 506–514. https://doi.org/10.1080/08959420.2020.1772002

Shepherd, V. (2016). Research involving adults lacking capacity to consent: The impact of research regulation on 'evidence biased' medicine. *BMC Medical Ethics*, 17(1), 55. https://doi.org/10.1186/s12910-016-0138-9

U.S. Department of Health and Human Services (2019). Pain Management Best Practices Inter-Agency Task Force Report: Updates, Gaps, Inconsistencies, and Recommendations. Retrieved from U. S. Department of Health and Human Services website: https://www.hhs.gov/ash/advisory-committees/pain/reports/index.html

3
SENIORS' POVERTY IN BRITISH COLUMBIA, CANADA

A social justice issue

Karen Lok Yi Wong

Introduction

Older adults' poverty is a topic of growing concern in many places around the world, including developed countries such as Canada. In this chapter, the author, who is a social worker practicing with older adults in British Columbia (BC), Canada, will discuss the issue of older adults' poverty in BC. Social justice is the fundamental value of the social work profession. The author will thus discuss why older adults' poverty in BC is a social justice issue. She will first define the issue of older adults' poverty in BC. She will then explain why this issue is a social justice one by referring to two social justice theories, which are the capabilities approach and the ethics of care perspective.

There are different definitions of the term "older adults" in the literature. Most literature defines older adults as people aged 65 or above because 65 years old is the age at which people begin to be eligible for most benefits for older adults (Ivanova et al., 2017; Office of the Seniors Advocate, 2015). Some literature defines older adults as people aged 55 or above because some agencies working with older adults find that people in their mid-50s and early 60s ask for help for problems experienced by older adults (e.g., high healthcare costs) (411 Seniors Center Society, 2018). The author will adopt this definition because most of the literature does, and it will be less complicated when the author refers to arguments and data. In 2018, 19% of the BC population was aged 65 or above (Office of the Seniors Advocate, 2018).

Older adults' poverty

This issue is defined in the following section by discussing that many older adults have low income but high spending and that some older adult groups are at a higher risk of poverty.

Low income—Older adults in Canada have three sources of income (Forum+, 2018). The first source is the public pension, that is, the Canadian Pension Plan (CPP), Old Age Security (OAS), and Guaranteed Income Supplement (GIS). The second source is the private pension. The third source is social assistance. However, most older adults can only rely on the public pension.

Many older adults have limited or no access to private pensions (Healthcare of Ontario Pension Plan, 2017). In Canada, two-thirds of the older adult population do not have a private pension funded by employers (Healthcare of Ontario Pension Plan, 2017). This is because they were not in employment, were not in employment long enough, and/or were not in employment which provides private pensions (Healthcare of Ontario Pension Plan, 2017). Even if they have a private pension, they need to bear the risks of the investment of their private pension due to changes in the private pension systems from defined benefits to defined contributions.

The amount of social assistance to older adults is minimal. For example, the amount of the older adults supplement in BC is the second-lowest in Canada, at only $49.30 per month (Office of the Seniors Advocate, 2018). Many older adults are not receiving the social assistance they are entitled to (411 Seniors Centre Society, 2018). The social assistance system requires them to apply. However, many older adults are not aware of social assistance, so they do not apply. Even if they are aware, the application processes are not accessible to them: many social assistance programs are now go online, assuming that applicants know how to use a computer. However, many older adults lack computer literacy (411 Seniors Centre Society, 2018). They try to apply by phone, but the waiting time is long. They want to apply in person but have mobility issues that prevent them from going to the agency.

The public pension system should be older adults' safety net. It successfully reduced older adults' poverty rate in BC from over 30% in the mid-1970s to less than 5% in the mid-1990s (Ivanova et al., 2017). However, from 1996 to 2014, this trend was reversed and older adults' poverty rate has risen from 2.2% to 12.7%.

Canada has no official poverty line (Ivanova et al., 2017; Veall, 2008). However, Statistics Canada uses different measures to indicate low income, including the low-income cut-off, low-income measure, and market basket measure, which are seen as the poverty lines of the government. The author adopts the low-income measure. The reason is that it is most used in

Canadian and international literature. The low-income measure "is set at 50 percent of median household income adjusted for family size" (Ivanova et al., 2017, p. 53). Most older adults in BC have an income above the poverty line, that is, having an annual income after tax above $15,000 (Ivanova et al., 2017). They are technically not in poverty. However, many of them have an income just slightly above this line. In BC, 44% of older adults reported an annual income after tax between $15,000 and $25,000 (Ivanova et al., 2017). They still have to pay for different things, especially increasing healthcare costs due to aging. Being above the poverty line obscures the reality of their lived experience from policymakers.

High spending

Housing and related costs—Whereas many older adults have low incomes, they have high spending. One main area of spending is housing and related costs (Ivanova et al., 2017; MacDonald et al., 2010). Older adults are more likely to own properties than working-aged adults because they or their partners worked for a longer time. However, they still need to pay the costs related to their properties (e.g., insurance, cable). Many older adults live in properties that are not in good condition and thus need to spend on repairs and maintenance. These costs are related to their safety and well-being.

A significant proportion of older adults rent. In BC, 19% of older adults rent (Ivanova et al., 2017). The rent in BC is rising rapidly and beyond the affordability of many older adult renters. For example, the average monthly rent for a one-bedroom apartment in Vancouver is $1,038 (Office of the Seniors Advocate, 2015). However, as suggested, most older adults only have an annual income between $15,000 and $25,000 (i.e., between $1,250 and $2,083 per month). Many older adults are not aware of the rent subsidies (e.g., Shelter Aid For Elderly Renters [SAFER]) (411 Seniors Centre Society, 2018). Even if they are aware, the rent subsidies are minimal compared with the rising rent. For instance, the maximum SAFER subsidies per month is only $765 for Vancouver, and many older adults are not receiving the maximum subsidies (Office of the Seniors Advocate, 2018).

We can imagine that an older adult has a monthly income of $1,250 with maximal monthly rent subsidies of $765, and the rent is $1,038 per month. After paying the rent, there is only $977 left. He still needs to spend on many other things, such as healthcare, transportation, and food. The waiting lists for subsidized housing are long. In BC, the average waiting time is 2.4 years (Office of the Seniors Advocate, 2018). In Vancouver, the waiting time is at least 2–3 years and can be up to 10 years (411 Seniors Centre Society, 2018). These older adults are at risk of being evicted by the landlords because they cannot afford the rapidly rising rent or the landlords want to sell the property for better profits (Greater Vancouver Shelter Strategy, 2013). Some older adults end up being homeless for the first time in their lives.

Healthcare costs—Another main area of spending is healthcare costs. Aging increases healthcare needs, especially with increased life expectancy (MacDonald et al., 2010). Canada in theory has a universal public healthcare system in which healthcare is accessible to all. However, in reality, many older adults find it difficult to meet their healthcare needs due to costs. Extended healthcare is not covered by the public healthcare system (e.g., dental care, foot care, home support, mobility aids) (MacDonald et al., 2010). Most older adults do not have private healthcare insurance. The reasons are similar to why many do not have a private pension. Thus, they have to pay for extended healthcare out-of-pocket. This "extended" healthcare sounds like basic healthcare needs. Are they really "extended"? (E.g., an older adult loses appetite because her denture is not fixed and ends up in malnutrition.)

The welfare state consists of three pillars, which are the state, market, and family (Esping-Andersen, 1999). When the first two pillars do not function well, the family pillar plays a larger role. This is the case with older adults who need home care (Ryser & Halseth, 2011). The public healthcare system cannot fulfill their healthcare needs. The private healthcare system is too costly for them to afford. They can only rely on their families. The Canadian government promotes deinstitutionalization and aging at home (Wong, 2016). In theory, these are good policy initiatives. However, there is not enough home care and support for family caregivers. Many family caregivers end up burnout (Turner & Findlay, 2012). Some family caregivers are older adults themselves and have their own health problems (e.g., older spousal caregivers).

Some older adults leave their healthcare needs unmet due to costs and not wanting to bother their families, and they end up in hospitals in emergency conditions (Kary, 2017). The cost of hospital care is far more expensive than home care. In BC, 1% of spending on acute hospital care per year is estimated to be equal to 5-year total spending on community and home care (Kary, 2017).

Food costs—Concerning food, older adults are in theory eating less as they need less energy compared with the working-age population (MacDonald et al., 2010). Therefore, it seems to make sense to consider lower costs on food for them when using the working-age population as the benchmark. However, many older adults need more specialized diets, so it turns out that they are spending similar or even more than the working-age population.

Transportation costs—The income of some older adults is just slightly above the threshold to qualify for the transportation subsidies (e.g., older adults' bus pass) and this makes them ineligible for the subsidies (411 Seniors Centre Society, 2018). Also, the current public transit system is not older adult-friendly enough (411 Seniors Centre Society, 2018). Older adults' mobility often declines with age. However, there is often not enough room for multiple wheelchair and scooter users or enough seats for walker and cane users. Some older adults have to turn to the automobile due to their mobility needs (MacDonald et al., 2010). Automobile ownership becomes a need instead of a want in these situations. However, many of them cannot afford automobile ownership, including the cost of insurance and/or gas. A taxi may not be an option because it can be expensive even if there are taxi savers.

Groups of older adults at higher risk of poverty

Older adults are a highly diverse population. Some groups are at a higher risk of poverty. One group is older adults who live alone. They live alone for different reasons, such as living in rural areas while having adult children living in urban areas due to the cost of living (Ryser & Halseth, 2011), or being single, separated, divorced, or widowed (Green et al., 2008; United Way, 2018). Living alone reduces the possibilities of in-cash and in-kind (e.g., food, clothes) transfers from families who co-reside with the older adults (Kaida & Boyd, 2011).

Another group is older adult women (Forum+, 2018; Ivanova et al., 2017). They might not be in employment, be in employment for a short time, or be in employment part-time due to care responsibilities at home (e.g., looking after children and older adult parents). Even if they were in employment for a long time and worked full-time, there is still a gender pay gap and women earn less than men. Since CPP is a pension plan based on employment history and earnings, older adult women receive less CPP than older adult men. In BC, the median annual CPP for older adult men is $1,700 higher than that for women (Ivanova et al., 2017). Older adult women are less likely to receive private pensions too. In BC, the average private pension older adult men receive is double that of older adult women (Ivanova et al., 2017).

One more group is the immigrant older adults, especially the recent immigrants. Many immigrant older adults reunite with their adult children through the sponsorship program (Kaida & Boyd, 2011). They are not entitled to benefits in the first 10 years under the program requirements. They are not entitled to OAS in the first 10 years either because OAS has a 10-year residency requirement. GIS is linked with OAS, so they are not entitled to it either. However, even if they have lived in Canada longer and are entitled to pensions and benefits, many do not apply because they are not aware that they are entitled to the pensions and benefits or they have different barriers with the application such as language and/or proof of residence (e.g., misplacing immigration certificate) (411 Seniors Center Society, 2018).

Even if they were employed, since they worked for a shorter period in Canada than their Canadian-born counterparts, they had fewer contribution years to CPP (Kaida & Boyd, 2011). Also, due to discrimination in the labor market, they were more likely to have lower wages. They were more likely to be in employment where they are not eligible for a pension (e.g., casual jobs). This is especially the case for racial minority immigrants. All these factors negatively affected the amount of their CPP.

Many immigrant older adults co-reside with family (Kaida & Boyd, 2011). Although this can be related to reasons such as culture, one main reason is to save costs. However, co-residence can lead to other problems. For example, in a recent immigrant family, an older adult is sponsored by her adult child. There are already a lot of issues going on in the family, such as unemployment of the adult child and intergenerational conflicts between the adult child and the grandchildren. The older adult might be seen as a burden by the family, or the family relies on the older adult to look after the grandchildren, and the older adult has care responsibilities all day long without respite.

The author acknowledges the limitation of this chapter in that it cannot include every group of older adults at a higher risk of poverty. However, some other groups at higher risk that are not discussed in this chapter include the Aboriginal Elders, racial minorities, and LGBTQ2S+ older adults (Greater Vancouver Shelter Strategy, 2013; Henriquez, 2019; Ivanova et al., 2017).

Why older adults' poverty is a social justice issue

The issue of older adults' poverty in BC, which is a social justice issue, can be explained by referring to two social justice theories, which are the capabilities approach and the ethics of care perspective.

Capabilities approach—The capabilities approach suggests that capabilities refer to functioning (i.e., being and doing), opportunities, and abilities (Morris, 2002; Robeyns, 2016). People need capabilities to actualize their good lives. There may be constraints for people building their capabilities, and support should be provided to them. There are differences between people, and they can value things differently, so they can define good lives and ways to achieve them differently. Each person should have the freedom of choice on the definition of good lives and ways to achieve them.

By applying the above definition of the capabilities approach in the context of older adults, suggested by Gopinath (2018) and Stephens and Breheny (2018), first, the approach recognizes the constraints older adults face in building their capabilities and suggests that support should be provided to older adults. Although older adults face different constraints, a common one is that as they age, their physical and cognitive conditions decline, and their needs increase. They are not able to meet these needs alone by themselves and/or their families. The government needs to provide adequate support to older adults.[1] Having these needs met, older adults can enhance their capabilities. Also, the approach suggests that each older adult should have the freedom of choice to define what good lives are and decide how they want to achieve the good lives defined by them.

However, the capabilities approach is not reflected in the issue of older adults' poverty. Older adults' poverty is therefore a social justice issue. As suggested, many older adults find it challenging to have their needs met due to costs. For example, if older adults define good lives as feeling comfortable and decide to achieve this by living in comfortable homes, they would need to be in housing in good condition. Their physical and cognitive conditions may not allow them to be in employment and earn enough income to rent housing in good condition. They need adequate pensions and rent subsidies for the high rent, or subsidized housing. However, as discussed, their low pensions and rent subsidies cannot afford high rent. Also, the subsidized housing waiting list is long.

If older adults define good lives as enjoyment and decide to achieve this by participating in leisure activities, they would need a certain level of health to participate. Their physical and cognitive conditions decline, requiring quality and affordable healthcare. However, as discussed, many healthcare costs are not covered by the public healthcare system and are too high for older adults to afford. Older adults cannot meet their needs and build their capabilities. Gradually, they see achieving good lives as something remote. They limit their thinking of options and possibilities. They lose their freedom of choices in defining good lives and ways to achieve them.

Some may argue that older adults' limitations on defining good lives and deciding how to achieve them are less related to inadequate support and more related to their physical and cognitive limitations. The author argues that if there is adequate support, older adults with physical and cognitive limitations can still have the freedom of choice in defining good lives and deciding how they want to achieve them (Payne, 2012). For example, an older adult with dementia and mobility issues lives in long-term care. She is not able to express herself clearly. However, she is happiest and most active when she participates in activities she chooses and enjoys. Through careful observation, families and staff understand that she defines good lives as enjoyment. She enjoys playing tennis. Her dementia and mobility issues do not allow her to play real tennis because she cannot run and cannot follow the complicated rules. However, with the support of recreation staff, she can still play balloon tennis, an adaptive version of tennis with less body movement and simplified rules, which she can participate in and enjoy.

The policymakers seem to think that what older adults need is just to be out of the poverty line. This is evidenced by the fact that there is a large proportion of older adults whose income is just slightly above the poverty line. However, from the capabilities approach, what older adults need should not just be to get out of the poverty line, but support to meet their needs and enhance their capabilities so that they can achieve what they consider to be good lives. There is a gap in understanding what older adults need from policymakers. This is because policymakers are used to defining for older adults what they need and how they should achieve this without listening to older adults' voices. For example, policymakers promote "successful aging." They define what "successful aging" should be and how it should be achieved (e.g., being active by doing exercises) (Calasanti, 2016; Ranzijn, 2010). This creates pressure on many older adults who do not fit the standards of "successful aging." An appropriate understanding by policymakers of what older adults need is crucial because this has implications when they design policies for older adults (MacDonald et al., 2010). Policymakers should consider how to build a policy-making process that can effectively include older adults' voices.

Ethics of care perspective

Another social justice theory the author will refer to is the ethics of care perspective (Engster, 2014; Hankivsky, 2004). The perspective suggests that people have diverse and complex features and relationships. They need to consider the contexts. They need to understand each other's perspectives, and this concept is known as responsiveness. This can be achieved through dialogue. People are dependent on each other and should take care of one another, and this concept is known as interdependency. Dependency and care are a normal and significant part of life. They are the universal human experience.

By applying the above definition of the ethics of care perspective in the context of older adults, first suggested by Ward (2015), the perspective considers that older adults are a diverse population. Older adults have different identities, and these identities place them in different positions of privilege and oppression in power relationships. Therefore, inequalities exist between different groups of older adults. As suggested, some groups of older adults are at higher risk of poverty. These identities intersect. Most older adults have some identities that give them privileges while some identities put them in oppressions. However, some older adults are particularly oppressed because they have multiple identities that subject them in multiple oppressions. For example, an immigrant racialized older adult woman faces oppression due to her immigrant status, racism, ageism, and sexism. The degree of privilege and oppression of these identities also changes in different contexts. A recent immigrant older adult who only speaks the language of her country of origin but no English may feel more powerful in her country of origin than in Canada. Because of these intersecting identities and changing contexts, older adults have complex features and relationships. Policymakers should consider all these identities, contexts, features, and relationships to design policies that cater to the needs of different older adult groups. Second, as suggested by Lloyd (2006), the perspective encourages older adults and other age groups to understand each other's perspectives. It promotes dialogues between them. As a result, older adults' voices are recognized in society. Third, as suggested by Lloyd (2006), the perspective considers that older adults and other age groups are dependent on each other and should take care of each other. For example, in many Aboriginal and Eastern cultures, younger age groups look after older adults while older adults share their life wisdom and provide guidance to younger age groups (Liu & Kendig, 2000; Sigafus & Ernst, 2014; Stiegelbauer, 1996).[2]

However, the ethics of care perspective is not reflected in the issue of older adults' poverty. Older adults' poverty is thus a social justice issue. First, policymakers fail to recognize the variations among older adults. For example, the public pension system continues to fail to recognize the problem that some older adult groups (e.g., women and immigrants) have more challenges accessing an adequate pension. Also, older adults' voices are marginalized in the policy-making process (Lloyd, 2006). For instance, despite advocacy by older adult groups, policymakers still fail to recognize the adequate costs older adults need (411 Seniors Centre Society, 2018). Third, society views older adults as a burden who increase the expenditure on healthcare and pension at the expense of other age groups (Lloyd, 2006). Policymakers in response suggest policies restraining the expenditure on these areas.

Instead of the ethics of care perspective, society views older adults through the lens of capitalism, the dominant ideology in society (Payne, 2012; Phillipson, 1982). Capitalism aims to maximize material profits (e.g., money, resources). It stresses competition for material profits among people. Therefore, the more material profits people produce, the more they are valued. Based on this logic, working-aged adults are most valued because they have the highest abilities to produce material profits. Children and youth are highly valued too because they will be the working-aged adults in the future. Older adults are least valued because they have the lowest abilities to produce material profits due to their physical and cognitive limitations.

However, older adults contributed to society when they were working-aged adults. Many indeed are still contributing. Some are still doing paid work (Government of Canada, 2012). Some contribute in non-material terms (e.g., looking after grandchildren, volunteering in the community, sharing their life wisdom) (Weiss & Bass, 2002). Society is dependent on these previous and current contributions of older adults. Older adults deserve a reasonable pension, healthcare, and other public expenditures.

Older adults' poverty is not only a concern for older adults (Lloyd, 2006). It is a common concern for everyone. This is because aging and care are universal. Everyone will age and will care or be cared for in life. Older adults cared for people older than them when they were young. They are cared for by young people now. Young people will be cared for by people younger than them when they are old. Due to our aging population, with more older adults but fewer young people, many of our current pension, healthcare, and other policies and systems are becoming unsustainable. However, this need not to develop into hostility toward older adults. What society needs are dialogues and collaboration between older adults and other age groups, and looking for solutions to improve our current policies and systems together (Engster, 2014; Hugman, 2008; Ife, 2008, 2012).

Conclusion

The author discussed the issue of older adults' poverty in BC. He also discussed why it is a social justice issue by referring to two social justice theories, which are the capabilities approach and the ethics of care perspective. The capabilities approach focuses on older adults. It talks about how older adults' needs are not met due to costs. This constrains older adults' building of capabilities and their freedom of choices in defining good lives and ways to achieve them. The ethics of care perspective focuses on the relationship between older adults and society. It talks about how society's view of older adults as a burden accelerates older adults' poverty. The theories explain why older adults' poverty is a social justice issue from different perspectives. They should complement instead of compete with each other.

Notes

1 Other social justice theories can be integrated into the capabilities approach. One of them is the human rights perspective. From a human rights perspective, there are rights attached to needs (Ife, 2012). For example, housing implies the right to be sheltered. Healthcare implies the right to have good health. These are positive rights. In other words, they need the government to provide and actualize them. This argument further strengthens the capabilities approach on the importance of government intervention in meeting seniors' needs and supporting them to build their capabilities.
2 However, with the spread and growth of Western influences including these ideologies, in these cultures, the seniors of these cultures are gradually less valued (Liu & Kendig, 2000).

References

411 Seniors Centre Society. (2018). *Submission on poverty reduction strategy for seniors*. 411 Seniors Centre Society.
Calasanti, T. (2016). Combating ageism: How successful is successful aging? *The Gerontologist*, *56*(6), 1093–1101. https://doi.org/10.1093/geront/gnv076
Engster, D. (2014). The social determinants of health, care ethics and just health care. *Contemporary Political Theory*, *13*(2), 149–167. https://doi.org/10.1057/cpt.2013.14
Esping-Andersen, G. (1999). *Social foundations of postindustrial economies*. Oxford University Press.

Forum+. (2018). *Rapid synthesis: Identifying indicators and rates of poverty among older adults*. McMaster University.
Gopinath, M. (2018). Thinking about later life: Insights from the capability approach. *Ageing International*, 43(2), 254–264. https://doi.org/10.1007/s12126-018-9323-0
Government of Canada. (2012). *Age-friendly workplaces: Promoting older worker participation*. Federal/Provincial/Territorial Ministers Responsible for Seniors.
Greater Vancouver Shelter Strategy. (2013). *Sheltering homeless seniors: Literature review*. United Way. http://hsa-bc.ca/wp-content/uploads/2018/02/Sheltering-Homeless-Seniors-Lit-Review-Dec-2013.pdf
Green, R. J., Williams, P. L., Johnson, C. S., & Blum, I. (2008). Can Canadian seniors on public pensions afford a nutritious diet? *Canadian Journal on Aging / La Revue Canadienne Du Vieillissement*, 27(1), 69–79. https://doi.org/10.3138/cja.27.1.069
Hankivsky, O. (2004). *Social policy and the ethic of care*. UBC Press.
Healthcare of Ontario Pension Plan. (2017). *Seniors and poverty: Canada's next crisis?* Healthcare of Ontario Pension Plan.
Henriquez, N. R. (2019). *What we need to know: Developing knowledge and awareness about LGBT older adults*. https://www.canadian-nurse.com/en/articles/issues/2019/september-2019/what-we-need-to-know-developing-knowledge-and-awareness-about-lgbt-older-adults
Hugman, R. (2008). Social work values: Equity or equality? A response to Solas. *Australian Social Work*, 61(2), 141–145. https://doi.org/10.1080/03124070801998400
Ife, J. (2008). Comment on John Solas: "What are we fighting for?" *Australian Social Work*, 61(2), 137–140. https://doi.org/10.1080/03124070801998392
Ife, J. (2012). *Human rights and social work: Towards rights-based practice* (3rd ed.). Cambridge University Press.
Ivanova, I., Daub, S., Cohen, M., & Jenkins, J. (2017). *Poverty and inequality among British Columbia's seniors*. Canadian Centre for Policy Alternatives.
Kaida, L., & Boyd, M. (2011). Poverty variations among the elderly: The roles of income security policies and family co-residence. *Canadian Journal on Aging / La Revue Canadienne Du Vieillissement*, 30(1), 83–100. https://doi.org/10.1017/S0714980810000814
Kary, M. (2017). *Strengthening seniors care delivery in BC*. BC Care Providers Association. https://bccare.ca/wp-content/uploads/2017/01/BCCPA_Roadmap_Full_Jan2017.pdf
Liu, W. T., & Kendig, H. (2000). *Who should care for the elderly? An east-west value divide*. Singapore University Press, National University of Singapore.
Lloyd, L. (2006). A caring profession? The ethics of care and social work with older people. *The British Journal of Social Work*, 36(7), 1171–1185. https://doi.org/10.1093/bjsw/bch400
MacDonald, B.-J., Andrews, D., & Brown, R. L. (2010). The Canadian elder standard: Pricing the cost of basic needs for the Canadian elderly. *Canadian Journal on Aging / La Revue Canadienne Du Vieillissement*, 29(1), 39–56. https://doi.org/10.1017/S0714980809990432
Morris, P. M. (2002). The capabilities perspective: A framework for social justice. *Families in Society: The Journal of Contemporary Social Services*, 83(4), 365–373. https://doi.org/10.1606/1044-3894.16
Office of the Seniors Advocate. (2015). *Seniors' housing in B.C.* Office of the Seniors Advocate. https://www.seniorsadvocatebc.ca/app/uploads/sites/4/2015/05/Seniors-Housing-in-B.C.-Affordable-Appropriate-Available.pdf
Office of the Seniors Advocate. (2018). *Monitoring seniors services*. Office of the Seniors Advocate. https://www.seniorsadvocatebc.ca/app/uploads/sites/4/2019/01/MonitoringReport2018.pdf

Payne, M. (2012). *Citizenship social work with older people*. Policy.
Phillipson, C. (1982). *Capitalism and the construction of old age*. Macmillan.
Ranzijn, R. (2010). Active ageing: Another way to oppress marginalized and disadvantaged elders?: Aboriginal elders as a case study. *Journal of Health Psychology, 15*(5), 716–723. https://doi.org/10.1177/1359105310368181
Robeyns, I. (2016). *The capability approach*. Stanford Encyclopedia of Philosophy. https://plato.stanford.edu/entries/capability-approach/
Ryser, L., & Halseth, G. (2011). Informal support networks of low-income senior women living alone: Evidence from Fort St. John, BC. *Journal of Women & Aging, 23*(3), 185–202. https://doi.org/10.1080/08952841.2011.587734
Sigafus, K., & Ernst, L. (2014). *Native elders: Sharing their wisdom*. 7th Generation/Native Voices.
Stephens, C., & Breheny, M. (2018). *Healthy ageing: A capability approach to inclusive policy and practice* (1st ed.). Routledge Ltd. https://doi.org/10.4324/9781315639093
Stiegelbauer, S. M. (1996). What is an Elder? What do elders do? First Nation Elders as teachers in culture-based urban organizations. *Canadian Journal of Native Studies, 16*(1), 37.
Turner, A., & Findlay, L. (2012). *Informal caregiving for seniors*. Statistics Canada. https://www150.statcan.gc.ca/n1/en/pub/82-003-x/2012003/article/11694-eng.pdf?st=6OSBy6qs
United Way. (2018). *B.C. seniors poverty report card*. United Way. https://www.uwlm.ca/wp-content/uploads/2018/06/B.C.-Seniors-Poverty-Report-Card.pdf
Veall, M. R. (2008). Canadian seniors and the low income measure. *Canadian Public Policy / Analyse de Politiques, 34*(4), 47–58. https://doi.org/10.3138/cpp.34.4.S47
Ward, N. (2015). Care ethics, intersectionality and poststructuralism. In T. Brannelly, L. Ward, & N. Ward (Eds.), *Ethics of Care* (pp. 57–68). Policy Press.
Weiss, R. S., & Bass, S. A. (2002). *Challenges of the third age: Meaning and purpose in later life*. Oxford University Press.
Wong, K. L. Y. (2016). Elder care in B.C.: Shifting to a proactive home and community care approach. *Monitor, March / April*, 40.

4
END OF LIFE CARE AND THE AGEING POPULATION

Asian perspectives

Jagriti Gangopadhyay

Caregiving in India continues to rest on the family. Despite the rise of the nuclear family system, later-life caregiving in India is expected from adult children and their families. Although paid caregiving is gradually increasing in India, policies focussing on end-of-life care for the elderly need more discussion. According to the WHO 2012 definition, palliative care is "an approach that improves the quality of life of patients and their families facing the problems associated with life-threatening illness, through the prevention and relief of suffering by means of early identification and impeccable assessment and treatment of pain and other problems, physical, psychosocial, and spiritual."

Although palliative care is quite popular across the globe, palliative care or end-of-life care started in the 1980s and, as a concept, is comparatively new in India (Khosla et al, 2012). Additionally, end-of-life care is mostly associated with cancer and other forms of chronic illness. The need for end-of-life care for the elderly in India has received limited attention in the gerontological scholarship of India. The older population of India suffers from a range of incurable diseases such as dementia, stroke, end-stage Parkinson's disease, refractory cardiac failure, end-stage renal failure, end-stage Chronic Obstructive Pulmonary Disease (COPD) on home oxygen therapy or non-invasive ventilation, vertebral fractures, and hip fracture and often physicians and nurses are not trained to provide palliative care to the geriatric population of India (Adhikari, 2017).

Against this backdrop, the present study seeks to understand the significance of palliative care among older adults with chronic illnesses. Relying on qualitative interviews with family caregivers (which are mostly spouses

DOI: 10.4324/9781003528432-5

and the adult children and their families) of the older patients suffering from chronic illnesses, this study demonstrates how end-of-life care is a crucial step to ensure quality of care in later lives. Finally, this chapter uses a policy lens and illustrates how end-of-life care has evolved across Asia.

A large number of studies have focused on end-of-life care among cancer patients in India. Studies examining end-of-life care among older adults are few in number. In a 2016 study located in two *gram panchayats* of Kerala, Jayalakshmi et al. (2016) found poor quality of ageing and dying services provided by home-based palliative care. In particular, the study demonstrated that home-based palliation in its current form does not endorse decent end-of-life care. Finally, the study concludes with concerns over the family home as the locus of ageing and dying for the poor and suggests the need for reorganization of the palliative programme. Chatterjee and Sengupta (2017), in their book "Death and Dying in India: Ageing and End of Life Care of the Elderly" suggest that death and dying of the elderly in India have received limited attention in academia as well as policy owing to the present obsession with the "active aging framework" in a neoliberal India. Additionally, this book also argues that older adults in India experience either a "medicalized death" or die due to inadequate socio-legal provisions for end-of-life care. As a result, end-of-life care often involves major psychological, social, and financial costs for the patients as well as the caregivers. Finally, this book provides evidence-based research to improve the dying conditions of the elderly and bring death and dying to the public health agenda (Chatterjee & Sengupta, 2017).

In another study examining end-of-life care among older adults attending a tertiary care hospital in the eastern part of India, Pany et al. (2018) found that a vast majority of their respondents preferred to die in their homes. Finally, in a recent editorial in the National Medical Journal of India, Gursahani et al. (2019) recommend a team of semi-skilled workers to aid elderly patients in their end-of-life care. Relying on the National Skill Development Mission, these workers can be trained and then employed to help older adults with their palliative care (Gursahani et al., 2019). A quick analysis of all these studies suggests that end-of-life care for the elderly in India has so far been neglected and needs immediate restructuring. Apart from these studies, reports by the Lien Foundation (2010, 2015) depicted the quality of death and dying in India as poor. Building on these studies, the present study highlights the challenges faced by family caregivers looking after older patients with chronic conditions. In the process, the present study also indicates how the quality of care for these elderly patients with chronic conditions can be improved. Finally, this study draws from policies on end-of-life care across Asia and suggests why end-of-life care in India needs urgent policy attention.

The present study

The present study used qualitative techniques to understand the different perspectives of family caregivers. Participants for this study were recruited through snowball sampling. Family caregivers who were providing end-of-life care to an older adult with a chronic illness for the last three years were included in the study. Owing to the pandemic, the study was conducted through telephonic interviews. Each interview lasted for an hour. In households where the older adult lived with their spouse as well as their adult children, the primary caregiver was interviewed. A total of ten family caregivers across India were interviewed for the purpose of this study. As the study relied on snowball sampling and the author relied on personal contacts to conduct the interviews, the study was spread all across India. However, the major cities covered were as follows: Kolkata, Manipal, and Ahmedabad.

The study was conducted based on a semi-structured questionnaire. This questionnaire was constructed using the deductive method. Existing literature on end-of-life care and the elderly in India was the main source for drawing up the questionnaire. The questionnaire was divided into four parts: Part I: Socio-Demographic Information; Part II: Quality of Care Received by the Older Adults; Part III: Challenges Faced by the Family; Part IV: Policy Suggestions. Some of the questions were as follows:

What forms of caregiving activities do you perform on a daily basis?
What are some of the problems faced by you as a caregiver?
How do you feel about the quality of care received by your spouse/father/
    father-in-law?
What form of policy changes would you recommend for elderly with chronic
    illnesses and requiring end-of-life care support?

Among the ten respondents, three of the family caregivers were spouses, three were adult children, and four were daughters-in-law. All the spouses interviewed as primary family caregivers were women, and among the adult children caregivers, two were daughters. In addition to the family caregiver, every household had hired domestic help to assist the family caregiver with end-of-life care services. However, none of these domestic helpers had any form of prior training, and all of them were hired through some domestic help agency. Although caste and religious intersections remained outside the scope of the study, information regarding these two demographic features was collected. The religious affiliations were as follows: four Hindus, three Christians, two Jains, and one Muslim. The caste affiliations were as follows: two Brahmins, two Kshatriyas, three Vaishyas, one OBC, and two SCs. The ethnic breakup of the respondents was as follows: two Bengalis, three Marwaris, three Malayalis, and two Gujaratis. All the older patients had two children. However, the end-of-life care responsibility was borne by either the spouse or by only one of the adult children and their families. In all the cases, the other sibling or both the adult children were situated in other cities or other countries. Although the adult children or the other sibling could not provide physical care, they provided monetary support. Owing to snowball sampling and limited access, all the households belonged to the middle-class income group. A detailed table (Table 4.1) with all the background information of the respondents is demonstrated below.

The study has a small sample size owing to the pandemic, with class and ethnic restrictions. Additionally, face-to-face interviews could not be conducted due to the nationwide lockdown imposed by the Government of India.

Results and discussion

Detailed interviews with the caregivers revealed that a lack of training among the primary family caregivers came across as the major problem associated with end-of-life care. All the family members indicated that they mostly felt guilty for not being able to provide the best care to their loved ones. The quotes below further substantiate these points:

> When my husband had his stroke and he became bed ridden, I was both heartbroken and scared. Each time I change his bed pan and his soiled clothes, I wonder if I am doing it right. I feel guilty that I have no training and I am worried that I might do something wrong which might cause

TABLE 4.1 Socio-demographic information of the respondents

Feature	Sample Representation
Living Arrangement of family caregivers	Two only with spouse; five with spouse and adult children and their families; three with adult children and their families
Religion	Four Hindus; three Christians; two Jains; one Muslim
Caste	Two Brahmins; two Kshatriyas; three Vaishyas; one OBC; two SCs
Ethnicities	Two Bengalis; three Marwaris; three Malayalis; two Gujaratis
Number of children of the older patient	Two for all the respondents
Chronic illnesses associated with older patients	Four cardiovascular failures; three stroke-related disability; two chronic kidney conditions; one dementia

Source: Author

some damage. There are no trained nurses or helpers who can come and stay with you guide you. The help we have is more like my assistant. She has no training and I cannot trust her either. It is a very difficult situation for all of us.

(Spouse, primary family caregiver, aged 75)

I have my own business. This is mostly run by my son and so I can be home and look after my mother. She has been suffering from dementia for the last seven years and I cannot trust her with anyone other than myself. I take her to the bathroom, feed her, and dress her up. I do everything. We have a helper who does separate cooking and cleaning for my mother. But the personal care is provided by me. I know I am not the best caregiver and also earlier I used to feel embarrassed while changing her clothes or taking her to the bathroom. But gradually you get used to. While there is no guarantee of quality of care provided by family members, I am not sure how institutional care is any good either. They often take large chunks of money and ill-treat the patient. At least at home I can monitor everything.

(Adult son, primary family caregiver, aged 67)

My mother-in-law has been terminally ill for the last five years and I have always taken care of her. After her heart attack, she got paralysis in various parts of the body and needs help with feeding, going to the bathroom, dressing and even lying down. I really do feel very sorry for her. My husband is busy with his work and my children have their own studies etc. Hence, it is my responsibility to look after her. I think I worry more because if anything goes wrong, I will be blamed for it. No matter how hard I try, I always feel that I am not doing enough and I can much more. The helper we have is mostly for cleaning the bed and the room. I cannot trust her with anything else.

(Daughter in law, primary family caregiver, aged 55)

Although all the primary family caregivers expressed concern over the quality of care they provided by them and did not rely on their domestic help for any major assistance, institutional support also did not emerge as a suitable alternative. All the respondents were wary of the type of care their parents/parents-in-law/spouses would receive in these caregiving homes. In particular, such homes or institutions providing end-of-life care support were critiqued for neglecting the older patients suffering from chronic illnesses and not delivering the promised quality care. Owing to the lack of state-funded institutional support, all the family caregivers chose to provide care within their household. These findings of the present study are in line with the findings of a study conducted by Bhattacharyya et al. (2017) in the private homes of end-of-life care homes for the elderly in Kolkata, West Bengal. Highlighting issues such as poor housing conditions, lack of skilled caregivers, and scarce funding, the study administered by Bhattacharyya et al. (2017) urge for remedial measures to improve the quality of care among end-of-life care elderly patients.

In contrast to institutional support, all the respondents emphasized the need for trained caregivers in India. As the quotes suggested, neither of the respondents could rely on their domestic help as the help was trained primarily in cooking and cleaning. As a result, the sole burden of care fell on one particular family member. As a policy suggestion, all the family caregivers indicated that the Government of India should train unemployed men and women through proper healthcare professionals to provide quality care to terminally ill elderly patients. With the rising ageing population, all the respondents stated that it is imperative for the Government to take end-of-life care for the elderly as a major policy decision and start creating skilled caregivers. In a 2014 article elaborating on end-of-life care received by elderly patients in India, Macaden et al. (2014), urge all healthcare providers with direct patient contact to undergo end-of-life care certification. Additionally, Macaden et al. (2014) in that same article also recommend end-of-life care training to be incorporated into the curriculum of healthcare education. Similar to the suggestions of the respondents, this article also stresses the need for proper end-of-life care training, knowledge, and certification to improve the quality of care received by terminally ill elderly patients in India.

Asian and South Asian countries have a long history of filial piety and, as this chapter indicated at the very beginning, later-life caregiving primarily rests on the family (Lamb, 2013; Kadoya & Khan, 2015; Gangopadhyay & Samanta, 2017). However, often this caregiving responsibility is viewed as a burden by caregivers, as it often impacts the everyday life of the caregivers (Gupta et al., 2009; Bastawrous, 2013; Ugargol et al., 2016). Similar to these studies, the respondents of the present study often found end-of-life care for their older relatives to be tedious and restrictive to their mobility. Additionally, as the relationship between the caregiver and the patient in the course of end-of-life care was not reciprocal, it became challenging for the caregiver to not complain and remain self-effacing throughout the process of caregiving. Some of the common problems listed by the caregivers were that their travel plans had come to a halt, and one member would always have to stay at home to be with the patient. In households where the patient lived only with their spouse, the challenge was larger as they would have to regularly plan regularly regarding their supply of groceries and other daily requirements. The quotes below further illuminate these findings:

> I sometimes feel like I live with a child. Like, when you have a baby in the house and you cannot do anything because of the baby, palliative care

often can be equated as a similar experience. I have all the shopkeepers delivering at my place because everybody knows that my husband has been terminally unwell for quite some time. Still at times I do get anxious and worry as to how I will manage on my own. It is very difficult as I am also growing old and I just hope that nothing happens to me physically. In fact, sometimes, I also wonder that who will look after me if something like this happens to me. My children are settled abroad. I might have to leave India then.

(Spouse, primary family caregiver, aged 72)

I feel frustrated every day to look after my father-in-law. My whole life changed and at times I cannot take it anymore. But I cannot abandon him either. My husband is his only son and if I stop caring for my father-in-law, then he will die of neglect. I feel life is unfair to me. Plus, I also worry that as I am not a blood tie, if anything ever happens to my father-in-law, I will be blamed by the entire family. At that time no one will understand my burden, pain or guilt. So, I do not share my struggles with my husband or children. I cannot go anywhere and I am confined to the home. There is no trained help and it really becomes difficult for us on a regular basis. I wish the Government did something.

(Daughter in law, primary family caregiver, aged 45)

My mother has been ill for a very long time and as my brother lives outside the country, it is impossible for him to do anything for her. He sends financial help. But that's about it. He cannot do anything more than that. I do feel that it is unfair to me that I do more for my mother when she has been a parent for both my brother as well as me. However, I cannot abandon her either. Someday I might be in her state and then might children my face the same thing that I am currently facing. I have stopped travelling and making plans with my family as my mother needs me to be here all the time. I often shout at my children to show my anger. But I know it is not their fault.

(Daughter, primary family caregiver, aged 49)

Apart from these quotes, the respondents also mentioned that end-of-life care more often than often impacted their mental health, and they faced stress on a daily basis. The lack of professionally skilled caregivers transferred the entire burden of caregiving to the family members. According to the recent Maintenance and Welfare of Parents and Senior Citizens (Amendment) Bill, 2019, introduced in the Lok Sabha on 11th December 2019, the description of children mentioned in the Maintenance and Welfare of Parents and Senior Citizens Act, 2007, was extended. In particular, the amendment went beyond the notion of biological children and incorporated daughters-in-law and sons-in-law as well as adopted and stepchildren to be responsible for later life caregiving for older parents in India (Gangopadhyay, 2019). Though this Bill was lauded by most policymakers, it is important to note that the Bill continues to burden the family with the sole responsibility of caregiving (Gangopadhyay, 2019). this Bill, most of the respondents highlighted that with the rise of globalization and neo-liberalization, joint living will gradually diminish, and unless the Government of India comes up with major alternatives, older patients with end-of-life care issues will face neglect and abandonment across India.

Apart from focusing on the law and the challenges faced by the caregivers on a daily basis, the respondents also elaborated on their own mental health. More often than often the family caregivers felt exasperated and were unsure of sharing their emotions with other family members. In all cases, the family caregiver felt guilty of complaining as they did not want to portray themselves as victims. As a result, most of the respondents suggested for counselling options to share their feelings and emotions regarding regular caregiving. All the respondents indicated that while mental health discussions are rising across the country, it is important for the Government of India to take note of the mental health conditions of the family caregivers and offer free telephonic counselling to reduce their everyday stress. This way, the interviewed family caregivers (the respondents) specified that their conflict with other family members would also reduce, and they would also receive a platform to voice their challenges and issues.

Although filial obligations are associated with adult children and their families, later life caregiving as a responsibility is mostly shouldered by women in India (Dhar, 2012; Ugargol et al., 2016; Ugargol & Bailey, 2018). Similar to these studies, in the present study, except for two, all the other caregivers were females. Lamb (2009), in her ethnographic account of the elderly in Kolkata, suggested that as per Indian traditions, daughters-in-law are mostly expected to provide caregiving arrangements for their older in-laws. According to a recent media report, Indian women spend 16 billion hours a day performing unpaid care (Times of India, 2020). Highlighting the gender disparities embedded in end-of-life caregiving arrangements, the respondents indicated that as women have been connected to care work for the longest time, they consider caregiving to be a part of their role. Throwing light on this fact, the quotes below illustrate the intersections between gender norms and end-of-life caregiving arrangements:

> When my husband became disabled, it was expected that I have to take care of him. Our children could not come and take responsibility. So I have to do everything. Though, I am not sure what would have happened if my husband had to take care of me and I was the one who was disabled.

Men are hardly trained. Women right from their birth have been trained to do all housework and basically take care of their husbands. All my life, I have been doing that. So I don't know how this is any different from what I was already doing.

(Spouse, primary family caregiver, aged 68)

I am at home and my husband has no time. So I have to look after my father in law. If I do not look after him, I will be blamed and called a bad daughter in law. I have to take full responsibility. My own mother also took care of her ageing parents in law and fulfilled her responsibilities. Maybe if I was working, we would have to think of other alternatives. But as I am not a working woman, the caregiving responsibility of both my children as well as my father-in-law falls on me.

(Daughter in law, primary family caregiver, aged 37)

I don't think I am taking care of my father because I am his daughter. It is because I live in India and my brother lives outside the country. However, I think I might have had to anyway take responsibility because my brother and his wife are working and I run my business which I can do from home. Hence, I think it might not always be gender, but it is more a matter of convenience and availability. I can monitor and keep an eye on all the activities, unlike my brother and his spouse who are very busy.

(Adult daughter, primary family caregiver, aged 41)

I take care of my father and I do not let my wife do anything. I mostly work from home and I like taking care of my father. I don't think caregiving should be performed only by women of the house. Men should also take some responsibility. I know most men do not and it comes on the women of the house, but everyone should at least take care of their own parents. My wife is also working and she has to go out every day as she works in a bank. So, it is easier for me to perform caregiving duties. There is no shame in this.

(Adult son, primary family caregiver, aged 67)

An analysis of the quotes suggests that while traditional gender roles do structure end-of-life caregiving arrangements, there are other factors as well. For instance, the narratives of the adult children indicated that convenience, availability, and intergenerational bonds also play a role in shaping end-of-life caregiving arrangements. Sharma et al. (2016), in their study, found that elderly caregiving among men is gradually increasing and more research needs to be done to explore the caregiving experiences of men.

Corroborating the findings of this study conducted by Sharma et al. (2016), the present study suggests that caregiving roles are steadily changing in a neoliberal India. Although this change should be celebrated, it is important to note that caregiving responsibility among female spouses continues to persist. In particular, this problem of older women taking care of their disabled husbands needs urgent policy attention as the caregivers themselves are old and have their own set of health issues as well.

As indicated in the Introduction of the chapter, one of the key goals of this chapter is to draw from end-of-life care policies of other Asian countries to enhance policy suggestions for India. This section will throw light on end-of-life care policies of those Asian countries which are currently dealing with a high ageing population.

China: In terms of an ageing population, by 2018, China accounted for 150 million people aged 65 years or older (Yan et al., 2020). Similar to India, China too stresses filial piety and adult children play a crucial role in providing end-of-life care to ageing parents. A recent study conducted by Yan et al. (2020) found that with a growing ageing population and increasing incidences of cancer and chronic illnesses within that ageing population, China will not be able to meet the palliative care demand of this ageing population. Additionally, owing to China's one-child policy, by 2010, one million Chinese parents had lost their only child. Another study conducted by Liang et al. (2018) found that most childless older couples in China preferred to shift to hospice or palliative care institutions for their end-of-life care. Thus, in both these studies, the authors urge for palliative care advocacy to improve end-of-life care for their elderly patients.

Japan: Similar to China, the ageing population of Japan is also increasing rapidly. Being inspired by Western countries, Japan has created several forms of palliative care services to assist the elderly with end-of-life care. For instance, Japan launched its Long-term Care Insurance (LTCI) system in 2000. This LTCI is a mandatory system that requires every person aged 40 and above to contribute by paying a premium which is income dependent. However, all older persons aged 65 years and above receive the same benefits, regardless of their income. The services and benefits of the LTCI, such as institutional, home, and community-based care, are accessed through a care manager (JHPN Main website, 2015). Critiquing the LTCI system, an analysis by Hirakawa (2012), suggests that while the LTCI was created to help the elderly and those with terminal illnesses, this policy fails to take note of the various cultural norms integrated among the Japanese. In particular, Hirakawa (2012), indicates that in Japan, family members and physicians play a more critical role in making decisions as opposed to the patient. Relatedly, in Japan, patients do not complain of pain as patience is a virtue, and life and death are often seen as matters of fate. Thus, generating an end-of-life care system that is motivated by Western countries may not be culturally appreciated by the elderly of Japan.

South Korea: A peaceful death at home, surrounded by friends and family, is the ideal definition of death for the elderly at South Korea. In the last ten years, Korea has witnessed more than a two-fold increase in the number of long-term care facilities for elderly people, including both long-term care hospitals and nursing homes, with around 2,930 nursing homes in South Korea (Park et al., 2019). This increase in institutional care could be attributed to increasing life expectancy, elderly people living independently and the decline of family caregiving. Elaborating on the rise of institutional care in South Korea, Park et al. (2019), in their study, found that the nursing home staff working in hospice care displayed a need for further education in end-of-life care. In particular, the staff mentioned that training and education should be specialized and focus on the following: Care Helpers: care in residents' last days of life; Nurses: spiritual care of residents; Social Workers: care for the bereaved families of residents. Thus, proper training and education among institutional caregivers are very important to provide quality end-of-life care services among the elderly population.

Singapore: A recent report titled "Leaving Well: End-of-Life Care Policies in Singapore", published by the Institute of Policy Studies (IPS), highlighted the need to change the administration of end-of-life care in Singapore. Drawing from the 2014, Lien Foundation survey, this report indicated that while 77% of Singaporeans wanted to die at home, in 2017, 70% of Singaporeans died in hospitals. A study conducted by Malhotra et al. (2012) among middle-aged and older Singaporeans found that the study participants identified eight components for quality end-of-life care. These eight components were as follows: 1) physical comfort at the end of life, 2) avoid inappropriate prolongation of the dying process, 3) maintain sensitivity toward religious and spiritual beliefs, 4) avoid burden on the family, 5) avoid expensive care, 6) be cared for by a trustworthy doctor, 7) maintain control over care decisions, and 8) achieve a sense of completion. Thus, in this study, the authors recommend that end-of-life care for the elderly should focus on these eight components to provide quality care to older Singaporeans.

Thailand: Highlighting the issue of long-term care and rural and urban inequality, a study conducted by Khongboon and Pongpanich (2018) suggests that to develop a comprehensive end-of-life care policy, it is important to assess the various inequalities present within the older cohorts as a group. Differences in terms of income, geographical area, and education need to be evaluated before developing any long-term end-of-life care policy for older adults (Khongboon & Pongpanich, 2018). Another study conducted by Supaporn et al. (2019), focusing on the perspectives of caregivers of older persons, found that the caregivers fulfil their caregiving responsibilities owing to Thai traditions of ancestral caregiving, to repay the kindness of the older person, and to avoid the abandonment of the elderly. Hence, this paper recommends designing various strategies to address caregivers' perspectives to improve the quality of care received by the older patients.

A summary of all the studies and policies indicated in this section suggests that cultural values, educational training of paid caregivers, and consulting family caregivers are very important for constructing a holistic end-of-life care policy. Given the stress on culture in Asian countries, policymakers need to take note of various cultural practices and the views of the patient as well as the caregiver to provide quality end-of-life care for the growing ageing population of Asia.

Conclusion and policy implications

One of the main goals of this chapter was to demonstrate the perspectives of family caregivers providing end-of-life care to their older parents, spouses, and parents-in-law. Findings from the study suggest that all the family caregivers were in constant guilt as they were not sure about the quality of care they were providing to their older relative suffering from chronic illnesses. Additionally, the study also found that constant caregiving restricted the mobility and freedom of family caregivers in their everyday lives. Owing to lack of trust and inadequate training, none of the family caregivers showed an inclination towards relying on paid caregiving. Similarly, institutional caregiving also did not come up as a major alternative as all the caregivers were wary of the quality of services provided by private palliative care homes for the elderly. Finally, several studies have demonstrated how the caregiving burden falls on women of the house and unpaid care work continues to be a major reason for gender inequality in India. Though most of the respondents of the present study were women, narratives from the adult children revealed that availability, geographical location, and convenience also act as important factors for end-of-life caregiving arrangements. Nonetheless, older women caring for their spouses was one of the main findings of this study.

Based on the findings of this study and drawing from the end-of-life care literature and policies of other Asian countries with a growing older population, this chapter will end by discussing some policy implications for end-of-life care for older adults in India. The first and foremost policy suggestion would be the need to create a trained pool of nonfamily caregivers. As mentioned by the respondents of the study, family caregiving can be shifted to paid caregiving only if the hired caregiver is trained and skilled. Taking note of this suggestion, the Government of India needs to invest in this sector and generate professional and skilled caregivers who are trained in providing end-of-life care services to elderly patients. In the course of the training, the caregivers should also be taught to be culturally sensitive, as cultural norms and ideologies form a core component of palliative care in Asia. Apart from training, these professional caregivers should be sent and monitored through central agencies to avoid any form of breach of trust between the caregiver and the patient's family. However, for families who choose to rely on family caregiving, mental health counselling must be provided to these family caregivers to reduce their everyday frustration. Finally, in households with older women taking care of their terminally ill older husbands, subsidized professional and domestic help should be provided to assist older women in coping with their own age-related challenges.

References

Adhikari, P. (2017). Palliative care needs of geriatric population in India. *Manipal Journal of Nursing and Health Sciences*, 3(2): 1–1.

Bastawrous, M. (2013). Caregiver burden—A critical discussion. *International Journal of Nursing Studies*, 50(3): 431–41. doi: 10.1016/j.ijnurstu.2012.10.005

Bhattacharyya, T., Chatterjee, S. C., Chand, D., Chatterjee, D., & Sengupta, J. (2017). Assessment of private homes as spaces for the dying elderly. *Indian Journal of Palliative Care*, 23(3): 325–30.

Chatterjee, S. C., & Sengupta, J. (2017). *Death and Dying in India: Ageing and End-of-life Care of the Elderly*. Routledge contemporary South Asia series: New Delhi.

Dhar, R. L. (2012). Caregiving for elderly parents: A study from the Indian perspective. *Home Health Care Management & Practice*, 24(5): 242–254. https://doi.org/10.1177/1084822312439466

Economic Intelligence Unit. (2010). The quality of death Ranking end-of-life care across the world. Lien Foundation. Accessed at http://www.lienfoundation.org/sites/default/files/qod_index_2.pdf

Economic Intelligence Unit. (2015). The 2015 quality of death index ranking palliative care across the world. Lien Foundation. Accessed at http://www.lienfoundation.org/sites/default/files/2015%20Quality%20of%20Death%20Report.pdf

Gangopadhyay, J. (2019). Senior Citizens Bill will fail to provide India's elderly the 'life of dignity' it claims to. Scroll. Accessed at https://scroll.in/article/946898/senior-citizens-bill-will-fail-to-provide-indias-elderly-the-life-of-dignity-it-claims-to

Gangopadhyay, J., & Samanta, T. (2017). 'Family matters': Aging and intergenerational social contract in urban Ahmedabad, Gujarat. *Contributions to Indian Sociology*, 51(3): 338–360. doi: 10.1177/0069966717720962

Gupta, R., Rowe, N., & Pillai, V. K. (2009). Perceived caregiver burden in India: Implications for social services. *Affilia*, 24(1): 69–79. doi: 10.1177/0886109908326998

Gursahani, R., Mani, R. K., & Simha, S. (2019). Making end-of-life and palliative care viable in India: A blueprint for action. *The National Medical Journal of India*, 32(3): 129–33.

Hirakawa, Y. (2012). *Palliative Care for the Elderly: A Japanese Perspective*, In Chang, E., & Johnson, A. (Eds.), *Contemporary and Innovative Practice in Palliative Care* (pp. 271–290), IntechOpen: Rijeka, DOI: 10.5772/30767. Available from: https://www.intechopen.com/books/contemporary-and-innovative-practice-in-palliative-care/palliative-care-for-the-elderly-a-japanese-perspective

IPS, https://lkyspp.nus.edu.sg/docs/default-source/ips/toc_report-calls-for-government-to-relook-at-end-of-life-care-schemes-and-giving-better-quality-of-life-netizens-back-the-call_150719.pdf

Jayalakshmi, R., Chatterjee, S. C., & Chatterjee, D. (2016). End-of-life characteristics of the elderly: An assessment of home-based palliative services in two panchayats of Kerala. *Indian Journal of Palliative Care*, 22(4): 491–8.
JHPN. (2015). http://japanhpn.org/en/longtermcare/#:~:text=Long%2Dterm %20care%20insurance%20(LTCI,17%25%20of%20this%20age%20 population.&text=All%20persons%20aged%2040%20and,that%20varies%20 according%20to%20income
Kadoya, Y., & Khan, M. (2015). The role of gender in long-term care for older parents: Evidence from India. *Economic Research Center Discussion Paper: E-Series*, E14–E15. doi: 10.1080/13229400.2017.1279561
Khongboon, P., & Pongpanich, S. (2018). Estimating long-term care costs among Thai elderly: A Phichit Province case study. *Journal of Aging Research*, 4180565. https://doi.org/10.1155/2018/4180565
Khosla, D., Patel, F. D., & Sharma, S. C. (2012). Palliative care in India: Current progress and future needs. *Indian Journal of Palliative Care*, 18(3): 149–54.
Lamb, S. (2009). *Aging and the Indian Diaspora: Cosmopolitan Families in India and Abroad*. Indiana University Press: Bloomington, IN.
Lamb, S. (2013). In/Dependence, intergenerational uncertainty and the ambivalent state: Perceptions of old age security in India. *South Asia: Journal of South Asian Studies*, 36(1): 65–78.
Liang, Y., Liang, H., Wang, J., Xu, H., & Wu, B. (2018). End-of-life care preference: Examination of Chinese adults with children and those who lost their only child. *Journal of Palliative Medicine*, 21(11): 1596–1603. http://doi.org/10.1089/jpm .2018.0043
Lien Foundation. (2014). http://lienfoundation.org/sites/default/files/Death %20survey%20Presser%20Final%20-%20Combined_0.pdf
Macaden, S. C., Salins, N., Muckaden, M., Kulkarni, P., Joad, A., Nirabhawane, V. & Simha, S. (2014). End of life care policy for the dying: Consensus position statement of Indian association of palliative care. *Indian Journal of Palliative Care*, 20(3): 171–81.
Malhotra, C., Chan, A., Do, Y. K., Malhotra, R., & Goh, C. (2012). Good end-of-life care: Perspectives of middle-aged and older Singaporeans. *Journal of Pain and Symptom Management*, 44(2): 252–63. doi: 10.1016/j. jpainsymman.2011.09.007
Pany, S., Patnaik, L., Rao, E. V., Pattanaik, S., & Sahu, T. (2018). End-of-life care and social security issues among geriatric people attending a tertiary care hospital of Eastern India. *Indian Journal of Palliative Care*, 24(4): 402–5.
Park, M., Yeom, H-A., & Yong, S. J. (2019). Hospice care education needs of nursing home staff in South Korea: A cross-sectional study. *BMC Palliative Care*, 18(2). https://doi.org/10.1186/s12904-019-0405-x
Sharma, N., Chakrabarti, S., & Grover, S. (2016). Gender differences in caregiving among family - caregivers of people with mental illnesses. *World journal of psychiatry*, 6(1): 7–17. https://doi.org/10.5498/wjp.v6.i1.7
Supaporn, K., Isaramalai, S. A., & Suttharangsee, W. (2019). Exploring caregivers' perspectives on improving care for older people at the end of life in Thailand. *International Journal of Palliative Nursing*, 25(7): 326–332. doi: 10.12968/ ijpn.2019.25.7.326
Times of India. (2020). Indian women spend 16 billion hours a day doing unpaid care. Accessed at https://timesofindia.indiatimes.com/india/indian-women-spend -16-billion-hours-a-day-doing-unpaid-care-work/articleshow/69699732.cms
Ugargol, A. P., & Bailey, A. (2018). Family caregiving for older adults: Gendered roles and caregiver burden in emigrant households of Kerala, India. *Asian Population Studies*, 14(2): 194–210.

Ugargol, A. P., Hutter, I., James, K. S., & Bailey, A. (2016). Care needs and caregivers: Associations and effects of living arrangements on caregiving to older adults in India. *Ageing International*, 41(2): 193–213. doi: 10.1007/s12126-016-9243-9

Yan, Y., Zhang, H., Gao, W., Liu, D., Endo, M., Deshpande, G. A., Uehara, Y., Watanabe, D., Yoshikawa, S., & Mizushima. A. (2020). Current awareness of palliative care in China. *The Lancet Global health*, 8(3): e333–e5. doi: 10.1016/s2214-109x (20)30006-1

5
WHY RESTRUCTURING RESIDENTIAL CARE MATTERS

A global perspective

Sumana Das

Introduction

The development of the academic and non-academic studies of aging started with the core concept of the "caregiving attitude and perspective." Overexposure to technology and declining sensibility towards elderly care in the contemporary epoch recognize and rejuvenate the relationship between "body, care and attachment," which needs to be studied under the macro and micro social lens. I am addressing elderly care issues particularly under the lens of gender and age, which are affected by many factors. Still, seldom are these factors reorganized, nor the contribution of elderly women in providing natural care or receiving care from their families and kin groups are acknowledged or rarely acknowledged. Very little research is "available to highlight the different aspects and, more importantly, to suggest remedies to improve the well-being of older women across the world. Many older women survive to avoid the death of their spouses who experience a drastic shift in their living arrangements during old age." One in ten women over 60 years live alone, and this is even more among widowed women, with many of them never having contact with their non-co-residing children (Shankardass Kapur Mala, 2021).

Care is a response that represents psychological, social, and biological actions towards a person or a group. It is a value-oriented and cultural practice loaded with responsibilities. Care is a process of giving warm affection and prayer for wellness. It nurtures the human heart and develops sensitiveness, a sixth sense to realize how to care for a care seeker. What do they want? And how to create a comfortable situation for a patient? Another central focus of related to care starts with who needs care? Caregiving aims

DOI: 10.4324/9781003528432-6

to offer a quality of services aimed to reduce pain, give support the targeted population. All these questions indicate the meaning the method of providing care (Shankardass Kapur Mala, 2021).

The natural way of caregiving is a process of healing that comes both from the self as well as from the family caregivers. Etymologically, care refers to providing what is necessary for the health, welfare, maintenance, and protection of someone or something. Care is a comprehensive and arbitrary word that can be applied in different contexts, ranging from child care to elderly care, the entire corpus of which mostly encompasses feelings like concern, love, responsibility, and, at times, selflessness, Close attention, ushering dignity, mutual adjustment, and respect for mutual opinions and perspectives are practically more caregiving than so-called protection and custody This can also be labeled as residential care, care within their known interior, and care from a micro perspective (Phillips Judith, Ajrou Kristine, and Nalletamby Sarah, 2010). According to a report by Help Age India, released in 2018, 65% of older adults found their families paying a lot of attention to phones and computers disrespectful. According to many elders, the installation of domestic gadgets by their young family members to smoothen the elders' day-to-day activities has often become a burden for older people. It is sometimes the reason behind elderly abuse. Their inability to cope with the pace of technological comfort gives rise to a sense of inferiority among them, making them further victims of elderly abuse and anticipated fear. This fear of abuse and the abuse itself gets accumulated into their mind, which hampers their confidence, flexibility of thinking, and willpower, which is instrumental in rendering them weak in practical reality (Shankardass, M. K., 2018). According to them, to 38% of elders, "the most effective way to deal with elder abuse is to sensitize children" (Jamuna, D., 2003). "Sensitization of children and strengthening inter-generational bonding is the way forward to bridge the technological gap and empower older people" (Technology Hurts the Elderly, 14th June 2018). Each society has its own method of caregiving system, usually care offered within instrumental and non-instrumental provisions. Macro and professional organizations like hospitals, nursing homes, and homes provide institutional care. In contrast, non-institutional care is provided by micro, non-professional, yet the core institutions like the family. Two main sources of non-clinical care are residential and family care (National Economic and Social Council, 2005). In some countries, residential care is provided by the community, thus it is also considered community care. Residential care functions as a bridge between these two types of care. This is also micro-level care, which is not so care with close attention, care from reliable and supportive source with basic infrastructure (Finch, J, 1989a). There are varieties of care depending on situation, needs and condition of the patient, for example, short-term and long-term care. Long-term care is this type of care, which is significant for those needing long-term maintenance, building a social and community network and supporting older people. Most older adults get scared about these settings, but why? The elderly, or mostly older adults, believe they are being thrown out of the house, alienated from their family members, and isolated. Consequently, it is often observed that after going to residential homes, elderly adults become mentally sick, depressed, and lonely. It has become an immense problem nationwide and needs to be resolved. Subsequently, the question arises: how can we restructure the residential care system? (Torrington Judith, 2005).

The subjective sense of social, cultural, and psychological gerontology emphasizes the life course's effect on older people's health status. Still, the applicability of health care within a residential structure needs more attention. Starting from Person's "Sick role" to Bourdieu's age habitat and Goffman's "body idioms" modern method methods of body care need to be restructured from a residential perspective. It helps to cultivate family attachment and give future benefits for generations, which demands educating family members to fulfill the knowledge of the residential caregiving method. Residential care settings provide a semi-institutional environment where older people can receive professional care from other associated facilities, such as helping with personal tasks. At present, many countries suffer from common elderly disabilities such as Alzheimer's disease, dementia, Parkinson's, arthritis, heart disease, hearing problems, weak eyesight, dental problems, problems with high blood pressure, etc. These elderly needs call for extra attention from professionals. Therefore, many countries provide government-subsidized accommodation for older people, in addition to accommodation and personally hired residential care centers, which are mushrooming all over the globe. These facilities are turning into business strategies and a marketing-based profit-gaining system. Many disciplines have considered different areas of aging, but sociology specifically studies the problems of aging from both subjective and objective views (Ramamurti, P. V., Jamuna, D. Reddy, L. K., 1996).

Sociologists are more concerned about the types of difficulties older adults are facing within society. They conduct surveys and prepare reports, construct theories, and recommend policies. The most significant problem that many sociologists have opined is that the breakdown of the joint family leads to family isolation, relationship breakdown, loose attachment, and finally leading to withering care for elderly members, rendering them helpless. Although in the societal structure, the family system performs the most significant role in the lifespan of the aged ones. New long-time work schedules, office distance, and migrated work are field-hampering the practices of traditional care methods. Modern constraints of life sometimes do not allow people to take all-around maintenance of their elderly ones. Autonomous social structures and new occupational patterns with over-urbanized ideologies working as social influences indicate that the traditional method of geriatric caregiving needs to be restructured.

Due to the high cost of housing and rapid urbanization, it is becoming impossible for mediocre families to arrange a comfortable and separate zone for their elderly parents. Modern-day 2 BHK apartment culture hardly places or can a separate room for older people or an elderly friendly zone, leading these people to become practical room sharers and thereby suffering the crisis of comfortable settlement. The developing care careers of their offspring, along with the increasing demands of their third generation, take a toll on their 8'*10' world. The scenario further aggravates when the older adult is diseased or bedridden, for as both conditions call for special residential care backed up with accommodations and amenities catering to the specific ailing demands of older adults (Hees Van Susan, Wanka Anna and Horstman Klasie, 2001).

For basic care services, the home plays an important role, for it is where individuals live and build their micro attachments, and bonding by establishing marital or blood relationships. All members perform their sense of duty and accountabilities toward other members within a household. The household care system is the most traditional resource that offers non-institutional attention, completely dependent upon family members, family structure, kinship system, and their relationship. Each needs care in their life, but the perception of care is multidimensional and varies with age. There is a deep correlation between care and age; as we know, children and elderly persons need maximum attention. A newborn baby gets the first care from the family, and at the same time, elderly persons get the last care of the family, thus they become more emotionally dependent on household care. Based on age differences, there are many discriminations against caregiving. Care is more of an area of concern as they started realizing the negative effects of, such as some stereotypical attitudes, common prejudices of disability or ill health or sickness, unattractive attractiveness or ugliness, low morale and physical strength, depression, and mental sickness gains gain in them (Singh, S, 2002).

To protect older people, the family must build a positive attitude toward those aging by giving them care, such as kindness, respect, importance, and freedom. The primary purpose of this study is to analyze the sense of caregiving to older people within their comfort zones, restructure the residential care system, and create a global guideline to set the treads for providing positive care for older adults. Japan, an example with the highest ratio of elderly citizens in the world, conforms to the new practice of age care in a traditional manner and has a more confident attitude toward ageing (Peine Alexander, Marshall Barbra and Martin Wendy, 2021).

Published work of World *Population Prospects: 2015* highlights that the 65+ population is increasing rapidly all over the world; between 2015 and

2030, the population aged above 60 will increase by 56 percent, from 901 million to 1.4 billion, and most importantly, by 2050, it will nearly touch 2.1 billion. As a result, every country must enhance its, policies, funding, and other areas; as for elderly care and benefits, with those better medical services and infrastructure, the elderly receive proper treatment and improved longevity. The rising graph of the elderly population indicates a level of demographic, a change in the fertility mortality ratio and demographic density. Many statistical reports show that elderly abuse, neglect, and ill-treatment are quite common, working against elderly care. Thus, the housing ambiance and architecture must be elderly friendly and comfortable. Professional practitioners provide medical care, but emotional care is only provided to one's family members (Higgs Paul & Jones Ian, 2009).

The major reason for introducing and restructuring elderly residential care lies in the root fact, as shown in the census reports, that almost all countries are facing high growth in the elderly population, declining fertility, reduction of mortality, advanced medical facilities, and moving towards quality living resulting in high life expectancy (Vaarama Marja, Pieper Richard, and Sixsmith Andrew, 2008). Here, the demand for senior care arises from the progress needed in elderly protection, supportive socio-economic and medical infrastructure for the elderly, education for employment, and community attachment to ethnic participation. All these aspects can indirectly or directly influence geriatric care. Moreover, it can be said that restructuring is necessary to establish a modern method for the advancement of the senior care system (Vaarama Marja, Pieper Richard, Sixsmith Andrew, 2008).

As a solution, healthy living, joyful ageing, and a supportive community set a new trend in senior care. The Madrid International Plan Action on Ageing (MIPAA; U.N., 2020) highlighted three aspects to analyse ageing issues and policy development: 1) older persons and development; 2) advancing health and well-being in old age; 3) ensuring an enabling and supportive environment. The last pillar aims to restructure and strengthen the area of formal and residential care in modern ways (Shankardass Kapur Mala, 2021). A country like India considers family as a source of traditional values followed by cultural norms, and family protects its members and fulfills all basic economic, social, physical, and psychological needs. This represents a structure of emotional bonding with family members, even if they care for their ancestors. In this manner, the notion of informal care develops as a result of family relationships, bonding, attachment, and increased dependency. The global perspective of residential care depends on a few aspects like the number of family members, economic conditions, and inner house spaces. These elements may differ from country to country. Globally, the role of relatives, neighbours, co-residents, and friends plays an important role. Other than this, governmental and non-governmental organizations, such as nursing homes, provide residential care and support to older adults in their comfort zones (Ramamurti, P. V., 2002).

Residential care institutions provide professional health care, execute caregiving responsibilities, and offer assistance and services to help older people within the residential home. They arrange doctors, nurses, attendants, physical assistants, medical technicians or physiotherapists, rehabilitation support and non-clinical support as well. They also arrange senior service events, cultural programs, and short and long travels, as well as provide essential services. We need to fill the gap between the practice of family care and professional care. Also, a smart move from household care to residential care may open a new avenue for care responses from responsible semi-professional institutes. There is a strong reason behind the regularization of residential homes, and that is a liberalized, self-aware, autonomous and self-determined elderly lifestyle.

A major blockage in the regularization of residents involves trust building, acceptance of strangers' interference, and attachment building with new, unknown co-residents. Thus, elder care services need a special design to meet all kinds of requirements, including security (Manchester Helen, 2021). The Facility of residential care services is in demand, especially in developing countries such as Thailand, the Philippines, Vietnam, and India. However, many poorer countries still face major challenges in providing support to the elderly. They are dependent upon family-based and community-based care. Globally, all countries launched policies for elderly care. Developed countries prefer to provide super-specialist on home-based professional care care, and underdeveloped countries depend on family members and neighborhood care. Here another problem arises: people are not skilled or trained to give geriatric care. There are a few areas where the elderly need professional care, such as 1) Mental Health consisting of Anxiety, Addiction, Bipolar Disorder, Depression, Eating Disorder, Personality Disorder, Schizophrenia, Stress and Suicide prone attitude, etc.; 2) Health and Wellness consists of Healthy lifestyle, workouts, well-being and happiness, sleep disorders; 3) Physical Health consists of Alzheimer and Dementia, etc.; 4) Relationship management consists of communication, bonding and attachment, emotional dependency, love and friendship (Shankardass Kapur Mala, 2021).

Residential care comprises all areas where the care of family members and professional help is demanding. We can see that the higher life expectancy trend is causing medical advancement and uplifting the healthcare management system. Advanced life expectancy also brings a new dimension to caregiving methods like seeking care from another, increasing trust and bonding, an adaptation of adopting some independent care measures, and noting your exact problem, etc. We can make age stratification of the elderly based on age, like young-older, middle-older, middle-older, and older elderly. The first section can take care of themselves if they are not critically ill; the second group sometimes needs extra care other than their family member, member; but the third group mostly needs professional care, with those who are suffering from long-term diseases seeking professional care at home settings (Wahl, H.-W. and Weisman, J., 2003).

Thus, the professional caregiver must restructure those old methods of the residential care system. They must know how to trigger different emotional variations in behavior and attitudes, must help them to improve and acknowledge the different feelings, and must involve friends, extended family members, and co-residents in developing a junction of care. Several sources of caregiving, which boosts the reciprocal relationship between caregiver and care seeker. The government or private clinics can initiate some training-based programs for family members to offer basic-level professional skills to give care to the elderly adults. Another's tendency for choosing residential care is the established economic capacity of the elderly like elderly, such as better retirement plans, after retirement plans, and post-retirement working policy policies, which push towards independent living. This which gives strength to a new economy controlled by the country's elderly population.

The Aged In-Home Care Project (ADHOC), one of the most valuable cross-national research projects, studied 11 countries and how they designed their community systems. All over the world, home care agencies were established around the 1900s to improve the care system, utilization of in-house space, building household attachment, professional care at home facilities, research orientation, cooperation and network building, and improvement in health care policy and family responsibility.

Organizations like HelpAge International, established in 1983, spread its network worldwide, especially in five countries named Canada, Colombia, India, Kenya, and the United States. They work with local community-based organizations to provide direct support to older people. They correspondingly arrange training programs for supporting the elderly, influencing governmental policies for older people, and conducting practical-based field fieldwork for better understanding.

An association like the International Association of Gerontology and Geriatrics (IAGG), established in 1950 and later renamed as the International Association of Gerontology, conducts the World Congress of Ageing. It promotes different medical advancements and advancements and advancements, focuses on diseases, and fosters high-quality education and training (Higgs Paul and Jones Ian, 2009).

An agency like the International Association of Home and Service for the Ageing (IASHA) was established in 1994 to provide aging care services across the globe. It is also an educational, business-oriented, research-based, and charitable organization. Members can exchange their knowledge in senior care and receive professional plans for business development.

Thus, home care or residential care is still in a growing phase. Argentina organizes a two-year geriatric fellowship after the Board Examination and provides a certificate for internal medicine or family medicine. In Australia, education in gerontology is available in universities like Technical and Further Education (TAFE). They offer courses like Age Care qualification, Community Services Training, Package, Personal Care Assistance, Home Care Assistant, etc. All Austrian universities provide special professional skill-based care management and nursing courses. These courses include lifestyle modification of older adults, life cycle and aging experience, management and leadership-based care, community, and, most importantly, residential care knowledge. The National Strategy for Ageing Australia (NSAA) emphasizes firstly self-provision aspects like employment, retirement, and savings schemes; secondly "Attitude, Lifestyles, and Community Support"; and third "Healthy Ageing" encompasses well-being, personal care, and life-course approaches. Subsequently, they started multidimensional research-based work to improve the care of older people. Denmark provides free home-help services from the municipality, they also offer training programs programs for skill enhancement in elderly care, and they established an aided house home for the elderly, which is granted from funded by social welfare (Department of Health and Ageing (DoHA), 2003).

In England, some residential care is free from government and welfare services, handled by local authorities. Around the 1980s, this concept emerged as "new rights" for older people in a commercial format. Over time, this business became very popular and encouraged investors, institutions, and professional organizations. In Ireland, residential care was established in 2009, and the government published national standards and quality guidelines for residential settings. Up to 80% and offered different courses with voluntary participation in home care activities. They divided their care services into parts: 1) personal care delivered at home supported by Community Long-Term Care Insurance Law, 2) Personal and recreational care services supported by daycare centres, and 3) local monitoring and supportive community care (Health Information and Quality Authority, 2007).

Italy provides public L.I.C. for older people, which consists of three main components: home care, residential care, and cash allowance. This country follows traditional family care norms; they use the home help method for critical and long-term care. The availability of infrastructure for residential care is quite unevenly distributed. A country like Malta also provides residential care, which includes three types of care services: first, a residential home, which is home run by the government; the second type of residential care run by the Catholic Church; and finally, residential home homes run for profit-oriented businesses. In 1996, the government announced a public-private partnership scheme, public-private model (Walker, A. (Ed.), 2005).

In New Zealand, the local community runs and governs the residential care system. This country also provides training for basic, advanced, community-based, and residential care-based geriatric courses. Presently, this service is semi-professional in reducing the burden on families and the community, and many caregiving organizations are developing such facilities. The statistical report says 19% of men and 13% of women receive residential care. However, they prefer to go for residential care only when they become highly disabled; otherwise, they stay within their home or in a community care household (Estes, C., 2001).

Social Policy and Aging

The aging world's highest population has started researching elderly care. The Development of China's Understandings for the Aged (China National Commission on Ageing, 2006) includes some aspects: 1) state supportive elderly mechanism, 2) old age security, 3) health and medical care, 4) social services for elderly, 5) elderly people's legitimate rights and interests. The Institute of Gerontology at Renmin University of China offers various courses, publishes articles, and conducts research (Du, P., Editor-in-chief, 2007).

India is the first-largest and second-largest populated country, as per country. According to the UNFPA report, by 2025, the expected growth of the elderly population will be 17.3 crores, and by 2050, it will reach 24 crores. Thus, the Government of India, Department of Ministry of Social Justice and Empowerment (M.S.J. & E) works for policy implementation for the elderly and announced the National Policy for Older Persons (NPOP) in the year 1999. Along with policy implementation, they provide guidelines for senior services, pension, and retirement benefits and also offer tanning-based programs in collaboration with different universities, universities, and N.G.O.s. They specifically highlight: 1) strengthening primary health care care, 2) endorsing geriatric training-based programs, 3) awareness for healthy aging, 4) subsidy on essential items for the elderly, 5) involving self-help groups for daycare and residential care, and 6) skill development and empowerment of older people. Other than this, the 2007 Care and Maintenance and Welfare of Parents and Senior Citizens Act was passed, which mandates the care of parents by their adult children. In a recent programme, The Ministry on Housing and Urban Affairs (MoHUA) announced the project "Retirement Home" in 2016, providing a model and guidelines for such housing. Universities like Sri Venkateswara Department of Psychology, Sri Padmavati Women's University, University of Calcutta, and Tata Institute of Social Science offer geriatric courses for elderly care and management (Jamuna, D., 2004).

Despite training and research activities, there is a very small number of model guidelines for developing and regulating residential and retirement homes in various countries. Residential care is not only to provide attention to older adults or assist them in different work but also to build intra-generational bonding, companionship, and dependency among the same age group. Therefore, structural change is very much needed at the city level, village level, and also town level, as well as the environment within the space, such as a priority room with an attached bathroom, room space, balcony, small stepping staircase and also decorated with old memories, pictures, flowers, and furniture. Currently, most countries are working on restructuring the home care model holistically. There are many available models, but none of them are methods that are internationally or globally followed. From the above discussion about the nature and types of residential care, some common methods can be applied holistically (Ramamurti, P. V. and Jamuna, D., 2007).

Structure of residential care centres

1. Locality-based residential care home based on affordability.
2. The patient's own house must be accessible to maintain family relations easily.
3. Residential homes can be rented, reverse mortgaged, or ownership-based.
4. The home structure must be full of greenery, have a balcony, and have spacious rooms and corridors. There must also be a religious place and a mandatory lift and ramps.
5. Sufficient light, ventilation, and CCTV cameras in all corners.
6. There must be one library with local language books covering religious to economic, social affairs to political books, dining hall, meeting hall, doctor's room, visitor's room, and yoga or exercise room.
7. Proper arrangement of medical services in collaboration with the nearest hospital and medicine store.
8. Internet service, laundry, wellness services, personal caregiving attendant.
9. Well-designed kitchen and toilet.
10. More emphasis on quality living.

Awareness guidelines for residential care

1. Awareness building for staying in residential care homes.
2. For service provision, include local self-helpgroups, NGOs, local clubs, nursing colleges, and medical colleges.

3. Elderly care education in practical or internship internship internship formats for the school and college students to build intra-generational bonding.
4. Creating a database or census report from the community level to monitor elderly care provided by local institutions, such as clubs and organizations.
5. Restriction or modification of in-house structure for the elderly can be aided by the government to the L.I.G.
6. Relationship metre reading (elderly with a family member) by local government and publication of the report.
7. Successful and quality caregiving families will receive acknowledgment and financial support from the state and central government.
8. Build a caregiving family association to boost training and skill development for others.

Residential homes, also known as elderly living houses, houses, and elderly family houses, fulfill the needs of the elderly for staying and caregiving facilities. The government, non-governmental organizations, associations, and personal interests regulate these housing systems. These houses mostly cater to the interests of the upper and middle-class classes by providing them with all types of assistance, assistance, and caregiving facilities. They ensure comfortable, attractive, healthy, and standard elderly living. Many N.G.O.s initiated this project to create profitable businesses. Still, the Indian government imposed various rules for this kind of home to ensure extreme security, benefits, and rights for the aged. There are numerous reasons for developing these residential homes like homes, such as working migrated children, loss of a spouse, and the nuclear family structure. Other than this process of globalization, excessive modernization and attraction towards Westernization resulted in a burden on life. In that case, in this context, both parents and children are moving towards a new ideology of a burden-free lifestyle. As a result, elderly people are losing support from family members and becoming more dependent on such semi-professional and professional organizations for the rest of their lives. Thus, the origin and development of residential homes have become socially impactful and have indicated a new social structure (Karmel, T., and Woods, D., 2004).

The ageing phenomenon has additional effects on a person's psychology and creates socio-psychological pressure. Many people find it difficult to accept the physical changes that occur in individuals' bodies, which results in many physiological disturbances as well. It is the responsibility of every individual to understand these changes and the mental turmoil that our elderly family members go through. Many times, elderly people face a lot of violence in their own families as well as in the outside world. The family family members tend to abuse them mentally or even physically, consider them to be a burden, and deny them basic needs such as food, shelter, and clothes. At times, family members may stoop so low that they even leave their parents on the road, at an old age home home, or may even kill them for property or maybe simply because they didn't feel like looking after them. Here, the cruelty comes in, and residential care becomes essential for the elderly to protect themselves. Besides this, the residential care system allows them to live burden-free or autonomously. It is also a safe and secure shelter within the protected care zone (Jamuna, D. and Ramamurti, P. V., 2000). It also gives a joyful life that is activity-based, participation-based, participation-based, and communication-oriented and provides a stress-free environment. Like Bourdieu's age habits and Goffman's body idiom is a modern method of body care that needs to be restructured from a residential perspective, a long journey to build awareness toward the positive impact of residential care. Still, primarily, the restructuring of household care must be considered. With aging, individuals understand the importance of "person-centered cases" and "self-centered cases." People are in a continuous hurry to secure their lives and are often preoccupied with their work and life problems. Children should be socialized in such a way that they learn to respect their elders and empathize with their changing situations. People should equally spend time with their parents or any elderly member of the family, as this would serve as an example for the children who will follow the paths of their parents. Even amidst the hustle and bustle of life, we cannot afford to neglect the aged members of our family or even outside our family. Hence, it is essential to teach and train children within a household atmosphere to take care of elderly members from childhood. Strict rules and regulations should be maintained to atrocities against elderly people. Proper investigation and punishment should be given to people who perform heinous crimes against elderly people. It is important to understand their condition and, give them a priority, and not treat them as a burden (Finch, J., 1995).

Many elderly people have to go through the agony of losing their loved ones, which causes a sense of loneliness in them. Our moral responsibility is to support the elderly in need and not isolate them. Isolation can cause even further damage to their mental and physical health. Many of them lose their sanity with increasing age. Not getting the right kind of attention or treatment can be quite detrimental; therefore, one should sympathize with them and help them to come out of the situation. Ignorance is another struggle that most aged people go through. We often become so involved in our daily lives that we tend to forget to interact with the elderly members of our family. Often, it has been noticed that the young members of the family go outside for recreational activities, leaving behind their aged parents and grandparents to look after their household. Such unexpected behavior from loved ones often causes a feeling of sadness in ageing people. Unable to convey their despair, they stay silent and accept everything (Harper, S., 2003).

Therefore, I have discussed why we need to build a new, healthy elderly care institution to give them a dignified, full life. It is essential to construct a bridge between residential care and social awareness. Fundamentally, living in a residential care institution gives a new identity to living. Many people face social stigma and become the topic of family gossip, which hammers the mental life of the elderly. They feel doubly marginalized, firstly, they feel isolated from their family, and secondly, they feel shameful of their residential living. As a result, residential living generates a critical image in society. In modern social settings, we need to re-conceptualize the importance of residential care facilities. Considering the current socio-cultural context, new living concepts must be socially accepted. We need to appreciate the advancement of new forms of living. In addition, affordable, peaceful end-of-life living needs to be formally evaluated. The residential care system must be more academically focused on different fields and incorporated into a training-based programme. This system must not bring any social stigma but rather ensure a life-enhancing system. Other than this, the residential care homes must restructure their internal infrastructure from service, facilities, and amenities as well as a promise to give comfortable living. It is an opportunity to shape new caregiving strategies and bring social revolution to meet the rising demand for friendly, supportive residential care homes.

References

Department of Health and Ageing (DoHA). (2003). *Framework for an Australian aging research agenda*. Canberra: Australian Institute of Health and Welfare.
Du, P. (Editor-in-chief). (2007). *The series of translated books on gerontology in the 21st century*. Beijing: China Population Press.
Estes, C. (2001). *Social policy and aging*. Thousand Oaks, CA: Sage.
Finch, J. (1989a). *Family obligations and social change*. Cambridge: Polity Press.
Finch, J. (1995). Responsibilities, obligations and commitment. In I. Allen & E. Perkins (Eds.), *The future of family care for older people* (pp. 261–267). London: HMSO.
Harper, S. (2003). *Changing families as societies age*. The Research Reports No. RR103. Oxford: Institute of Ageing, University of Oxford.
Hees Van, S., Wanka, A., & Horstman, K. (2001). *Making and unmaking ageing-in-place, towards a co-constructive understanding of ageing and place*. London: Routledge.
Higgs, P., & Jones, I. (2009). *Medical sociology and old age*. Routledge. India.
Jamuna, D. (2001). Intergenerational issues in eldercare. *Indian Journal of Gerontology*, 15 (3 & 4), 287–295.
Jamuna, D. (2003). Issues of elder care and elder abuse in the Indian context. In P. S. Liebig & S. I. Rajan (Eds.), *An ageing India: Perspectives, prospects and policies* (pp. 125–142). New York: The Haworth Press, Inc.
Jamuna, D. (2004). The statics and dynamics of elder care in the Indian context. In P. V. Ramamurti & D. Jamuna (Eds.), *Handbook on Indian gerontology* (pp. 208–242). New Delhi: Serials Publications.

Jamuna, D., & Ramamurti, P V. (2000). *Psychological correlates of long-lived individuals. Project report.* New Delhi: University Grants Commission.

Karmel, T., & Woods, D. (2004). *Lifelong learning and older workers.* National Centre for Vocational Education Research Ltd., India.

National Economic and Social Council. (2005). *The developmental welfare state* (No. 113). Dublin: National Economic and Social Council.

Peine, A., Marshall, B., & Martin, W. (2021). *Socio-gerontechnology, Interdisciplinary Interdisciplinary Critical studies of aging and technology.* Routledge, India.

Phillips, J., Ajrou, K., & Nalletamby, S. (2010). *Key concepts in social gerontology.* Sage Publication. India

Ramamurti, P. V. (2002). Geropsychology—East–west scenario. *Journal of Community Guidance and Research*, 19 (2), 265–272.

Ramamurti, P. V. (2003a). Empowering the older persons in India. *Research and Development Journal*, Help Age (India), 9 (1), 16–21.

Ramamurti, P. V., & Jamuna, D. (2007). Senior citizens' service and information centers. *Research and Development Journal*, Help Age (India), 13 (3), 33–36.

Ramamurti, P. V., Jamuna, D., & Reddy, L. K. (1996). Psychosocial profiles of centenarians: The Tirupati centenarian study. In V. Kumar (Ed.), *Aging: The Indian perspective and global scenario* (pp. 63–65), *Indian Journal of Gerontology*, New Delhi.

Shankardass, M. K. (2018). *Perspective on abuse and neglect of the elderly in India.* Springer. India.

Shankardass, K. M. (2021). *Older Women: Global Concerns and Responses Toward Their Well-Being is a serious issue- an introductory note.* Springer. India.

Singh, S. (2002). Issues of emotional integration, peace, and happiness—The pedantic view. *Journal of Gerontology*, 17 (1 & 2), 205–212.

Torrington, J. (2005). *Care homes for older people: A briefing and design guide.* Taylor & Francis. London.

Vaarama, M., Pieper, R., & Sixsmith, A. (2008*). Care-related quality of life in old old age. European Journal of Ageing*, 6, 113–125.

Wahl, H.-W., Iwarsson, S., & Oswald, F. (2012). Aging well and the environment: Toward an integrative model and research agenda for the future. *The Gerontologist*, 52 (3), 306–316. https://doi.org/10.1093/geront/gnr154

Walker, A. (Ed.). (2005). *Growing older in Europe.* London: Open University Press.

6
DEVELOPING A MODEL FOR CAREGIVER'S TRAINING AND SUPPORT

Ruchika Kuba and G. Mythili

Introduction

With a rise in life expectancy, the number of elderly people is increasing globally. This causes the morbidity and mortality rates to escalate. It is therefore expected that there will be a greater need for caregivers over time (Hajek & König 2016). Society expects family members or close relatives to shoulder the responsibility of care for each other. These family members, often referred to as informal caregivers, provide partial or complete care concerning self-care, aiming towards their well-being and facilitating them in different tasks and activities (Grant & Graven, 2018). However, the limits of filial and spousal obligations vary among cultures, families, and individual family members. Various demographic and social factors have resulted in fewer family members caring for older persons. These include reduced family size, more women joining the workforce, the breakdown of the joint family system, and children moving out of nuclear families for jobs. An increase in life expectancy results in the children of older persons also being in the geriatric age group with their own set of problems (MSD Manual Professional version). This then brings in the need for formal caregivers from outside the family for short-term or long-term care (Schulz & Eden, 2016).

The caregiving role has been changing over the years. In the past, family members provided emotional support and assistance for activities of daily living and other household tasks. However, over a period of time, they have also involved in providing health and medical care and other surrogacy responsibilities. This could have ethical and legal implications.

Some family members continue to provide support even after moving out of the house. Long-distance caregivers are those who live at least one hour

DOI: 10.4324/9781003528432-7

from the care recipient. These caregivers provide social and emotional support, advanced care planning, financial assistance and care coordination.[2]

Caregiving, whether formal or informal, requires some prerequisite knowledge and skills to be able to provide supportive, assistive and emergency care. Formal training is required so that the caregiving can be proficient. Caregivers are often confronted with situations in which they are unable to find a solution and do not know whom to turn to. Training provides them with the competencies to deal with the same.

We are proposing a dynamic model wherein the caregivers can get trained to gain the prerequisite knowledge and skills. Through this model, they will also find resources for solutions to their problems, whether it is managing their own stress or supporting the elderly they care for.

Need for training caregivers

Caregiving for older persons could range from providing minimal support to full-time care depending upon the requirements of the elderly based on their physical and mental condition. Sixty-three percent of the older persons being cared for have long-term physical conditions, and 29% of them have cognitive impairment, as per a caregiver's report.[1] A caregiver's role is dynamic and variable during the course of caregiving. It may be of short duration, but intense for short-term illness in which the older person is incapacitated and requires support, to long-term progressive support for persons having chronic ailments like Parkinsonism, dementia, advanced stages of cancer, etc. (Essential Competencies in the Care of Older Adults, 2014).

According to some studies, 15% of the caregivers had provided care for less than or equal to one year, and an equal number had provided care for 10 years at the time of the survey.[1] The remaining percentage of the caregivers fell within this period. For high-need elderly, which included those with dementia or who needed help with two or more self-care activities, the median years of caregiving was 4 years. This rose to 5 years when the elderly had both dementia and required help with two or more self-activities.[2]

The range of tasks that a caregiver may be required to perform has been enumerated as (Schulz & Eden, 2016):

1. Assisting in activities of daily living, which may include bathing and grooming, dressing, feeding, toileting, transferring from and to beds, chairs, and wheelchairs.
2. Emotional and social support – companionship, facilitation and participate in hobbies or leisure activities, help managing emotional responses, managing family conflict.
3. Household tasks – shopping, transportation, bills, bank transactions, preparing meals, laundry and household work.

4. Health and medical care – health promotion activities which include exercise, proper diet, personal care and hygiene, immunization, fall prevention, timely and proper medication including giving injections, operating medical equipment, wound care. They are also required to pick up signs of progression of disease and notify the appropriate person, look for adverse events and positive responses to treatment, manage emergencies and take appropriate and timely action for further management.
5. Coping with and managing the reduction of functional and cognitive capacity of the older person as the disease progresses.
6. Advocacy and care coordination – collect information, communicate with healthcare providers including fixing appointments, ordering medicines, and arranging for specialized care like nursing care and physiotherapy.
7. Surrogacy – handle financial and legal matters, manage personal property and participate in advanced planning and treatment decisions.
8. End of life caring – functional and palliative needs of the patient, information about long-term care and assisted living facilities.

Caregivers can play an important role in delaying and to a large extent preventing the hospitalization or institutionalization of chronically ill older persons. Studies have shown that the high rate of hospital readmissions is related to inadequate preparation of informal caregivers to care for their dependent elderly at the time of discharge (Parry et al., 2008).

Many family caregivers have expressed that they do not have the necessary knowledge to provide standard care to their dependent older persons with chronic illness. They also do not have access to resources, nor the knowledge of how to use the resources. (Given & Given, 2002). Some of the areas where the need has been expressed are monitoring management, personal care delivery and handling emotional stress, especially after the discharge of the older person from the hospital (Shyu , 2000). Studies have shown that family caregivers consider the concepts of mastery, preparedness and competency as important components for problem solving and effective decision making (Archbold, et al., 1995; Silver et al., 2004).

However, not many of the caregivers receive any formal or informal training. Many caregivers receive inadequate preparation for the tasks they are expected to assume. In the 2015 National Alliance for Caregiving and AARP Public Policy Institute survey, half (51%) of caregivers of older adults aged 50 and older with Alzheimer's disease or dementia reported that they provide medical/nursing tasks without prior preparation. Thirty percent of Alzheimer's disease caregivers had informational needs about managing challenging behaviours, and 21% wanted more help or information about incontinence. In the Home Alone study, more than 60% of the caregivers reported learning how to manage at least some medications on their own

(Reinhard et al., 2008; Reinhard et al., 2012). Forty-seven percent reported never receiving training from any source. Caregivers described learning by trial and error.

Information and skills other than health care are also desired. Some researchers have found that caregivers received more information with respect to the illness suffered and self-care in the management of medication as compared to the self-care areas of bathing, dressing and toilet use. They hardly received any information about financial support and auxiliary equipment (Dixe et al., 2019; Floriano et al., 2012). The nurses were the main health professionals to give information except regarding illness, which was given by the doctor. However, in spite of receiving the information, this is not enough for a majority of caregivers as observed in studies (Rotondi et al., 2007; Rabow et al., 2004).

Providing knowledge and skills is not only important to equip the caregiver to perform better but also to remove the feeling of uncertainty regarding caring for their dependent elderly, which can contribute to stress (Northouse, et al., 2000; Shyu, 2000).

Various researchers have expressed the strain and stress that a caregiver is confronted with during the process of caring. This, commonly referred to as a caregivers burden is defined as the emotional, social and financial stress that is imposed on a dependent person due to his/her illness on the caregiver (Tan et al., 2017; Rha et al., 2015). Part of the training programmes should also include teaching how to mitigate the caregiver's stress.

The vast arena of caregiving, coupled with the fact that the ambit of caregiving is bound to change with time, means that caregivers need to be equipped with the basic knowledge and skills to perform their tasks proficiently. Besides medical knowledge and other ancillary knowledge, they also need to inculcate problem-solving and communication skills (Gitlin & Wolff, 2011). There is also a need for this to be a perpetual process over a period of time.

Competencies required for caregiving

According to Parry (Parry, 1998) competencies are "a cluster of related knowledge, skills and attitudes that affect a major part of one's job (i.e. one or more key roles or responsibilities); that correlated with performance on the job; that can be measured against well-accepted standards; and that can be improved via training and development" (Kaplan & Berkman, 2021).

The competencies that a caregiver should be equipped with can be divided into the cognitive, affective and psychomotor domains. The objectives for the competencies to be achieved under each domain are listed in Table 6.1.

TABLE 6.1 Competencies for cognitive domain

After the training, the caregiver should be able to:

- Describe different medical problems in an elderly
- Enumerate the complications and adverse events of diseases and their treatment
- Explain diet planning for elderly
- List and discuss the health promotion measures in elderly
- Discuss the activities of daily living, and assess the activities that may require support or assistance in different situations
- Assess of the cognitive impairment in an elderly
- Describe the end-of-life caring issues
- Identify the agencies necessary for emergency management, referral, legal or financial advice or assistance
- Outline the recreational activities for an elderly
- Enumerate the signs of elder abuse or neglect by family members
- Discuss the emotional, social and financial stresses of a caregiver

Table 6.2 lists the competencies for the affective domain.

TABLE 6.2 Competencies for the Affective domain

After the training, the caregiver should be able to:

- Listen to the elderly with patience
- Communicate with clarity, firmness, and allow for discussions and explanations where required and helpful
- Support the elderly in all activities with willingness, empathy and compassion
- Create an atmosphere of positive demeanour, instil positivity in the elderly, uplifting their mood and instilling hope
- Demonstrate patience in dealing with the elderly and take decisions in a time bound manner
- Navigate among the various members of the healthcare team
- Advocate interest of the elderly in different situations
- Maintain a positive attitude and manage your own emotions such that they do not interfere with the caring

Table 6.3 lists the competencies for the psychomotor domain.

TABLE 6.3 Competencies for the psychomotor domain

After the training, the caregiver should be able to:

- Identify the medical problems of the elderly
- Recognize signs of progression of a disease, its complications, adverse events and their treatment
- Prepare a diet plan for the elderly as per nutritional requirements and availability of resources
- Prepare an exercise plan, medication schedule, suggestions for fall prevention and a plan for other health-promotional activities like meditation, yoga, etc.
- Provide support or assistance for activities of daily living and adapt the same as per the requirements of particular situations or disabilities (i.e., bathing, grooming, toileting feeding, transferring from bed, etc.)
- Identify the deterioration in functional and cognitive impairment
- Alter care plans and provide support for the end of life
- Collect information, communicate with healthcare providers including fixing appointments, ordering medicines and arranging for specialized care like nursing care and physiotherapy., nutritional assessment, diet planning, or legal or financial experts as and when required
- Facilitate and participate in leisure or recreational activities with an elderly
- Recognize any abuse or neglect of elderly
- Reach out for help in case of stress, strain or burn out is felt

Available training models

Studies have recommended the implementation of different training models for caregivers in which information can be provided to empower them in all care domains. They suggest the use of ICT tools and digital materials like videos, websites and apps to address different caring tasks in different domains (Dixe et al., 2019).

Other studies have suggested the provision of basic written material that can teach caregivers about the progression of a disease, treatment plans, adverse events and strategies for managing these. The skills that a caregiver needs to be proficient in could be related to the cognitive domain, such as monitoring, decision making and problem solving (Nigolian et al., 2011); the psychomotor domain, such as catheter and wound care; or affective domain, such as offering emotional support. Cognitive behavioural intervention is another method suggested to help caregivers of cancer patients with symptom management (Sherwood et al., 2005; Sikorskii et al., 2007).

One of the methods adopted includes problem-solving skills (Blanchard et al. 1996) and psychoeducational interventions (Barg et al., 1998). This type of intervention is aimed at providing information and also psychological/counselling to the caregiver to reduce the stress.

Group interventions were effective in improving care-recipient symptoms, while interventions targeted at the individual caregivers helped improve their well-being (Sörensen et al., 2002). Researchers suggest that multicomponent interventions, rather than single interventions like support groups, can reduce the burden of the caregivers to a large extent. (Acton & Kang, 2001; Gitlin et al., 2003).

Some studies have documented that interventions designed to improve specific caregiving tasks are helpful, e.g., in pain education for caregivers of cancer patients (Ferrell et al., 1995), problem-solving abilities in caregivers of Alzheimer's disease (Gitlin et al., 2005), and weekly telephone interventions in stroke survivors (Grant et al., 2002). Safe medication administration (Griffiths et al., 2004).

Creating a Website to meet all needs

Before creating a website, it is required to assess certain parameters which may vary according to the target audience we are catering to. These include:

1. The care demands of the patient
2. Role and expectation of family
3. The disease condition and competencies of a caregiver expected
4. Pre-existing knowledge, skills and capability the caregiver (assessing oneself)
5. Available resources and resources required
6. Support for the caregiver

The second step is to draw out the outcome objectives of the training and support portal. These could be enumerated as:

1. Provide the requisite knowledge and skills in the cognitive, affective and psychomotor domains and bridge the gap
2. Provide access to related and relevant resources
3. Make available contact information for support to the elderly, which could range from medical, social, rehabilitative, etc.
4. Create a trained manpower resource of caregivers
5. Create a platform which can be used by trained caregivers to access to information regarding their placement
6. Have a consortium of caregiving-related experiences in the form of discussions, stories, videos and research papers

Implementation of the training programme requires drawing out a methodology to enable the caregivers to develop the various competencies. The instructional strategies and delivery mechanisms that can be drawn out for the cognitive, affective and psychomotor objectives are provided below (Table 6.4).

TABLE 6.4 Instructional strategies and delivery mechanisms of the three domains

A. Cognitive Domain

S.No	Cognitive Outcome Objectives	Instructional Strategies	Delivery Mechanisms
	Knowledge about the different medical problems of the elderly, complications and adverse events of diseases and their treatment, diet planning, health promotion measures, activities of daily living and assessment of the activities that may require support or assistance in different situations, cognitive impairment, end-of-life care issues, agencies necessary for emergency management, referral, legal or financial advice or assistance, recreational activities, signs of elder abuse or neglect by family members, and identifying own emotional, social and financial stresses	E-content with pictures and short videos coupled with assignments and tutorial, formal and informal discussions and interactions, workshops, case studies, scenario-based learning, problem-based learning	Synchronous and asynchronous discussions, webinars, virtual classrooms, game-based learning, interactive multimedia, 3-D virtual worlds

B. Affective Domain

S.No	Affective Outcome Objectives	Instructional Strategies	Delivery Mechanisms
	Listen to the elderly with patience	Videos – both recorded and live streaming, reverse demonstration recorded or live by caregiver, role play, drill, situational analysis and problem-solving scenario-based learning, storytelling, gamification, etc.	Interactive video, audios, interactive multimedia, web conferencing, web of thoughts, gamification, etc.
	Communicate with clarity, firmness, and allow for discussions and explanations where required and helpful		
	Support the elderly in all activities with willingness, empathy and compassion		
	Create an atmosphere of positive demeanour, instil positivity in the elderly, uplifting their mood and instilling hope		
	Patience in dealing with the elderly, family and making decisions in a time bound manner		
	Navigating among the various members of the health care team		
	Advocate interest of the elderly in different situations		
	Maintain a positive attitude and manage your own emotions such that they do not interfere with the caring		

C. Psychomotor Domain

S.No	Psychomotor Outcome Objectives	Instructional Strategies	Technological Interventions
	Recognize the medical problems of the elderly – signs of progression of a disease, its complications and adverse events of the diseases and their treatment. Prepare a diet plan for the elderly as per nutritional requirements and availability of resources. Prepare an exercise plan, medication schedule, suggestions for fall prevention and a plan for other health-promotional activities like meditation, yoga, etc. Provide support or assistance for activities of daily living and adapt the same as per the requirements of particular situations or disabilities (i.e., bathing, grooming, toileting feeding, transferring from bed, etc.). use and teach the use of assistive devices. Identify deterioration in functional and cognitive abilities. Alter care plans and provide support for the end of life. Collect information, communicate with healthcare providers including fixing appointments, ordering medicines, and arranging for specialized care like nursing care and physiotherapy, nutritional assessment, diet planning or legal or financial experts as and when required. Facilitate and participate in leisure or recreational activities with an elderly person. Recognize any abuse or neglect of elderly. Reach out for help in case of stress, strain, or burn out is felt	E content of self-instructional material should contain steps for all activities, videos – both recorded and live streaming, reverse demonstration recorded or live by caregiver, role play, drill, practical face-to-face practice of skills in designated centres, simulations, projects or practical activities, field trips, survey, problem-based learning, etc.	Mobile apps with gamification, artificial intelligence, IOT

Conceptual model for the caregiver training and support

Learning management system

A robust learning management system can be incorporated with the portal (Figure 6.1) The portal will provide general information to anyone who wants to learn more about the training programmes and the support that is being offered through this platform:. For those who enrol in the training programmes, the portal would be used to organize training programmes, manage the content of the training programmes, track the participants' performances and maintain the archives for all the training programmes. The portal will also provide resources which will enable the caregiver to provide support to the elderly as well as support for oneself in case they experience

82 Ruchika Kuba and G. Mythili

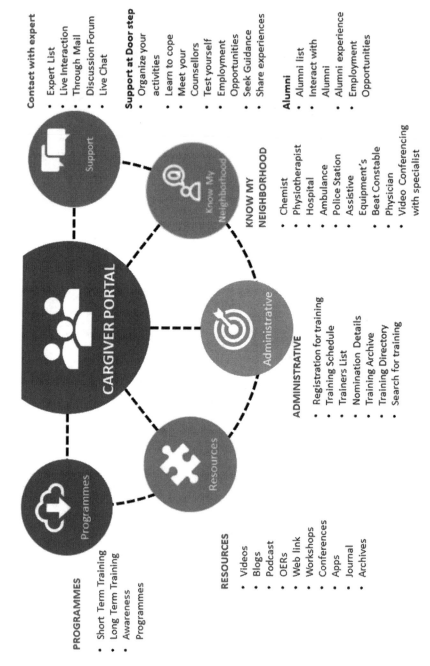

FIGURE 6.1 Model for caregiver portal.

stress or burnout. Alumni will be able to register, provide personal information for those who wish to use their services, as well as find employment opportunities.

The conceptual model will thus have various components as elaborated below, and should be dynamic and evolve as per the requirements of the users. The home page should display all information. The information available to all those who visit the portal is elaborated below:

1. Home page
   This page will provide an overview of the organization, it's vision and mission, the team members and contact details. An e-brochure giving information about the components and facilities provided by the portal will also be available.
2. Programmes
   This page will provide information regarding the various training programmes available, their dates, duration, syllabus covered, multimedia packages used for their delivery, assessment methods used and certification. The details of the programmes will also be available in the brochure on the home page.
3. Resources
   All people who visit the portal can access the resources page. The resources made available are videos, podcasts, blogs, OER's relevant web links to other resources and information regarding workshops and conferences. Subject matter experts can be invited to prepare small clips of videos/audios and can place them in the repository of the portal. These videos/audios can be used by the caregivers whenever they have time to enhance their knowledge. These can be made mobile-friendly or developed as apps. Topics, images, videos, audios and stories to disseminate information through the web. The author of a blog can publish it for public use to get views/opinion from like-minded people or use as personal journal. The blog should be updated frequently to provide relevant information about caregiving, which facilitate both caregivers and relatives as well.

   An online journal which can be subscribed to, accessed and to which articles can be submitted. Apps which can help caregivers in their day-to-day activities will also be placed here.
4. Contact with experts
   A caregiver will have access to an expert list with whom they will be able to request live interactions, interactions through emails, live chat, and through discussion forum.
5. Know my neighbourhood
   Most of the caregivers are occupied with the routine work of taking care of older people. Gathering information from various sources or websites

is very difficult for the caregivers. This page will use geoinformatics to provide relevant contact details and information on useful resources near the location of the caregiver. The following facilities can be in the portal:
a. Chemist shop
b. Physiotherapist
c. Emergency/hospital
d. Ambulance services
e. Beat constable/police station
f. Day care centres
g. Family doctor or physician
h. Links for video conferencing with specialists
i. Links for assistive devices

6. **Support at the doorstep**
The caregivers may require support anytime for stress, abuse, or inability to cope with the situation at hand and may also need to look for opportunities for employment. Hence, the following facilities can be made available through this platform:
a. Test to know yourself – Through a structured questionnaire a psychoanalysis can be done to analyse personality traits, and this information can be used to provide advice or suggestions regarding which type of job would be best for the person, which training programmes would be useful and what kind of support the caregiver may require for self-help.
b. Building a support system for tips and guidance for day-to-day work – this could be with the help of professional guidance from other professionals by establishing contact through the 'contact experts' page, participating in discussion forum with peers, short videos or through apps.
c. Organizing one's schedule and routines can be done using machine learning, where customized schedules are created based on the information provided by the caregiver in a structured questionnaire.
d. Share your experiences with other caregivers and remain connected with the community. This can be done using integrated social media like WhatsApp groups, Facebook, Twitter, blogs, etc.
e. Learn to cope – Self-help videos and information may be provided to help cope with the issues like stress, abuse, etc.
f. Counselling or support services – Recognition of burnout is possible by testing yourself through structured assessment tests. The caregiver should be able to get in touch with personalized counselling services or group therapy services as and when required. This can be possible through apps.

g. Employment opportunities – the caregivers may be provided with various opportunities which could be uploaded here from time to time. They can use blogs/app.
7. **Frequently asked questions**
Frequent questions that can be asked by caregivers will be compiled and made available to all those who visit the web portal. This will be a dynamic page which will be updated regularly as and when inputs are received from the viewers.

Those who would like to undergo specific training programmes will be required to register and will then have access to the following additional information and support for training.

A. **Administrative activities**

The administrative activities related to managing training programmes will be accessible through this page. The administrative page should have two components – one which has access to the registered students and the other which has access only to the administrator. The following sub-components can be considered for access by the caregiver students

1. *Training directory*
   This component provides a list of training programmes and workshops. A link will direct them to the details of each training programme which they may wish to learn more about. This could be viewed as the calendar activities of the organization. The details of cancellation and rescheduling training programmes should be updated regularly.
2. Search for training icon
   This icon will provide the facility to find the desired training or workshop for a particular theme, month, and cater.
3. Registration for training
   The clients/users should be able to register for the selected training programmes. The registration form can collect information about their qualification, competencies already possessed by them, their interest areas of the training, nature of their occupation or the work connected with the elderly, expectations from the training programmes. They should have access to the information regarding the maximum number of seats available for the particular training or workshop at any time. Users can see the acceptance and rejection status of the application, and they can view the status of their application.

4. Assess your requirements and find your programme. Artificial intelligence and machine learning will be used to analyse the information provided in the registration form, and the programmes/courses best suited for the applicant will be suggested. The applicant can take the programmes as per the suggestion or customize their own programmes as per available modules.
5. *Details related to the training programme*
   After successful registration, the students should have access to the following:
   a. *Training coordinator's details*
      The details of the training or workshop coordinators for each programme should be available to users so they can interact with the coordinators for further information about the training programmes.
   b. Choose your language
      All the course material should be multilingual.
   c. Customize your programme – choose how you would like to study the subject, depending upon your personal learning styles – hard copies of the printed modules, audio, video, interactive e-modules, etc.
   d. Track your progress – provides alerts, suggests other modules or resources to be taken up based on the progress, e.g., video or audio, discussion forum., artificial intelligence or machine learning, etc.
   e. Upgrade to a higher programme or lateral shift into another programme based on your progress and/or specific skill set requirements.
   f. Connect with peers in the same programme or in a different programme but with similar skills – this can be achieved through discussion forums.
   g. Feedback
      Feedback provisions should be there for the quality of course material, delivery mechanisms, and various components of the programme. The students should also be able to suggest updates which can be included in the course material and any corrections required to be made.
   h. Pick up your certificate
6. Communication channels for information exchange and academic exchange
7. Readily available anywhere assistant – that can be accessed anywhere, including through mobile to provide ready solutions to the problems posed by the caregiver and navigate the LMS.
8. Alumni association – all interested participants can join the Alumni group through registration. The alumni can be regularly provided with all the relevant information, updated course material and OERs from

time to time. The alumni could also be an important resource for those who may require trained caregivers, and their details should be available online if consented to by the respective participant.

The controls or components available to the administrators are given as under.

1. Training directory updation
   The administrator should take up the responsibility of updating the training directory. Options should be available to update, delete and modify the training programmes and workshops being offered through the portal. The details of cancellation and rescheduling of training programmes should be listed and communicated to the users.
2. Devise compatibility with multiple devices
   The same programme should be accessed from different devices like a mobile phone, tablet, and also have printable options.
3. Locate the trainee
   The will help locate the trainee and find out how many times he/she attended in different training programmes.
4. Mass SMS and mailing facility
5. This facility should be used by the administrators to communicate and provide information to all the registered students.
6. Training archives

The training archives will preserve the records and history of training and workshops organized by the IUC. This will help in future planning and the designing and development of training programmes.

B. **Academic activities**
   a. Academic programmes – these range from awareness packages to short-term and long-term programmes. They could be just for providing knowledge or for skill development in the cognitive, affective and psychomotor domains, or a mix of all three. The programmes would be modular in nature. The participants can choose the modules based on specific competencies catering to different diseases/disorders like dementia, cancer, unconscious patient care, palliative care, etc. The participants could pick up any one or more of the packages successively as per recommendations on registration or customize them themselves, depending upon their needs. In this way, the students would take successive modules and accumulate credits. For some of the programmes, lateral entries would also be feasible. The programmes could have interactive audios and videos as part of or as a supplement to the Self-Learning Materials (SLMs).

Gamification, simulations, virtual patients and augmented reality can be used for delivering the skills, especially the psychomotor skills, more effective. The various types of training programmes are provided below.

i. *Awareness programmes*

These programmes aim only at building the knowledge of the participants. Such programmes can also help the caregivers learn about new initiatives in the area of caregiving, clear misconceptions, and update themselves all of which will enhance their roles and responsibilities as caregivers. They will not have any built-in assessments. These could be accessed as per the topics. The programme could have the following components:

a. OERs – OERs, as resources that can be accessed by the participants according to their requirements can be placed on the LMS and made readily available to participants. The OERs could be in the form of PDFs of books, relevant articles, videos, etc.

b. Audios Videos – customized audio videos could be prepared and placed in the portal as part of the package for the awareness programmes.

c. Discussion forum – A platform can be created where the participants are provided few scenario-based situations in which all the enrolled participants can interact. Experts can also be asked to pitch in to clear doubts and provide additional information. This discussion forum. would be asynchronous in nature, although a synchronous component can also be built in as and when needed.

d. Web conferencing – Online synchronous presentation of lectures and group discussions followed by case presentations and discussion by participants can be made feasible. Crowdsourcing and YouTube can be used to prepare and share the presentations by the participants.

e. Conferences – Conferences with specific themes could be organized and the students participate in these either as only participants or by presenting papers related to their work.

f. Seminars – these will help to update the caregivers and also provide them with an opportunity to connect with eminent and resourceful people.

g. Formative assessments – these could be inbuilt in the course material as non-marked in-text questions or Google Forms for marked formative assessments. Other methodologies to be used could include written assignments to be uploaded on the classroom platform, scanning and sending the PDF of completed assignments, or uploading audio or videos prepared.

ii. *Short-term training programmes*

Short-term training programmes could range from a few hours to a few weeks and could be chosen by the caregivers depending on the knowledge or skills they desire to enhance. The programme could also help them in their career path or build up competencies to perform better.

Short-term training could include workshops, personal upgrading courses, specialized courses, etc.

iii. *Long-term training programmes*

Long-term training programmes could be full-time or part-time, distance, online or blended courses/programmes where some face-to-face components can be integrated at identified centres for providing training. The goal of a long-term programme is generally to achieve a certificate or degree, which can help with career development. The web portal could be used for placing various components of the training programmes.

You can also access a sample of a website with the following QR code. The sample includes many of the elements discussed in this chapter.

Or learn more about the components of the website through the video by clicking on the QR code.

References

Acton, G. J., & Kang, J. (2001). Interventions to reduce the burden of caregiving for an adult with dementia: A meta-analysis. *Research in Nursing & Health*, 24(5), 349–360. https://onlinelibrary.wiley.com/doi/abs/10.1002/nur.1036. Last accessed on 26th November 2021.

Archbold, P. G., Stewart, B. J., Miller, L. L., Harvath, T. A., Greenlick, M. R., van Buren, L., Kirschling, J. M., Valanis, B. G., Brody, K. K., & Schook, J. E., & Hagan, J. M. (1995). The PREP system of nursing interventions: A pilot test with families caring for older members. *Research in Nursing & Health*, 18(1), 3–16. https://onlinelibrary.wiley.com/doi/abs/10.1002/nur.4770180103. Last accessed on 26th November 2021.

Barg, F. K., Pasacreta, J. V., Nuamah, I. F., Robinson, K. D., Angeletti, K., Yasko, J. M., & McCorkle, R. (1998). A description of a psychoeducational intervention for family caregivers of cancer patients. *Journal of Family Nursing*, 4(4), 394–413. https://journals.sagepub.com/doi/abs/10.1177/107484079800400406. Last accessed on 26th November 2021.

Blanchard, C. G., Toseland, R. W., & McCallion, P. (1996). The effects of a problem-solving intervention with spouses of cancer patients. *Journal of Psychosocial Oncology*, 14(2), 1–21. https://www.tandfonline.com/doi/abs/10.1300/J077v14n02_01. Last accessed on 26th November 2021.

Dixe, M. D. A. C. R., da Conceição Teixeira, L. F., Areosa, T. J. T. C. C., Frontini, R. C., Peralta, T. D. J. A., & Querido, A. I. F. (2019). Needs and skills of informal caregivers to care for a dependent person: A cross-sectional study. *BMC Geriatrics*, 19(1), 1–9. https://link.springer.com/article/10.1186/s12877-019-1274-0. Last accessed on 26th November 2021.

Essential Competencies in the Care of Older Adults. *Journal of Physical Therapy Education: Spring 2014*, 28(2), 91–93.

Ferrell, B. R., Grant, M., Chan, J., Ahn, C., & Ferrell, B. A. (1995). The impact of cancer pain education on family caregivers of elderly patients. *Oncology Nursing Forum*, 22(8), 1211–1218. https://europepmc.org/. Last accessed on 26th November 2021.

Floriano, L. A., Azevodo, R. C. S., Reiners, A. A. O., & Sudré, M. R. S. (2012) Care performed by family caregivers to dependent elderly, at home, within the context of the family health strategy. *Text Context Nursing*, Florianópolis, 21(3), 543–548.

Grant, J. S., & Graven, L. J. (2018). Problems experienced by informal caregivers of individuals with heart failure: An integrative review. *International Journal of Nursing Studies*, 80, 41–66. https://www.sciencedirect.com/science/article/abs/pii/S0020748917302912. Last accessed on 26th November 2021.

Gitlin, L. N., Belle, S. H., Burgio, L. D., Czaja, S. J., Mahoney, D., Gallagher-Thompson, D., Burns, R., Hauck, W. W., Zhang, S., Schulz, R., & Ory, M. G. (2003). Effect of multicomponent interventions on caregiver burden and depression: The REACH multisite initiative at 6-month follow-up. *Psychology and Aging*, 18(3), 361. https://psycnet.apa.org/doiLanding?doi=10.1037%2F0882-7974.18.3.361. Last accessed on 26th November 2021.

Gitlin, L. N., Hauck, W. W., Dennis, M. P., & Winter, L. (2005). Maintenance of effects of the home environmental skill-building program for family caregivers and individuals with Alzheimer's disease and related disorders. *The Journals of Gerontology Series A: Biological Sciences and Medical Sciences*, 60(3), 368–374. https://academic.oup.com/biomedgerontology/article/60/3/368/630603?login=true. Last accessed on 26th November 2021.

Gitlin, L. N., & Wolff, J. (2011). Family involvement in care transitions of older adults: What do we know and where do we go from here? *Annual Review of Gerontology & Geriatrics*, 31(1), 31.

Given, C. W., & Given, B. (2002). *Palliative care for patients with advanced cancer (grant project)*. East Lansing: Michigan State University in collaboration with Walther Cancer Institute.

Grant, J. S., Elliott, T. R., Weaver, M., Bartolucci, A. A., & Giger, J. N. (2002). Telephone intervention with family caregivers of stroke survivors after rehabilitation. *Stroke*, 33(8), 2060–2065. https://www.ahajournals.org/doi/full/10.1161/01.STR.0000020711.38824.E3. Last accessed on 26th November 2021.

Griffiths, R., Johnson, M., Piper, M., & Langdon, R. (2004). A nursing intervention for the quality use of medicines by elderly community clients. *International Journal of Nursing Practice*, 10(4), 166–176. https://onlinelibrary.wiley.com/doi/abs/10.1111/j.1440-172X.2004.00476.x. Last accessed on 26th November 2021.

Hajek, A., & König, H. H. (2016). Informal caregiving and subjective well-being: Evidence of a population-based longitudinal study of older adults in Germany. *Journal of the American Medical Directors Association*, 17, 300–305.

Kaplan, D. B., & Berkman, B. J. Family caregiving for older adults. MSD Manual Professional version. https://www.msdmanuals.com/en-in/professional/geriatrics/social-issues-in-older-adults/family-caregiving-for-older-adults. Last accessed on 26th November 2021.

Nigolian, C. J., & Miller, K. L. (2011). Supporting family caregivers: Teaching essential skills to family caregivers. *AJN The American Journal of Nursing*, 111(11), 52–58. https://journals.lww.com/ajnonline/Fulltext/2011/11000/Supporting_Family_Caregivers__Teaching_Essential.28.aspx. Last accessed on 26th November 2021.

Northouse, L. L., Mood, D., Templin, T., Mellon, S., & George, T. (2000). Couples' patterns of adjustment to colon cancer. *Social Science & Medicine*, 50(2), 271–284. https://www.sciencedirect.com/science/article/abs/pii/S0277953699002816. Last accessed on 26th November 2021.

Parry, C., Mahoney, E., Chalmers, S. A., & Coleman, E. A. (2008). Assessing the quality of transitional care: Further applications of the care transitions measure. *Medical Care*, 317–322. https://www.jstor.org/stable/40221660?c. Last accessed on 26th November 2021.

Parry, S. B. (1998). Just what is a competency ? (And why should you care?). *Training and Education in Professional Psychology*, 35(6), 58–64. https://www.proquest.com/openview/3c866ef4e98055bbfa2cc64b6bb0a1d6/1?pq-origsite=gscholar&cbl=28852. Last accessed on 26th November 2021.

Rabow, M. W., Hauser, J. M., & Adams, J. (2004). Supporting family caregivers at the end of life: They don't know what they don't know. *Jama*, 291(4), 483–491. https://jamanetwork.com/journals/jama/article-abstract/198062. Last accessed on 26th November 2021.

Reinhard, S. C., Given, B., Petlick, N. H., & Bemis, A. (2008). Supporting family caregivers in providing care. *Patient Safety and Quality: An Evidence-based Handbook for Nurses*. https://www.ncbi.nlm.nih.gov/books/NBK2665/. Last accessed on 26th November 2021.

Reinhard, S. C., Levine, C., & Samis, S. (2012). *Home alone: Family caregivers providing complex chronic care*. Washington, DC: United Hospital Fund and AARP Public Policy Institute. giaging.org/documents/family-caregivers-providing-complex-chronic-care-spouses-AARP-ppi-health.pdf. Last accessed on 26th November 2021.

Rha, S. Y., Park, Y., Song, S. K., Lee, C. E., & Lee, J. (2015). Caregiving burden and the quality of life of family caregivers of cancer patients: The relationship and correlates. *European Journal of Oncology Nursing*, 19, 376–382. https://doi.org/10.1016/j.ejon.2015.01.004. Last accessed on 26th November 2021.

Rotondi, A. J., Sinkule, J., Balzer, K., Harris, J., & Moldovan, R. (2007). A qualitative needs assessment of persons who have experienced traumatic brain injury and their primary family caregivers. *The Journal of Head Trauma Rehabilitation*, 22(1), 14–25. https://journals.lww.com/headtraumar. Last accessed on 26th November 2021.

Schulz, R., Eden, J., & Committee on Family Caregiving for Older Adults; Board on Health Care Services; Health and Medicine Division; National Academies of Sciences, Engineering, and Medicine (eds). (2016). Family Caregiving Roles and Impacts. In *Families caring for an aging America*. Washington, DC: National Academies Press. Available from: https://www.ncbi.nlm.nih.gov/books/NBK396398/. Last accessed on 26th November 2021.

Sherwood, P., Given, B. A., Given, C. W., Champion, V. L., Doorenbos, A. Z., Azzouz, F., Kozachik, S., Wagler-Ziner, K., & Monahan, P. O. (2005). A cognitive behavioral intervention for symptom management in patients with advanced cancer. *Oncology Nursing Forum*, 32(6), 1190–1198.

Shyu, Y. I. L. (2000). The needs of family caregivers of frail elders during the transition from hospital to home: A Taiwanese sample. *Journal of Advanced Nursing*, 32(3), 619–625. https://onlinelibrary.wiley.com/doi/abs/10.1046/j.1365-2648.2000.01519.x. Last accessed on 26th November 2021.

Sikorskii, A., Given, C. W., Given, B., Jeon, S., Decker, V., Decker, D., Champion, V., & McCorkle, R. (2007). Symptom management for cancer patients: A trial comparing two multimodal interventions. *Journal of Pain and Symptom Management*, 34(3), 253–264. https://www.sciencedirect.com/science/article/pii/S0885392407003326. Last accessed on 26th November 2021.

Silver, H. J., Wellman, N. S., Galindo-Ciocon, D., & Johnson, P. (2004). Family caregivers of older adults on home enteral nutrition have multiple unmet task-related training needs and low overall preparedness for caregiving. *Journal of the American Dietetic Association*, 104(1), 43–50. https://www.sciencedirect.com/science/. Last accessed on 26th November 2021.

Sörensen, S., Pinquart, M., & Duberstein, P. (2002). How effective are interventions with caregivers? An updated meta-analysis. *The Gerontologist*, 42(3), 356–372. https://academic.oup.com/gerontologist/article/42/3/356/614446?login=true. Last accessed on 26th November 2021.

Tan, J-Y., Molassiotis, A., Lloyd-Williams, M., Yorke, J. (2017). Burden, emotional distress and quality of life among informal caregivers of lung cancer patients: An exploratory study. *European Journal of Cancer Care*. March:e12691. https://doi.org/10.1111/ecc.12691.

7
EMERGING CHALLENGES OF CARE OF ELDERLY

Need for newer strategies for nurses in India

Sandhya Gupta

What is the decade of healthy ageing?

The Decade of Healthy Ageing (2020–2030) is an opportunity to bring together governments, civil society, international agencies, professionals, academia, the media, and the private sector for ten years of concerted, catalytic, and collaborative action to improve the lives of older people, their families, and the communities in which they live. Populations around the world are ageing at a faster pace than in the past, and this demographic transition will have an impact on almost all aspects of society. The world has united around the 2030 Agenda for Sustainable Development: all countries and all stakeholders pledged that no one will be left behind and determined to ensure that every human being can fulfil their potential in dignity and equality and in a healthy environment. A decade of concerted global action on Healthy Ageing is urgently needed. Already, there are more than 1 billion people aged 60 years or older, with most living in low- and middle-income countries. Many do not have access to even the basic resources necessary for a life of meaning and dignity. Many others confront multiple barriers that prevent their full participation in society (United Nations Population Fund (UNFPA), 2017).

A longer life brings with it opportunities, not only for older people and their families, but also for societies as a whole. Additional years provide the chance to pursue new activities such as further education, a new career, or pursuing a long-neglected passion. Older people also contribute in many ways to their families and communities. Yet the extent of these opportunities and contributions depends heavily on one factor: health. Increased human lifespan as witnessed in the preceding decades has not been accompanied by

DOI: 10.4324/9781003528432-8

a good quality of life for the majority of older Indians. Of the many determinants of the quality of life – financial security, emotional security, and health and well-being – the last one occupies the prime position, as all other issues become irrelevant in poor health. Research in social gerontology and geriatrics in past decades has provided insight into various aspects of the status of older people in India. A large volume of authentic data on demographic trends, impact of changes in the family structure and migration, physical and behavioural status, and organization and dynamics of health systems exists in Indian literature. However, very little effort has been made to develop a model of health and social care in tune with the changing needs and time. As no model for older people exists in India, as well as in most other societies with similar socio-economic situations, it may be a challenge as well as an opportunity for innovation in health system development. This is a major challenge because no clear policy or strategy for the development of health care for older people exists, there are differences in opinion about whether there is a need for such segregation, there is dilemma about the most effective way of satisfying the health needs of the elderly, and there is no unanimity regarding the minimum knowledge and skills required in the curriculum of health professionals (India current affairs, 2011).

It is often simplistically considered that health problems in old age are a constellation of issues such as increased susceptibility to infection, inability to cope with physical and psychological stress, degenerative arthritis, atherosclerotic and vascular diseases of the heart and brain, cancer of various organs, and cognitive impairment due to declining brain size, or, more importantly, various types of cognitive disorders (Economic and Social Affairs, 2015).

How does society has to face the challenge? A strategy is the need of the hour.

The components of the old age care strategy could be an iterative process of policy and strategy formulation, focus on primary health care, age-friendly health systems, strong participation of the older population in society, development of human resources for quality health care, creation and maintenance of multidisciplinary networks to facilitate care of the elderly, research, surveys, and studies for the establishment of a database for evidence-based care, and raising the awareness of the population to active ageing. Health in old age is affected by social and economic issues apart from the inherent disadvantage of biological decline. The aim of health care for older people is to provide quality services closest to their homes, to keep them functional, and to help them return to normal life in the community from the hospital as soon as possible after illness (National Health Profile, 2019).

The health system which cares for older people must have full knowledge of its users, such as their financial status, social and cultural resources, and living arrangements, apart from other disadvantages they may be facing. The care provided should be tailored to meet each individual's needs. A comprehensive care package that includes preventive, curative, and rehabilitative services is essential for this population group. Easy accessibility, continuity, and good quality of care can only can earn the respect and satisfaction of these consumers. A high degree of coordination is essential in such a model so that different services do not function at cross-purposes but are complementary to each other (World Health Organization (WHO), 2015b).

Most importantly, the services should be complete in terms of clinical consultation, paramedical services, drugs, and restorative interventions. The design of services for older people has been an object of debate in most developed countries. Till now, no consensus has been reached on whether these services should be age-based or need based. What would be ideal: to have all people above the age of 60 cared by the services, or only those people with multiple disabilities included in the system? For a society like ours, probably a balanced mix of both these models would be more pertinent and of great value.

Long-term care is the system of activities undertaken by informal caregivers (family, friends, and/or neighbours) and/or professionals (health, social and others) to ensure that a person who is not fully capable of self-care can maintain the highest possible quality of life, according to his or her individual preferences, with the greatest possible degree of independence, autonomy, participation, personal fulfilment, and human dignity. Long-term care for older persons in India has always been a matter of family functioning.

Key components of healthy ageing

Diversity: There is no typical older person. Some 80-year-olds have levels of physical and mental capacity that compare favourably with 30-year-olds. Others of the same age may require extensive care and support for basic activities like dressing and eating. Policy should be framed to improve the functional ability of all older people, whether they are robust, care-dependent, or in between.

Inequity: A large proportion (approximately 75%) of the diversity in capacity and circumstance observed in older age is the result of the cumulative impact of advantage and disadvantage across people's lives. Importantly, the relationships we have with our environments are shaped by factors such as the family we were born into, our sex, our ethnicity, level of education, and financial resources (Beard et al., JR, 2016).

Healthy ageing is replaced with active ageing

Healthy Ageing is the focus of WHO's work on ageing between 2015 and 2030. Healthy Ageing replaces the World Health Organization's previous Active ageing: a policy framework developed in 2002. Healthy Ageing, like Active Ageing, emphasizes the need for action across multiple sectors and enabling older people to remain a resource to their families, communities, and economies. Societies that adapt to this changing demographic and invest in Healthy Ageing can enable individuals to live both longer and healthier lives and for societies to reap the dividends. Healthy Ageing is an opportunity and also a challenge to bring together governments, civil society, international agencies, professionals, academia, the media, and the private sector for ten years of concerted, catalytic, and collaborative action to improve the lives of older people, their families, and the communities in which they live. It will increase demand for primary health care and long-term care, require a larger and better-trained workforce, and intensify the need for environments to be made more age-friendly.

Yet, these investments can enable the many contributions of older people – whether it be within their family, to their local community (be it the formal or informal workforce), or to society more broadly.

Integrated Care for Older People (ICOPE)

As people grow older, their health needs are likely to become more complex and chronic. However, existing health systems are fragmented and lack coordination, which makes it difficult to effectively address these needs. The WHO Integrated Care for Older People (ICOPE) approach helps key stakeholders in health and social care to understand, design, and implement a person-centred and coordinated model of care (WHO, 2017a).

The World Health Organization (WHO) recently endorsed the proposal for a Decade of Healthy Ageing (2020–2030). The WHO defines "healthy ageing" as "the process of developing and maintaining the functional ability that enables wellbeing in older age." Among the strategies for the Decade of Healthy Ageing, the WHO has suggested enhancing intrinsic capacity, promoting functional ability, and implementing the Integrated Care for Older People (ICOPE) package.

The WHO has defined steps for ICOPE evaluation and scale-up and is performing a prospective study in 2–3 countries (low and middle income, high income) to test its feasibility in 2021–2022 and a multinational randomized study to validate its clinical efficacy and effectiveness in 2022–2024 (Tavassoli et al., 2021).

The WHO defines "healthy ageing" as "the process of developing and maintaining the functional ability that enables wellbeing in older age."

Functional ability is the capability of people to do what they have reason to value. Being free of disease is not a requirement for healthy ageing as many older adults have one or more health conditions that, when well-controlled, have little influence on their functional abilities. By its definition, functional ability includes a person's capacity to: meet his or her basic needs; learn, grow, and make decisions; be mobile; build and maintain relationships; and contribute to society. Therefore, "functional ability" depends on the intrinsic capacity (IC) of the individual, relevant environmental characteristics, and the interaction between them (UN Decade of Healthy Ageing, 2021–2030).

The concept of intrinsic capacity (IC) is related to an individual's functional status, the follow-up of which over time may be useful to achieve healthy ageing. IC comprises all the mental and physical capacities upon which a person relies and includes their ability to walk, think, see, hear, remember, etc. In addition, several factors, including diseases, injuries, and age-related changes, may influence the level of IC. The environment includes the home, community, and broader society and all the factors within them, such as the facilities, people and their relationships, attitudes and values of society members, health and social policies of the government, and the systems and services that support them.

As one of the strategies to implement the Decade of Healthy Ageing by enhancing IC, promoting functional ability, and minimizing care dependency, the WHO provided the Integrated Care for Older People (ICOPE) package in 2017. Another concept associated with reduced intrinsic capacity (IC) is frailty. Frailty is related to functional deficits, and IC refers to functional reserve. Therefore, efforts to diagnose and manage frailty may help assess and prevent declines in intrinsic capacity (IC).

The current ICOPE guidelines are organized into three modules

Module I: Declines in IC, including mobility loss, malnutrition (vitality), visual impairment, hearing loss, cognitive impairment, and depressive symptoms.
Module II: Geriatric syndromes associated with care dependency, including urinary incontinence and risk of falls.
Module III: Caregiver support that includes interventions to support caregiving and prevent caregiver strain.

These guidelines cover evidence-based interventions to manage common declines in capacity in older age, including mobility, nutrition or vitality, vision, hearing, cognition, and mood, as well as important geriatric syndromes such as urinary incontinence and risk of falls. These conditions were selected because they are strong independent predictors of mortality and care dependency in older age (World Health Organization, 2020).

The general care pathways for those with functional declines comprise the following five steps:

Step 1: Screen for declines in intrinsic capacity (IC).
Step 2: Undertake a person-centred assessment in primary care.
Step 3: Define the goal of care and develop a personalized care plan.
Step 4: Ensure a referral pathway and monitor the care plan with links to specialized geriatric care.
Step 5: Engage communities and support caregivers.

IC and frailty represent the two faces of the same coin, with one indicating the reserves of the individual and the other the deficits that accumulate with ageing. Although both frailty and IC are dynamic entities, frailty is mainly used in cross-sectional assessments, while IC is applied in longitudinal approaches. However, instead of the frailty phenotype, a frailty index can be used in longitudinal approaches. The frailty index is related to physical, psychological, cognitive, sensory, and social functional declines, and the index is used not only to identify frail persons but also those at risk of frailty. In addition, the frailty index and IC are based on the assumption that ageing individuals can be adequately assessed and managed only if comprehensively evaluated and followed in a novel healthcare model based on service integration and multi-disciplinarity (World report on Ageing and Health, 2015).

Therefore, the integrated care of older patients with frailty or risk of frailty using the frailty index is as important for achieving healthy ageing as reducing frailty levels is for promoting it.

ICOPE implementation pilot programmes

The first phase of the ICOPE implementation pilot programme started in France, Andorra, China, India, Italy, Kenya, Mexico, Qatar, and Vietnam to assess its feasibility and acceptability.

Step 1: screening of the ICOPE-CARE programme is performed every 4–6 months by professionals or the seniors themselves. If a deterioration in one or more domains of IC is identified, an alert is generated by an algorithm, which allows rapid intervention by health professionals (Table 7.1).
Step 2: person-centred assessment
Step 3: personalized care plan

Experienced trained nurses in Gerontology perform geriatric evaluations of older people in community health centres close to their homes. These nurses, with the support of a physician, propose personalized care plans for the older people evaluated. This plan is then sent to the clinic physician to ensure its implementation and follow-up.

The WHO ICOPE's Ready-Set-Go approaches to test and learn from the feasibility and acceptability of pilot studies, as well as studies to evaluate clinical effectiveness and efficacy, are planned to be completed by 2024. From 2025, ICOPE will be rolled out within primary healthcare settings in a wider range of countries.

The intrinsic capacity (IC) and frailty represent the two faces of the same coin. One indicates individual reserves, while the other indicates deficits that have accumulated with ageing. Although both frailty and IC are dynamic entities, frailty is mainly evaluated in cross-sectional assessments, while IC is often used in longitudinal approaches. However, instead of the frailty phenotype, the frailty index can also be used in longitudinal approaches. The frailty index is related to declines in physical, psychological, cognitive, sensory, and social functions and can be used to identify not only frail persons but also those at risk of frailty. In addition, the frailty index and IC are based on the assumption that ageing individuals can be adequately assessed and managed only if comprehensively evaluated and followed in a novel healthcare model based on service integration and multidisciplinarity (Belloni et al., 2019).

Therefore, the integrated care of older patients with frailty or risk of frailty based on the frailty index is as important for achieving healthy ageing as reducing frailty is for promoting healthy ageing (Kim et al., 2017).

The WHO has described steps to evaluate and scale-up ICOPE, including a prospective study in 2–3 countries (low and middle income, as well as high income) in 2021–2022 to test its feasibility and a multinational randomized study in 2022–2024 to validate its clinical efficacy and effectiveness.

Comparisons of the eight core items of WHO ICOPE and 53 items of ICOOP_Frail showed that all the eight core items of the ICOPE were well integrated. In addition, WHO ICOPE and ICOOP_Frail both (1) are designed to be implemented in primary care at the community level, (2) are integrated programmes that consider not only medical but also social and psychological aspects, (3) develop personalized care plans, and (4) aim to promote healthy ageing (Table 7.1).

However, ICOOP_Frail does not include the referral pathway and caregiver support addressed in ICOPE (Nwagwu et al., 2020).

Present status of ICOPE training in India and other SEARO counties

Primarily, health and social care workers in the community and primary care settings will be the training targets of these modules. The guidance will enable them to screen, assess, and identify older adult with loss of intrinsic

TABLE 7.1 Example of identified frailty risk factors (functional declines) and recommendations

Identified problem	Recommendations
Sarcopenia suspected	Rule out underlying diseases. Protein intake of 20 g per meal. Resistance exercise twice weekly and aerobic exercise for 30 minutes daily.
Hearing problem	Refer to ENT doctor.
Sleep problems	Investigate the causes. Improve the sleep environment and increase daytime outdoor activities. Stop unnecessary psychotropic use of medications/substances. Treat depression if indicated.
Daytime drowsiness	Stop unnecessary use of psychotropics or sleep pills. Investigate the presence of sleep problems at night. Investigate the presence of snoring during sleep (sleep apnea).
Urinary incontinence	Urinalysis. Evaluate bladder movement. Urge incontinence: try bladder-specific anticholinergics or consult a urologist.
IADL impairment	Arrange the help of family or caregiver (or formal paid care-giver).
Insufficient social contact	Link to nearby community resources or services; search for home visiting service if needed. A health visitor, ASHA, may visit the patient's home.
Fewer than two meals per day	Check for the cause of infrequent meals, e.g., economic problems, no person to provide meals, or disease. Link to nearby community resources or services; search for food delivery services. ANM, MPHW, PHN, village guide, or ASHA may visit the patient's home.

ICOPE, Integrated Care for Older People; ENT, ear-nose-throat; IADL, instrumental activities of daily living.
Referenced by World Health Organization. Guidelines on Integrated Care for Older People (ICOPE).
Available from: https://www.who.int/ageing/publications/guidelines-icope/en/.

capacity and functional ability, as well as the need for specialized knowledge for a person-centred care plan.

Recently, the Indian Academy of Geriatrics, with the support of WHO SEARO, conducted training for master trainers of primary care physicians on Integrated Care for Older People. In addition, members of the professional bodies of the region, viz. Bangladesh Association for the Aged and Institute of

Geriatric Medicine, Sri Lankan Association of Geriatric Medicine, Geriatric Society of Nepal, Indonesian Geriatric Association, Mahidol University, Thailand, and Non-Governmental Organizations (HelpAge India, Jan Seva Foundation, ACMERI) actively participated in the online training. As a result, one hundred thirty-six physicians from India, Indonesia, Thailand, Nepal, Sri Lanka, and Bangladesh were trained by facilitators from India, Thailand, Nepal, Sri Lanka, and Myanmar. These master trainers will deliver training to primary care physicians, nurses, and community health-care workers, which will help them impart easily accessible, effective, and comprehensive health care to every older adult (WHO, 2017b).

Nurses in primary care and physicians could easily adopt the ICOPE approach in clinical practice. Besides comprehensive clinical evaluation, the ICOPE approach emphasizes supporting social care and caregivers. A partnership involving the older person, treating physician, community health officers, primary healthcare workers, family, and community as envisaged in ICOPE, will sustain people's well-being as they age. The ICOPE will contribute significantly to achieving the decade's goals of healthy ageing.

Advancing nurse leadership

Nurses are committed to advancing nurse leadership in the design, governance, and provision of high-quality, person-centred, and professional aged care. Nurses contribute to planning, delivering, and evaluating clinical and other care and lifestyle outcomes in all aged care settings. Nurses have a critical role in providing quality and safe aged care that includes: contributing to clinical governance systems, upholding older peoples' rights to dignity, respect, and autonomy and making care decisions consistent with their values and goals; and delivering quality, safe care irrespective of care environment.

- Nurses, as part of clinical governance systems, contribute to measuring, monitoring, and improving the quality, safety, and appropriateness of clinical care.
- Older people are a diverse group whose care needs vary depending on the care environment and their presenting health issues. Care must be personalized to meet the expressed needs of the individual and in consultation with the individual or family where appropriate.
- Older people have the right to receive quality evidence-based care consistent with their needs.
- Nurses support individual older people and their families to access evidence-based care.
- Enabling older people to participate in their care decisions, undertake self-care, and seek help early are core components of safe, quality care.

- Nurses lead and support aged care teams to provide safe, quality care for older people through the application of their knowledge, skills, and mentorship. Nurses have a responsibility to continuously reflect on and develop their knowledge and skills (World Health Organization-Eastern Mediterranean Region (WHO-EMRO), 2018).

Indian Scenerio

While the Indian population is ageing, most older people care for themselves within the community. However, over time age-related and other factors impact their health, well-being, and ability to function independently. Many older people have more than one chronic condition and live with significant self-care, disease, and treatment burdens. Thus, they are at risk of being prescribed potentially or actually inappropriate medicines and of medicine-related adverse events, including unnecessary hospitalizations. Many older people require polypharmacy to manage their health conditions, some of which are high-risk medicines. Thus, they are at risk of being prescribe potentially/actually inappropriate medicines and of medicine-related adverse events, including unnecessary hospitalizations. These medicine-related adverse events occur in hospitals, residential aged care facilities, and community settings, and can contribute to morbidity and mortality. As such, many older people require comprehensive, holistic, and high-quality clinical care (Takeda, 2020).

Quality and safety

The aged care system fails to meet the needs of older, often very vulnerable, citizens. It does not deliver uniformly safe and quality care for older people. It is unkind and uncaring towards them.

There is a need to address deficits identified in numerous internal reviews, indicator monitoring, studies, and consultancies conducted over the past 40 years into the aged care system.

Specifically focus on the points below:

- focus on the rights-based approach to care, supported by legislation
- shift towards a system that supports the most vulnerable and marginalized
- emphasis on addressing workforce deficits that influence poor care outcomes
- monitoring of care outcomes through effective clinical indicators
- prioritizing strategies for vastly improved quality and safety of aged care provision.

The role of nurses in supporting older people to access quality, safe aged care and further opportunities to influence policy and the provision of quality and safe aged care into the future (Sustainable Development Goals).

Clinical governance frameworks support nurses in providing safe, evidence based, cost-effective quality care. Clinical governance is an integrated set of leadership behaviours, policies, procedures, responsibilities, relationships, planning, monitoring, and improvement mechanisms implemented to support safe, quality clinical care and positive clinical outcomes for individuals. Integral to the success of effective clinical governance systems is the ability of nurses to lead, influence, and contribute to the delivery of evidence-based care, and continuously improve care outcomes to support older people's health and well-being through monitoring and evaluation. Specifically, nursing leadership is essential in engaging older people in health and aged care design and analysing whether care outcomes reflect the individual's values, rights, and needs. A review into aged care approved providers for the current clinical governance structures in aged care has found that they have failed to support quality care. Indian aged care can only be improved with a focus on clinical governance systems to ensure monitoring and advancement in care systems, and improved cooperation and collaboration between aged care and healthcare services.

There are five themes to improve effectiveness and consistency in the interface between aged and healthcare systems.

These would improve:

- access to primary health care for those in aged care
- access to and integration with secondary and tertiary health systems, including acute and sub-acute care
- access and integration with palliative care services
- transfer of older people between residential care, hospital, ambulance transfer, rehabilitation, and transition care
- key mechanisms and processes needed for the integrated interface between aged care and healthcare systems, including digital innovation and streamlined data sharing.

These changes can only be implemented through the provision of quality nursing and interdisciplinary care systems that offer older people both in- and out-reach health services to meet their complex care needs. Nurses' unique position in providing high-quality evidence-based clinical care and leadership (Tavassoli et al., 2021).

The spaces where nurses and patients meet become the area where practice develops. Older people have unique needs. Person-centred approaches, clinical governance frameworks, and evidence-based care should underpin all care provision for older people. These frameworks will ensure each person's needs are identified and supported in a way that is responsive to the care environment and best utilizes nurses' full expertise and scope of practice (Shaji & Reddy, 2012).

Nurses play a critical role in promoting healthy ageing

Nurses are best placed to deliver quality and safe clinical care, including advocating for person-centred, culturally safe and respectful care relationships and supporting the health, well-being, and independence of older people. Further, nurses are responsible for the supervision and development of non-government (unregulated healthcare workers) in order to support older people to undertake many of their daily activities, such as personal hygiene, mobilization, maintaining nutrition and hydration, and participating in recreational activities (Won et al., 2020).

A key element of the nurse's role is recognizing, preventing, and managing deterioration to promote greater functional ability for older people. This element supports the health and well-being of the older person and prevents inappropriate or avoidable hospitalizations and early entry into residential care. Nurses have the expertise, through assessment, care planning, and interdisciplinary collaboration, to identify and manage chronic health issues impacting the well-being and longevity of older people such as diabetes, dementia, pain, impaired mobility, and nutrition. Nurses play a significant role in promoting health literacy through education to support the older person in making decisions about their life including advance care planning. Nurses are key to providing appropriate and person-centred palliative care to support the older person and their families at the end of life (Kim et al., 2017).

Recommendation of gerontological nursing

The WHO advocates for nurse-led, evidence-based clinical care and governance in aged care that encompasses:

- personalized, dignified care to determine the individual's needs and preferences with the older person; achieving optimal clinical care outcomes consistent with their values, goals, and capabilities
- contemporary application of nursing knowledge, skills, and capability in multidisciplinary teams of well-educated, proficient healthcare workers to improve outcomes for older people
- relevant clinical guidelines that set standards for evidence-based clinical care, as well as identification, monitoring, and evaluation for a range of clinical risks, conditions, co-morbidities, and multi-morbidities
- quality indicators to ensure care can be measured, monitored, evaluated, and improved (Roth et al., 2015)

Role of nurses in maintaining good health and well-being of the elderly

The role of geriatric nurses is essential and diverse, encompassing various responsibilities. What sets them apart is their expertise and sensitivity to the unique needs of elderly patients. Nurses act as a support function to motivate and empower the elderly, utilizing their expertise in age-related issues to promote independence and functional abilities. With a holistic approach to promoting the health and well-being of the elderly, their responsibilities are:

- Administering medications and treatment plans under the guidance of a doctor
- Collaborating with doctors and medical team members to administer treatment for chronic conditions most likely to affect the elderly (e.g., heart disease, arthritis, diabetes, osteoporosis, Alzheimer's disease)
- Early identification of complex comorbid physical and mental conditions
- Assisting with and training patients on daily living activities, such as hygiene, toileting, medication management, and nutritional needs
- Assessing different levels of the functional, mental, and emotional status of older patients
- Implementing interventions and preventive care to reduce the risk of falls, malnutrition, and other health problems
- Promoting healthy lifestyles that can prevent or delay the onset of chronic diseases
- Skills to provide optimal pain management and end-of-life care
- Provide training and motivation to patients and caregivers to handle age-related conditions

The role of nurses in the care of elderly patients is essential in ensuring that patients fully understand their health conditions, illnesses, medications, and treatments. They counsel patients on recommended self-care practices and assist in overcoming any obstacles that prevent them from making healthy decisions. With support and encouragement, nurses play a significant role in guiding older adults on their wellness journeys (Takeda et al., 2020).

Role of nurses in socializing

Positive social connections help improve the cognitive health of the elderly. Those above 50 may experience risk factors like living alone, losing loved ones, chronic illness, or sensory impairments that lead to social isolation or loneliness. It can be a serious and often overlooked issue that affects many. The focus of elderly nursing care is on discovering new social opportunities, building self-confidence, and leading a happier, purposeful life.

In India, it's uncommon for seniors to engage in hobbies, and only a few participate in community work. To stay mentally stimulated and active, gerontologists recommend that seniors create a daily routine of activities such as gardening, reading, writing, music, dancing, and playing board games.

Elderly nursing care facilitates participation in daily activities by providing a structured routine. It allows them to engage in various activities such as:

- Physical exercise, yoga, or walking in local parks or outdoor spaces
- Facilitating connections with family members and loved ones who may be living in other parts of the country or abroad through video calls or messaging apps
- Brain-stimulating activities like crossword puzzles or Sudoku for mental stimulation
- Participating in traditional social events and cultural activities, such as festivals or religious ceremonies
- Enabling them to access to technology

Overall, the role of nurses in the care of the elderly is multifaceted. It encompasses not only socialization and engagement but also learning, empathy, and increased self-esteem (World Health Organization, 2015a).

Additionally, older persons need more care as cure options become limited due to degenerating health conditions. They need a long time to either recuperate after acute illness or develop chronic conditions, resulting in the inability to perform daily routine activities and, therefore, becoming dependent on others for the rest of their lives. In India, although notions of ageing and care are changing, there is a continued preference among families for home-based care of elderly relatives. Bedridden elderly people may need help with bathing and dental care. Preference among families for home-based care of elderly relatives is on the rise (WHO Clinical Consortium on Healthy Ageing, 2018).

Conclusion

Nursing plays a vital role in improving and maintaining the health of the older person. Nurses are often the primary care providers for the older person, particularly when their health needs require them to be placed in an aged care facility. However, nurses are also crucial in ensuring the health and well-being of people to enable them to live their lives to their potential. Nurses also play an active role in the diagnosis and treatment of many conditions in the older person. The International Council of Nurses (ICN, Geneva) supports the active role of nurses, which requires major changes in their work patterns. As a result of advances in communication and medical technology, many interventions that were earlier possible only in hospitals are now possible at home. The elderly need more care as cure options become limited due to degenerating health conditions. They need a long time to either recuperate after acute illness or develop chronic conditions, resulting in the inability to perform daily routine activities and, therefore, becoming dependent on others for the rest of their lives. In India, although notions of ageing and care are changing, there is a continued preference among families for home-based care of elderly relatives. Preference among families for home-based care of elderly relatives is on the rise. The National Program for Health Care of the Elderly (NPHCE) is a very substantive contribution from MOHFW towards health goals for the elderly, formulated in the National Policy on Older Persons as well as the Maintenance and Welfare of Parents and Senior Citizens Act 2007 (WHO Clinical Consortium on Healthy Ageing, 2018).

References

Beard, J.R., Officer, A., de, Carvalho I.A, et al. (2016). The world report on ageing and health: A policy framework for healthy ageing. *Lancet*, 387, 10033, 2145–54.

Belloni, G., & Cesari, M. (2019). Frailty and intrinsic capacity: two distinct but related constructs. *Front Med (Lausanne)*, 6, 133.

India Current Affairs (2011). National Programme for Health Care of the Elderly. A leading resource of online information of India. [Last accessed on 2 May 22]. http://www.indiacurrentaffairs.org.

Kim, H., Park, Y.H., Jung, Y.I., et al. (2017). Evaluation of a technology-enhanced integrated care model for frail older persons: protocol of the SPEC study, a stepped-wedge cluster randomized trial in nursing homes. *BMC Geriatr*, 17, 88.

National Health Profile. (2019). *Global burden of mental disorders and the need for a comprehensive, coordinated response from health and social sectors at the country level.* https://apps.who.int/gb/ebwha/pdf_files/EB130/B130_9-en.pdf.

Nwagwu, V.C., Cigolle, C., & Suh, T. (2020). Reducing frailty to promote healthy aging. *Clin Geriatr Med*, 36, 613–30.

Roth, D.L., Fredman, L., & Haley, W.E. (2015). Informal caregiving and Its impact on health: a reappraisal from population-based studies. *Gerontologist*, 55, 309–319. doi: 10.1093/geront/gnu177.

Shaji, K.S., & Reddy, M.S. (2012). Caregiving: a public health priority. *Indian J. Psychol. Med*, 34, 303–5. doi: 10.4103/0253-7176.108191.

Sustainable Development Goals. *THE 17 GOALS*. New York, United Nations; (https://sustainabledevelopment.un.org/sdgs).

Takeda, C., Guyonnet, S., Sumi, Y., & Vellas, B. (2020). Integrated care for older people and the implementation in the INSPIRE study. *J Prev Alz Dis*, 2(7), 70–4.

Tavassoli, N., Piau, A., Berbon, C., De, K.J., Lafont, C., & De, S.B.P. (2021). Framework implementation of the INSPIRE ICOPE-CARE program in collaboration with the World Health Organization (WHO) in the Occitania region. *J Frailty Aging*, 10, 103–9.

UN Decade of Healthy Ageing: Plan of Action. (2021–2030). https://www.who.int/initiatives/decade-of-healthy-ageing.

United Nations, Economic and Social Affairs. (2015). *Population Division: World population ageing 2015*. New York (NY): United Nations (https://www.un.org/development/desa/pd/content/world-population-ageing-2015).

World Health Organization (WHO). (2015a). *The growing need for home health care for the elderly*. https://apps.who.int/iris/bitstream/handle/10665/326801/EMROPUB_2015_EN_1901.pdf?sequence=1&isAllowed=y.

World Health Organization (WHO). (2015b). *World report on ageing and health*. Geneva. (https://apps.who.int/iris/handle/10665/186463).

World Health Organization (WHO). (2017a). *Global strategy and action plan on ageing and health*. Geneva. http://www.who.int/ageing/global-strategy.

World Health Organization (WHO). (2017b). *Integrated care for older people: Guidelines on community-level interventions to manage declines in intrinsic capacity*. http://apps.who.int/iris/handle/10665/258981.

World Health Organization (WHO). (2018). *Clinical Consortium on Healthy Ageing*. Report of Consortium meeting held 11–18 December 2018 in Geneva, Switzerland https://www.who.int/publications/i/item/WHO-FWC-ALC-19.2

World Health Organization. (2020). *Ageing: healthy ageing and functional ability*, Geneva, Switzerland: [cited 2021 Mar 25]. https://www.who.int/news- room/q-a-detail/ageing-healthy-ageing-and-functional-ability.

Won, C.W., Lee, Y., Lee, S., & Kim, M. (2020). Development of Korean frailty index for primary care (KFI-PC) and its criterion validity. *Ann Geriatr Med Res*, 24, 125–38.

World Health Organization-Eastern Mediterranean Region (WHO-EMRO) (2018). *Regional guide for the development of nursing specialist practice*.

World Report on Ageing and Health. (2015). *World report on ageing and health*. World Health Organization. https://apps.who.int/iris/handle/10665/186463.

PART II
Family care, community care and long-term care

8
SENSE OF BELONGING IN COMMUNITY-BASED CARE AMONG SOUTH AFRICAN OLDER PERSONS

A rapid review

Keshenaa Fakir, Erika Hitge, and Jaco Hoffman

Introduction

The aim of this chapter is to explore how existing literature describes sense of belonging in relation to community-based care (CBC) among South African older people. The South African policy sets out the protection of the older population and offers a framework for what CBC and residential care entail in the *Older Persons Act* 13 of 2006. However, gaps remain in practically incorporating older people into society and enabling their independent living (Lombard & Kruger, 2009). This article specifically addresses the gap on the conceptual level of sense of belonging.

Background

In contextualising this research, a brief background to the nature of the older population is necessary. Globally, there has been an unprecedented increase in the older population (United Nations [UN], 2011; United Nations Department of Economic and Social Affairs [UNDESA], 2017), prompted by a demographic transition (Guseh, 2016) which co-occurs with an epidemiological transition (United Nations Population Fund [UNFPA] & HelpAge International, 2012). From a South African perspective, the older population is projected to increase by 15.9% within the next 30 years, to an estimated absolute number of 11.5 million people (UNDESA, 2017). Furthermore, it was established in 2019 that South African older people were affected predominantly by non-communicable diseases (NCDs) (Institute for Health Metrics and Evaluation [IHME], 2020).

DOI: 10.4324/9781003528432-10

The demographic and epidemiological transitions are important because of their relationship to a growing need for long-term care (LTC) (UNFPA & HelpAge International, 2012). Alongside this need for LTC for older people, the concept of sense of belonging in the South African context is of particular interest because older people are encouraged to continue living in their communities (*Older Persons Act* 13 of 2006). Relevant to this focus, the concepts of care and belonging in relation to South African older people are addressed, followed by the theoretical background that underpins this chapter.

Care and belonging

According to the World Health Organization (WHO, 2017), LTC refers to assisting individuals to preserve a certain degree of functional ability. This type of care is intended for individuals who present with or are at risk of prominent and enduring intrinsic capacity deterioration, and the assistance provided should be in line with the due rights, dignity, and freedom of the person (WHO, 2017). Even though the demand for LTC is not met in South Africa, it is nevertheless one of only three countries in sub-Saharan Africa that presents with efforts, at a national level, to develop LTC systems (WHO, 2017).

The *Older Persons Act* 13 of 2006 in South Africa gives prominence to older people within policy, and the marked shift from a focus on institutional care for older persons to an emphasis on CBC is critically relevant to this study. Similarities between CBC and the international concept of *ageing in place* are evident from older persons' continued residence in the community and their relative independence (Davey et al., 2004; *Older Persons Act* 13 of 2006). CBC is a form of LTC (National Institute on Aging, 2017) and is defined as care that is accessible within close proximity to the home, responsive to people's needs, and fosters participation, responsibility, and traditional community life (Department of Health, 2011). The rights associated with CBC allow older people to engage in opportunities for growth, and to obtain care and protection in a culturally appropriate manner from family and community systems (*Older Persons Act* 13 of 2006). As set out in policy, CBC programmes are composed of two parts: (a) prevention/promotion programmes, and (b) home-based care (*Older Persons Act* 13 of 2006). While the prevention/promotion programmes are put in place to ensure older persons are able to live in their communities at an independent level, home-based care is directed towards older people who are frail, to ensure maximum care by means of an all-inclusive scope of integrated services in the community environment (*Older Persons Act* 13 of 2006).

While policy accommodates the intention of CBC for older people (*Older Persons Act* 13 of 2006), Strydom (2008) states that unfortunately to date the provision both to promote independent living and to provide for the frail older persons in the community remains very limited and unevenly spread across the country. In rural areas, the envisaged provision is almost non-existent. Even emergency provision hardly exists. Basic transport and communication systems are not yet in place. The absence of an infrastructure capable of ensuring clean drinking water, an adequate diet, and proper sanitation undermines the development of services to older persons. (p. 108) Taking into account the prevalence of factors such as unemployment, and HIV and AIDS in South Africa, Madhavan et al. (2017) point out that these circumstances hamper an ideal ageing trajectory. An ideal ageing trajectory possibly encompasses older people making use of pension money as per their needs and the ability to decide on the use of their money, obtaining care from their adult children who are working, and inclusion in a considerable network of social support that offers emotional support, practical assistance, and friendship (Madhavan et al., 2017).

Considering care for older persons on a national level, the Department of Social Development, with the South African Older Persons Forum, presents the Active Ageing Programme (Department of Social Development, 2019), with the intention of enhancing older persons' quality of life (Department of Social Development, 2019). Some of the ways in which it proposes to do this are by (a) participation (cultural, social, and sport-related) that attempts to counteract diseases associated with older ages, and (b) supporting independence (Department of Social Development, 2019).

At a provincial level, however, a study by the Western Cape Department of Social Development (2015) identified loneliness and social isolation to be among the obstacles encountered by older people. Being ignored by kin, especially in the case of older people living independently, and having limited opportunities for interaction were noted in the study (Western Cape Department of Social Development, 2015). The COVID-19 pandemic prompted measures for limiting movement, such as "stay-at-home restrictions, quarantines, and lockdowns" (United Nations [UN], 2020, p. 9), with the idea that such seclusion of older people could help to curtail the spread of the virus (Armitage & Nellums, 2020). However, an international study warns that self-isolation will greatly affect older people whose social lives comprise solely of those activities outside their home environment, as well as those who were already socially disconnected (Armitage & Nellums, 2020). The distancing measures put in place also affect older people who are recipients of home/community care (UN, 2020). In the case of older people in South Africa who lack care from family members (Kasiram & Hölscher, 2015; Rankin, 2019), the issue about isolating during the COVID-19 pandemic became especially concerning.

In view of this evidence of isolation and distancing, Diener and Seligman's (2004) view that social connections are important for wellbeing is noteworthy. Furthermore, from a perspective of maintaining wellbeing, there is a need for social belonging and helpful, positive relational bonds (Diener & Seligman, 2004). Similarly, the social connections that older people have in their neighbourhood or community were identified as fulfilling a crucial role in wellbeing (Cramm et al., 2013). In response to (a) the concept of CBC and concern for wellbeing by policy (*Older Persons Act 13 of 2006*), and (b) the importance of belonging for wellbeing (Cramm & Nieboer, 2015; Fletcher, 2015; Visser, 2012), it becomes essential for this chapter to consider the underlying theoretical foundations in the field of psychology in relation to older people.

Theoretical and conceptual background

Community psychology contributes to a foundation that can be used to reflect on the community elements that might increase the possibility of a good old age (Provencher et al., 2014). While Cheng and Heller (2009, p. 162) note that "community psychologists pride themselves on their values of social equity and their advocacy in championing the needs of socially disenfranchised groups", addressing the challenges associated with ageing is limited. Furthermore, Cheng and Heller (2009) state that the branch of community psychology has (a) infrequently paid attention to concerns associated with ageing, and (b) seldom gained the interest of individuals who work with older people and their community environments. The abovementioned statements highlight the need for the care and sense of belonging of the older population to be addressed.

This study is therefore positioned in the field of community psychology, premised on care for individuals and concern for their wellbeing (Nelson & Prilleltensky, as cited in Visser, 2012). Visser (2012) states that wellbeing is encouraged by establishing mutual emotional connections and sentiments of belonging. Such interventions also highlight the goal of achieving a sense of community, which is indicative of mutual care and belonging (Visser, 2012). This chapter contributes to knowledge of the older population from the basis of community psychology, with particular reference to a sense of community.

Sense of community is composed of four components: (a) reinforcement (McMillan & Chavis, 1986), (b) influence (McMillan & Chavis, 1986; Prezza & Constantini, 1998), (c) shared emotional connection, and (d) membership (McMillan & Chavis, 1986). The principal component related to this study, and thus discussed, is membership. *Membership* indicates affiliation and a feeling of belonging at a community level or the ability to connect at a personal level (McMillan & Chavis, 1986; Prezza & Constantini, 1998). From the perspective of a sense of community,

McMillan and Chavis (1986) state that *sense of belonging* "involves the feeling, belief, and expectation that one fits in the group and has a place there, a feeling of acceptance by the group, and a willingness to sacrifice for the group" (p. 10). Similarly, Pretty et al. (2006) hold that belonging enables community members to communicate freely – in a safe environment – who they are, their background, their individual feelings, and common historical aspects. Furthermore, in the community context, members are able to occupy status that is considered important and they are able to connect in a relatable manner to group members with comparable backgrounds (Pretty et al., 2006). Peter et al. (2015) identify a sense of belonging as the need to form close relationships, which provide a person with feelings of care, love, and safety.

In terms of social relationships, Lambert et al. (2013) point out that when relationships provide a perception of fitting in safely, there is a sense of belonging. Furthermore, there is evidence that a sense of belonging adds meaning to life (Lambert et al., 2013). Finally, Ryan and Deci's (2004) description of *relatedness* appears comparable to the sense of belonging defined above. Relatedness is described in psychological terms as feeling connected to other individuals in a secure manner (Ryan & Deci, 2004). Reflecting on the conceptualisations presented here, it is clear that there are various ways of referring to a sense of belonging, such as membership, fitting in, and relatedness.

Policy in South Africa prioritises the wellbeing of older persons (*Older Persons Act* 13 of 2006). However, at the level of implementation, discrepancies have been noted in the current inconsistent quality of community care and in the lack of organised services for older people (Rankin, 2019; Strydom, 2008; WHO, 2017). In the quest to assure the wellbeing of older persons, evidence revealing that belonging is an important feature (Cramm & Nieboer, 2015; Fletcher, 2015) must be seriously considered.

The importance of belonging to wellbeing is confirmed by community psychology (Visser, 2012). The interconnected nature of a sense of community and sense of belonging in the field of community psychology (Visser, 2012) is at the core of this chapter. The aim is to explore how existing literature describes sense of belonging in relation to CBC among South African older people, who naturally experience challenges and adjustments commonly associated with old age. The exploration and development of an understanding of how sense of belonging is described in CBC could be used to inform any relevant decisions that emerge (Khangura et al., 2012; Scientific Resource Centre, 2016) regarding the care of the older population. Against this background, the methods that directed this exploration are presented.

Methods

In accordance with the aim of this research, a rapid review of available literature was undertaken. The review question that was asked, "How does existing literature describe sense of belonging in relation to community-based care among South African older people?" guided the review.

Research design

This study employed a rapid review to access existing literature. The rapid review approach is one of the methods used to synthesise evidence (Scientific Resource Centre, 2016). In contrast to traditional systematic reviews, rapid reviews expedite the process of synthesising evidence in a shorter amount of time (Ganann et al., 2010; Khangura et al., 2012). The methods of expediting this study involved refining the research question, confining the inclusion of grey literature sources to those most strongly related to the topic, making use of English language sources only, and employing a rigorous process to formulate the keywords/search fields; however, the keywords were not exhaustive. In addition to the researcher (primary author), three other reviewers – the second and third authors, and an external reviewer – were involved in the research.

Scoping review

A preliminary scoping search presented an adequate amount of literature and was deemed viable after consultation with two reviewers and acceptance by two initial review committees.

Search strategy

Databases and identification of data

Three strategies were conducted to search for existing literature:

1) The EBSCO Discovery Service search platform, available on the North-West University library website (North-West University, 2020). The EBSCO Discovery Service search platform comprises 73 databases, including South African and international databases, such as Academic Search Premier, Africa-Wide Information, JSTOR, ProQuest Theses & Dissertations Full Text, PsycINFO, SAGE Publications, SAGE Journals online, SCIELO, ScienceDirect, and Wiley Online Journals (North-West University, 2020).
2) Google Scholar search: The first 200 results were searched.

3) Identifying relevant grey literature sources (policy documents, organisational documents) from reputable organisations. Examples include government publications, national/international non-governmental organisations, and intergovernmental organisations.

There is no absolute standard for systematic and robust grey literature searching, and few recommendations for performing this search are recorded (Godin et al., 2015). Hence, the researchers were aware that grey literature was to be treated in a slightly different manner compared with research articles while the method remained ethical. The list of grey literature data sources was developed by the researchers engaging with literature on the topic, hand searching websites of reputable organisations by exploring their publications/resources, and in consultation with two reviewers.

Keywords

The formulation of the keywords involved the researchers engaging with various literature sources, identifying closely related synonyms of core terms, and consulting with the faculty librarian and two reviewers. The following keywords, Boolean operators, and search fields (indicated in square brackets) were used for the EBSCO Discovery Service search:

Level 1 [title]: "older people" or elderly or aging or aged or "old people" or senior* or "older person*" or "older adult*" or "senior citizen*" or pensioners or ageing AND

Level 2 [abstract]: "community based care" or "community-based care" or "community care" or "community support" or community* or "family care" or "family support" or "aging in place" or "community caregiving" or "community assistance" or "community services" or "community based" or "community living" or "age-friendly environment" or "informal care" or "home-based care" or "home care" or "ageing in place" or "community dwelling" AND

Level 3 [all text]: "sense of belonging" or belong* or isolation or connection or lonely* or relationship or relatedness or abandonment or solitude or remoteness or seclusion or rejection or "fit* in" or "feel* of belong*" or membership or affiliation or acceptance AND

Level 4 [all text]: "South Africa*" or Gauteng or KwaZulu or Limpopo or "Western Cape" or "Eastern Cape" or "North West" or Mpumalanga or "Free State" or "Northern Cape"

For the Google Scholar search, the following search terms were used:

With all of the words: belong* lonely* elderly community care South Africa
With the exact phrase: "South Africa"

Inclusion and exclusion criteria

EBSCO Discovery Service and Google Scholar search. Inclusion criteria were restricted to individuals 60 years and older; older people living in CBC; older people residing in South Africa; English-language text; and studies conducted and published between January 2009 and June 2020. The timeframe was restricted due to the *Older Persons Act* 13 of 2006 only having been assented to (Mathiso, 2011) and commencing into operation just over a decade ago, on 1 April 2010 (President of the Republic of South Africa, 2010).

The limiters pre-selected for the EBSCO Discovery Service search were (a) January 2009 to June 2020, (b) English language, and (c) selecting the application of related keywords, equivalent subjects, and searching within full-text articles and e-books on the search website. For the Google Scholar search, a pre-selected time range limiter of 2009 to 2020 was applied.

Full-text journal studies, peer-reviewed studies, non-peer-reviewed studies (for contributions by policy documentation), quantitative studies, qualitative studies, mixed-methods studies, PhD studies, and master's dissertations/mini-dissertations were included. Studies were excluded on the basis of being review studies or conference proceedings, studies published in languages besides English, or studies of older people living in institutional settings or similar settings (e.g., residential care facilities or old age homes).

Grey literature. The above inclusion/exclusion criteria were broadened due to the sparseness of grey literature that focused specifically on South Africa. Inclusion criteria for grey literature were broadened in terms of location to employ a global perspective given the nature of international policy documents/instrumentation as a basis for policies in Africa. Grey literature documents followed the same time range, with an exception made for acts and policy documents which have been in effect prior to 2009 and remained unchanged since then. The abovementioned parameters of inclusion/exclusion criteria were applied after consultation with one of the reviewers, who is an expert in gerontology.

Appraisal of sources

Stage 1 (determining relevance) and stage 2 (quality appraisal) were conducted by the first author and overseen by all three reviewers. For the research studies, the first author independently screened the titles, abstracts, and the inclusion/exclusion criteria to determine relevance and compliance. If the title and abstract provided insufficient information, the researcher screened the full text of the source to determine relevance. Data sources initially classified as uncertain underwent a second review by the researcher. Sources that remained classified as "uncertain" after the second review were discussed in consultation with the three additional reviewers in order to make a collective decision.

The contents page, introduction, and recommendations sections of grey literature sources were screened for relevance. These sections were selected and deemed important in consultation with a study reviewer, who is an expert in gerontology, and are comparable to a study focused on a systematic review (Godin et al., 2015). Compliance with the grey literature inclusion/exclusion criteria and terms amongst those used in the search keywords was considered to determine if grey literature contained relevant information.

One of the grey literature sources, *Global age-friendly cities: A guide* (WHO, 2007), did not meet the inclusion criteria in terms of time range. Nevertheless, in consultation with the reviewers, a decision was made to include this source as a seminal document with valuable data directly related to this research, whereas none of the other documents contained similar information relative to the explicit focus on the features of an age-friendly city.

The quality appraisal instrument used in this study was a compilation of the following established instruments: (a) Joanna Briggs Institute [JBI] Reviewer Manual (The JBI, 2014), (b) Developing National Institute for Health and Care Excellence [NICE] guidelines: the manual (NICE, 2020), and (c) the AACODS (Authority, Accuracy, Coverage, Objectivity, Date, and Significance) Checklist (Tyndall, 2010). The quality appraisal instrument was developed by the researcher in consultation with, and reviewed by, the three reviewers.

Journal articles were also compared against a list of predatory journals to omit untrustworthy sources, none of which corresponded. Following the researcher's quality appraisal of the literature sources, one reviewer cross-checked several of the appraisals in conjunction with the researcher. This process warranted the remainder of the quality appraisal forms to be reviewed a second time by the first author and to be given final scores. Articles evaluated as "uncertain" were reviewed by the two additional reviewers. A small number of articles yielded dissimilar evaluations by the first author and reviewers, which reflected low inter-rater reliability. To address the low inter-rater reliability and inconsistency, a meeting with all the reviewers was conducted, and justification for the individual evaluations was discussed. To conclude the final decision-making process of this stage and achieve consistency, a collective decision was reached in accordance with the quality

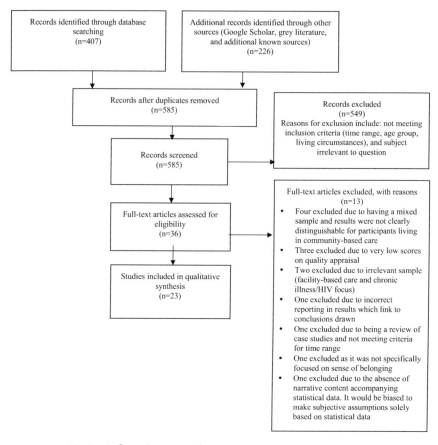

FIGURE 8.1 PRISMA flow diagram of search strategy and appraisal process.
Source: Moher et al. (2009)

appraisal tools and relevance to the review question. Figure 8.1 represents a summary of Stages 1 and 2.

Data extraction

Altogether, 23 existing literature sources were included to explore the review question. The data to be extracted were determined by the first author, guided by existing data-extraction tools and consultation with all three reviewers. Data extraction was conducted by the researcher and overseen by two reviewers.

Data analysis

Thematic synthesis (Thomas & Harden, 2008) was used to analyse and synthesise the data. Thematic synthesis is an inductive approach (Nicholson et al., 2016) and involves three stages, namely coding, development of descriptive themes, and development of analytical themes (Thomas & Harden, 2008).

During Stage 1 (coding), the researcher read the findings (results, discussion, and conclusion sections) of the included research studies. Grey literature sources varied in structure compared to research articles. In consultation with the three reviewers, the following sections were deemed important to analyse: glossary, the chapter relevant to the research topic, the conclusion/summary/next steps, the preface (where appropriate to the topic), and recommendations in policy documents. Accordingly, the first author reviewed each grey literature source and documented the sections to be analysed; this was overseen by a reviewer, thus limiting bias. In the case of research studies or grey literature being quantitative/statistical in nature, the first author extracted and coded the relevant narrative content. For Stage 1 the researcher highlighted and coded the core concepts and information in these paragraphs line by line (Thomas & Harden, 2008).

During Stage 2, the researcher developed descriptive themes by reviewing the developed codes and looking for differences or congruency among these preliminary codes (Thomas & Harden, 2008). The researcher grouped codes that were similar and created descriptive themes based on the connections between the different codes formed in Stage 1 (Thomas & Harden, 2008). Stages 1 and 2 were performed by the researcher, and each stage was comprehensively reviewed before the next was performed. The last stage, Stage 3, dealt with the development of analytical themes and involved an iterative process by the first author and consultations with two reviewers. The ethical considerations employed in this study are subsequently discussed.

Ethical considerations

Ethical approval for the study was granted by the North-West University Health Research Ethics Committee, who declared it a no-risk study (ethics number: NWU-00425-20-A1). The quality appraisal process was carried out by the researcher and overseen by three reviewers. This process was crucial to ensuring that the literature used in the review was in line with ethical standards and quality (Vergnes et al., 2010). In order to minimise the ethical risk of subjectivity (Vergnes et al., 2010) and to ensure credibility, the project as a whole was overseen by the two primary reviewers associated with this exploration, who were consulted throughout the process. The third reviewer, uninvolved in the project, was also consulted and provided an additional objective perspective.

The American Psychological Association (APA) 7th edition publication guidelines (APA, 2020) were followed. The study obtained a Turnitin similarity report within acceptable norms. When information in data sources was not clearly stated or was incorrectly reported, the information was cross-checked by the third reviewer and omitted accordingly. The process of omission during data coding was overseen by a primary reviewer. The researcher conducted the exploration in a rigorous manner, and a comprehensive account of all the procedures followed in this project is clearly stated to convey transparency.

Results

By means of a rapid review, the review question was explored using 23 existing literature sources. Due to the variety of features that exist in the concepts of sense of belonging and CBC, the first two stages of data analysis produced multiple codes and descriptive themes related to the study. The preliminary codes resulted in a total of 39 primary descriptive themes and 155 sub-themes. The descriptive themes and sub-themes were compiled into a mind map chart by the researcher and scrutinised by a primary reviewer, who also engaged in the preliminary coding in an in-depth manner.

An analysis of the descriptive themes produced a total of three core themes: (a) belonging as tangible and intangible inclusion, (b) belonging manifests as contribution and expectations/reciprocity, and (c) belonging as intersectoral inclusion. Information originating from the data sources and a discussion on how they contribute to the core themes are presented below.

Belonging as tangible and intangible inclusion

"Tangible" in this context implies something that is of a material nature and/or can be touched, such as money, a building, or amenities. "Belonging as tangible inclusion" therefore refers to that which exists physically and can be shown, while allowing for aspects such as social care, accessibility, and life satisfaction (considered here as intangible aspects). Intangible aspects were also highlighted in the data and are indicative of that which is abstract and unable to be physically touched. Addressing or considering feelings, behaviours, relational connections, and frame of reference are considered as comprising intangible inclusion in this data. From the descriptions above, it becomes evident that tangible features present with connections to those that are intangible.

Four studies alluded to tangible features, such as infrastructure and resources (Du Preez & De la Harpe, 2019; Rankin, 2019; Roos et al., 2014; Van der Pas et al., 2015). Infrastructure related to day care centres was highlighted in two studies (Rankin, 2019; Roos et al., 2014). Roos et al.'s (2014) study drew attention to physical place and found contrasts in the experience of living in a community where respective participants grew up (before apartheid forced relocation) and their current community of residence (where they have lived since the apartheid-forced relocation). Whereas the former community presented physical components that were valued, such as space (for privacy) and land (for raising cattle), it also allowed for co-existence and for feeding family members (Roos et al., 2014). However, in participants' current community, no features of place/land were highlighted as important. A participant in the study by Roos et al. (2014) highlighted that in their present community, houses were shacks that were close to each other. It was, however, noted that "the only connection to place that they [participants] mentioned was the day care centre, which was a setting that allowed for the development and maintenance of strong social connections with other women" (Roos et al., 2014, p. 18).

Rankin (2019) found that the day care centre services were experienced as good care; however, having transport to the day care centre would improve accessibility. In addition, the safety and comfort of these day care centres would be imperative for what is perceived as good care. The "social care in the community is mainly provided by the church and the day care centre" (Rankin, 2019, p. 48), which highlights the role played by these two types of infrastructure in social care (Rankin, 2019). With reference to resources, personal financial resources and day care centre funding were indicated to lead to better accessibility to the day care centre (Rankin, 2019). Furthermore, regarding the provision of home-based care by clinics, it was noted that the delivery of chronic medication and blood pressure/sugar level monitoring were predominantly experienced as poor care, with specific reference to access (Rankin, 2019). The unreliability of life-sustaining medication due to the medication either (a) causing illness or (b) being insufficient was highlighted (Rankin, 2019). Occasionally, healthcare workers were found to be incompetent and lacking in their provision of skilled medical care (Rankin, 2019).

Van der Pas et al. (2015) found several resources in the home to be associated with life satisfaction. These include electricity, a toilet indoors, outdoor water, and the belief of having greater or maintained financial status in comparison to two years ago (Van der Pas et al., 2015). In relation to technology as a resource, Du Preez and De la Harpe (2019) identified that the majority of their participants viewed technology as an instrument assisting to accomplish a goal. Furthermore, in response to available information about the increasingly strained healthcare systems globally, Du Preez and De la Harpe (2019) noted that technology might be able to assist with various methods of helping and interacting with older people.

Intangible aspects were also brought to the fore for the development of this theme. Intangible aspects, in this study, refer to attention, dignity, respect (Hayes, 2014; Rankin, 2019), feelings (Van der Pas et al., 2015), social participation or engagement (Geffen et al., 2019; Rankin, 2019; Roos et al., 2014; Van der Pas et al., 2015), and technology (Du Preez & De la Harpe, 2019; Geffen et al., 2019).

Proceeding from the former aspects, Rankin (2019) reported good care as being attentive to needs and being treated with respect. Moreover, when receiving care, dignity and patience were highlighted as a want and an expectation respectively (Rankin, 2019). In terms of social engagement, one study pointed to the contrast between sense of belonging for participants in their respective community where they grew up (before apartheid forced relocation) and their current community of residence (where they have lived since the apartheid-forced relocation) (Roos et al., 2014). It was noted that, "belonging arose or was constrained through close connections to others and sharing of resources, shared rituals and generational relations" (Roos et al., 2014, p. 18). Although it was noted that current circumstances involved a smaller community, the focus was on strong bonds present among those in the daycare centre (Roos et al., 2014). Present circumstances of generational relationships were described as strained in contrast to the "strong, reciprocal generational relationships" of the past (Roos et al., 2014, p. 20). Lastly, the practice of shared rituals fostered and maintained belonging (Roos et al., 2014). The specific example of ancestral worship was and is important for a sense of support and upholding connections (Roos et al., 2014). Furthermore, it was mentioned that individuals continued to perform these forms of worship jointly, despite the rituals and worship being different from their past experiences (Roos et al., 2014). Recalling the past, participants in Roos et al.'s (2014) study noted care for the vulnerable, the experience of safety from the close community, and the ability of the community to meet its members' needs without reservation. The sense of belonging of participants in Roos et al.'s (2014) study was a main feature of their sense of community.

Rankin (2019) identified external community-based social care as complementing the informal social care, despite participants in her study reporting that they "do not feel the need of 'outsiders' to supplement the care received from their families" (p. 47). Informal social care included tangible and intangible aspects, such as instrumental support, physical care, financial assistance, and companionship (Rankin, 2019). Supplementing informal social care, Rankin (2019) highlighted companionship, sports activities, and being treated as important in the day care centre as good care. Spiritual care, provided by the church, was highly valued; and food and treats were also occasionally provided by the church (Rankin, 2019).

In Van der Pas et al.'s (2015) study, feelings of safety at home and aspects of accessibility – the time taken to reach the closest healthcare service and being able to do grocery shopping without assistance – were related to older people's life satisfaction. Regarding engagement in the community, regular organisational participation was also related to life satisfaction (Van der Pas et al., 2015). Considering the usefulness of peer support, Geffen et al.'s (2019) findings indicated that it led to improvements in wellbeing, social support, physical activity, social activity, and decreased anxiety, depression, withdrawal, and loneliness. The peer supporters, who were also older people, benefited at the same time by feeling empowered, less isolated, feeling a renewed sense of purpose and increased self-esteem, and "felt more connected to each other and their community" (Geffen et al., 2019, p. 7). Technology also featured among the peer supporters, who were enthusiastic to learn and use it, and their new skills fostered feelings of empowerment (Geffen et al., 2019). Furthermore, Du Preez and De la Harpe's (2019) study presented a proposed process of decision-making that older technology users go through in deciding whether or not to engage with supportive technology services. This process was described as iterative and featured components such as perceived benefits and the web-based user context that is influenced by the social and use context (Du Preez & De la Harpe, 2019). Du Preez and De la Harpe (2019, p. 11) reported that "product and service design projects and initiatives encourage contributions from aging users to varying degrees", which highlights a sense of inclusion of older people.

The abovementioned aspects are comparable to features mentioned in the grey literature sources. For example, the *Older Persons Act* 13 of 2006 accounts for aspects such as participation, residing in an accommodating environment, respect, and dignity. Furthermore, in keeping with the theme of belonging as tangible and intangible inclusion, there is the comparable aim of the Political Declaration and Madrid International Plan of Action on Ageing (UN, 2002, Point 10, Part 2), which is to "ensure that persons everywhere are able to age with security and dignity and to continue to participate in their societies as citizens with full rights".

According to findings by Hayes (2014), respect, love, and care were closely related. Hayes' (2014) study focused specifically on older persons' relationships with middle adolescents. Within the study, Hayes (2014) identified respect to be conveyed by older persons' acts of caring, the words used when talking to and in front of each other, older people's approval of the use of respectful titles, and expecting vocal expression of gratitude from adolescents for care received as well as the respect taught by the older people. Older people in this study were also aware of the reciprocal nature of respect (Hayes, 2014).

It was noted that three studies highlighted a somewhat one-dimensional perspective of older people in their relations with adolescents (Mabaso, 2011; Oosthuizen, 2014; Wheeler, 2014). One study referred to the absence of empathy, indicating that older people perceived the intergenerational relationship from their own perspective only, judged younger people on the basis of their own evaluation of what is right or wrong, and presented a conditional acceptance of younger individuals (Wheeler, 2014). A concluding remark in the same study indicated that "empathy has been identified as a scarce commodity in some low-resourced rural areas and this was also seen in this study" (Wheeler, 2014, p. 48). Similarly, regarding a one-dimensional perspective, Mabaso (2011) highlighted the instances of older people making use of their own frame of reference and taking on a controlling position in relation to younger individuals.

Yet another study, focused on care, referred to the scarcity of emotional care and a larger focus on physical care by older people (Oosthuizen, 2014). Furthermore, older people had particular parameters in which the expectation of reciprocity in the caring relationships with adolescents could take place. The study suggested that older people appeared to be somewhat set in a traditional view of limitations for care (Oosthuizen, 2014). With reference to literature, this study indicated that "the low resource environment could provide an explanation for the limited and simplistic description of care, offering limited possibilities to explore and few options for alternatives (Evans & Thomas)" (Oosthuizen, 2014, p. 58). Wheeler (2014) highlighted the consequences of the absence of empathy, indicating the young as being invisible and rejecting teachings and reprimands of older people, older people's increasing use of violence, and the use of help from external resources, such as the police or church, to discipline the young (Wheeler, 2014). By referring to other sources, Oosthuizen (2014) noted that, in the absence of emotional care, there were implications for the wellbeing of individuals in both generations. Furthermore, "if the young people continue to withdraw from relationships with the older people, due to the unwillingness of the latter to compromise through empathic understanding, the result could be serious neglect of the older generation by the young" (Wheeler, 2014, p. 47). In cited data regarding the young rejecting the older generation, it was found that this predominantly occurs "because the young no longer need to rely solely on the older generation for care because they have the energy to look after themselves or can turn to other adults when assistance is needed" (Wheeler, 2014, p. 46).

Belonging manifests as contribution and expectations/reciprocity

All articles related to this theme focused on intergenerational relationships with adolescents. The theme conveys that while older people feel a sense of belonging in contributing in their specific way to intergenerational relationships with adolescents, the contribution should not merely be one-sided.

Rather, this feature of belonging joins up with the adolescent's mutual contribution to the intergenerational relationship.

Four studies highlighted aspects related to the nature of contribution and expectations/reciprocity (Hayes, 2014; Oosthuizen, 2014; Roos et al., 2014; Wheeler, 2014). Two studies indicated that physical care contributed by older people (Oosthuizen, 2014; Wheeler, 2014) was accompanied by expectations of assistance with household chores, doing homework (Oosthuizen, 2014), and obeying and complying with instructions (Wheeler, 2014). Furthermore, Oosthuizen (2014) highlighted the older participants' expression of frustration because of the younger individuals' seeming unacceptance of what was taught. If older people displayed that they cared by disciplining, adolescents were expected to follow by complying and keeping to the boundaries the older person had laid down (Oosthuizen, 2014).

Roos et al. (2014) indicated that, previously, strong generational relationships were characterised by reciprocal respect; any parent was a parent to all children in the community and engaged in disciplining them when necessary, which in turn saw younger individuals assisting older people. This experience was contrasted with strained relationships found in the community that was researched, highlighting that "participants felt used by young people who showed no interest in elders' expectations of intergenerational relationships. They said that the unspoken obligation of young people to support older people and to protect them from exploitation was not being honoured" (Roos et al., 2014, p. 20).

Hayes's (2014) study highlighted the awareness of reciprocity of respect in that, if older people respected younger individuals, they would, in turn respect older people. Older people contributed respect in various ways, such as caring, their manner of communicating and behaving, and teaching respect. This was accompanied by older people indicating forms of reciprocal respect by younger people, conveyed via communication, which included the way they spoke, the use of respectful titles, the expectation of expressing gratitude, and expecting the respect that older people taught the younger people (Hayes, 2014). The following statement highlights this reciprocity: "The respect is not just freely given, but has to be earned by certain actions from the older generation" (Hayes, 2014, p. 40).

Belonging as intersectoral inclusion

Intersectoral inclusion, as derived from the data, refers to addressing concepts related to belonging for older people in various sectors, including financial, social, cultural, political, health, and familial sectors. While pivotal policy documents, guidelines, and frameworks address the older population in a range of different fields, cutting across the health, social, and financial sectors, amongst others, the concept of sense of belonging was not explicitly evident. However, components that predominantly addressed aspects related to belonging and inclusion were the following:

1) Active participation (AU, 2016; *Older Persons Act* 13 of 2006; UN, 2002; WHO, 2019), with a focus on contribution and recognition, decision making, and preferences in participation.
2) Work and ageing, education, knowledge, training, and income security (AU, 2016; AU & HelpAge International, n.d.; *Older Persons Act* 13 of 2006; Stats SA, 2013, 2017; UN, 2002) addressed matters of being able to continue with income-generating work, employment opportunities, having equal opportunities, access to education, and the elimination of discrimination.
3) Living environment (AU, 2016; AU & HelpAge International, n.d.; *Older Persons Act* 13 of 2006; Stats SA, 2013, 2017; UN, 2002; WHO, 2007, 2019) focused on housing, promoting ageing in place, accessible/accommodating infrastructure, and transport, among others.
4) Intergenerational solidarity (*Older Persons Act* 13 of 2006; UN, 2002; WHO, 2007) was embraced and recognised as important, and intergenerational programmes were indicated.
5) Poverty and finance (AU & HelpAge International, n.d.; UN, 2002; WHO, 2019) featured awareness of addressing the rights/needs of older people in the case of strategies to reduce poverty, and considering older people in poverty-reduction plans and data on the South African older people living below the lower-bound poverty line.
6) Health and wellbeing (AU, 2016; AU & HelpAge International, n.d.; *Older Persons Act* 13 of 2006; Stats SA, 2013, 2017; UN, 2002) included equal access, indicating health-related services in CBC, training of care providers, and involvement of older people in developing primary and LTC services.
7) Social welfare (AU & HelpAge International, n.d.) addressed the creation and implementation of suitable social welfare strategies that are inclusive of older people's concerns.
8) Care for older persons (AU, 2016; Department of Health, 2011; Department of Social Development, 2017; *Older Persons Act* 13 of 2006; UN, 2002) included a focus on home-based care and CBC (including the definition, rights, principles, and proposed stakeholder roles/responsibilities), providing a continuum of care and services, the concept of care, the aim of care programmes, and the multiple aspects defining care.
9) Rights (AU & HelpAge International, n.d.; *Older Persons Act* 13 of 2006; UN, 2002) considered aspects of their recognition and protection; rights were also addressed in the context of enabling and supportive environments and CBC and support services, among others.

10) Neglect, abuse, and violence (AU, 2016; UN, 2002; WHO, 2019) were directed towards their elimination, as well as protection, assessment, management, and referral.
11) Gender (AU & HelpAge International, n.d.; UN, 2002) related to its integration into policy relative to older people and programmes and aiming for equality in social protection systems.
12) The concept of an older person (AU, 2016; Department of Social Development, 2017; *Older Persons Act* 13 of 2006; Stats SA, 2013) was addressed by defining the age of an older person, defining ageing, and associated words related to older people.
13) Family (AU & HelpAge International, n.d.; *Older Persons Act* 13 of 2006; UN, 2002) included, *inter alia*, recognition of importance, strengthening their role in caring, and developing ways in which older people are empowered to contribute to the family.

The ability to work and reduce discrimination in employment opportunities for older people emerged in the grey literature (AU, 2016; AU & HelpAge International, n.d.; *Older Persons Act* 13 of 2006; UN, 2002). However, none of the South African research studies reviewed in this project focused on the concept of employment in relation to a sense of belonging. Only one study reported on paying a group of peer supporters a small salary that "gave both monetary value to their work and allowed them to become economically active"; however, this was not the main aim of the study (Geffen et al., 2019, p. 7).

One source provided crucial practical recommendations relative to LTC systems in the context of sub-Saharan Africa, which included developing understanding and commitment, national coordination systems, and indicators of the current circumstances of, and what is needed for, LTC (WHO, 2017). In a continental context, one document provided recommendations to the AU Commission, AU member states, and international development partners with regard to LTC (AU, 2017).

At a global level, the WHO (2015) advised that there is a pressing need for all-inclusive public health action focused on ageing. Moreover, it is necessary for countries/regions to assess their specific contexts and determine what is likely to be effectively implemented prior to mapping the WHO's highly suitable recommendations (WHO, 2015). The WHO *World Report on Ageing and Health* (WHO, 2015) presented a large focus on areas in which action can be taken in working towards the concept of healthy ageing. These involve aligning health systems to the needs of older populations served, developing systems for LTC provision, "creating age-friendly environments", and "improving measurement, monitoring, and understanding" (WHO, 2015, p. 213). The WHO (2015) addressed the concept of an age-friendly city/community and pointed out that:

an age-friendly city or community is a good place to grow old. Age-friendly cities and communities foster healthy and active ageing and, thus, enable well-being throughout life. They help people to remain independent for as long as possible, and provide care and protection when they are needed, respecting older people's autonomy and dignity.

(p. 161)

Similarly, the WHO (2007) indicates that enablement is a core element in an age-friendly city and highlights the importance of accessibility of spaces and structures. The same source also specifies "integrated and mutually enhancing urban features" (WHO, 2007, p. 73). It was mentioned that action was necessary in several sectors and government levels for the creation of age-friendly environments (WHO, 2015). Countering ageism and enabling autonomy and support for healthy ageing in all policies at various government levels were recognised as key approaches (WHO, 2015). In order to accomplish an integrated 2030 Agenda, it is imperative to make arrangements for an ageing population (United Nations Development Programme [UNDP], HelpAge International & the American Association of Retired Persons [AARP], n.d.). The final document used in this rapid review addressed policy changes that are required in relation to the 2030 Agenda for Sustainable Development, which addressed the need for a multifaceted and integrated approach (UNDP, HelpAge International & AARP, n.d.). By means of collaboration, initiatives, and research, UN agencies can, *inter alia*, "mainstream ageing issues in their programmes of work, while stressing the need to ensure that the rights of older persons, including to income, health, education, security, voice and participation are addressed" (UNDP, HelpAge International & AARP, n.d., p. 19).

Discussion

To our knowledge, this is the first study to undertake an explicit exploration of how sense of belonging is described in relation to CBC among South African older people. This was unexpected, taking into consideration (a) that the South African older population is projected to more than double over the next 30 years (UNDESA, 2017), (b) the shift to CBC for older people in policy (*Older Persons Act* 13 of 2006), (c) the relevance of community psychology in relation to older people (Cheng & Heller, 2009; Provencher et al., 2014), and (d) the evidence that belonging is important for wellbeing (Cramm & Nieboer, 2015; Fletcher, 2015).

Although not explicit in the literature, sense of belonging in relation to CBC among South African older people appears to feature at multiple levels. The mutual dependence of tangible and intangible inclusion that emerged from the data is imperative for understanding a sense of belonging in CBC for older people in the context of South Africa. For example, relationships, participation, and engagement (as intangible) were fostered in a day care centre (as tangible). This mutual dependence is comparable to a statement by Rankin (2019) that "although infrastructure itself does not constitute good care, it has an impact on care and contributes to the care experience. Care does not meet needs if those in need cannot access it" (p. 50). Similarly, in this exploration, it is apparent that tangible and intangible aspects work in unity, with the tangible facilitating the development of the intangible, which in turn allows for a sense of belonging.

In the South African context of CBC for older people, tangible and intangible inclusions are not distinct, independent concepts but rather have the intrinsic potential to work in tandem towards achieving a sense of belonging. This conceptual understanding of the mutual and interrelated dependence of tangible and intangible inclusion impacts the methodological measures to be taken when addressing the sense of belonging of older people in the South African context. While tangible inclusion, intangible inclusion, and their mutual dependence promote the autonomy of the older person, the additional preference for interdependence among South African older people emerged noticeably from this review. Findings indicate that interdependent connections are crucial for older people's sense of belonging. This premise is in clear contrast to the comprehension of CBC or ageing in place in international policy and other documentation that focus more on the independence of an older person (Davey, 2006; UN, 2002; UNFPA & HelpAge International, 2012). The concept of independence has also been identified in South African policy, relative to community-based prevention/promotion programmes (*Older Persons Act* 13 of 2006) that reflect, for example, its agreement with the Political Declaration and Madrid International Plan of Action on Ageing (TAFTA, 2020; Western Cape Department of Social Development, 2015).

The promotion of independence in policy frameworks is concerning because this review reveals that co-occurring with the autonomous nature of most older persons is interdependence. In relation to CBC, the ambiguity in South African policy became apparent. While policy accommodates the older person's right to "benefit from family and community care and protection in accordance with society's system of cultural values", the development of community-based "prevention/promotion programmes, which ensure the independent living of an older person in the community" obscures the positioning of older persons in CBC (*Older Persons Act* 13 of 2006, p. 12). The development of a best practice exemplar for service centres or CBC necessitates the consideration of specific needs associated with a community and thus should be purpose-built for those needs (Western Cape Department of Social Development, 2015). This is also referred to as "goodness of fit for the community" (Western Cape Department of Social Development, 2015,

p. 6). South African policy should therefore consider the nature of the older population, their needs, and their sense of belonging if it is to fit CBC to the South African community.

The finding of interdependence, which is more evident in the South African than in the international literature, becomes an important contribution to community psychology, which has paid little attention to concerns associated with ageing (Cheng & Heller, 2009). In community psychology, the nature of interdependence found in this study highlights the following: (a) a holistic focus, (b) the attention paid to how people and their context fit together (Visser, 2012), and (c) the relationships that individuals have with their community and society (Kloos et al., 2012). In African cosmology, "it is the responsibility of all individuals as a collective to uphold this interdependence through a conscious effort to ensure that the flow remains unbroken" (Semenya & Mokwena, 2012, p. 76). The relationships with other people are valued and emphasised (Semenya & Mokwena, 2012). Furthermore, "to Africans, a person, though he or she is other things as well, is primarily a being in the community. It is in the human community that an individual is able to realize himself or herself as a person" (Mnyaka & Motlhabi, 2015, p. 223). In view of this information, the finding of interdependence becomes crucial, and its acknowledgement in a practical sense is essential.

Apt (as cited in UNFPA & HelpAge International, 2012) states that fading cultural views of older people as conveyors of knowledge and wisdom, and deteriorating respect towards older people, arise from urban society in sub-Saharan Africa. Globally, alongside increased longevity and decreased fertility, family structures are altering (Powell, 2010). In turn, these changed family structures result in (a) fewer alternatives of care for older people (Powell, 2010) and (b) an impact on older people's wellbeing (Treas & Marcum, as cited in Higo & Khan, 2015; Wahab & Adedokun, 2012). Furthermore, the study's finding of interdependence becomes crucial knowledge that requires attention in the context of (a) globalisation and urbanisation influencing increases in migration and the possibility of older people living on their own, and (b) in the future, family care might fall short of addressing older people's expanded needs in view of changing gender roles and the wearing away of orthodox familial values (Jesmin et al., 2011).

Given that culture is dynamic (Semenya & Mokwena, 2012), community psychology's characteristic of being socially relevant and the perception of behaviour being influenced by multiple levels (Visser, 2012) are important. The findings in this exploration draw attention to the level of policy and address the concurrent importance of policy when considering sense of belonging. While policies, frameworks, and guidelines consider intersectoral inclusion, there remains a gap in the level of sense of belonging. Lacking an explicit focus on sense of belonging in policies, frameworks, and guidelines, countries appear to be guided by recommendations that are disconnected from a sense of community as a contributor to wellbeing. This absence of focus is crucial, considering that in order to accomplish an integrated 2030 Agenda for Sustainable Development, it is imperative to plan for an ageing population (UNDP, HelpAge International & AARP, n.d.). With less than ten years to meet the intended time frame of the Sustainable Development Goals (SDGs), a "Decade of Action" has been highlighted by leaders at the SDG Summit in 2019 (UN, n.d.). However, belonging, in CBC or as an independent concept, was not explicitly addressed in the *Ageing, Older Persons and the 2030 Agenda for Sustainable Development* (UNDP, HelpAge International & AARP, n.d.) source reviewed. Alongside the noteworthy ten-year timeline, it is important that South Africa should be contextually aware of what constitutes older people's sense of belonging in order to attend to the growing ageing population, who are encouraged to remain living in their communities (*Older Persons Act* 13 of 2006).

In understanding the literature on South African older people's sense of belonging in CBC, there appears to be broad similarities with existing theoretical definitions; however, no direct links are evident. McMillan and Chavis (1986) emphasise fitting into, acceptance by, and sacrificing for the group in defining a sense of belonging, in keeping with the broad finding of inclusion in this review. Furthermore, the idea of sacrificing for the group (McMillian & Chavis, 1986) could, in some ways, be linked to the finding of interdependence/interrelatedness, which appears to be pronounced in the South African literature. This finding of interdependence, distinctly obvious in this review, is therefore a crucial contribution to understanding the nature of sense of belonging in South African CBC. Sense of community highlights the two components of integration and fulfilment of needs, as well as mutual influence and importance (McMillan & Chavis, 1986; Prezza & Constantini, 1998), which, in this review, emerged broadly as interdependence, and specifically as a close descriptor of a sense of belonging.

While grey literature lacks an explicit focus on sense of belonging for older people living in CBC, scientific literature also demonstrates the same lack. Only one of the studies considered in this research focused explicitly on sense of belonging (Roos et al., 2014). Thus, there appears to be a scarcity in addressing sense of belonging at the scholarly, research, professional, and government levels. As this study presents scholarly research underpinned by the paradigm of community psychology, it offers a vital contribution to understanding sense of belonging. This research contributes to filling an explicit conceptual research gap regarding a sense of belonging in relation to CBC among South African older people. A sense of belonging in the context of this study may thus be described as the mutual dependence of tangible and intangible inclusion, interdependence, and intersectoral inclusion. Overall, belonging is highlighted as interdependent inclusion.

This study is not without limitations, which should be considered in the interpretation of its findings. The primary limitations include search keywords, databases/grey literature searched, and language. Regarding context, this research did not include studies where the results were not clearly differentiated for community-based participants who were mixed with participants living in a form of residential/institutional environments. Studies focusing specifically on older people in caregiver roles were not included. Information about the older person as caregiver was not always clearly distinguished when authors mentioned in the sample description only that participants lived in the community. Because this research was exploratory, such studies were included because participants were residing in the community and the author had not specified their role as caregiver. The aim of the exploration was not gender-specific. However, it was noted that the reviewed research articles had a greater number of female participants in their samples. This limitation should be taken into consideration whilst being aware of the sparse research on this topic. The research method was transparently delineated alongside the reasoning for various decisions, which should be taken into account with the abovementioned limitations.

Proceeding from this exploration, the core recommendation is for future research to conduct empirical studies based on the paradigm of community psychology, which works in conjunction with the community to establish credible knowledge (Kloos et al., 2012). It is essential that recommendations are addressed to develop theories and to direct practical application (Kloos et al., 2012) relative to the sense of belonging of older people in South Africa. Lastly, it is recommended that policy should elaborate and clarify the particulars of CBC, the stakeholders/professionals involved, and should account for a sense of belonging in policy and programmes for older people.

Conclusion

This scoping review, which foregrounded the older population and their sense of belonging, can serve as a catalyst for further investigation. From a review of 23 existing literature sources, it appears that sense of belonging in CBC is compressed into and impacts multiple levels and systems. The Political Declaration and Madrid International Plan of Action on Ageing (UN, 2002) cut across a diverse range of fields and efforts; hence it is recognised that a concerted effort is required to attend to population ageing.

These findings are thus an integral contribution to the field of community psychology, which has seldom attended to concerns associated with ageing (Cheng & Heller, 2009). The study contributes to filling the research gap by providing a conceptual description of sense of belonging, relative to the South African older people living in CBC. The mutual dependence of tangible and intangible inclusion, interdependence, and intersectoral inclusion feature as descriptors of a sense of belonging. Importantly, this review revealed that belonging does not entail one component only, but rather features as a link between all three components and, in essence highlights belonging as interdependent inclusion.

References

African Union. (2016). *Protocol to the African charter on human and peoples' rights on the rights of older persons in Africa.*
African Union. (2017). *Common African position on LTC system for Africa.*
African Union & HelpAge International. (n.d.). *AU policy framework and plan of action on ageing.* https://www.helpage.org/silo/files/au-policy-framework-and-plan-of-action-on-ageing-.pdf
American Psychological Association. (2020). *Publication manual of the American psychological association* (7th ed.).
Armitage, R., & Nellums, L. B. (2020). COVID-19 and the consequences of isolating the elderly. *The Lancet Public Health*, 5(5), e256. https://doi.org/10.1016/S2468-2667(20)30061-X
Cheng, S. T., & Heller, K. (2009). Global aging: Challenges for community psychology. *American Journal of Community Psychology*, 44(1–2), 161–173. https://doi.org/10.1007/s10464-009-9244-x
Cramm, J. M., & Nieboer, A. P. (2015). Social cohesion and belonging predict the well-being of community-dwelling older people. *BMC Geriatrics*, 15(1), 1–10. https://doi-org.nwulib.nwu.ac.za/10.1186/s12877-015-0027-y
Cramm, J. M., Van Dijk, H. M., & Nieboer, A. P. (2013). The importance of neighborhood social cohesion and social capital for the wellbeing of older adults in the community. *Gerontologist*, 53(1), 142–152. https://doi-org.nwulib.nwu.ac.za/10.1093/geront/gns052
Davey, J. A. (2006). "Ageing in place": The views of older homeowners on maintenance, renovation and adaptation. *Social Policy Journal of New Zealand*, 27, 128–141. Retrieved December 4, 2020 from https://www.msd.govt.nz/about-msd-and-our-work/publications-resources/journals-and-magazines/social-policy-journal/spj27/ageing-in-place-the-views-of-older-homeowners-27-pages128-141.html
Davey, J. A., De Joux, V., Nana, G., & Arcus, M. (2004). *Accommodation options for older people in Aotearoa/New Zealand.* Report prepared for the Centre for Housing Research Aotearoa/New Zealand (CHRANZ). Retrieved December 6, 2020 from http://citeseerx.ist.psu.edu/viewdoc/download?doi=10.1.1.460.8794&rep=rep1&type=pdf
Department of Health (South Africa). (2011). *National guideline on home-based care (HC) community-based care (CC).* https://www.westerncape.gov.za/sites/www.westerncape.gov.za/files/documents/2003/define_homebased.pdf
Department of Social Development (South Africa). (2017, June 2). Older Persons Amendment Bill, 2017 (Notice 426 of 2017). *Government Gazette*, 40883, 227–244. https://www.gov.za/sites/default/files/gcis_document/201706/40883gen426.pdf
Department of Social Development (South Africa). (2019). *Minister Lindiwe Zulu opens 2019 Active Ageing Programme in Port Elizabeth, 21 to 25 October.* https://www.gov.za/speeches/nelson-mandela-bay-municipality-18-oct-2019

-0000#:~:text=The%20Active%20Ageing%20 Programme%20was,Older%20P ersons%20Act%20(Act%20No.
Diener, E., & Seligman, M. E. P. (2004). Beyond money: Toward an economy of well-being. *Psychological Science in the Public Interest*, 5(1), 1–31. https://doi .org/10.1111/j.0963-7214.2004.00501001.x
Du Preez, V., & De la Harpe, R. (2019). Engaging aging individuals in the design of technologies and services to support health and well-being: Constructivist grounded theory study. *JMIR Aging*, 2(1), e12393. https://doi.org/10.2196 /12393
Fletcher, C. (2015). *Wellbeing: The importance of belonging. Summary report.* http://www.barnwoodtrust.org/wp-content/uploads/2017/08/Importance_of _Belonging_ Summary_v12-web.pdf
Ganann, R., Ciliska, D., & Thomas, H. (2010). Expediting systematic reviews: Methods and implications of rapid reviews. *Implementation Science*, 5, Article 56. https://doi.org/10.1186/1748-5908-5-56
Geffen, L. N., Kelly, G., Morris, J. N., & Howard, E. P. (2019). Peer-to-peer support model to improve quality of life among highly vulnerable, low-income older adults in Cape Town, South Africa. *BMC Geriatrics*, 19, Article 279. https://doi .org/10.1186/s12877-019-1310-0
Godin, K., Stapleton, J., Kirkpatrick, S., Hanning, R. M., & Leatherdale, S. T. (2015). Applying systematic review search methods to the grey literature: A case study examining guidelines for school-based breakfast programs in Canada. *Systematic Reviews*, 4, Article 138. https://doi.org/10.1186/s13643 -015-0125-0
Guseh, J. S. (2016). Aging of the world's population. In C. L. Shehan (Ed.), *The Wiley Blackwell Encyclopedia of Family Studies* (pp. 1–5). John Wiley & Sons. https://onlinelibrary.wiley.com/doi/epdf/10.1002/9781119085621.wbefs352
Hayes, J. M. (2014). *Older persons' experience of respect from middle adolescents in an economically vulnerable environment* (Unpublished master's dissertation). North-West University.
Higo, M., & Khan, H. T. A. (2015). Global population aging: Unequal distribution of risks in later life between developed and developing countries. *Global Social Policy*, 15(2), 146–166. https://doi.org/10.1177/1468018114543157
Institute for Health Metrics and Evaluation. (2020). *GBD compare: South Africa, Both sexes, 70+ years, 2019, DALYs.* Retrieved June 3, 2020 from https://vizhub .healthdata.org/gbd-compare/
Jesmin, S. S., Amin, I., & Ingman, S. R. (2011). Ageing and caregiving crisis in the low- and middle-income societies. *Indian Journal of Gerontology*, 25(3), 309–328.
Kasiram, M., & Hölscher, D. (2015). Understanding the challenges and opportunities encountered by the elderly in urban KwaZulu-Natal, South Africa. *South African Family Practice*, 57(6), 380–385. https://doi-org.nwulib.nwu.ac.za/10.1080 /20786190.2015.1078154
Khangura, S., Konnyu, K., Cushman, R., Grimshaw, J., & Moher, D. (2012). Evidence summaries: The evolution of a rapid review approach. *Systematic Reviews*, 1(1), 1–10. https://doi.org/10.1186/2046-4053-1-10
Kloos, B., Hill, J., Thomas, E., Wandersman, A., & Elias, M. J. (2012). *Community psychology: Linking individuals and communities.* Washington, D.C.: American Psychological Association.
Lambert, N. M., Stillman, T. F., Hicks, J. A., Kamble, S., Baumeister, R. F., & Fincham, F. D. (2013). To belong is to matter: Sense of belonging enhances meaning in life. *Personality and Social Psychology Bulletin*, 39(11), 1418–1427.

Lombard, A., & Kruger, E. (2009). Older persons: The case of South Africa. *Ageing International*, 34(3), 119–135. https://doi.org/10.1007/s12126-009-9044-5

Mabaso, T. P. (2011). *An exploration of the intergenerational relationships between young adults and older people in the Khuma community* (Unpublished master's dissertation). North-West University.

Madhavan, S., Schatz, E., Gómes-Olivé, F. X., & Collinson, M. (2017). Social positioning of older persons in rural South Africa: Change or stability? *Journal of Southern African Studies*, 43(6), 1293–1307. https://doi-org.nwulib.nwu.ac.za/10.1080/03057070.2017.1365522

Mathiso, S. (2011). Realising the rights of older persons in South Africa: Feature. *ESR Review: Economic and Social Rights in South Africa*, 12(1), 3–5.

McMillan, D. W., & Chavis, D. M. (1986). Sense of community: A definition and theory. *Journal of Community Psychology*, 14(1), 6–23.

Mnyaka, M., & Motlhabi, M. (2015). The African concept of ubuntu/botho and its socio-moral significance. *Black Theology*, 3(2), 215–237. https://doi-org.nwulib.nwu.ac.za/10.1558/blth.3.2.215.65725

Moher, D., Liberati, A., Tetzlaff, J., Altman, D. G., & The PRISMA Group. (2009). Preferred reporting items for systematic reviews and meta-analyses: The PRISMA statement. *PLOS Medicine*, 6(7): e1000097. https://doi.org/10.1371/journal.pmed.1000097

National Institute for Health and Care Excellence. (2020). *Developing NICE guidelines: The manual.* Retrieved August 27, 2020, from https://www.nice.org.uk/process/pmg20/resources/developing-nice-guidelines-the-manual-pdf-72286708700869

National Institute on Aging. (2017). *What is long-term care?* Retrieved November 5, 2020, from https://www.nia.nih.gov/health/what-long-term-care.

Nicholson, E., Murphy, T., Larkin, P., Normand, C., & Guerin, S. (2016). Protocol for a thematic synthesis to identify key themes and messages from a palliative care research network. *BMC Research Notes* 9, Article 478. https://doi.org/10.1186/s13104-016-2282-1

North-West University. (2020). *EDS Search*. https://library.nwu.ac.za/eds-search

Older Persons Act 13 of 2006.

Oosthuizen, S. J. (2014). *Older persons' experiences of care in relation to adolescents in a resource-constrained environment* (Unpublished master's dissertation). North-West University.

Peter, M. Z., Peter, P. F. J., & Catapan, A. H. (2015). Belonging: Concept, meaning, and commitment. *US-China Education Review*, 5(2), 95–101. https://doi.org/10.17265/2161-6248/2015.02.003

Powell, J. (2010). The power of global aging. *Ageing International*, 35(1), 1–14. https://doi-org.nwulib.nwu.ac.za/10.1007/s12126-010-9051-6

President of the Republic of South Africa. (2010). Commencement of the Older Persons Act, 2006 (Act No. 13 of 2006) (Proclamation no. R. 11 of 2010). *Government Gazette*, 33075, 3.

Pretty, G., Bishop, B., Fisher, A., & Sonn, C. (2006). Psychological sense of community and its relevance to well-being and everyday life in Australia: A position paper of the Australian Psychological Society. *The Australian Community Psychologist*, 19, 6–25. http://www.groups.psychology.org.au/Assets/Files/Community-Updated-Sept061.pdf

Prezza, M., & Constantini, S. (1998). Sense of community and life satisfaction: Investigation in three different territorial contexts. *Journal of Community and Applied Social Psychology*, 8, 181–194.

Provencher, C., Keating, N., Warburton, J., & Roos, V. (2014). Ageing and community: Introduction to the special issue. *Journal of Community & Applied Social Psychology*, 24(1), 1–11.

Rankin, S. M. (2019). *Older adults' experiences of formal community-based care services in Sebokeng: Implications for long-term care management* (Unpublished master's dissertation). North-West University.

Roos, V., Kolobe, P. S., & Keating, N. (2014). (Re)creating community: Experiences of older women forcibly relocated during apartheid. *Journal of Community & Applied Social Psychology*, 24(1), 12–25. https://doi-org.nwulib.nwu.ac.za/10.1002/casp.2177

Ryan, R. M., & Deci, E. L. (2004). Overview of self-determination theory: An organismic dialectical perspective. In E. L. Deci, & R. M. Ryan (Eds.), *Handbook of self-determination research* (pp. 3–33). University of Rochester Press.

Scientific Resource Center. (2016). *EPC methods: AHRQ end user perspectives of rapid reviews*. Retrieved 15 April 2020, from https://www.ncbi.nlm.nih.gov/books/NBK362006/ pdf/Bookshelf_NBK362006.pdf

Semenya, B., & Mokwena, M. (2012). African cosmology, psychology and community. In M. Visser, & A-G. Moleko (Eds.), *Community Psychology in South Africa* (2nd ed., pp. 2–19). Van Schaik.

Statistics South Africa. (2013). *Social profile of vulnerable groups 2002–2012*. https://www.statssa.gov.za/publications/Report-03-19-00/Report-03-19-002012.pdf

Statistics South Africa. (2017). *Vulnerable groups series II: The social profile of older persons, 2011–2015*. http://www.statssa.gov.za/publications/Report%2003-19-03/Report%2003-19-032015.pdf

Strydom, H. (2008). The future of community-based services for older persons in South Africa. *Practice*, 20(2), 103–111. https://doi.org/10.1080/09503150802059002

TAFTA. (2020). *Getting old is not something that happens to 'other people'*. Retrieved February 12, 2020, from https://www.tafta.org.za/ageing.html#law

The Joanna Briggs Institute. (2014). *The Joanna Briggs Institute reviewers' manual: 2014 edition*. The JBI.

Thomas, J., & Harden, A. (2008). Methods for the thematic synthesis of qualitative research in systematic reviews. *BMC Medical Research Methodology*, 8(1), Article 45. https://doi.org/10.1186/1471-2288-8-45

Tyndall, J. (2010). *AACODS checklist*. https://dspace.flinders.edu.au/xmlui/bitstream/handle/ 2328/3326/AACODS_Checklist.pdf

United Nations. (n.d.). *The sustainable development agenda*. https://www.un.org/sustainabledevelopment/development-agenda/

United Nations. (2002). *Political declaration and Madrid international plan of action on ageing*. https://www.un.org/en/events/pastevents/pdfs/Madrid_plan.pdf

United Nations. (2011). *Current status of the social situation, wellbeing, participation in development and rights of older persons worldwide*. https://www.un.org/esa/socdev/ageing/documents/publications/current-status-older-persons.pdf

United Nations. (2020). *Policy brief: The impact of COVID-19 on older persons*. https://unsdg.un.org/sites/default/files/2020-05/Policy-Brief-The-Impact-of-COVID-19-on-Older-Persons.pdf

United Nations Department of Economic and Social Affairs, Population Division. (2017). *World population ageing 2017 – Highlights*. https://www.un.org/en/development/ desa/population/publications/pdf/ageing/WPA2017_Highlights.pdf

United Nations Development Programme, HelpAge International & the American Association of Retired Persons. (n.d.). *Ageing, older persons and the 2030 agenda for sustainable development.* https://www.undp.org/content/undp/en/home/librarypage/ poverty-reduction/ageing--older-persons-and-the-2030-agenda-for-sustainable-develo.html

United Nations Population Fund & HelpAge International. (2012). *Ageing in the twenty-first century: A celebration and a challenge.* https://www.unfpa.org/sites/default/files/pub-pdf/Ageing%20report.pdf

Van der Pas, S., Ramklass, S., Cassim, B., O'Learly, B., Anderson, S., & Keating, N. (2015). Features of home and neighbourhood and the liveability of older South Africans. *European Journal of Ageing,* 12(3), 215–227. https://doi-org.nwulib.nwu.ac.za/10.1007/s10433-015-0343-2

Vergnes, J. N., Marchal-Sixou, C., Nabet, C., Maret, D., & Hamel, O. (2010). Ethics in systematic reviews. *Journal of Medical Ethics,* 36(12), 771–774. http://dx.doi.org/10.1136/jme. 2010.039941

Visser, M. (2012). Community psychology. In M. Visser, & A-G. Moleko (Eds.), *Community psychology in South Africa* (2nd ed., pp. 2–19). Van Schaik.

Wahab, E. O., & Adedokun, A. (2012). Changing family structure and care of the older persons in Nigeria. *International Union for the Scientific Study of Population,* 25, 1-25. https://iussp.org/sites/default/files/event_call_for_papers/IUSSP%202013%20B.pdf

Western Cape Department of Social Development. (2015). *An evaluation of service centres for older persons in the Western Cape.* https://www.westerncape.gov.za/sites/www.westerncape.gov.za/files/evaluation_of_service_centres_for_older_persons_final_report_branded_cover.pdf

Wheeler, A. (2014). *Exploring empathy in intergenerational relationships from the perspective of a group of older people* (Unpublished master's dissertation). North-West University.

World Health Organization. (2007). *Global age-friendly cities: A guide.* https://www.who.int/ageing/publications/Global_age_friendly_cities_Guide_English.pdf

World Health Organization. (2015). *World report on ageing and health.* https://apps.who.int/iris/bitstream/handle/10665/186463/9789240694811_eng.pdf?sequence=1&isAllowed=y

World Health Organization. (2017). *Towards long-term care systems in sub-Saharan Africa: WHO series on long-term care.* https://www.who.int/ageing/long-term-care/WHO-LTC-series-subsaharan-africa.pdf?ua=1

World Health Organization. (2019). *Integrated care for older people (ICOPE): Guidance for person-centred assessment and pathways in primary care.* https://apps.who.int/iris/ bitstream/handle/10665/326843/WHO-FWC-ALC-19.1-eng.pdf?sequence=17&is Allowed=y

9
POPULATION AGEING AND CARE ARRANGEMENTS IN LATER LIFE IN THE NETHERLANDS

Louise Meijering and Tobias Vogt

Introduction

Population ageing is a phenomenon experienced by most countries around the world. On a global scale, the United Nations estimates that the absolute number of individuals above age 60 surpassed 1 billion in 2019 and will increase further to 2.1 billion in 2050 (United Nations 2020). This means that by 2050, 22% of the world population will be older than 60 years (ibid). The increase in the share of older adults in a population puts societies under increased pressure to adapt. One major concern is associated with the rise of chronic disease prevalence and disability as more and more individuals in a society live to old ages. As a result, it is expected that older adults will spend extended periods of their lives in need of support and care. This support is usually provided by families or organized via statutory welfare programmes. Still, the extent to which families or the state provide support for the needs of older adults differs greatly between countries in the world with certain countries relying almost exclusively on the family while others predominantly on the state (Vogt, Kluge & Lee 2020).

Although much of the overall increase in population ageing is experienced in low- and middle-income countries (United Nations 2020), high-income countries mostly in Europe are at its forefront. Despite the common challenge, national policymakers have adapted different strategies and priorities in dealing with increasing shares and numbers of older adults and their care needs. In this chapter, we present the ageing dynamics and the organization of care in the Netherlands. In particular, we focus on the aspect of organizing care at home, which is sought to allow older adults to maintain a certain degree of self-determination and autonomy. We start with a discussion of

DOI: 10.4324/9781003528432-11

the specific ageing dynamics and the current and expected care needs in the Netherlands.

Population ageing and care needs in the Netherlands

The Dutch population is ageing. Between 1950 and 2018, life expectancy at birth increased from 72.6 to 83.3 years for women and from 70.3 to 80.2 years for men (Human Mortality Database 2020). If this trend continues, half of a cohort born after 2000 can expect to live to more than 100 years like in other high-income countries (Christensen et al. 2009). The rising average life spans together with below-replacement fertility since the mid-1970s have led to an ageing of the Dutch society (Human Fertility Database 2020). In the last five decades, the share of the population older than 65[1] years has increased from 10.1% to 20.0% and the share of those aged 75 and above grew from 3.6% to 8.6% in the same period. These substantial changes make the Dutch population among the older ones in Europe. Figure 9.1 shows the variety of median ages of European populations for

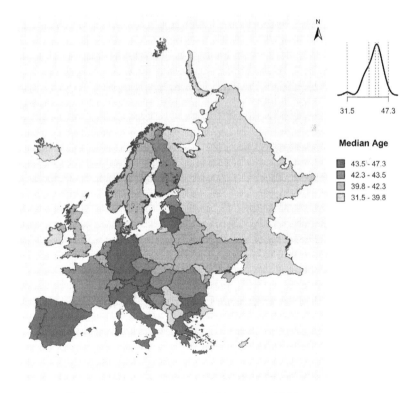

FIGURE 9.1   Median age of populations in Europe in 2020.

Source: United Nations 2020 (own illustration)

2020. Although the median age of the Netherlands is not as high as in Mediterranean countries or Germany, with 43.3 years it is still considerably higher than in most Northern or Eastern European countries.

Also, within the Netherlands, we see marked regional differences in the median ages. Figure 9.2 shows the median age of the 12 Dutch provinces.

In 2019, there was a 10-year differential between the youngest province, Flevoland, in the centre and the oldest province, Limburg, in the South of the country. Since 2015, the median age of the population has increased by up to 1.9 years in the North Eastern provinces of Friesland and Drenthe while it remained stable in the central provinces of North-Holland, South-Holland and Utrecht (EUROSTAT Demography and Migration Database 2020). These are the economically important areas around the major towns of Amsterdam, Rotterdam and Utrecht which are still comparatively young due to labour migration, high number of students and retirement migration to other parts of the country.

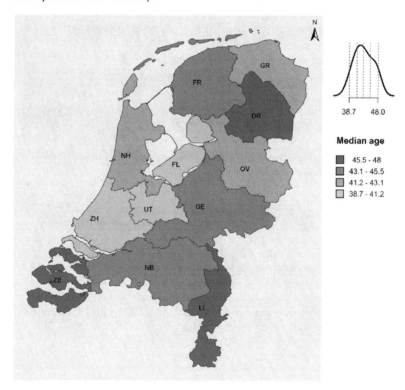

FIGURE 9.2   Median age of Dutch provinces in 2019.

Source: EUROSTAT Demography and Migration Database (2020) (own illustration)Note: ISO 3166-2 Codes for the 12 Dutch Provinces: Drenthe (DR), Flevoland (FL), Friesland (FR), Gelderland (GE), Groningen (GR), Limburg (LI), North Brabant (NB), North Holland (NH), Overijssel (OV), Utrecht (UT), Zeeland (ZE), South Holland (ZH)

The increase in the median age of the Dutch provinces shows that there is a relative increase in the share of the older population and a relative decline in those age groups that provide familial and public support. It is important to note that not only the proportion of older adults in the population increases but also that they can expect to live longer than in the past. In the last decades, not only life expectancy at birth but remaining life expectancy at age 65 in the Netherlands has increased substantially as well. In 1970, a 65-year-old woman could still expect to live on average another 16.1 years while a man of the same age had 13.6 years of remaining life expectancy (Human Mortality Database 2020). By 2019, this number of years has further increased to an average remaining life time of 21.7 years for women and 19.2 years for men (CBS 2020a). Also, for remaining life expectancy, there are regional differences within the Netherlands and most importantly between women and men (Figure 9.3 a and b). It becomes apparent that there is a North-South gradient in remaining life expectancy for women and a Northeast-Southwest gradient for men. Even though the regional differences for men are less substantial than for women, we observe that the provinces with the highest remaining life expectancy for both sexes are at the centre and the South of the country. We also observe that women can on average expect to live longer than men across all provinces. Men in the provinces with the highest remaining life expectancy, Zeeland and Utrecht, can expect to live for another 19.2 years which is still one year lower than for women in the provinces with the lowest life expectancy.

Although the levels and past increases in Dutch life expectancy indicate that there is an overall improvement in population health, there are larger parts of these gained life years that are spent in need of support and care. The main drivers for rising support needs are age-related deteriorations in mental and physical health. Of the 21.7 remaining life years for Dutch women in 2019, 8.7 years are spent with moderate or severe physical limitations and 4.1 years without chronic morbidity[2] (CBS 2020a). In the same year, Dutch men aged 65 and older could expect to live on average for another 19.2 years but would spend 6.8 years of their remaining lifetime with moderate and severe physical limitations and 15,4 years with chronic health conditions (ibid.). As nearly 89% of Dutch men and 92% of Dutch women can expect to survive to age 65 (Human Mortality Database 2020), we will face larger proportions of the population facing difficulties with their activities of daily living (see Table 9.1).

These limitations refer to the abilities of taking care of personal basic needs such as bathing, preparing meals, doing housework or shopping groceries. It becomes also apparent that with increasing age, the majority of men and women face limitations in performing ADLs and may rely on support from others. Also, the shares of older adults who report severe problems in ADLs increases markedly after age 75. In this age group, 37% of men

144 Louise Meijering and Tobias Vogt

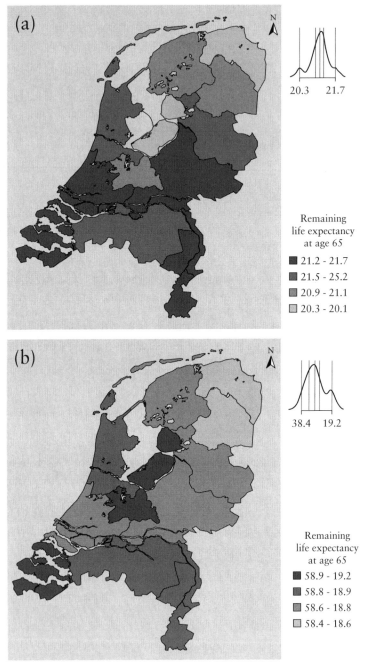

FIGURE 9.3   Remaining life expectancy at age 65 for women (left) and men (right) in Dutch provinces 2019.

Source: EUROSTAT Demography and Migration Database (2020) (own illustration)

TABLE 9.1 Share of Dutch population aged 65 with difficulties with Activities of Daily Living and contribution of selected diseases and health conditions to years lived with disability

Share of Dutch population aged 65+ with difficulties in activities the daily living (ADL)[a]				
Difficulties in personal care and household activities			Limited	Severe
	Men	65–74	40.1	14.0
		75 and above	62.8	36.9
	Women	65–74	57.4	23.3
		75 and above	76.3	51.6
Self-perceived long-standing limitations in usual activities due to health problem			Some	Severe
	Men	65–74	35.9	4.2
		75 and above	41.8	8.8
	Women	65–74	39.1	7.8
		75 and above	43.5	16.5

Contribution of selected diseases and health conditions to all years lived with disabilities (YLD) for Dutch population aged 65+ in %[b]			
Cardiovascular diseases	Men	65–74	7.4
		75 and above	8.9
	Women	65–74	5.0
		75 and above	7.5
Stroke	Men	65–74	2.0
		75 and above	2.9
	Women	65–74	2.0
		75 and above	3.4
Diabetes mellitus	Men	65–74	8.0
		75 and above	6.7
	Women	65–74	5.8
		75 and above	5.0
Alzheimer's disease and other dementias	Men	65–74	1.3
		75 and above	5.9
	Women	65–74	1.6
		75 and above	8.3
Chronic obstructive pulmonary disease	Men	65–74	6.8
		75 and above	10.3
	Women	65–74	5.5
		75 and above	8.4
Musculoskeletal disorders	Men	65–74	19.8
		75 and above	14.2
	Women	65–74	25.6
		75 and above	16.6

Source: [a] EUROSTAT Health Database (2020), [b] Global Burden of Diseases Study (2019)

and more than 50% of women are in need of support due to their substantial limitations in taking care of themselves. Also, severe limitations become more prevalent at ages above 65. More than every third man and every second woman in this age group had considerable problems in managing their everyday lives. This overall pattern changes substantially when older men and women report their self-perceived limitations in activities of daily living. Still, around 35–44% of Dutch men and women aged 65 and older report limitations in their ADLs but there is only a small increase in the prevalence of limitations between age 65–74 and 75 and older. More importantly, only a small fraction of older adults perceive their limitations as severe. Apart from the population group of women above age 75, less than 10% of older adults report severe limitations in household and personal care activities. These discrepancies suggest that despite increasing health problems in later life, older adults adapt to declining physical and cognitive capabilities and still maintain their abilities to take care of themselves despite perceived limitations.

Understanding the underlying causes of disabilities is a central aspect in determining care and support needs at older ages. Table 9.1 also provides an overview of the contributions of selected diseases and health conditions to the overall disability burden in the Netherlands. This selection represents a number of health conditions that lead to higher support needs at later life. For each age group, their joint contribution to the YLD is more than 40%. In 2019, Dutch men above age 65 lived in total 353.000 years with disabilities and women in the same age group 467.000 years (Global Burden of Disease Study 2019). These are around 50.000 years lived with disabilities among 100.000 persons alive in the same age group (or a half year per person above age 65). Musculoskeletal disorders, such as osteoarthritis in different forms, contribute a substantial share to the overall years lived with disabilities. This holds especially true for the age group 65–74 where these health conditions contribute up to 25% to all YLDs in the Netherlands. Also, chronic obstructive pulmonary diseases, diabetes or circulatory diseases including stroke contribute considerably to the overall disability burden but to a lower extent.[3]

Preventing or postponing disease and health conditions that lead to increased care needs has a high societal priority in the Netherlands. Still, larger parts of the population are expected to require a form of assistance at older ages. This holds especially true as remaining life expectancies are rising and more and more Dutch men and women can expect to survive to higher ages. A central concern of policymakers and societal organization has been to help older adults to cover their care needs while allowing them to remain an integrated part of society.

Addressing care needs in the Netherlands

In order to support care needs in later life, and to allow older adults to function as part of society, policies around care arrangements in the Netherlands centre on *ageing in place*. Ageing in place is a loosely defined term, which essentially refers to the ideal of "community living" or "ageing at home" (Boyle et al., 2015: 1501). Enabling older adults to age in place is a policy ideal in most Western countries. However, this has not always been the case. After World War II, older adults were encouraged to spend some well-deserved free time at the end of their lives in so-called rest homes, which were typically located on the outskirts of towns and villages, literally separated from the rest of society. In the 1980s, these rest homes turned out to be unsustainable economically, and there were also social disadvantages to locating older adults away from society. Since then, institutionalized care for older adults in residential care and nursing homes has decreased and older adults are expected to age in the community. Moreover, arranging suitable care and support has increasingly become an individual and market responsibility, rather than a societal one (Boyle et al., 2015).

The care system in the Netherlands is financed through a combination of social health insurance and managed competition. Curative care is paid from compulsory health insurance, which is partly income-dependent. The Dutch Health Care Authority oversees the managed competition between healthcare providers (Kroneman et al., 2016). Intensive long-term care is paid from income-dependent fees, and arranged through the Law Long-Term Care (Wet Langdurige Zorg (WLZ), 2014). With a recommendation for long-term care, vulnerable older adults can be admitted to a nursing home, but can in some cases choose to continue living at home, with intensive care. Older adults and other vulnerable groups who need less intensive support, need to arrange this through the municipality where they live. Since 2015, the responsibility for enabling all citizens to participate in society, and to provide the required support where necessary, has been transferred from the Dutch central government to municipalities, by means of the Law Societal Support (Wet Maatschappelijke Ondersteuning (WMO), 2015). The underlying principle of this law is that all citizens are responsible for their own lives and living environments, exemplified by the so-called participation society (Hurenkamp, 2020). However, simultaneously with the decentralization, budgets for care and support have been reduced. As a result, practice has bureaucratized and it can be difficult to find out where to get the required support and what forms to fill out. Also, it is not always clear whether support will be funded through the WMO or the WLZ. Table 9.2 presents what types of care and support are funded through each of these provisions and it shows indeed that there is some overlap.

TABLE 9.2 Care and support paid from the different provisions (Zorgwijzer, 2020)

Support type	WMO	WLZ
Meals and social activities	• Grocery service • Meal service (e.g. meals on wheels) • Organized activities (e.g. in a neighbourhood centre)	
Housing	• Annex to the residence • Adaptations to the residence, such as a stair lift, widened doors, removing obstacles, provisions in bathroom and toilet.	• Residence in a healthcare facility • Intensive care at home • Devices
Care		• Supervision, nursing and grooming • Medical care and treatment in the context of one's illness, limitation or disorder
Individual support	• Domestic help • Daytime activities • Personal alarm	• Domestic help • Daytime activities • Devices
Transport	• Shared taxi or wheelchair taxi • Adaptation to a car • A mobility scooter • A wheelchair • A leased car • Compensation for transport by own car	• Transport to the place where supervision, nursing and grooming take place
Transport-related	• Compensation for certain insurances and maintenance • Medical supervision during transport (if necessary) • Charging costs for electric vehicle • A parking space • A disabled parking card	

As a combined result of the above legislations and their application in local policies, the vast majority of older adults in the Netherlands is ageing in place. Indeed, as on January 1, 2020, 119.911 persons were living in an old age or nursing home, which is less than 4% of the total population aged 65 and above (CBS, 2020b). We now turn to discuss the experiences of community-dwelling older adults in need of care. We also discuss how these experiences and care arrangements are related to wellbeing in later life.

Care arrangements among community-dwelling older adults in the Northern Netherlands

Drawing on qualitative data collected in several research projects on the living environments of community-dwelling older adults in the Northern Netherlands, we discuss some of the challenges around care arrangements in later life that older adults face.

Arranging care in later life

In terms of housing, many older adults in the Netherlands live in either a rented or owner-occupied dwelling that is not adapted to live in when experiencing age-specific health problems. However, many older adults would prefer to age in their current dwelling. In our research project, we have met participants who experience a strong attachment to their house but struggle to maintain it and live there comfortably. In such situations, it is possible to make one's home "age-proof", for instance by building a stair lift, a safe shower cabin, a toilet that's adjustable in height, and automated control of lights, heating, or hatches. For such measures, there are subsidies available, such as life course proof intervention subsidies for homeowners. For those living in rental housing, housing associations have to provide life course proof houses and adapt houses for their current tenants (Ontzorg Experts, 2020).

Some older adults choose to move into a smaller residence, in anticipation of or upon increasing care needs. We have met several people who have chosen to move into an even-floored apartment, accessible with a lift, with built-in adaptations that have made it age-proof, prior to the onset of age-related disabilities, or just afterwards. When older people live in such a setting, it is typically easier to arrange the care they need. Here, too, it is important to underline the creativity that older adults display in arranging support and care: we met people who were eligible to get help with showering thrice a week but choose to get that only once because they can manage to wash themselves the other days. Others arrange a friend to support with cleaning and other household tasks, and in return take out their friend to do fun activities, to establish a reciprocal routine.

Bureaucratic barriers in arranging care

As we have discussed above, many older adults are able to arrange their care well while living in the community. However, we also observe that there are barriers that prevent people from getting what they need. As a result, there are also many older adults who live in unsupportive environments and who are, in turn, at risk of becoming socially isolated or lonely and experiencing reduced general well-being. In Box 9.1, we discuss the experiences of one of our research participants, who tried to get a parking spot designated for people with a disability. His story illustrates how difficult it can be to organize the needed support, and what impact that can have on well-being in later life.

> **BOX 9.1 THE STRUGGLE TO GET ACCESS TO A DESIGNATED DISABLED PARKING SPOT**
>
> More than three years ago, Mr. Kraima and his wife moved to an apartment which is located beside a shopping centre with a large parking area. Their previous residence was a terraced house with a private parking spot. Having a parking spot close to the entrance of the apartment building was important for Mr. Kraima since he has difficulties walking because of a foot injury and he cannot cover more than 100 metres on foot. However, to his surprise, his request to get a designated parking spot for his car was denied. The motivation was that, according to the municipality, there would always be a parking spot available within 100 metres of the entrance to the apartment building. When there would be many people in the shopping centre, such as on Fridays, Saturdays or market days, that was not the case based on Mr. Kraima's experiences. Moreover, he still has to walk about 60 metres within his apartment building before reaching his front door.
>
> Since the rejection of his application coincided with severe health problems of his wife, Mr. Kraima decided not to object at first. However, with time, his physical health deteriorated and he recently decided to submit a renewed application.
>
>> So I was tested by the municipal doctor. And he said again, ok you will get a designated parking space when there is one available. That advice was rejected again. So now I have written an appeal [...] and that is still pending. So, there is a spot available, but I cannot have a sign with my license plate number on it.
>
> Mr. Kraima told us how he does feel frustrated with the municipal organisation. He feels he is entitled to get a designated parking spot, the doctors underline this, but then somewhere in the municipal organisation, his application hits a blind wall and is rejected. As a result of a combination of his physical health problems and his frustration with not being able to get what he needs, he mentioned how his mental health also deteriorated:

> It's such a big hassle and these things do have an impact emotionally. [...] I didn't sleep and those things, and then I got more problems, also in terms of becoming more depressed. Well, now that's a bit better. But also because of those circumstances, the jibber-jabber about the parking spot, that does impact your health.
>
> The impact that the time, effort and frustration around the parking place have on Mr. Kraima should not be underestimated. It makes him feel depressed and only after getting medication for that, he feels slightly better.
> Mr. Kraima's story illustrates how difficult it can be to get the support that one needs to age in place. Although a disabled parking space is not directly care-related, it does enable older adults such as Mr. Kraima to live more comfortably in their own home. To deny such support to older adults has a detrimental effect on their health and well-being.

Ageing in place and well-being

In the Netherlands, the organization of care has been decentralized in recent years. In theory, this should help older adults to organize what they need, and better cope with the health-related challenges they experience. This should, in turn, have a positive impact on their experienced well-being. In any case, a familiar living environment can be conducive to well-being, since an older adult knows his or her way around, has a social network in place and is familiar with the shops and services in the neighbourhood (Lager et al., 2015). Overall, it is vital to enable older adults to "age in place", which means that it is necessary to offer different types of housing and care (or adapting existing forms) in neighbourhoods (Boyle et al., 2015; Pani-Harreman et al., 2020; Wiles et al., 2012; 2017). In such a familiar living environment, we observe different potential pathways towards well-being, because older adults have different preferences as to what a pleasurable living environment looks like. Some may never want to give up a garden or an outside space, while for others, a spacious living room may be more important. All this depends on the activities that an older person enjoys doing, both at home, at other places, and outdoors – be it reading, needlework, cooking, gardening, cycling, playing billiards or tennis, going to the cinema or eating out. Therefore, there are different pathways to well-being when ageing in place, based on the preferences with regard to activities that older adults want to do in their living environment.

Furthermore, older people, as was discussed above, are a very diverse group in terms of age and ability. In this context, especially the group of older adults in their 60s and 70s faces a high care burden: they sometimes are informal caregivers for people of an older generation, such as their parents, aunts and uncles, as well as older siblings or cousins. Sometimes they combine this with care for grandchildren. This means that the demands placed on them in terms of caring for may be quite high, even more so in the current context of the Netherlands, where people are first and foremost expected to arrange care within their own social circle.

Discussion and conclusion

The organization of care and support for older adults is a central challenge for Dutch society. With rising life expectancies, more and more individuals will reach old and very old ages, during which they will require assistance. At these later ages, disabilities are to a large extent caused by diseases that are preventable or whose onset could be potentially delayed. Diseases such as diabetes, dementia, musculoskeletal disorders or cardiovascular diseases account for larger shares of the overall disability burden today and may cause a higher care demand in the future. During the last 30 years, the Netherlands has witnessed a qualitative change in the organization of care with a stronger emphasis on allowing older adults to age in place while organizing the care and support they need. Although older adults face (bureaucratic) barriers in getting the needed assistance to age in place, ageing in place allows them to remain an integrated part of the Dutch society.

The ageing and care situation in the Netherlands, as we documented it here, may change in the coming years and decades. Care needs depend to a large extent on the risk of suffering from certain chronic diseases. These diseases are often avoidable either by amending unfavourable health behaviours such as smoking, unhealthy nutrition or a sedentary lifestyle. The care needs in the older age groups that we reported above are a result from past life experiences and exposures over the life of cohorts. Younger cohorts, that were born less than 65 years ago, may exhibit very different health behaviours and face a higher risk of suffering from certain diseases. Exemplary for this development is the smoking prevalence and the subsequent health problems of older cohorts in comparison to younger ones (Barendregt, Looman & Brønnum-Hansen 2002; Holford et al. 2014; Janssen, El Gewily & Bardoutsos 2020). An underlying determinant of committing to unhealthy lifestyles is socioeconomic status and most importantly education. For example, Nagelhout et al. (2002) found that low education was associated with earlier smoking initiation, higher smoking prevalence and later or no cessation of smoking. Apart from health behaviours, education was also found to be protective against the development of dementia (see Meng & D'Arcy (2012) for a review) and a decline in physical functioning (Zajacova & Karas Montez, 2017). Future Dutch cohorts will have higher education attainment than the ones that are in a higher need of care now. In 2015, 11,8% of men in the age group 65 and older had primary education and 25.1% lower secondary education while 37.8% had upper secondary and 23.4% post-secondary education. Among women in the same age group, 23.8% had primary education, 37% lower secondary education, 25.5% upper secondary education and 10.5% post-secondary education (Wittgenstein Center 2020). These numbers will change considerably in the next decades and gender inequalities in education will decline. In 2040, 5.9% of men and 8.9% of women above age 65 will have primary education, 16.7% and 20.7% lower secondary education, around 40% of men and women will have higher secondary education and 33.5% and 28.4% post-secondary education (ibid). This higher educational attainment may not only translate into more favourable health behaviours and lower care burden but it may also imply that the higher educated have a higher resilience and the capabilities to age in place independently.

Not only care needs but also care arrangements may change in the future. The digitalization of working processes and the ability to work from home may enable older employees in need of care to remain active in the labour market. Likewise, informal care provision of family members may be facilitated by new forms of labour where informal caregivers can reconcile care commitments with work requirements and career ambitions. This holds especially true for labour market inequalities for those informal caregivers that have to withdraw from employment or reduce their working hours because of care commitments (Bauer & Souza-Posa, 2015).

An important development that we want to emphasize in the context of population ageing is the fact that technological devices that enable ageing in place will probably become more widespread. Here, one can think of technology such as the internet of things or care robots. Similar to the bureaucratic barriers that exist in accessing care and support, we anticipate that there will also be barriers to getting and working with appropriate technology in later life. In part, this can be explained by the different experiences earlier in life that older adults will have had with technology. Moreover, a lack of engagement and participation of older adults as end users in the design and development of technology does explain that many older adults experience barriers in using technology (Hill et al., 2015; Wang et al., 2019). Thus, we echo Wang et al. (2019) in calling for co-design processes in development of technology geared at facilitating ageing in place that engage older adults right from the start, i.e. in identifying what their actual needs are. Only in that way can appropriate and usable technology be designed.

Based on this chapter, we conclude that needs in terms of care and living arrangements are shaped by the population composition of the Netherlands. There are regional differences in population structure, for instance in terms of education, socio-economic status, migration background and household structure. As a result of these differences, we anticipate that the specific needs with regard to care arrangements in later life will differ between regions and that a one-size-fits-all approach in policy is not sustainable. We therefore suggest that it will be good to invest in region-specific living and care arrangements that accommodate, for instance, the specific needs of older migrant groups (see Carlsson et al., 2020; Meijering & Lager, 2014). Such more fine-grained living and care arrangements are likely to result in more positive lived experiences. Further research in this field will contribute to understanding the drivers that shape what care and support is needed in later life.

Acknowledgements

We would like to thank the Dutch research participants in the *Meaningful Mobility* project for sharing their stories with us.

Funding statement

Louise Meijering's contribution was made possible with funding received for the *Meaningful Mobility* project, from the European Research Council (ERC) under the European Union's Horizon 2020 research and innovation programme (Grant Agreement No. 802202).

Notes

1 Throughout this text, we define ages above 65 as older ages for the Netherlands. This age threshold is widely used to differentiate between adult and older ages and refers often to the classical retirement age when adults leave the labour market and rely on support, e.g. via pensions from others.
2 Chronic health conditions refer to the presence of at least one chronic disease ranging from hypertension, stroke or heart conditions over diabetes or rheumatic joint disorders to cancers, asthma or bronchitis. Severe and moderate physical limitations are measured as having problems in a) cognitive function like hearing, eyesight or having conversations and b) general mobility with walking, keeping balance or lifting items (see CBS 2020a for further details).
3 The contribution of further diseases and health conditions to age-specific and overall YLD can be found at http://ghdx.healthdata.org/gbd-results-tool.

References

Barendregt, J. J., Looman, C. W., & Brønnum-Hansen, H. (2002). Comparison of cohort smoking intensities in Denmark and the Netherlands. *Bulletin of the World Health Organization*, 80, 26–32.

Bauer, J. M., & Sousa-Poza, A. (2015). Impacts of informal caregiving on caregiver employment, health, and family. *Journal of Population Ageing*, 8(3), 113–145. https://doi.org/10.1007/s12062-015-9116-0

Boyle, A., Wiles, J. L., & Kearns, R. A. (2015). Rethinking ageing in place: the 'people' and 'place' nexus. *Progress in Geography*, 34(12), 1495–1511. https://doi.org/10.18306/dlkxjz.2015.12.002

Carlsson, H., Pijpers, R. & van Melik, R. (2020). Day-care centres for older migrants: spaces to translate practices in the care landscape. *Social & Cultural Geography*, 23(2), 250–269. https://doi.org/10.1080/14649365.2020.1723135

CBS (2020a). Health Expectancy; since 1981. Retrieved from: https://opendata.cbs.nl/statline/portal.html?_la=en&_catalog=CBS&tableId=71950eng&_theme=1043 [3.12.2020]

CBS (2020b). Household and population data. Available through: https://www.cbs.nl/nl-nl/cijfers/detail/82905ned.

Christensen, K., Doblhammer, G., Rau, R., & Vaupel, J. W. (2009). Ageing populations: the challenges ahead. *The Lancet*, 374(9696), 1196–1208. https://doi.org/10.1016/s0140-6736(09)61460-4

EUROSTAT Health Database (2020). Retrieved from: https://ec.europa.eu/eurostat/web/health/data/database. [4.12.2020].

EUROSTAT Demography and Migration Database (2020). Retrieved from: https://ec.europa.eu/eurostat/web/population-demography-migration-projections/data/database [3.12.2020]

Global Burden of Diseases Study (2019). Retrieved from: http://ghdx.healthdata.org/gbd-results-tool [1.12.2020].

Hill, R., Betts, L.R. & Gardner, S.E. (2015). Older adults' experiences and perceptions of digital technology: (dis)empowerment, wellbeing, and inclusion. *Computers in Human Behavior* 48: 415–423. https://doi.org/10.1016/j.chb.2015.01.062

Holford, T. R., Levy, D. T., McKay, L. A., Clarke, L., Racine, B., Meza, R., Land, S., Jeon, J. & Feuer, E. J. (2014). Patterns of birth cohort–specific smoking histories, 1965-2009. *American Journal of Preventive Medicine*, 46(2), e31–e37. https://doi.org/10.1016/j.amepre.2013.10.022

Human Fertility Database (2020). Retrieved from: https://www.humanfertility.org/cgi-bin/country.php?country=NLD&tab=si [3.12.2020]

Human Mortality Database (2020). Retrieved from: https://www.mortality.org/cgi-bin/hmd/country.php?cntr=NLD&level=1 [3.12.2020]

Hurenkamp, M. (2020). Participation society: the rise and fall of a concept. [Participatiesamenleving: de opkomst en neergang van een begrip]. *Sociale Vraagstukken*. January 22, 2020. https://www.socialevraagstukken.nl/participatiesamenleving-de-opkomst-en-neergang-van-een-begrip/.

Janssen F., El Gewily S., Bardoutsos A. (2020). Smoking epidemic in Europe in the 21st century. *Tobacco Control* 30(5), 523–529. http://dx.doi.org/10.1136/tobaccocontrol-2020-055658

Kroneman M., Boerma W., van den Berg M., Groenewegen P., Jong J. de & Ginneken, E. van (2016). The Netherlands: health system review. *Health Systems in Transition*, 18(2), 1–239. https://apps.who.int/iris/handle/10665/330244

Lager, D., Hoven, B.v. & Huigen, P.P.P. (2015). Understanding older adults' social capital in place: obstacles to and opportunities for social contacts in the neighbourhood. *Geoforum*, 59(1), 87–97. https://doi.org/10.1016/j.geoforum.2014.12.009

Meijering, L. & Lager, D. (2014). Home-making of older Antillean immigrants in the Netherlands. *Ageing & Society*, 34(5), 859–875. https://doi.org/10.1017/S0144686X12001377.

Meng X. & D'Arcy C. (2012). Education and Dementia in the context of the cognitive reserve hypothesis: a systematic review with meta-analyses and qualitative analyses. *PLOS ONE*, 7(6), e38268. https://doi.org/10.1371/journal.pone.0038268

Nagelhout, G.E., de Korte-de Boer, D., Kunst, A.E., van der Meer, R.M., de Vries, H., van Gelder, B.M. & Willemsen, M.C. (2002). Trends in socioeconomic inequalities in smoking prevalence, consumption, initiation, and cessation between 2001 and 2008 in the Netherlands. Findings from a national population survey. *BMC Public Health*, 12(303). https://doi.org/10.1186/1471-2458-12-303

Ontzorg Experts (2020). Subsidies en Leningen Woningaanpassingen [Subsidies and loans for adapting houses]. Available through: https://ontzorgexperts.nl/kennis-en-inspiratie/subsidies-en-leningen-woningaanpassingen/.

Pani-Harreman, K., Bours, G., Zander, I., Kempen, G., & Van Duren, J. (2020). Definitions, key themes and aspects of 'ageing in place': A scoping review. *Ageing & Society*, 41(9), 1–34. https://doi.org/10.1017/S0144686X20000094

United Nations (2020). UN Population Prospects 2019. Retrieved from https://population.un.org/wpp/DataQuery/ [3.12.2020].

Vogt, T., Kluge, F. & Lee, R. (2020). Intergenerational Resource Sharing and Mortality in a Global Perspective. *Proceedings of the National Academy of Sciences*, 117(37), 22793–22799. https://doi.org/10.1073/pnas.1920978117.

Wang, S., Bolling, K., Mao, W., Reichstadt, J., Jeste, D., Kim, H.C. & Nebeker, C. (2019). Technology to support aging in place: older adults' perspectives. *Healthcare*, 7(2), 60. https://doi.org/10.3390/healthcare7020060

Wet Langdurige Zorg (2014). *Law Long-term Care [Wet Langdurige Zorg]*. Available through: https://wetten.overheid.nl/BWBR0035917/2020-03-19.

Wet Maatschappelijke Ondersteuning (2015). *Law Societal Support 2015 [Wet Maatschappelijke Ondersteuning 2015]*. Available through: https://wetten.overheid.nl/BWBR0035362/2020-07-01.

Wiles, J.L., Leibing, A., Guberman, N., Reeve, J. & Allen, R.E.S. (2012). The meaning of "ageing in place" to older people. *The Gerontologist*, 52(3), 357–366. https://doi.org/10.1093/geront/gnr098

Wiles, J.L., Rolleston, A., Pillai, A., Broad, J., Teh, R., Gott, M. & Kerse, N. (2017). Attachment to place in advanced age: a study of the LiLACS NZ cohort. *Social Science & Medicine*, 185, 27–37. https://doi.org/10.1016/j.socscimed.2017.05.006

Wittgenstein Centre (2020). Human Capital Data Explorer. Available through: https://dataexplorer.wittgensteincentre.org/wcde-v2/

Zajacova A. & Karas Montez, J. (2017). Physical Functioning Trends among US Women and Men Age 45–64 by Education Level. *Biodemography and Social Biology*, 63(1), 21–30, https://doi.org/10.1080/19485565.2016.1263150.

Zorgwijzer (2020). WMO: wat is het? [WMO: what is it?] and WLZ: wat is het? [WLZ: what is it?]. Available through: www.zorgwijzer.nl.

10
AGED PEOPLE CARE IN POLAND

Artur Fabiś and Joanna K. Wawrzyniak

Introduction

According to the projections of the Polish Central Statistical Office, by 2030 the population in Poland will decrease by around 1.3 million, but at the same time, the number of citizens aged 60 and more will increase to about 10 million (GUS 2019). At present, Poland has 38.35 million citizens. Regular and significant growth of the individual life span all over the world (Roser 2016)—including Poland (even though this trend has visibly slowed down recently)—creates opportunities for improving not only longevity but also the quality of life. It is a fact now that for years people have been not only living longer but also healthier. In the last decade of the previous century and the first decade of the present century, the average life expectancy in developed countries increased by 4.7 years, out of which 3.8 years is life in good health (Murray et al. 2012). The demographic changes in Poland prognosed for the next decade stimulate reflection on the quality of life in old age and health is one of the significant contributors to reaching the highest indicator of wellbeing. Health is considered a good from both individual and social perspective. It is listed as a top value in life not only by older citizens but also by other generations. When asked about the priority values in their lives, two-thirds of Poles declare it is health, and nine out of ten list health as one of the three most important life values (GUS 2015). Paradoxically, healthcare services are not publicly recognized, and two-thirds of Polish citizens negatively evaluate health services available in Poland (CBOS 2018). It is a challenge for senior policy, social work, the healthcare system, and professional and family care dedicated to the elderly.

DOI: 10.4324/9781003528432-12

Health condition and disabilities among seniors

According to the most recent reports from the nation-wide quantitative research POLSENIOR 2 (2020), one in five respondents aged 70 and more declares the need to receive support from outside, and one in twenty respondents declares a definite need for such help. This declarative demand for assistance increases greatly with age. Among the respondents aged 80 and more, almost one in three persons declared they needed support, whereas almost every fourth senior aged 80–89 needed it definitely. In the oldest age group (90 years and more), almost eight respondents in ten declared they needed assistance, and more than half of them signaled that they definitely needed such help. Women are much more willing to receive help than men. The research also shows a clear relation between socio-economic status (education and financial situation) and cases of depression, dementia, disability, as well as two or more existing severe diseases. The POLSENIOR 2 study also investigated also the scope of the so-called major geriatric problems. In the population studied, 16% experienced at least one fall in the last year, and 7.9% fell down at least twice. The frequency of falls is positively correlated with age—one in three respondents aged 80+ has already experienced such an incident. Women fell almost twice as often. Another one of the major geriatric problem is connected with bladder control. It is a common problem among Polish women aged 60 and more—more than half of the female respondents admitted they struggle with urinary incontinence. One in five male seniors mentioned it as a problem. The condition becomes more prevalent with age. Another major issue is the loss of vision and hearing. Moderate sight problems affect more than 40% of Polish seniors, and 10% reported moderate hearing disorders. There are no big differences between the genders, even though hearing problems are slightly more common in men. The loss of both vision and hearing increases with age. It is impossible to determine the exact number of dependent persons due to differences in determination systems based on different criteria. The complex PolSenior study report indicated that the percentage of dependent individuals among the citizens aged 65 and more does not exceed 40% (Błędowski 2012).

The older the Poles, the lower they evaluate their health condition. In 2012, more than half of the people aged 75 and more evaluated their health as bad (CBOS 2012). At the same time, as they get older, patients show less and less critical attitude toward the healthcare system. The most satisfied are the oldest respondents aged 65 and more (45% of the satisfied). Even though Polish healthcare services are not rated high by the total of Polish population, 66% are rather satisfied or definitely dissatisfied (CBOS 2018). Surely, geriatrics is one of the most neglected areas in Poland. According to the data of the National Consultant in Geriatrics, there are 427 specialists in geriatrics in Poland (as of 2017), about half of whom are active in their specialization. This means that there are slightly more than 200 specialists available for about 7 million citizens aged 65+, whereas the estimated demand is 3,000. Assuming that about 30% of seniors require geriatric help, at present there are 12 thousand seniors per specialist (Kostka 2019).

The European statistics indicate that Polish male citizens live in good health up to 60.5 years on average, whereas female seniors up to 64.3 years. This is nine years less than the European highest (Malta, 73.4 years) and over 9 years longer than ill female seniors in Lithuania (53.7 years). Polish male seniors, in turn, are over three years below the European average. However, they live in good health 8.5 years longer than Lithuanians and more than 13 years shorter than the healthiest Swedes (73.7 years) (Eurostat 2020). It is impossible to determine the exact number of dependent persons due to differences in determination systems based on different criteria.

Social policy and senior policy in Poland

The necessity to take care of the oldest citizens results directly from the principles of social and senior policies implemented in Poland. The report "Poland 2030. Developmental challenges" (2009) developed by the Prime Minister's Strategic Advisors Team points out to the need to modify the healthcare system to improve the quality of services and optimize health care and access to specialized care and therapy for older patients, especially those with multiple diseases/polypathology.

The document "Long-term Senior Policy in Poland for years 2014–2020" (2013) emphasizes the necessity to integrate the healthcare policy and the senior policy to support and provide opportunities for active aging in health and opportunities for a continued self-reliant, independent, and fulfilling life, even with some functional and health limitations. The main areas of implementation are social policy and health care. Piotr Błędowski writes that "the effectiveness of the senior-oriented activities is determined by several factors, of which the most important are:

- adequate and regularly updated diagnosis of the situation and the needs of the older generation,
- monitoring activities taken by different subjects at national and local level,
- rational management of the public funds assigned to implement these activities" (2012a, p. 201–202). Thus, senior policy (including healthcare policy) cannot be implemented separately from the social policy structures (Kurpas 2016).

Social policy instrument is **social assistance** described in the Act of 12 March 2004 on Social Assistance (Journal of Laws 2004, No. 64, Item 593) as an institution designed to help individuals and families overcome difficult life situations which they are not able to overcome using their own resources, abilities, and rights. The social assistance system in Poland is based, to a large extent, on local governments—in every municipality and city there are social assistance centers and the main governing institution is the Ministry of Family and Social Policy.

Systemic care and support solutions for the elderly usually include financial and material benefits, providing services, and institutional support in the form of places in long-term care facilities (Chabior, Fabiś, Wawrzyniak, 2014).

Social assistance systems were developed in response to social needs and their main goal is to ensure proper education, health, and living conditions for citizens in need. The support is eligible for 15 reasons, called *social risks*, and eleven of them can apply to older people. The most common risks in the senior population are: homelessness, disability, prolonged or severe illness, family violence, incompetence in running a household, addictions (e.g., drug abuse, alcoholism), unforeseeable events, and crisis situations.

Any activities taken to provide support to seniors in the above-mentioned situations should be organized based on the principle of voluntary and free decisions regarding one's life, maintaining full participation in social life and entrusting care and support activities to institutions and organizations that are monitored and controlled. For example, family abuse victims receive social assistance in, among others, 24-hour assistance centers where their basic needs are met and where they receive professional medical, social, psychological, and legal support, but only upon their will and consent (Maćkowicz, 2017). In 2019, in Poland, there were 24-hour support centers for family abuse victims (MRPiPS, 2020), which function based on the ministerial resolution (Journal of Laws 2011, No. 50, Item 259) and are managed by local governments. Another important principle, together with autonomy, integration, and organization, is that assistance is provided when it is needed, rather than as relief in unjustified situations.

Assistance and care tasks dedicated to seniors are fulfilled through social work, the goals of which have been described according to international standards. The most important global principles of social work include: removing barriers; facilitating the inclusion of socially excluded, weak, and vulnerable groups; helping people receive services and resources; developing and implementation of policies and programs that improve well-being and promote development and human rights; assisting individuals who are incapable of independent living; and engaging in social and political campaigns to influence social policy and eliminate inequalities (Marynowicz-Hetka, 2006). An important criterion during the implementation of social work is the necessity to trigger the activity and independence of seniors because—as mentioned before—it is not about giving as such but rather about activating the potential of individuals and social powers to act in order to improve the situation.

In this perspective, the main tasks of social workers among seniors, besides providing information and assistance in solving severe problems, include showing them opportunities to improve their personal situation, initiating different forms of assistance including access to benefits and services for individuals and groups in difficult life situations. In order to complete these tasks successfully, social workers must cooperate with seniors or facilitate their contacts with institutions, organizations, and specialists in different fields, whose involvement is necessary or can improve the chances of solving given problems.

Senior care

Models of senior care are determined based on the types of caregivers. In the present Polish realities, there is family care provided by spouses, children, grandchildren, and other relatives; informal home care provided by neighbors, friends, or caregivers hired privately or sent by NGOs; community care ensured by special centers with professional staff, for example, day-care facilities and community self-help homes; and institutional care provided by qualified staff in long-term, 24-hour care facilities or as care services delivered to seniors at their homes (Szarota 2010).

Senior care models—home care

If their living conditions allow it, patients with chronic diseases are being taken care of at their homes. This means that while living at home, patients receive the necessary medical and nursing care, and their families can also count on support as they prepare to take over the care responsibilities.

Poland is one of the countries where the family is primarily responsible for caring for elderly members. Family's role is to fill the gaps in systemic health and social care. In many regions, access to medical services is limited. Local authorities engage in senior care only when family members do not cope with it, and even then, the family has to participate as much as possible (e.g., financially) in providing care services. According to the 2012 survey, one in three adult Poles had helped (in different forms) some elderly in need (CBOS, 2012). When asked about their needs, seniors (aged 55 and more) mentioned care during an illness (40%) and personal hygiene (17%). The most common caregivers are children (69%), spouses (47%), siblings (26%), and neighbors (26%). One in five seniors can also count on help from their grandchildren, friends, and other relatives (CBOS 2019). The tradition of home care for the elderly is so strong in some regions that moving an older family member to a care facility is a source of controversy or even stigmatization in the community. Although weakening, cultural, historical, and religious realities are still very powerful. According to a CBOS survey, almost 60% of the respondents think older people should live with one of their children who should take care of them (CBOS 2018). It is the highest (twice the average) rate among the European countries (EUROFAMCARE 2002).

According to the definition adopted in Eurofarmacare research, a **family caregiver** is a person who considers themselves a caregiver, provides care services for at least 4 hours a week, and supports a close person aged 65 and older. Family caregivers are recruited from the closest family members of a senior who requires care due to health condition and/or disability. However, they do not have to formally belong to the family. Seniors who live with their families can rely on the care of their spouses, children, or adult grandchildren most often (Eurofarmacare 2012). It is estimated that there are about 2 million informal caregivers in Poland. They are mainly women, that is, daughters and sons aged 50–60 (Racław 2012). The most common problems connected with this type of care are overload with responsibilities, especially in cases of patients with chronic or terminal illnesses, physical and emotional exhaustion of the caregiver, lack of professional support, and low level of satisfaction from this work. The model of the Polish family has been changing in recent years. More and more often, children gain their independence sooner and leave their family home, there are fewer multi-generational families and more migrations—mainly among young people. As a consequence, there is a growing need for support for senior citizens provided by people from outside the family. It can be assumed that in the near future, this type of senior care will change its name to **informal caregiver** as it is broader and describes the relationship between caretakers and caregivers more accurately (Czekanowski 2018).

Research on Polish family caregivers who look after chronically ill seniors has revealed some regularities. Care provided to those with chronic illnesses is mainly based on an informal network of family caregivers. Women are the main driving force here. It turns out that the main motivation to remain engaged is the satisfaction from the role of a caregiver. Care responsibilities are overwhelming, but chronic fatigue and stress are ignored. The caregivers do not notice their negative influence on their bodies (Zysnarska et al. 2010). Such results imply the necessity to introduce complex solutions to ensure proper support for family caregivers in their voluntarily assumed care responsibilities. These are expectations addressed in particular to legislative authorities but also to local governments.

The vast majority of informal caregivers are left alone with the problems resulting from caring for the elderly. Research in this area points out to the need to provide constant support to such caregivers on several levels. It is mainly the psychological support to help them maintain the right relationships with senior family members and prevent depression and burnout. Another important aspect is first aid training and learning practical skills needed to care for temporarily or permanently bed-ridden patients, such as changing diapers and bedding, feeding, and personal hygiene. There is also a significant need to learn how to perform simple medical procedures, dosage procedures, patting to prevent bedsores, simple massages and rehabilitation exercises, and how to measure pressure and dress wounds (NMCE 2012).

Home care is a popular model of senior care in highly developed countries. It is not very common in Poland due to financial reasons—this type of caregiver is usually paid from the private funds of seniors and their families. This type of care is usually provided by professional businesses or organizations, or individuals who are paid to perform the necessary care and nursing tasks. In Poland, home care services are delivered mainly by privately hired individuals, with the help of NGOs or as part of social projects (e.g., neighborhood help financed from EU funds).

A relatively new form of senior care is the role of a **personal assistant for the elderly**. This role functions within the social assistance area as a family assistant who most often works with dysfunctional families. In the near future, there might be a necessity for these assistants to provide assistance to families of seniors, by accompanying them in their daily activities and duties. The demographic situation has been developing definitively toward feminization, singularization, and deficits in old age, thus the required help can be delivered as support for the families of seniors who require permanent care.

Personal assistant for the elderly is a form of care dedicated to relatively independent and healthy individuals who, nevertheless, need support with their everyday activities such as cleaning, cooking, dressing, shopping, dealing with administrative affairs, or involvement in different activities. The curriculum for personal assistant for people with disabilities training can be used to formulate the specific tasks for personal assistants for the elderly (Journal of Laws 2011 No. 49). These tasks can include:

- assist older persons, especially if they are not fully physically/motorically able, in fulfilling their social and professional roles,
- participate in identifying and solving problems (family, social, formal),
- cooperate with social workers and other specialists to improve the quality of senior's life,
- provide help with using medical and rehabilitation services and leveraging the opportunities for education and development of interests/hobbies,
- help initiate social contacts and organize free time,
- recognize and solve social, health, nursing, and care problems,
- help seniors meet their essential needs,
- help seniors maintain their social and neighborly activities,
- activate seniors to increase their life independence,

- help ensure safe living conditions,
- cooperate with care and therapeutic team,
- popularize health-oriented and preventive activities.

Assistant's job focuses mainly on activating the older person and improving the quality of their life to prevent social exclusion and empower them to live an independent life.

Save for dependence, one of the important reasons to hire a personal assistant for the elderly may be the difficult social and personal situations seniors face in their home environments. This problem is egalitarian; it is present in every society, and its scope has been increasing. Seniors are particularly vulnerable to pathologies such as violence, abuse, or frauds, as they are less able—also technologically, have limited access to help offered by different organizations and services, and can be depressed, closed, withdrawn, and lonely. One of the determinants of senior exclusion is the lack of abilities to use and access modern information tools. In addition, family structures have been transformed, often resulting in the crisis of the multigenerational family model and poor relationships of the elderly with other family members.

Thus, a well-prepared assistant should possess wide knowledge about old age as a stage of life and its accompanying crises and problems. Certain social and ethical competencies are also necessary.

Personal assistants can work both with seniors' families and lonely seniors. The second case may turn out to be more important as lonely elderly are at risk of marginalization and social exclusion.

In every case, and particularly when there is risk of any pathology, personal assistants play not only a significant preventive role but also contribute to improving the quality of seniors' lives and help to meet their needs.

Community caregivers, in turn, function within the framework of institutional care—city or municipal social assistance centers. They implement many different care, assistance, and nursing tasks. They provide care (including specialist services) which can be commissioned by a city or municipal social assistance center to institutions or organizations providing this type of support at the place of residence of an older, lonely person.

As part of their community care services, social assistance centers can also provide financial and material help, social work, contracted care services, and places in day-care facilities—day nursing homes or community self-help homes. These centers are an indirect form of community and institutional help. Both assistance from the caregivers and providing places in day-care homes are intended to prolong independence, autonomy, and prevent loneliness, passivity, and helplessness, which significantly decrease the quality of life of seniors. Being able to live in one's own apartment and environment is equally important. Thanks to this, seniors can stay in their familiar living environment and maintain contacts with it, which seems to be particularly important in the situation of the disappearance of social interactions and the necessity to compensate for various deficits.

Long-term patient care

In the present healthcare system in Poland, many older citizens use the specialized help of care and medical institutions. These institutions include social assistance (nursing) homes, medical care centers, hospices, and geriatric departments. They provide services in stationary facilities and at patients' homes.

Long-term, stationary care centers address their services to the chronically ill and people who have undergone treatment but do not need to stay in a hospital. There are two types of facilities: medical-care and nursing-care. They admit patients who require temporary but 24-hour nursing and continued treatment. This is due to their physical disability or general health condition and, at the same time, their inability to take care of themselves and the need to ensure medical control, professional nursing, and rehabilitation.

According to the Resolution of the Minister of Health of 27 August 2004 (Journal of Laws, No. 210, Item 2135), seniors, that is, individuals who have the need to stay in a care facility, apply to get a referral to such a center. In case of individuals who stay at home, the referral is issued by a family practitioner in consultation with a health visitor (community nurse). When the applicant stays in a hospital, it is the hospital that refers the patient directly to the facility. Waiting time for admission depends on the number of available beds in a given center. For example, out of 23 centers in the Silesian region, three received patients on an ongoing basis, but the average waiting time is about three months. There are also centers where the waiting time is as much as eight months (data from the website (NFZ 2020). People who require immediate permanent care are treated as a priority. A stay in a care facility is paid for, and the amount due is determined individually by the facility manager, depending on the patient's income. The monthly fee is calculated based on 250% of the lowest pension, but it cannot exceed 70% of the patient's income. The fee covers accommodation and boarding costs; other expenses (medicines, medical supplies, etc.) are provided by the center. The duration of the stay in a care facility depends on health. If the patient's condition is rated more than 40 points in the Barthel Index, the National Health Fund shall cease the funding. Services are delivered following the diagnosis of needs and include, as needed: medical observation and continuation of treatment, professional nursing, and rehabilitation. These supportive benefits focus on psychological support, speech therapy, occupational therapy, dietary treatment, as well as health education addressed to the family to prepare the patient and their loved ones for self-care and self-nursing at home.

A desired form of care and activation is **day social assistance homes** (day care homes), which are an open form of the communal system of social support. The facilities are open on working days for eight hours a day and provide access to qualified specialists: therapists, animators, caregivers, and physiotherapists. They are dedicated to seniors—residents of a given region who are lonely, have limited mobility or intellectual abilities, live under harsh conditions, have dysfunctional relationships with their family, or whose families cannot provide them full care during the day.

Apart from living services, day care homes also provide rehabilitation, development, education, and recreation activities, as well as different forms of therapy—individual, group, and occupational to activate patients in different areas. These activities also compensate for the lack of family interactions.

Community self-help homes are facilities for people with mental disorders, intellectual disabilities, dementia, or Alzheimer's disease. These centers provide specialist care and nursing services and promote the activity, ability, and independence of their patients in order to maximize their self-care potential and ability to function in the community.

The main advantage of the day-care centers is that they relieve family members in caring for their seniors and thus facilitate their daily functioning and enable them to pursue professional careers. In addition, staying in a familiar environment optimizes the help given and received. Such a form of care builds seniors' faith in their own abilities, raises their self-esteem and self-worth. Seniors who benefit from day care in their community feel safe and useful, gaining a sense of dignity and social integration (Zielińska-Więczkowska 2016). This form of assistance enables them to remain independent for longer and defers the obligation of maintenance payments and the necessity to move to a long-term facility.

The main form of long-term stationary care is **social assistance homes** (nursing homes), which are closed-type facilities providing 24-hour assistance to individuals who need constant care due to their advanced age, illness, disability, and loneliness. Nursing homes function under the Resolution of 12 March 2004 of the Minister of Labor and Social Policy on social assistance homes. Nursing homes are substitutes for the home environment. These facilities deliver their services based on referrals from social assistance centers and/or doctors in cases of an illness or disability, which require patient to be placed in a facility providing specific treatment and help. The purpose of nursing homes is to ensure 24-hour care, meet basic living, educational, social, and religious needs, and access to healthcare services for their residents. Homes are managed by poviats (regional administrative units) and co-financed from the state budget. They can also be also managed by religious associations, churches, social organizations, foundations, individuals, and legal persons.

Residents of the nursing homes are mainly people with significantly limited psychophysical abilities, in advanced age, and in difficult material-social situations: poor, lonely, unaccompanied, living in poor living and sanitary conditions, and with difficult family situations. The fee is paid by the residents in the amount of up to 70% of their income, and if this is not enough (and usually it is not), the remaining part of the costs is covered by other family members and/or the municipality which has referred the senior to the nursing home. For example, according to the data of the regional office of the Małopolska region (MUW 2019), the monthly cost of accommodation in a nursing home for the elderly is about 3,900 PLN per person (approx. 900 €). The average pension **in the first half of 2019** was 2,352.91 **PLN, but the majority of pensions did not exceed 1,100 PLN (GUS 2019).**

The functions and tasks of the assistance homes include: provision of 24-hour care (daily care, boarding, dressing, hygiene); satisfying the residents' needs (care services, helping in basic activities, nursing, activation and rehabilitation, assistance in dealing with daily affairs); ensuring conditions for peaceful, safe and dignified living, intimacy, independence, and personality development (educational services, personal and spiritual development, occupational therapy, contact with family, specialist counseling, visiting places of religious cult and culture, development of interests, psychological and medical support, access to social activities, participation in celebrations, regional life, integration and social events) (Leszczyńska-Rajchert 2006). To fulfill these requirements, assistance homes must also meet some standards set in the resolution. The building and its surroundings must be barrier-free. There must be elevators and call-alarm systems. The maximum recommended number of residents is 100. Single bedrooms should be no less than 9 m^2 and multiperson bedrooms should ensure not less than 6m^2 of personal space per person; the building must have day rooms, an eating room, medical office, rehabilitation rooms as well as an additional kitchen, laundry room, smoking lounge, guest room, and a place to perform religious practices. Bathrooms must be adapted to the needs of persons with disabilities and one bathroom can be available to a maximum six persons. Toilets must be accessible for the disabled, with a maximum one toilet per four people. Residents are guaranteed at least three meals a day, with options to choose the menu and time of the meal (2-hour timeframe), and basic groceries are available 24 hours.

Optimization of the tasks in an assistance home is supported by: the assistance home resident's individual plan of support, the first contact staff member, and therapeutic-care team. The individual support plan is created for individual residents, and its goal is the optimization of work with the senior according to his or her needs, individual situation, and problems, as well as a specific approach that enables the widest possible plan of support and care provided by the first contact staff member in cooperation with all home personnel. The individual support plan is particularly helpful in crisis situations such as aggressive or asocial behaviors or addictions of the resident, but it is it also important for addressing the senior's daily needs.

First contact staff member is a person who coordinates activities resulting from the individual support plan. Residents can choose such a person themselves, it should be a person with the necessary social and care competencies and skills. This role requires an individual approach to the senior resident, empathy and understanding of their needs, as well as determination in efforts to optimize the conditions and quality of their life.

Specific tasks are performed by the **therapeutic-care team** consisting of the first contact workers and specialists who help the caregivers in professional activities: nurses, physiotherapists, occupational therapy instructors, psychologists, and priests. The team is responsible for coordinating aspects related to the senior's stay in the nursing home and identifying individual needs to support the resident's development. They also evaluate the psychosocial condition of the residents and diagnose the level of their motor functioning, resourcefulness, self-care, and interpersonal functioning.

While the above-mentioned forms of care have been functioning successfully for decades, **family care homes** are the most recent form of supporting the elderly who require 24-hour assistance. Such homes can be managed by individuals or families as their business activity and are based on agreement signed with the municipality, describing the conditions for the functioning of family care homes. Their roles are very similar to those of social assistance homes. The number of residents is what is different (3–8 persons)—family care homes are smaller than traditional nursing homes, so it is easier to create a friendly and family-like atmosphere. The stay is financed similarly to traditional care homes. In both types of facilities, the stay can be of a commercial character when there is no referral from the municipality and the potential resident decides for the full package of services. There are homes which function only in this way, guaranteeing a higher standard of life. The key characteristic of family care homes is their size, as the conditions resemble a home environment. It is assumed that every resident and caregiver has their own bedroom but they manage the household together. As much as possible, seniors take part in housework even though the responsibility to provide for the residents' needs rests on the caregiver(s). Certain qualifications needed to manage this type of assistance home. The most preferable are persons with medical and related education (nursing, rehabilitation, care, social work). Practical and professional experience in working with the elderly is an advantage. The required skills and competencies include: communication skills, stress resilience and decisiveness, management, administrative, teaching, nursing and organizational skills, and the ability to deal with issues like suffering and death (Mirewska 2011).

Another new form of care is assisted living apartments (sheltered housing) for seniors, which are something between their own apartments where seniors do not always have the right conditions or are not able to function independently and maintain them, and nursing homes, which are treated as a last resort. Assisted living apartments are a special form of housing that provides access to professional care and assistance, while ensuring the relatively autonomous functioning of the residents. These facilities do not function as total institution and allow seniors to remain independent as long as possible (Mielczarek 2010).

Palliative and hospice care

Palliative and hospice care is dedicated to those with chronic illnesses who finished their causal treatment (most often cancer) and need pain treatment. Its goal is pain reduction and support for patients during the final, terminal stage of their chronic illness. Activities of a multidisciplinary team of specialists and volunteers focus on improving the quality of everyday life, preventing, and alleviating pain and suffering of the patients and their families. The core of the team comprises nurses, doctors, psychologists, and physiotherapists; however, hospice volunteers play a unique role as individuals who work without payment. Aside from young people, a large part of this group consists of older persons.

Referrals for palliative and hospice care are issued by physicians, but patients must give their consent. Palliative and hospice care services are delivered at home or in outpatient and inpatient centers. Palliative outpatient clinics serve individuals who are independent enough to use stationary support temporarily or receive home visits. Outpatient palliative and hospice services include medical advice, medical-nursing advice at the patient's home, psychological consultations, and support for the family. Advice includes patient examination, medicine management, necessary diagnostic tests, ordering and administering treatment procedures, ordering nursing procedures, referring to consultations, referring to a hospital, and issuing the required opinions about the patient's health condition. When the patient is not able to move on their own and is bedridden, he or she may receive complex care at home when there are the right conditions and their family ensures the basic care. In such cases, the hospice team provides support according to the patient's needs. Patients who cannot stay home are referred to stationary hospices. Despite the development of the palliative and hospice care idea, the number of facilities and "hospice beds" is insufficient in Poland. In some regions, especially in rural areas, patients wait too long for support, and the palliative and hospice care system does not provide access to proper quality services to all patients who need them. The list of eligible illnesses is too narrow. According to the Supreme Audit Office, every year,

45 thousand patients die with diagnosed cancer that could qualify them for palliative care (NIK 2019).

Conclusions

The growing number of older citizens and the quickly progressing aging of society mean changes in the functioning of the state as a whole and its structures. These changes include not only the reorganization of social benefits, the healthcare system, and public finances but also generate the necessity to adopt a new approach toward widely understood education. Many of these challenges are being solved on a regular basis. Hospice care seems to be the area where, besides greater accessibility, no major changes are required. Thanks to European funds utilized by non-governmental organizations, the solutions within social policy—even though not perfect—more and more often respect the needs of the elderly. However, there is an urgent need to increase the number of medical professionals, including geriatricians and geriatric nurses, who would work with older patients. Polish healthcare services require major changes in the field of geriatrics. Apart from the typically medical professions, there is a demand for trained specialists to work with seniors in different types of facilities and in different areas: older person caregivers, social workers, or animators and therapists. They should have competencies in coordination and cooperation with patients' families and institutions providing medical services, therapy, care, and activation of seniors. Over the years, a lot has changed in long-term 24-hour senior care. Many nursing homes for the elderly are now model facilities, and the only limitation is finances. However, the most common, culturally and historically established form of care in Poland is home care, and to maintain this positive trend of aging and struggling with illness among loved ones, the family caregivers need support. Today, they are mostly left on their own, which generates many problems for them and lowers the quality of care services they provide.

Health-related, financial, or social issues that older people struggle with often lead to social exclusion. Lack of resources to meet basic needs or lack of social acceptance when they want to create their old age individually results in broken social relationships, failure to participate in culture, and self-exclusion. These negative factors strongly affect the well-being of older people. Qualified professional staff who ensure medical care, activation, psychological, material, or spiritual support in a family environment, local educational and cultural institutions, within the healthcare and social work systems, as well as financing care services, may significantly improve the quality of life of older Polish citizens.

References

Błędowski, P. (2012). Problem niesamodzielności ludzi starych w Polsce, In M. Mossakowska A. Więcek & P. Błędowski (Eds.), *Aspekty medyczne, psychologiczne, socjologiczne i ekonomiczne starzenia się ludzi w Polsce* (pp. 449–466). Poznań: Termedia.

Błędowski P. (2012a), Polityka wobec osób starych – cele i zasady, *Studia BAS*, 2 (30), s. 201–202.

Chabior, A., Fabiś, A., & Wawrzyniak, J. K. (2014). *Starzenie się i staroś ć w perspektywie pracy*.

Czekanowski, P. (2018). Dylematy w badaniach opiekunów rodzinnych ludzi starych. Refleksje socjologa starości i opiekuna. *Pedagogika Społeczna*, 3 (69), 81–90.

Dziennik Ustaw, Nr 210, poz. 2135, Ustawa z dnia 27 sierpnia 2004 r. o świadczeniach opieki zdrowotnej finansowanych ze środków publicznych.

Dziennik Ustaw, Nr 49. poz. 254, Rozporządzenie Ministra Edukacji Narodowej z dnia 21.01.2011 r. Podstawa programowa kształcenia w zawodzie asystent osoby niepełnosprawnej i opiekun medyczny.

Dziennik Ustaw, Nr 64. poz. 593, Ustawa o Pomocy Społecznej z dnia12 marca 2004.

Dziennik Ustaw, Nr 50 poz. 259, Rozporządzenie Ministra Pracy i Polityki Społecznej z dnia 22 lutego 2011 r. w sprawie standardu podstawowych usług świadczonych przez specjalistyczne ośrodki wsparcia dla ofiar przemocy w rodzinie http://isap.sejm.gov.pl/isap.nsf/download.xsp/WDU20110500259/O/D20110259.pdf

Kurpas, D. (2016), Polityka senioralna w Polsce i wybranych krajach Europy oraz USA. In M. Cybulski & E. Krajewska-Kułak (Eds.), *Opieka nad osobami starszymi. Przewodnik dla zespołu terapeutycznego*, (pp. 159–169). Warszawa: PZWL.

Leszczyńska-Rejchert, A. (2006). *Człowiek starszy i jego wspomaganie – w stronę pedagogiki starości*, Olsztyn: Wyd. UWM.

Maćkowicz, J. (2017). *Osoby starsze jako ofiary przemocy domowej. Ujęcie wiktymologiczne*, Krakow: Oficyna Wydawnicza Impuls.

Marynowicz-Hetka, E. (2006). *Cele pracy socjalnej w wymiarze międzynarodowym w: Pedagogika społeczna. Podręcznika akademicki*, Warszawa: Wydawnictwo Naukowe PWN.

Mielczarek, A. (2010). *Człowiek stary w domu pomocy społecznej. Z perspektywy polityki społecznej i pracy socjalnej*. Toruń: Wyd. Edukacyjne Akapit.

Mirewska, E. (2011). Rodzinny dom pomocy jako alternatywa dla domu pomocy społecznej, In Z. Szarota (Ed.), *Staroś ć zależna – opieka i pomoc społeczna*, Biblioteka Gerontologii Społecznej, Tom 3, (pp 81–92). Kraków: Wyd. Akademia Frycza-Modrzewskiego.

Murray C.J. et al. (2012). Disability-Adjusted Life Years (DALYs) for 291 Diseases and Injuries in 21 Regions, 1990–2010: A Systematic Analysis for the Global Burden of Disease Study 2010, *The Lancet*, 380, s. 2197–2223.

Racław, M. (2012). Opiekunowie nieformalni. Krótkookresowa funkcjonalność nieopłacanej pracy, In J. Hrynkiewicz (Ed.), *O sytuacji ludzi starszych*. Warszawa: Rządowa Rada Ludnościowa, s. 71–82.

Szarota Z. (2010). *Starzenie się i staroś ć w wymiarze instytucjonalnego wsparcia*. Kraków: Wyd. Uniwersytetu Pedagogicznego.

Zysnarska M., Wojnicz-Michera I., Taborowska M., Kołecki P., & Maksymiuk T. (2010). Kobieta – opiekun osoby przewlekle chorej – wyznaczniki przeciążenia, *Nowiny Lekarskie*, 79 (5), 386–391.

Zielińska-Więczkowska, H. (2016). Wpływ domów pomocy społecznej i uniwersytetów trzeciego wieku na proces starzenia się społeczeństwa, In M. Cybulski & E. Krajewska-Kułak (Eds.), *Opieka nad osobami starszymi. Przewodnik dla zespołu terapeutycznego*, (pp. 241–253). Warszawa: PZWL.

Online references:

CBOS (2018). Centrum Badań Opini Społecznej, https://cbos.pl/SPISKOM.POL/2018/K_089_18.PDF
CBOS (2012). Centrum Badań Opini Społecznej, https://www.cbos.pl/SPISKOM.POL/2012/K_083_12.PDF
CBOS (2019). Centrum Badań Opini Społecznej, https://www.cbos.pl/SPISKOM.POL/2019/K_116_19.PDF
Eurofamcare (2012). www.uke.de/extern/eurofamcare/documents/deliverables/teusure_web_080215.pdf (dostęp: marzec 2013)
Eurostat (2020). https://ec.europa.eu/eurostat/statistics-explained/index.php?title=Healthy_life_years_statistics
GUS (2015). Główny Urząd Statystyczny https://stat.gov.pl/obszary-tematyczne/warunki-zycia/dochody-wydatki-i-warunki-zycia-ludnosci/wartosci-i-zaufanie-spoleczne-w-polsce-w-2015-r-,21,1.html
GUS (2019). Główny Urząd Statystyczny, https://stat.gov.pl/obszary-tematyczne/warunki-zycia/dochody-wydatki-i-warunki-zycia-ludnosci/emerytury-i-renty-w-2019-r-,32,11.html
Kostka, T. (2019). https://www.prezydent.pl/aktualnosci/
MRPiPS (2020). Sprawozdanie z realizacji Krajowego Programu Przeciwdziałania przemocy w Rodzinie za okres od 1 stycznia do 31 grudnia 2019r. https://www.senat.gov.pl/download/gfx/senat/pl/senatdruki/11047/druk/229.pdf
MUW (2019). Małopolski Urząd Wojewódzki, https://www.malopolska.uw.gov.pl/doc/koszt%20domy%20pomocy%20spo%C5%82ecznej%202019.pdf
NIK (2019). Najwyższa Izba Kontroli, https://www.nik.gov.pl/aktualnosci/opieka-paliatywna-i-hospicyjna.html
NFZ Kraków (2020). https://www.nfz-krakow.pl/
NMCE (2012). Nurse Managed Care for Elderly – NMCE, WP 2. Analysis of Needs. Final Report, http://www.nmce.eu/images/stories/articles/analysis_of_needs_en.pdf
Polsenior 2 (2020). https://konferencjapolsenior2.pl/
Roser M. (2016). Our World in Data, https://ourworldindata.org/grapher/life-expectancy?tab=chart&region=World
Wyzwania rozwojowe (2009). Polska 2030. http://kigeit.org.pl/FTP/PRCIP/Literatura/001_PL_2030_wyzwania_rozwojowe.pdf
Założenia Długofalowej Polityki Senioralnej w Polsce na lata 2014–2020 (2013). https://das.mpips.gov.pl/source/Dlugofalowa%20Polityka%20Senioralna%20w%20Polsce%20na%20lata%202014-2020%20w%20zarysie.pdf

11

CARE FOR THE ELDERLY IN SINGAPORE

Policies, delivery systems, and paradigms

Ho Mun Wai

Introduction

As in many countries, Singapore is facing the challenges of an ageing population. The issue results from a combination of increasing life expectancy and decreasing birth rate.

Challenges

Singapore has one of the highest life expectancies in the world. The average life expectancy at birth has increased from 72.1 in 1980 to 83.6 in 2019. On the other hand, Singapore is one of the countries with the lowest fertility rates in the world. Its Total Fertility Rate (TFR) has decreased from 3.07 in 1970 to 1.14 in 2019. This is substantially lower than the replacement rate of 2.1 (Craig, 1994). Correspondingly, the median age of the resident population has increased from 34 in 2000 to 41.5 in 2020 (Department of Statistics, 2020). Hirschmann (2020) further projected that the median age will rise to 53.4 in 2050. By 2035, it is estimated that around 32 percent of Singaporeans will be aged 65 and above. Meanwhile, the old-age support ratio of residents, computed as the ratio of residents aged 20–64 years for each resident aged 65 years and over, declined from 13.5 in 1970 to 4.3 in 2020. This has exerted tremendous pressure on the economy as well as on families and adult children, who need to support the elderly in the family. This demographic shift is therefore is placing tremendous pressure on Singaporean society as the shrinking workforce struggles to support an ageing population. The challenge is further compounded by the pace at which this is happening (Table 11.1 & Table 11.2, Figure 11.1, Figure 11.2, Figure 11.3).

DOI: 10.4324/9781003528432-13

TABLE 11.1 Life expectancy of Singapore residents (Department of Statistics, 2020)

Year	At Birth			At Age 65 Years		
	Persons	Males	Females	Persons	Males	Females
1980	72.1	69.8	74.7	14.0	12.6	15.4
1990	75.3	73.1	77.6	15.7	14.5	16.9
2000	78.0	76.0	80.0	16.9	15.6	18.1
2010	81.7	79.2	84.0	19.8	18.0	21.4
2019	83.6	81.4	85.7	21.3	19.6	22.9

TABLE 11.2 Singapore's total fertility rate (Department of Statistics, 2020)

Year	Total Life-Births	Resident Life-Births	Crude Birth Rate[a]	Total Fertility Rate[b]	Gross Reproduction Rate[b]	Net Reproduction Rate[b]
1970	45,934	n.a.	22.1	3.07	1.49	1.42
1980	41,217	40,100	17.6	1.82	0.88	0.86
1990	51,142	49,787	18.2	1.83	0.88	0.87
2000	46,997	44,765	13.7	1.60	0.77	0.76
2010	37,967	35,129	9.3	1.15	0.56	0.55
2018	39,039	35,040	8.8	1.14	0.56	0.55
2019	39,279	35,330	8.8	1.14	0.56	0.56

[a] Per 1,000 residents. [b] Per Female.

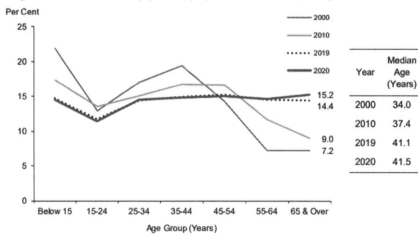

FIGURE 11.1 Age distribution of resident population (Department of Statistics, 2020).

Age pyramid of resident population (Department of Statistics, 2020)

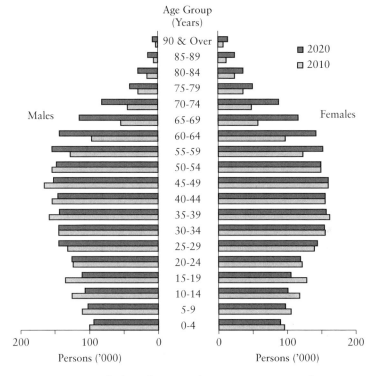

FIGURE 11.2 Age pyramid of resident population (Department of Statistics, 2020).

Resident Old-Age Support Ratio (Department of Statistics, 2020)

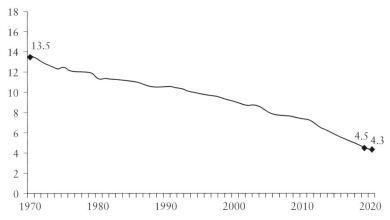

FIGURE 11.3 Resident old-age support ratio (Department of Statistics, 2020).

Singapore's approach to the demographic challenges was laid out since the 1980s (Mehta, 2019). A number of high-level committees were formed to look at issues related to ageing. These included the Committee on the Problems of the Aged (1982), the Advisory Council on the Aged (1988–1989), the National Advisory Council on the Family and the Aged (1989–1998), and the Inter-Ministerial Committee (IMC) on Health and Care for the Elderly (1997–1999).

Whilst not dismissing the need for the traditional solution of providing institutional care with nursing homes, it was also recognised that this itself would not be adequate nor sustainable (Mehta and Vasoo, 2000). For instance, the specific challenges in this regard are not just about cost but also manpower. Singapore is already facing a tight labour market situation and is heavily dependent on the foreign workforce. By 2020, there were already some 1.42 million foreign workers in Singapore. They constitute about a quarter of the country's population of 5.7 million people (Phua and Chew, 2020). The manpower required to staff the further capacity expansion in nursing homes will exert additional pressure to hire even more foreign workers, who constituted about 26% of the total healthcare workforce in 2011 (NPTD, 2012). The fear is that if this trend continues unabated, it will result in undesirable social and political problems.

Hence, community care for the elderly has been identified as an essential approach to address the issue of the ageing population. Indeed, the establishment of a strategic policy direction as such is a fundamental step towards addressing the problem in a sustainable manner. Beyond that, it is also necessary to unpack such a strategic policy direction and delve deeper into the issues of capacity building and resource mobilisation. Eventually, somebody must do the work. Hence, it is also necessary to ensure the delivery system to do the work on the ground is properly set up and implemented.

Framework of analysis

Hence, this chapter will adopt a framework of analysis as shown in Figure 11.4. Beginning with the end in mind, the focal point of the analysis is the overall strategic intent of Singapore towards the issue of the ageing population. Thereafter, the ensuing discussions will encompass an examination of some of the key policies, delivery systems, and paradigms that are needed to steer the implementations towards such strategic intent in the long term. Whilst it is beyond the scope of this chapter to provide comprehensive details of all the programmes that have been put together to support elderly care, the discussions will nonetheless highlight some enabling legislation that have been promulgated, as well as some of the major initiatives that are taken by the public, private, and the non-for-profit sectors towards the desired outcome. Finally, it will conclude with the development of an integrated model

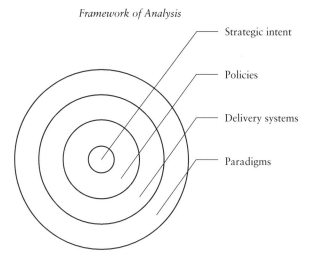

FIGURE 11.4 Framework of analysis.

for sustainable elderly care using the systems thinking methodology, which can be leveraged to support further research with data analytics.

Policies

Population planning

It is recognised that the issues of an ageing population are multi-faceted. Whilst healthcare services to support the elderly are the first thing that comes to mind, there are also non-healthcare issues that need to be addressed. These include housing, financing, and insurance. Hence, policies need to be developed and coordinated from the Whole-Of-Nation perspective. Accordingly, various government agencies have been set up to address the issues holistically.

In 2016, the National Population and Talent Division (NPTD) was set up within the Strategy Group of the Prime Minister's Office. The NPTD is intended to provide Singapore's overall direction and policies with regard to population-related matters at the strategic level. In particular, it comprises the Population Policy & Planning Directorate (PPD), which analyses data, conducts research, reviews, and formulates policies to support Singapore's immediate and longer-term population strategies. These include those that are needed to tackle the challenges of a declining birth rate and an ageing population (NPTD, 2020).

Corresponding with the strategic insights provided by the NPTD, one of Singapore's visions is to be a city that is friendly to seniors. This is being effected at three levels. At the national level, Singapore aims to be a City for All Ages. At the community level, Singapore wants to be a 'Kampong' or a 'Village' for All Ages. At the individual level, Singapore promises Opportunities for All Ages (Teoh and Zainal, 2018). In order to provide guidance at the implementation level, the Action Plan for Successful Ageing was published in 2016 (MOH, 2016). Specifically, it envisaged Singapore to be a good place for people to grow old in. While Singapore is a large modern city, it will retain the 'human touch' and the spirit of a village, where there is inter-generational harmony and understanding. Hence, the city will be designed sensitively and lovingly for seniors to age gracefully among family, friends, and neighbours, leveraging the potential of modern technology.

Healthcare manpower

As part of Singapore's effort to address the long-term challenges with regard to economic development, the government has spearheaded the development of Industry Transformation Maps (ITM) to steer the various sectors towards more sustainable development in the 21st century.

The ITM for the healthcare industry, as shown in Figure 11.5, was launched in 2017. This is a tripartite effort involving the government, labour union, and employee unions to ensure Singapore is equipped with sufficient manpower who are appropriately trained and skilled to sustain the level and quality of care needed to deal with the healthcare needs of the country. At the strategic level, the key challenges faced by the healthcare industry include increasing demand due to overall population growth as well as an ageing population. On the other hand, there are also the challenges of not having sufficient workers to work in the healthcare industry. This, in turn, is due to two problems. First of all, it is difficult to attract young school leavers to join the healthcare profession due to the perceived challenging nature of the work. This is further aggravated by some of the existing workers in the industry leaving the profession as they grow older and find the nature of the work too demanding physically or mentally. Hence, the ITM for the healthcare industry was intentionally developed to steer the healthcare industry so that it may better attract talents, develop them with better skills, and support them with better working conditions so that they can deliver better care for Singaporeans.

The number of healthcare professionals and support care staff in Singapore is projected to increase from 50,000 in 2011 to 91,000 in 2030 (NPTD, 2012). These include those working in primary care such as the polyclinics and General Practitioner (GP) clinics, acute care institutions like hospitals, as well as various set-ups in the community that provide community care. To help the ageing workforce in the healthcare industry and to make the healthcare profession more attractive, the ITM incorporates initiatives to reduce

TABLE 11.3 Healthcare personnel in Singapore in 2009 and 2019 (Department of Statistics, 2020)

Variables	Year 2009	Year 2019	Change (%)
Doctors	8,323	14,279	72
Dentists	1,531	2,475	62
Oral Health Therapists	264	429	63
Pharmacists	1,658	3,408	106
Registered Nurses	19,733	34,609	75
Enrolled Nurses	6,765	8,059	19
Advanced Practice Nurses	37	267	622
Optometrists and Opticians	2,324	2,636	13
Physiotherapists	NA	2,020	
Speech Therapists	NA	686	
TCM Physicians	2,203	3,045	38
Acupuncturists	218	259	19

TCM = Traditional Chinese Medicine

the physical strain of healthcare jobs. This will entail job redesign as well as the use of more ergonomic equipment like bed transporters to reduce physical exertions. In order to encourage more Singaporeans of all ages to join the healthcare sector, especially nursing, the government has also launched nursing scholarships and provided incentives to help more mid-career professionals, managers, executives, and technicians (PMETs) to consider nursing as their second career. It has also expanded and set up new programmes in universities, polytechnics, and the Institute of Technical Education (ITE) to train allied health professionals and other workers to work in clinical as well as non-clinical roles in the healthcare industry. These include programmes in nursing, diagnostic radiography, physiotherapy, occupational therapy, dietetics and nutrition, healthcare promotion, health services management, integrated care management, etc. Hence, in addition to increasing the healthcare workforce, the ITM for the healthcare industry will also support ongoing shifts in the healthcare system towards health promotion, moving care more into the community instead of acute hospitals, and having cost-effective care (Table 11.3).

Enabling legislations

The Chinese word 'XIAO' means filial piety. This notion is central not only to the Chinese but also to many cultures in Asia. 'XIAO' calls for adult children to take care of their aging parents not only in terms of their physical lives but also their mental needs and general well-being. Hence, traditionally,

Healthcare Industry Transformation Map (Ng, 2017)

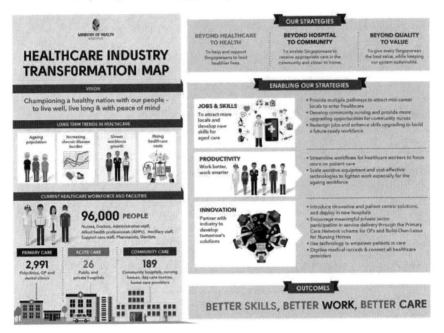

FIGURE 11.5 Healthcare industry transformation map (Ng, 2018).

the societal norm is that adult children and their young families will live in the same household as their ageing parents. This will allow the younger members of the household to care for the older ones.

However, changing socio-economic configurations in recent years have created challenges for such co-residence between the younger and the older generations. As a result, the feasibility of relying upon the family to care for the elderly in the household has become more challenging. Whilst it has been common for adult children in Singapore to look after their aged parents, financial realities are, however, making it more difficult for them to do so. Hence, governments in many countries, including Singapore and those in Asia that embrace the Confucian heritage of filial piety, have begun to take a more proactive role in choreographing fresh paradigms to provide care for the elderly. In essence, this entails an emerging "triadic relationship" amongst the government, family, and individual in sharing such responsibility.

That shift has been visible in Singapore for many years. A key milestone occurred in 1995, when the Government passed a Maintenance of Parents Act (Maintenance of Parents Act, 1995). This legislature provides for elderly or needy parents, who are unable to maintain themselves adequately, with a legal recourse to seek maintenance from their children, who are capable of supporting them but are not doing so. Specifically, it allows anyone 60 years or older living in Singapore and who is unable to maintain himself to apply for an order for his children to pay him a monthly allowance.

Although the Maintenance of Parents Act is well-intentioned, it was not without controversy. Indeed, when the legislation was first introduced, it generated some heated debate which polarised society. This was not surprising, as a key criticism of it was that the legislation subsumed the Asian value of filial piety into a legalistic Western framework. There was also criticism that it was unnecessary, as the number of parents being neglected by their children was relatively small. There was also feedback that the root cause of a lot of the issues was not the adult children, but the aged parents who were not exhibiting responsible behaviours, such as being addicted to gambling or involved in extramarital affairs (Tan 2015). Notwithstanding, the number of elderly Singaporeans who have resorted to the Act cannot be neglected, albeit small.

The Mental Capacity Act is another piece of legislature geared towards the protection of the well-being of the elderly. This law, which was passed by Parliament in 2008 and came into effect in 2010, enables individuals to make a Lasting Power of Attorney to appoint someone they trust to make decisions on their behalf in case they lose mental capacity. This law is becoming more and more useful in light of the increasing incidence of dementia cases (Ng, Ang, and Kandiah, 2015). More recently, in 2018, the Vulnerable Adults Act also came into effect. While not limiting to seniors, this law enables the State to intervene more effectively to protect vulnerable persons including seniors and persons with disabilities who are suffering or at risk of harm due to abuse, neglect, or self-neglect (MSF, 2020).

Medical financing and insurance

Working Singaporeans have to contribute to their Central Provident Fund (CPF) through the compulsory withdrawal of a part of their monthly income. There are three components in each of their CPF accounts. The Ordinary Account (OA) is dedicated primarily to housing and tertiary education of their children. The Special Account (SA) serves primarily as a form of forced savings for retirement. The Medisave Account (MA) is dedicated solely to helping individuals pay for their medical and hospitalisation expenses, which are already subsidised if these services are received at public hospitals.

However, the Medisave itself may not be sufficient to meet all the medical expenses of a person for his or her lifetime. This is especially so if one is saddled with critical illnesses for a prolonged period. Hence, the government has set up a compulsory medical insurance programme called the MediShield Life. In essence, this is a low-cost medical insurance initiative to help Singaporeans pay for the more substantive hospitalisation bills. The premiums for the MediShield Life can be paid from their Medisave.

In addition, Medisave has been expanded for more outpatient uses such as long-term treatment for chronic illnesses, including cancer, diabetes, and hypertension. It can also be used to pay for preventive health measures such as health screenings and vaccinations for newborns. The needs for outpatient treatments for such conditions are greater in old age when one is more likely to have more health problems and incur higher medical expenses, especially towards the end of life.

Through Medisave and Medishield Life, Singapore's government ensures affordable, dependable, and accessible healthcare for the masses. Even then, the need for more support is still keenly felt at the personal level. It is estimated that from 2030, long-term care will cost $22,950 a year or about $1,900 a month in Singapore. This is about 48% of the average income of each working member of the household, which was $3,940 in 2018. Based on an estimate done in 2017, Singaporeans live on average to 82 years old, with 8 of those years experiencing ill health. Furthermore, unhealthy years are not exclusive only to seniors or the elderly. A relatively younger person may also experience years of ill health requiring long-term care after suffering from accidents such as a motor accident or a serious illness such as a stroke.

Hence, the question of who will pay for the healthcare costs when a person is old and needs medical care is a critical issue. Whilst the government may provide such services at a subsidised level or even free of charge, such public funding will still need to be recovered by the government through fiscal measures. Fundamentally, these or at least a part of these expenses will have to be paid for from the savings of the elderly person who needs the care. If he or she is not able to pay for it, such long-term care costs may eventually end up being paid for by someone else, usually an immediate family member. In addition to the direct costs of nursing, medical, and therapy-related expenses, the caregiver from the family may also have to stop working or reduce working hours and hence experience some loss of income. These may lead to tension and disputes within the family. The need for the introduction of the Maintenance of Parents Act, as discussed earlier, is a case in point.

In order to mitigate the problem, the government set up a long-term care insurance in the form of ElderShield in 2002. Essentially, it provides funding support when a person loses their independence due to ageing and the deterioration of health, such as stroke, heart attack, or severe dementia. Specifically, the scheme provides a payout of $400 monthly for 6 years when severe disability is determined. It was, however, found that the quantum of the payout and the limit to the number of years of payout made the scheme rather impractical and unattractive. As part of the continuous process of improvement, ElderShield was enhanced in 2020 to become CareShield Life

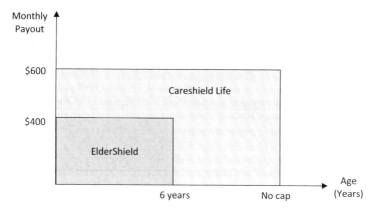

FIGURE 11.6 Comparison of Eldershield and Careshield Life.

(Ang, 2020). As shown in Figure 11.6, CareShield Life provides a higher payout and for as long as the person live.

Finally, there is also a Medifund set up in 1993. Essentially, Medifund is a government endowment fund to ensure no Singaporean is denied good basic medical care due to financial reasons. It is a safety net for needy patients who still face financial difficulties with their remaining medical bills after receiving government subsidies and drawing on other means of assistance such as MediShield Life, private Integrated Shield Plans, MediSave, and cash. In 2007, Medifund Silver was launched as an extension of Medifund to deliver targeted assistance to needy elderly Singaporean patients (MOH, 2016).

Housing

In order to reduce the dependency on nursing homes, one of the measures is to encourage Singaporeans to live with and take care of the elderly at home. However, for this to be feasible, one has to examine if the type and design of housing for the population are conducive for this to happen. The study of this issue has to begin with an understanding of the overall housing situation in Singapore.

Singapore is a city-state of some 5.8 million people, including foreign workers. To house so many people within a small island of only 700 square kilometres, housing in Singapore is predominantly in the form of high-rise apartments.

The government takes an active role in the provision of housing in Singapore. About 80% of the population lives in apartments or flats built by the Housing and Development Board (HDB). The remaining 20% consists of the 20% housing that includes condominiums and landed properties built by private developers. The sizes of the bulk of HDB flats range from about

70 sqm to 110 sqm and comprise two to three bedrooms. They are designed primarily to cater to the nuclear family of a pair of parents with an average of two children. As can be seen, if a family wants to accommodate a pair of grandparents to live with them as well, the space available in the flat may become too little for comfort (Figure 11.7).

Hence, HDB is called upon to play an indirect but significant role in enhancing the robustness of the overall approach for the care of the elderly in Singapore. The implementation levers that HDB pursued include designing flats that are conducive for housing three generations of the extended family within the same unit and providing incentives for people to purchase such flats.

In this regard, the HDB has introduced 3Gen flats since 2013 that are specifically designed for multi-generation families who wish to live together, including the parents, the children, and the grandparents (Koo, 2020). The area of these flats is typically about 115 sqm, which is about 5 to 10 percent larger than the typical flats. The defining feature of 3Gen flats is that there are four bedrooms including two that have attached bathrooms. Essentially, 3Gen flats have two master bedrooms for the married couple and one set of grandparents. There was also an older design of the multigenerational flats offered in the 1980s which comprised a flat with an adjoining studio

FIGURE 11.7 Public housing development by the Housing and Development Board (HDB) in Singapore (HDB, 2020).

apartment that had a separate entrance. This allowed the nuclear family and the aged parents to live in the 'same' flat while each of them could enjoy the privacy of having their respective entrances.

Since 2012, the HDB has also introduced the Enhancement for Active Seniors (EASE) programme. This is targeted at helping families to make the home safer for the elderly by incorporating features to minimise the risks of falls at home. Essentially, the EASE programme provides subsidies for home modifications such as the provision of slip-resistant treatment to floor tiles as well as grab bars in the bathrooms or toilets. It also supports the provision of ramps to facilitate wheelchair access to the flats (Figure 11.8).

In order to incentivise young couples to live with their parents and to take care of them, couples who apply for 3Gen flats with their parent(s) are eligible for the Enhanced Housing Grant (EHG) in addition to the usual housing grants for first-time home buyers. Thus, with such 3Gen flats, grandparents can live with their children and grandchildren for as long as possible, and defer the need to progress to a nursing home for care for as long as possible.

For those young families who are unable to or do not want to buy a 3Gen flat, or find it not feasible to live with their aged parents in the same household, they can instead buy a flat that is near to their parents' flat. This way, the adult children can send their young children to the grandparents' home nearby for babysitting while they go to work. On the other hand, when the grandparents get older, it is also more convenient for the adult children to take care of the grandparents, such as being able to help the elderly parents with doctor's visits and other needs. In order to encourage Singaporeans to

FIGURE 11.8   Layout of a 3Gen flat (HDB, 2020).

adopt this approach and maintain a robust intergenerational support system, the HDB also offers the Proximity Housing Grant (PHG) which provides substantive monetary incentives if the distance between the HDB flat of the grandparents and adult children is within 4 km from one another.

In 2017, the concept for integrated housing that is intentionally designed to be elderly-friendly reached a new milestone in the form of Kampung Admiralty. The word 'Kampung' in the Malay language means 'village'. Located in the new town of Admiralty, Kampung Admiralty is the first-of-its-kind development in Singapore which intentionally integrates housing for the elderly with a wide range of social, healthcare, communal, commercial, and retail facilities. The project involved the collaboration of various government agencies including the HDB, the Ministry of Health (MOH), Yishun Health Campus (YHC), National Environment Agency (NEA), National Parks Board (NParks), Land Transport Authority (LTA), and Early Childhood Development Agency (ECDA). Some of the key design principles adopted in Kampung Admiralty that were intentionally geared towards making it elderly-friendly include (Yap, 2019):

- Provide scale to create opportunities for collaboration and co-programming, and amenities to facilitate seniors leading independent and active lifestyles.
- Integrate healthcare facilities within the same development so that medical staff and volunteers can actively work with senior residents, particularly on chronic disease management; this also eases the patient load at hospitals.
- Co-locate child care with senior care facilities to promote intergenerational bonding.
- Be barrier-free and wheelchair-friendly.
- Design social communal spaces, such as a community park, playground, and fitness corner that cater to the young and old to promote interaction of all ages.

Building on the success of Admiralty Village, HDB has continued to innovate with further housing solutions that support the independent living of the elderly for as long as possible. In 2021, a new type of public housing with senior-friendly design features and subscription to care services will be launched (Lin, 2020). These flats, known as Community Care Apartments, have to be bought with a compulsory subscription to care packages, which include access to 24-hour emergency monitoring and response, basic health checks, and simple home fixes. In addition, residents may also opt for extra care services at additional costs, including personal home care, medical transport, meal delivery, laundry, and housekeeping.

Delivery system

The delivery system of healthcare services for the elderly is operated both by the public sector, the Not-for-Profit sector, as well as the private sector. Specifically, the Not-for-Profit sector refers to facilities that are run by the Voluntary Welfare Organisations (VWO). The range of services includes the entire spectrum, including acute hospitals, residential long-term care facilities, non-residential long-term care facilities, primary care facilities, dental clinics, and pharmacies. The public sector however focuses on operating hospitals that provide acute care and transition care. It also provides subventions to some nursing homes that are operated by the Not-for-Profit sector.

Acute hospitals and residential long-term care facilities

As can be seen from Table 11.1, there has been a substantive increase in the capacity of the overall delivery system for healthcare services in Singapore between 2009 and 2019. For example, the number of acute hospitals has increased by 36%. While the bulk of this was contributed by the public sector, the private sector has also increased its investment in this space. In addition to supplementing the capacity of the public hospitals, this will also provide more choices to consumers in terms of cost and the range of services offered, as summarised in Table 11.4 and Table 11.5 (Evlanova, 2020).

TABLE 11.4 Indicative cost (for Singapore citizen after subsidies) of staying at public acute hospitals subsidised by the government (Evlanova, 2020)

Acute Hospital (for SG Citizen)	Ward C	Ward B2	Ward B1	Ward A
Alexandra Hospital	$33	$72	$224.70	$457
Changi General Hospital	$41	$80	$251	$464
Khoo Teck Puat Hospital	$35	$81	$215	$430
KK Women's and Children's Hospital	$35	$179	$273.95	$533.95
National University Hospital	$41	$75	$224.70	$527.51
Ng Teng Fong General Hospital	$38	$77	$235	$469
Sengkang General	$41	$80	$252	$467
Singapore General Hospital	$35	$79	$251.45	$466.52
Tan Tock Seng Hospital	$43	$77–$87	$250	$303–$438

TABLE 11.5 Indicative cost of staying at private acute hospitals (Evlanova, 2020)

Ward Type	Cost per Day	No. Of Beds
4-Bedded	$240–$281	4
2-Bedded	$305–$345.61	2
Single Room	$642–$798	1
Deluxe Room	$708–$1,398	1
Low-End Suite	$808–$2,618	1
High-End Suite	$3,304–$9,838	1

Acute hospitals provide acute care to patients who need immediate assistance for severe illnesses, medical conditions, and post-surgery recovery. Community hospitals provide medical services for patients who require a short period of continuation of care, usually after they are discharged from acute hospitals (Figure 11.9). Hence, community hospitals are the next step for patients who are discharged from acute hospitals to carry on with medical, rehabilitation care, sub-acute care, and palliative care. Typically, acute and community hospitals work closely together to optimise the use of resources while maintaining a seamless quality care. In recognition of the benefits of having such differentiated and yet interconnected roles of the acute and community hospitals, the government has invested heavily in enhancing the number of community hospitals by 50% between 2009 and 2019, as shown in Table 11.6.

Beyond community hospitals, elderly individuals who still need residential long-term care may consider nursing homes where they can receive assistance in daily life activities, such as using the toilet, showering, eating, and walking. Usually, there will be professional nursing care that will address medical needs ranging from changing urine catheter to dressing wounds, as well as exercises and games with other elderly residents. For the elderly who are suffering from mental conditions such as dementia or psychiatric disorders, nursing homes can be safe havens where someone will be on constant lookout for them, and they can participate in cognitive stimulation programmes and activities to slow down the loss of mental capacity.

The general cost for nursing homes is around $1,200 to $3,500 a month before government subsidy, which ranges from 10% to 75%. This cost varies based on the number of people sharing a bedroom and the level of care required. As shown in Table 11.7, the cost of staying in nursing homes is very high. The government, however, has provided some subsidy for eligible families to defray the cost as shown in Table 11.8.

TABLE 11.6 Healthcare establishments in Singapore (MOH, 2020)

	2009	2019	Change (%)
Hospitals			
Acute Hospitals	14	19	36
Public	7	10	43
Not-for-Profit	1	1	0
Private	6	8	33
Psychiatric Hospitals	1	1	0
Public	1	1	0
Not-for-Profit			
Private			
Community Hospitals	6	9	50
Public		5	
Not-for-Profit	5	4	-20
Private	1		
Residential Long-Term Care Facilities			
Nursing Homes	60	77	28
Public		23	
Not-for-Profit	30	23	-23
Private	30	31	3
Inpatient Hospices	2	2	0
Public			
Not-for-Profit	2	2	0
Private			
Non-Residential Long-Term Care Facilities			
Centre-based Care Facilities5	35	143	309
Home Care Providers6	9	24	167
Home Palliative Care Providers7	5	9	80
Primary Care Facilities			
Public - Polyclinics	18	20	11
Private - General Practitioner Clinics	1628	2304	42
Dental Clinics			
Public (Total)	240	246	3
Polyclinic Dental Clinics	9	10	11
Hospital/Institution Dental Clinics 8	5	8	60
School Dental Clinics	226	228	1
Private	582	851	46
Pharmacies	211	256	21
Public	58	67	16
Private	153	189	24

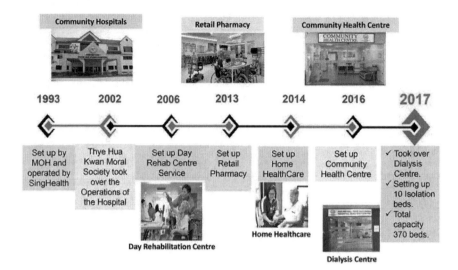

FIGURE 11.9 Ang Mo Kio Thye Hua Kwan Hospital located at the Yio Chu Kang Constituency is a community hospital (AMKH, 2020). It provides a comprehensive range of services including residential step-down care, palliative care, day care, dialysis services, etc.

TABLE 11.7 Indicative cost of nursing homes in Singapore (Moneysmart, 2019)

Nursing homes	Price range (SGD)/month
VWO Nursing Homes under MOH Subsidy	
Grace Lodge	(Most of the nursing homes in this
All Saints Home (certain branches)	category will cost an estimated
Jamiyah Nursing Home	price range of $700 – 1,600 after
Lion's Home for the Elders	subsidy. The amount of the subsidy
Ren Ci Nursing Home	depends on the means test.)
Assisi Hospice	$8,850 (before subsidy)
Kwong Wai Shiu Hospital	$1,460–$2,289 (before subsidy)
St. Andrew's Nursing Home	$1,300–$2,300 (before subsidy)
NTUC Health Nursing Home	$2,000–$3,500 (before subsidy)
Apex Harmony Lodge	$3,150–$3,400 (before subsidy)
VWO Nursing Homes not under MOH Subsidy	
All Saints Home (certain branches)	$1,400–$2,800
Private Nursing Homes under MOH Subsidy	
Econ Medicare Centre and Nursing Home (certain branches)	$1,200–$4,500 (before subsidy)
Orange Valley Nursing Home (certain branches)	$1,200–$4,500 (before subsidy)
Private Nursing Homes not under MOH Subsidy	
Econ Medicare Centre and Nursing Home (certain branches)	$1,200–$4,500
Orange Valley Nursing Home (certain branches)	$1,200–$4,500

TABLE 11.8 Subsidy for staying in nursing home (Moneysmart, 2019)

Household Per Capita Monthly Income	Subsidy Rate (%)	
	Singapore Citizens	Permanent Residents
$700 and below	75	50
$701 to $1,100	60	40
$1,101 to $1,800	50	30
$1,801 to $2,600	40	20
$2,601 to $3,100	20	10
$3,101 and above	0	0

Community healthcare services for the elderly

While the number of nursing homes has increased by 28% to meet the increasing demand, it is apparent that even with subsidies, not every Singaporean will be able to afford them. On the other hand, some elderly may prefer to live in a familiar environment with their family members and friends. While the elderly stay in their own home, they can still access support for their care through community healthcare services, which may be provided at centres in the vicinity of their homes during the day.

Indeed, during the period from 2009 to 2019, there has been an increase in the capacity for such non-residential long-term care facilities. Specifically, Centre-based Care Facilities have increased by 309%; Home Care Providers and Home Palliative Care Providers have increased by 167% and 80%, respectively. The growth in such non-residential long-term care facilities reflects the commitment of the government to step up the capacity for community care to complement institutional care.

In home-based care, healthcare services are provided within the homes of older persons. They include medical, nursing, and palliative care services. Basically, care receivers will enrol in programmes whereby the organisations which provide such care will arrange for professional care service officers to visit them and deliver the care services at their homes periodically. Such services can be organised by the Agency for Integrated Care (AIC), as will be elaborated later.

In Centre-based care, healthcare services are provided within a centre located within the residential neighbourhoods. The elderly will visit these centres during the day, usually on a regular basis, but will go back to their own homes in the evenings to sleep. These centres include Day Rehabilitation Centres, Dementia Day Care Centres, Psychiatric Day Care Centres, and Rehabilitation Homes.

Other than Day Care Centres, another form of Community Care is the Senior Activity Centres (SACs). The SACs help seniors age with dignity and grace. There are more than 50 Senior Activity Centres located all over Singapore. These are located at most rental blocks or studio apartments, targeting those living alone. Operated by Voluntary Welfare Organisations (VWOs) or commercial operators, senior citizens have the chance to make new friends and partake in social activities such as lunch treats, singing, arts and crafts, and outings; there are also be services such as health checks and talks at these centres. The centres also provide lunch and tea breaks. For those who are homebound, there are volunteers who assist to deliver meals to their homes. With such activities and care given to the elderly, it gives families peace of mind while they are at work.

Some of these centres also offer caregiver training for caregivers, including foreign domestic workers.

Informal caregiving

Other than day care centres, a portion of Singaporeans care for the elderly themselves. This is known as informal caregiving.

Within the family, it is not uncommon for daughters and daughters-in-law to play the relatively more major roles in taking care of the elderly at home, usually unpaid. If the aged parents have more children, then the burden of taking care of the older parents can be shared among them. However, in society today, economic necessity and changing family structures mean more women are in employment. Hence, they will not be able to stay at home to care for aged parents or parents-in-law. As shown in Figure 11.10, female participation in the workforce in Singapore has increased from 50.2% in 2000 to 61.2% in 2020. This trend directly contradicts efforts to reduce the need for nursing homes as a solution for elderly care.

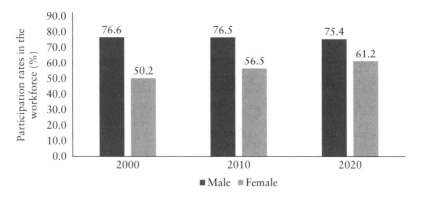

FIGURE 11.10 Participation rates of residents in the workforce (Department of Statistics, 2020). Residents refer to Singapore citizens and permanent residents.

Hence, many families resort to hiring Foreign Domestic Workers (FDW) to take care of the elderly at home and to assist with household chores. These workers help to reduce the stress of the caregivers and also provide emotional support. However, this can be rather costly, as the salary cum foreign workers' levy can come up to some $1500 a month. In order to mitigate the problem, eligible families, such as where the care is for an elderly member of the family who is 67 years old or older, can apply for a concessionary levy of $60 instead of the normal $300 per month. Furthermore, if the elderly person is unable to perform three or more Activities of Daily Living (ADLs), the family may also apply for the Home Caregiving Grant (HCG), which gives them a monthly grant of $200 to defray the expenses of hiring of an FDW to help care for their frail elderly (AIC, 2020).

National care integrator

As can be observed from the discussions earlier, while the importance of acute and residential long-term care cannot be over emphasised, the strategic intent is to enhance the capacity of elderly care in the community. Over the years, many organisations in the public and not-for-profit sectors have been set up to deliver various forms of services and support towards the overall strategic intent. Whilst there is no shortage of help, it is also important that these myriad forms of assistance are stitched together in a seamless manner such that all those who need them are able to access them. Since 1992, the Ministry of Health (MOH) has already set up the Care Liaison Services (CLS) to coordinate and facilitate the placement of the elderly sick in nursing homes and chronic sick units. In 2001, the CLS expanded its role to become the Integrated Care Services (ICS). Essentially, the ICS planned and facilitated the transition of patients from hospitals to the community. In 2008, the ICS was renamed the Agency for Integrated Care (AIC). A year later, the AIC was established as an independent corporate entity under MOH Holdings and assumed the role of National Care Integrator.

In 2018, AIC was designated the single agency to coordinate the delivery of aged care services and to enhance service development and capability-building across both the health and social domains. As more assistance schemes were being rolled out to support seniors in various ways, it was also recognised that support is needed to help them understand how they can benefit from such schemes and how they can access them. Hence, the Silver Generation Office (SGO) was set up to honour, assure, and empower the seniors through personalised outreach and support to help them age gracefully. It does this by deploying Silver Generation (SG) Ambassadors to reach out to the seniors. Some 3,000 SG Ambassadors are trained with information and knowledge of senior-related policies and schemes. They are also equipped with soft skills to communicate and connect with the seniors. Thus, the SG

Ambassadors will share information with them and help them make applications for the various government schemes (e.g., Pioneer Generation Package, Merdeka Generation Package, MediShield Life, and eldercare schemes) and connect them to health services and activities in the community.

Today, AIC continues in what it is tasked and seeks to create a vibrant care community enabling Singaporeans to live well and age gracefully. It works closely with Community Care partners in supporting them in service development and manpower-capability building to raise the quality of care and bring care support closer to those in need.

Capability development

As discussed earlier, the Not-for-Profit sector plays a major role in the delivery system for services to support seniors. Such Voluntary Welfare Organisations (VWO) offer the full range of services, from residential long-term care facilities like nursing homes to Day-Care Centres and Senior Activities Centres.

Whilst these VWOs are independent organisations registered under the Registry of Societies, the government provides them with various support for their capability development. Such a support system is organised centrally under the National Council of Social Service (NCSS), which is umbrella body for some 450 member social service agencies in Singapore.

Specifically, the mission of NCSS is to provide leadership and direction in social services, to enhance the capabilities of social service agencies, and to provide strategic partnerships for social services. It does this by spearheading the following:

Advocacy and research: The NCSS conducts research to make sense of social issues and advocates the importance of enabling applied research in developing impactful solutions.

Capability and capacity building: NCSS helps VWOs innovate and enhance productivity and human resource practices. It also scaffolds them to improve their customer service through the NCSS Service Standard Framework.

Corporate engagement: NCSS engages corporate donors with the causes of the various VWOs so that they can develop long-term and sustainable corporate partnerships to support them with money, time, people, or skills.

Innovation and Productivity: Productivity projects are initiatives designed to help VWOs improve organisational capabilities and productivity through technology and innovation. Some of these initiatives include Tech Booster and Back-to-Basics that will offer ready technologies and innovative solutions at attractive subsidies to alleviate manpower challenges in the sector.

Membership and Funding: NCSS engages and support the VWOs by providing them with funding based on their organisational needs and stage of development.

Social Service Planning and Development: There are six areas of focus in NCSS's work, including eldercare services. The other five include disability services; children, youth and family services; mental health services; standards and impact; and integrated service planning.

New paradigms

The issue of care for the elderly in Singapore has been discussed from the perspective of policies and delivery systems that are designed to deliver the services. As can be seen, the approaches involved are multi-prong and multi-tier. In the early days, many of these measures were driven by reactive forces to address healthcare, economic, and social problems. But, to ensure sustainability and that new aspirations of the population are met, new paradigms are needed. Whilst it is not possible to prevent ageing, measures can be taken to delay the onset of the negative effects of ageing for as long as possible. In other words, people must be made to stay healthy physically and mentally for as long as possible. They can do so through lifestyle adjustments in terms of diet and engagement in physical and recreational activities.

In recognition of the importance of moving healthcare upstream to place emphasis on prevention in addition to acute care, the Health Promotion Board (HPB) was established in 2001 as a government statutory board to promote healthy living in Singapore. It seeks to provide evidence-based health information that empowers the Singapore public with knowledge and skills to take ownership of their health and live healthy lifestyles. HPB achieves this through its wide range of health promotion and disease prevention programmes that are encapsulated in its Healthy Living Master Plan (HPB, 2014). These include health and dental services for school children, workplace health programmes, and physical activity programmes, to name a few.

But, a healthy lifestyle is more than eating well, medical check-ups, and disease control. People must also engage in sports and exercises to stay healthy both physically and mentally. There are two statutory boards within the Ministry of Culture, Community and Youth working in these areas. Sport Singapore's (SportSG) core purpose is to inspire the Singapore spirit and transform Singapore through sport. Beyond competitive sport, SportSG also seeks to reach out to all ages of the community to embrace a sporting lifestyle. This is encapsulated in its Vision 2030, which is Singapore's sports master plan (SportSG, 2020). SportSG uses sport to create greater sporting opportunities and access, more inclusivity and integration, as well as broader development of capabilities. Working alongside SportSG is the Peoples'

Association (PA), whose charter is to foster racial harmony and social cohesion. Through its Senior Citizens' Executive Committees (SCECs), the PA supports a wide array of activities and courses to enrich the life experiences of senior citizens. These are implemented through its network of more than 100 Community Clubs, 550 Residents' Committees, and 100 Neighbourhood Committees set up at every corner of Singapore (PA, 2020). For example, in the Yio Chu Kang Constituency, there are sports, dance, or other communal activities that are specially designed to help participants stay fit and healthy. Specifically, there is an Active Ageing Committee (AAC) that organises programmes like the Silver Generation Times (SG Times) that organises outings for seniors to help them stay healthy and engaged. There are also courses for lifelong learning, such as classes for learning new languages, improving one's cooking, and even using computers and social media. With new skills acquired, some seniors may even rejoin the workforce and be engaged in fulfilling roles that are more befitting to their stage of life. In this regard, there are Not-for-Profit VWOs like the Centre For Seniors (CFS), which was set up in 2006 to promote the total well-being of older persons in Singapore in terms of their vocational, financial, and psychosocial health (Silverjobs, 2020). They achieve this outcome by helping them explore work in various sectors for meaningful retirement. Correspondingly, the government also encourages employers to provide more employment opportunities for seniors by extending the retirement age and creating opportunities for reemployment or part-time work. Financial incentives like the Senior Worker Early Adopter Grant (SWEAG) and Part-Time Re-Employment Grant (PTRG) are provided by Workforce Singapore (WSG) to support employers in such initiatives. This is mutually beneficial to the employers and the older workers as the employers will be able to tap into their rich experience and skillsets.

In summary, the journey of Singapore in recognising and tackling the issue of the ageing population was not a static one. Indeed, it had to keep redefining and innovating with new ideas and solutions, partly necessitated by the pace of demographic changes, which can be crystallised in the following paradigm shifts:

- Moving beyond treating the sick to preventive medicine, i.e., helping people to stay healthy.
- Moving from the provision of care driven by the clinical perspective to care integration, so that the elderly will receive seamless care through the integrated delivery system.
- Moving beyond the provision of facilities for institutional care to developing innovative housing solutions that are elderly-friendly.
- Going beyond physical care by leveraging on technology such as telehealth to improve access to healthcare.

- Redesign jobs and create micro jobs so that the elderly can stay meaningfully engaged and secure their mental well-being.

More recently, the strategy of preventive health received a further boost with the launch of the Healthier SG initiative in 2023. A particular highlight of Healthier SG is that it seeks to provide every Singaporean with a dedicated family doctor who will support them in their health needs throughout their lives. This programme is also inclusive from the supply side, whereby doctors from both public institutions and private practices are involved to work collaboratively in this overarching national framework (HealthierSG, 2023).

Moving forward, Singapore will have to continue to monitor and review the outcome of the various policies and programmes and make appropriate adjustments as may be necessary. An Integrated Model for Policy Development for Elderly Care (IMPDEC) developed on the basis of the systems thinking methodology is proposed to support such further analysis (Forrester, 1999). As shown in Figure 11.11, the causal loop S_1 shows that a direct response to the increasing demand for healthcare services for the elderly is being met by the supply of more healthcare services. While these are essential, they may create an unintended side effect where the availability of such services at affordable prices may lead to even more demand for such services, a phenomenon anticipated in Say's Law (Sowell, 2015) as indicated in causal loop S_3 in Figure 11.11. As shown in Table 11.9, the per capita expenditure on healthcare by the government has more than trebled from $498 in 2007 to $1744 in 2017. Few countries can sustain such continuous increases in healthcare costs. The debates in the National Health Service (NHS) in the United Kingdom and the Affordable Care Act in the United States are two examples that other countries can learn from (West, 2020). Furthermore, as resources are finite, the more resources drawn for supporting healthcare services will result in fewer resources available for other public services, as shown in causal loop S_4 and O_1 respectively in Figure 11.11. Hence, instead of overly relying on such "symptomatic

TABLE 11.9 Government expenditure on healthcare in Singapore (Department of Statistics, 2020)

Variables	2007	2017	Increase (%)
Per Capita Government Health Expenditure ($)	498	1,744	350
Government Health Expenditure (Million $)	2,283.2	9,764.3	428

response", more pre-emptive measures, as informed by the new paradigms, may need to be prioritised to ensure sustainability and holistic treatment of the issues. This is shown in the balancing loops S_2 and O_2 in Figure 11.11, respectively.

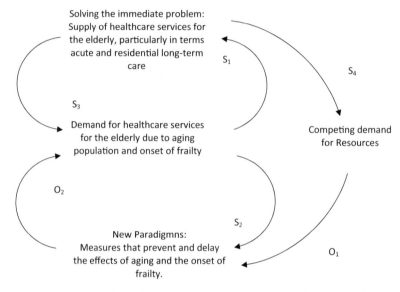

FIGURE 11.11 Integrated model for policy development for the care of the elderly.

References

AIC. (2020). Home Caregiving Grant. Retrieved from https://www.aic.sg/financial-assistance/home-caregiving-grant

AMKH. (2020). Retrieved from https://www.amkh.org.sg

Ang, H. M. (2020). CareShield Life and MediSave Care to Launch in October. *Channel News Asia*, 28 August 2020. Retrieved from https://www.channelnewsasia.com/news/singapore/careshield-life-medisave-care-launch-october-13062186

Craig, J. (1994). Replacement Level Fertility and Future Population Growth. *Population Trends*, 20–22.

Department of Statistics. (2020). Retrieved from https://www.Department of Statistics.gov.sg/

EASE. (2020). Enhancement for Active Seniors. Retrieved from https://www.hdb.gov.sg/residential/living-in-an-hdb-flat/for-our-seniors/ease

Evlanova, A. (2020). Guide to Finding the Best Hospital in Singapore. Retrieved from https://www.valuechampion.sg/guide-finding-best-hospital-singapore

Forrester, J. W. (1999). *System dynamics: The foundation under systems thinking*. Sloan School of Management. Massachusetts Institute of Technology, 10.

HDB. (2020). Types of Flats. Retrieved from https://www.hdb.gov.sg/cs/infoweb/residential/buying-a-flat/resale/getting-started/types-of-flats

HealthierSG (2023). Retrieved from https://www.healthiersg.gov.sg/about/what-is-healthier-sg/

Hirschmann, R. (2020). Aging Population of Singapore – Statistics & Facts. Retrieved from https://www.statista.com/topics/5821/ageing-population-of-singapore/#:~:text=Singapore%20is%20currently%20facing%20an,only%200.83%20children%20per%20woman.

HPB. (2014). One in Two Singaporeans to Have Access to At Least Three Healthier Options by 2020. Retrieved from https://www.hpb.gov.sg/article/one-in-two-singaporeans-to-have-access-to-at-least-three-healthier-options-by-2020

Koo, A. (2020). Living under One Roof With A 3Gen HDB Flat. Retrieved from https://dollarsandsense.sg/guide-buying-3gen-hdb-flat-singapore/

Lin, C. (2020). New Flats for the Elderly to Be Launched in February BTO Exercise, with Subscription to Care Services. Retrieved from https://www.channelnewsasia.com/news/singapore/bto-flats-elderly-bukit-batok-care-services-assisted-living-13742262

Maintenance of Parents Act. (1995). Retrieved from https://sso.agc.gov.sg/Act/MPA1995

Mehta, K. (2019). Positive Ageing: How Can We Make It Happen? Ethos. Civil Service College. Issue 20, 28 Jan 2019. Retrieved from https://www.csc.gov.sg/ethos

Mehta, K. K., & Vasoo, S. (2000). Community Programmes and Services for Long-Term Care of the Elderly in Singapore: Challenges for policy-makers. *Asian Journal of Political Science*, 8(1), 125–140.

MOH. (2016). Action Plan for Successful Ageing. Ministry of Health.

MOH. (2020). Heath Facilities. Retrieved from https://www.moh.gov.sg/resources-statistics/singapore-health-facts/health-facilities

Moneysmart. (2019). Nursing Homes in Singapore – How Much Does It Cost? Retrieved from https://blog.moneysmart.sg/family/nursing-homes-singapore/

MSF. (2020). Protection For Vulnerable Adults. Retrieved from https://www.msf.gov.sg/policies/Helping-the-Needy-and-Vulnerable/Pages/Protection-for-Vulnerable-Adults.aspx

Ng, K. (2018). Innovation, Skills Upgrading Part of Healthcare Transformation Roadmap Unveiled. Retrieved from https://www.todayonline.com/singapore/innovation-skills-upgrading-part-healthcare-transformation-roadmap-unveiledhttps://www.todayonline.com/singapore/innovation-skills-upgrading-part-healthcare-transformation-roadmap-unveiled.

NPTD. (2012). Projection of Foreign Manpower Demand for Healthcare Sector, Construction Workers and Foreign Domestic Workers. Retrieved from https://www.strategygroup.gov.sg/images/Press%20Release%20images/PDFs/occasional-paper-projection-of-foreign-manpower-demand-healthcare-construction-foreign-domestic-workers.pdf

NPTD. (2020). Retrieved from https://www.population.gov.sg.

PA. (2020). Active Ageing. Retrieved from https://www.pa.gov.sg/our-programmes/active-ageing

Phua, R., Chew, H. M. (2020). Can Singapore Rely Less on Foreign Workers? It's Not Just About Dollars And Cents, Say Observers. CNA. Retrieved from https://www.channelnewsasia.com/news/singapore/singapore-foreign-workers-reliance-challenges-12806970#:~:text=Experts%20say%20that%20while%20Singapore,population%20of%205.7%20million%20people.

Silverjobs. (2020). A Platform for Seniors. Retrieved from https://silverjobs.sg/

Sowell, T. (2015). *Say's Law: An Historical Analysis*. Princeton University Press.

SportSG. (2020). Vision 2030 – Live Better Through Sport. Retrieved from https://www.sportsingapore.gov.sg/about-us/vision-2030.

Tan, T. (2015). Parent Maintenance Cases 'Often Down to Strained Ties'. Retrieved from https://www.straitstimes.com/singapore/parent-maintenance-cases-often-down-to-strained-ties

Teoh, Z. W., Zainal, K. (2018). Successful Ageing: Progressive Governance and Collaborative Communities. Ethos. Issue 19, 8 Jul 2018. Civil Service College. Retrieved from https://www.csc.gov.sg/articles/successful-ageing-progressive-governance-and-collaborative-communities

West, J. (2020). What the NHS Can Learn from the US Obamacare System. Retrieved from https://www.theguardian.com/healthcare-network/2015/feb/03/obamacare-lessons-nhs-healthcare

WSG. (2020). Senior Worker Early Adopter Grant and Part Time Re Employment Grant. Workforce Singapore. Retrieved from https://www.wsg.gov.sg/programmes-and-initiatives/senior-worker-early-adopter-grant-and-part-time-re-employment-grant-employers.html

Yap, C. B. (2019). Kampung Admiralty: Building for All Ages. Ethos. Digital Issue 4, 29 Apr 2019. Civil Service College. Retrieved from https://www.csc.gov.sg/articles/kampung-admiralty-building-for-all-ages

12
FROM POLICY TO PRACTICE

A comparative Anglo-German view of long-term care provision for older people

Ingrid Eyers, Kimberly Stoeckel, and Laura Allen

Introduction

Whilst celebrating the success of increasing longevity, there is also a need to give due consideration to health and social care policies aiming to meet the needs of vulnerable older people. The population is diverse and the high COVID-19 death rates among older people residing in long-term care settings (International Long-Term Care Policy Network 2022) highlight the need to reassess governmental policies that influence the quality of later life in these settings. This will help to ensure the continuation of longevity while also promoting quality of life and well-being.

In this chapter, two northern European country welfare states are compared: Germany and England. This comparison highlights how government policies regulating the provision and funding of long-term care impact the lives of older people, their families, and professional caregivers. Person-Centred Care (PCC) can be seen to be fundamental to all service delivery in both countries. However, country-specific differences in how integrated care (WHO 2021) can be facilitated are noteworthy.

Germany has a state-regulated long-term care insurance linked to its health insurance system and a care sector that is dominated by "not for profit" service providers. As a member state of the United Kingdom (UK), England has a National Health Service that segregates the social care needs of older people, and service providers are predominantly established as "for profit" organisations. Germany and England both have government policies regulating and supervising the provision of health and social care services. Workforce retention and training of health and social care workers who support and care for older people in long-term care settings are essential parts of these policies because of the widely acknowledged global shortage of these workers. In Germany and England, the funding system expects participation from each older person requiring care. The difference, however, lies in how governmental legislation financially supports long-term care within these two welfare states. This contrast between the German long-term care insurance and the UK health and social care funding, alongside the differing professional training systems, should be carefully analysed by other countries.

Evaluating how the differing policy frameworks of these two countries influence each country's ability to provide integrated person-centred care identifies different approaches towards addressing very similar health and social care needs. In this chapter, the discussion of these differences between two well-established welfare states contributes to the global debate focusing on how best to meet the needs of an ageing population.

Within the current global focus on the Decade of Healthy Ageing (WHO 2020b), there is a need to give due consideration to how integrated, person-centred care can be provided in long-term care settings. Due to the acute situation caused by the COVID-19 pandemic that arose in 2020 and the disproportionate number of deaths (International Long-Term Care Policy Network 2022), there is greater awareness of how older people are cared for in long-term care settings. As a result, government policies relating to long-term care are being re-evaluated and examined in many countries. It is time for all countries to reassess where they are and to decisively plan how best to move forward in redefining priorities for long-term care. Comparing England and Germany, as two Northern European countries with long-established but also differing welfare systems, provides a solid basis from which to develop an informative, fruitful discussion.

The aim of this chapter is to stimulate thought processes that will support care providers and policymakers in individual countries to find the best way to achieve this objective in their own environment. By comparing England and Germany, the intention is not to evaluate and categorically state what is better or best, but to consider why something is the way it is in one or both countries. The onus is then upon the reader to give thought to whether or not this aspect could be reflected in their own country.

Brief introduction to welfare systems in England and Germany

The well-known National Health Service (NHS) of the United Kingdom was introduced in 1948. For many years, the population was led by Winston Churchill and other politicians to believe this service would provide and care for them from "the cradle to the grave". What was not necessarily obvious to many was the fact that there is a clear distinction to be made between "health" and "social care".

The provision of medical care-related services is "health needs" based and provided free, at the point of delivery, by the NHS in their facilities and by their staff. In contrast, social care needs that are often linked to long-term medical conditions are met by local municipalities based and funded on a needs-based evaluation under the umbrella of social care and are "means" tested.

This dual health and social care system is funded by National Insurance contributions from a working adult's income. The social care services required, however, are not provided by the municipalities but are contracted out to the "Independent Sector". These are predominantly for-profit organisations that operate independently of the NHS and Social Care Services. At the governmental level, this structure is regulated and guided by Acts of Parliament under the auspices of the Department of Health and Social Care (DHSC). An independent Care Quality Commission (CQC) is tasked with guiding and inspect all health and social care services, whether they are part of the NHS or independent (Legislation.gov.uk 2012).

The welfare system in Germany has its roots in the social developments that became a necessity throughout the industrialisation of the country in the 19th century. The German "Iron Chancellor" (1871–1890), Otto von Bismarck, was instrumental in establishing a welfare state (Ştefan 2015) that has continuously grown and developed into what it is today.

Whilst legislation governs the system, the provision of health and social care services is independent of the State. It is the patient's choice when accessing any medical care services. Many providers, from hospitals to home care services, are linked to charitable organisations that are often connected to the Catholic (Caritas) or Lutheran Church (Diakonie). Overall, health and allied professionals working outside a hospital setting are self-employed, either in group practices or as individual practitioners. The services provided are paid for via a task-based oriented system used by all health insurance companies operating in accordance with legislative guidance.

When it comes to health and social care, the most important legislation is found in the German Social Code XI (WHO 2020a). After many years of debate and negotiation between the government, trade unions, and employers' organisations, Germany introduced statutory Long Term Care Insurance in 1995. With the passing of the legislation, Germany became one of the few countries within Europe to establish statutory long term care insurance.

These highlighted differences between how the welfare states of Germany and England function regarding health and social care provision are the first indicators of complex key factors that influence the ability to facilitate integrated care in long-term care settings.

Defining person-centred care

As healthcare became more science- and data-driven throughout the 20th century, it started to receive criticism for overlooking the personal side of care. In the United States in the 1980s, a counterculture movement arose, known today as *culture change* in healthcare practice and policy, to improve both the quality of care and the quality of life of the care recipient (Koren 2010). This culture change brought about what is known today as *Person Centred Care*, which rapidly spread across the globe and especially throughout Europe (Paparella 2016). In recent years, Person-Centred Care has become a widely used term with a variety of definitions. In this instance, the use of the term grows out of the publications of Thomas Kitwood (1997a, b), which have continued to be developed by many others (McCormack 2003; Koren 2010). The most important feature of person-centred care is the relationship between the caregiver and the care recipient.

Both the care recipient and caregiver interact with each other, having highly individualised and differing experiences, needs, and expectations. The older person is supported by their personal social capital (Bourdieu 1986, Eyers & Backes 2009) whilst the employed caregiver is supported by an integrated care system of service delivery (WHO 2020b, Sustain Consortium 2019).

Each older person has their individual comorbidities, and no one else will have experienced exactly the same as that individual has throughout their complex life. From the cradle to the grave, the personal circumstances of each of us are undeniably unique. Focusing on these individual aspects is central to the successful implementation of person-centred care. The caregiver is no different from the older person in experiencing unique life circumstances and patterns, and therefore, mutual respect and acknowledgement of the differences between caregiver and the care recipient are vital.

Due to the older person's need for guidance and support in many of their everyday activities, the power relationship between the caregivers and care recipients can easily be put out of balance. For this reason, it is essential for the rights of older people to be foundational in how care delivery is structured. Integrating the rights of older people into care settings ensures their voices are heard and empowers older people to be actively engaged and participatory in the care they receive (HelpAge International 2021).

Together, an older person and their caregiver interact with each other within a policy framework that structures their relationship and is imposed upon them by government legislation. No matter where you are in this world, the core framework presented in this chapter (Figure 12.1) is likely to be applicable. To ensure the best possible quality of life for older people, each country has:

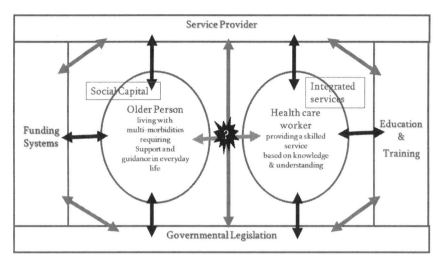

FIGURE 12.1   Caregiving framework.

- specific Acts of Parliament or legislation relating to health and social care
- considered how LTC is funded
- addressed how the service is provided
- established health and social care-relevant education programmes

However, as the comparison between England and Germany will highlight, the material used for each of the four sides will differ considerably and can be seen to be constructed out of very finely compressed and interwoven layers.

Government legislation

In Germany and in England, all long-term care services operate under the countrys' laws that relate to health and safety, building regulations, and employment laws. However, in the context of this section, the focus is on government legislation that relates directly to the long-term care sector providing services to older people.

English legislation

At the start of the 21st century, a considerable change took place in the provision of care services for older people in England. At this time in history, there was a growing awareness of human rights issues, and this factor is referred to in the legislation (Legislation.gov.uk 2000). The UK parliament passed the Care Standards Act 2000 (Legislation.gov.uk 2000) that enforced noticeable changes in the long-term care sector. Service providers were assessed and required to meet the standards set out by a well-established Care Quality Commission. In 2014, the government also passed the Care Act 2014 (Legislation.gov.uk 2014) that has a strong influence on how care is funded and eases the divide between health and social care. This Act will be addressed in the section focusing on funding.

The Care Standards Act 2000 ultimately led to the closure of many small, family-run "cosy" care homes with often less than 20 beds that had been established in the 1980s. Such small businesses were initially established by adapting and converting larger family houses, often in buildings dating back to Victorian days. By the nature of the architecture, such care homes were, for example, often unable to meet the minimum building regulations. For example, these homes may have failed to meet the minimum size of a bedroom and door width, and construction to alter the structure was often cost-prohibitive. Importantly, shared bedrooms in care homes were also to become a thing of the past.

The change in legislation has also led to the development of purpose-built care homes that initially aimed to take on a more hotel-like character. Over the years, a trend towards developing care facilities based on smaller units and offering day care services can be observed. Despite the visible increase in more extensive purpose-built care homes, the average number of 29.5 beds per care home (GOV.UK 2020) continues to be relatively small. All care homes are registered with CQC and are inspected regularly.

A further noticeable change that came about as a result of the Care Standards Act 2000 related to the staffing levels, training requirements, and qualifications for all staff. The minimum number of staff required to be on duty in each home is negotiated with CQC as it is dependent on the type of specialist care the provider is registered to provide. A strong focus in the care sector since then has also been on safeguarding, dignity, and quality of life of the older person. One of the greatest developments has been the focus on "activities" in care homes, which has vastly improved the quality of life now experienced by older people living in care homes. A visit to the website of any care home in England will highlight the importance they place on the "activities" on offer.

It is undoubtedly UK government legislation that has brought about change for the better in the provision of services to older people who, for many diverse reasons, need to move into a care home. The strong focus on staff training has also professionalised the workforce and potentially empowered care staff to empower older people to actively participate in everyday life. Establishing ground rules for the built environment of the care home also has a positive impact on the daily life of both the care recipient and caregiver.

German legislation

In Germany, the legal system includes a "Social Code" that governs social care, generally referred to as "SGBXI" (Sozialgesetzbuch XI). It is regularly reviewed, and major amendments are made after consultation, debate, and negotiation with all relevant parties. In addition to the legislation governing the provision of long-term care, the rights of an individual to lead a self-determined life are supported by a "Patients' Rights Act" introduced in 2013. This is accompanied by a "Charter of Rights for People in Need of Long-term Care" (WHO 2020a).

The governance of the system is undertaken by the Medizinischer Dienst der Krankenversicherungen (Medical Services of the Health Insurance Providers) known as the MDK. This is an independent organisation tasked by the German government with overseeing the implementation of SGBXI. The role of this organisation is also outlined within this legislative framework. In the context of long-term care, they have two separate but very important tasks. The first is to register and regulate care home standards, and the other is to assess a patient's level of dependency. As the name implies, there is a strong focus on the medical aspect of long-term care, and this is a factor that is very noticeable when visiting German care homes that are, in the norm purpose built.

The strong medicalised approach towards long-term care is also influenced by the insurance system. The long-term care insurance providers are the same as the health insurance providers and can initially be seen to have systematically transferred the task-focused medical care funding methodology into long-term care funding. Initially, this resulted in a focus on a very restrictive time-based system (Eyers 2007) that failed to address the needs of older people living with dementia or other mental-health oriented conditions. It was acknowledged that this needed to change and in 2017 the law was amended accordingly. There is now an improved and stronger focus on the quality of life and the needs of an older person living with dementia.

The legislation in Germany determines the minimum amount of space that must be available for each older person but currently does not exclude shared rooms. Shared rooms are not uncommon and tend to be allocated to residents who are receiving financial support from the local social services department or to accommodate a couple.

A further important factor that is guided by SGBXI relates to the staffing of a care home, where it is expected that 50% of the care staff should be qualified healthcare professionals. This requirement is currently under review. The number of staff members on duty at any given time is predominantly determined by the assessed dependency levels of all the older people living in the facility. The death of an older person or a short stay in the hospital can result in a reduction in staffing levels.

The governments of both countries have given considerable thought to the legislation put into place to face the demographic challenge of providing support and care for an increasing number of older people in later life. There is a clear emphasis on policies respecting the individual while also needing to provide an affordable service for the good of all. This is a challenge for any government.

The government legislation is of considerable importance. It plays a powerful role in the actual daily delivery of care, extending from the environment in which care is provided to the daily "hands on" provision of care. However, the way in which long-term care is funded in England and in Germany is very different and highlights the role of family and the responsibility of an individual to take care of themselves across their life-course.

Funding

As welfare states, England and Germany have complex safety nets to capture those most in need of support in later life. However, it is expected that individuals with personal resources will contribute towards the costs associated with long-term care. The financial thresholds determining the circumstances that will yield access to long-term care funding provided through government-led resources do differ, however, when comparing these two countries.

England

Throughout the working life of every adult in England, National Insurance contributions are paid to the government. In times of need this insurance entitles you to medical care provided by the NHS, sick leave pay, unemployment benefits, and ultimately a State Pension. The amount of these payments is standardised across England. Should you require social care services to give you guidance and support in your everyday life, as your dependency increases at any stage of life, you turn to your Local Authority Social Services Department. Your needs will be assessed by the department, and you will be means-tested to determine eligibility for financial support.

If this situation arises in conjunction with a discharge from the hospital, a multi-disciplinary discharge team will assess your needs. A Local Authority social worker will be assigned to organise your long-term care needs. This is a process informed by the Care Act 2014 (Legislation.gov.uk 2014) which has clarified the legal framework governing the role of Local Authority Social Services.

Should healthcare needs arise, the NHS may make financial contributions towards your medically determined nursing care requirements. In contrast, your social care needs come under the auspices of your Local Authority Social Services, where you will be guided and advised on the available services. A financial needs test will be undertaken to assess your ability to pay for these services.

Should the means test establish the value of your assets is above £23,250 (March 2022 = US$ 30,756), you must pay for social care from your own resources (NHS2022). This is consistent throughout the UK. However, the funds available from the budget of each municipality (Local County Council) to pay for Social Services is unavoidably variable.

Knowing what you can afford becomes key to selecting the care home you move into. The lowest price of a care home placement in a region tends to be determined by the amount their Local Authority has budgeted to pay for a care home placement. The choice of care home is up to the individual and is often a family decision. There is no reason for a Local Authority to prevent an older person living in the north of England from moving to be near an adult child living in the south of the country. However, the amount of available funding will be determined by the Local Authority in the North and could well be lower than the amount paid by the authority in the south. This could mean that on a voluntary basis, family or friends pool funds to make up the difference in the cost between available funding for the individual and the care home fees. It is entirely up to the family or friends to do this; there is no legal requirement or framework support for such contributions. Once an older person has moved into a care home, they receive the same medical services from the NHS as they would in their own home. However, access to therapists is more complex as home visits are more difficult to arrange, and it is rare to encounter independent therapists if you wanted to self-fund, for example, physiotherapy.

Each older person is seen by both the NHS and Local Social Services as an individual. However, the needs of a partner or a dependent also required to be addressed and taken into consideration (Legislation.gov.uk 2014). The involvement of family members or friends is not expected. Any participation in this process depends on the family dynamics and the social capital an older person has acquired over their life course. In such a situation, asking for or accepting assistance and guidance from family members in the selection of a home is very valuable, as is the assistance to physically move to the new surroundings.

For an older person with sufficient assets to meet the cost of life in a care home, it is up to them to organise their affairs accordingly. Any family involvement is voluntary, and where needed, professional advice is sought from a solicitor (attorney) and financial advisor. Should a lonely older person without family or friends be faced with this situation, the social workers will reach out to a solicitor for professional services. Which care home an older person decides to move into is entirely up to them; however, selection may be limited by availability.

Germany

In Germany, throughout their working life, an adult will have made statutory contributions towards their health and social care insurance. Currently, legislation states that 3.05% of your gross income is deducted to pay for your long-term care insurance, 2.025% is covered by the employee (plus 0.25% if you are childless) and 1.025% by the employer (Bundesgesundheitsministerium 2022a).

When needed, this insurance will cover your formally assessed long-term care needs but does not include the "hotel cost" of a care home placement. The outcome of a needs assessment undertaken by specifically trained healthcare professionals working for the MDK will place an individual into one of five categories. The level of need is determined by six areas of impairment:

1. mobility
2. mental and communication-related abilities
3. Behaviour and psychological issues
4. Self-care
5. Independent handling of requirements and challenges associated with illness or therapy and their management
6. Everyday life and social contacts

(Bundesgesundheitsministerium 2022b)

If a care home placement is required as part of hospital discharge planning, the health insurance will initially cover the cost for up to four weeks (Bundesgesundheitsministerium 2020c). Thereafter, the Long-Term Care insurance will cover the care costs in accordance with the assessed level of need.

Should your personal financial situation be such that you are unable to cover the "hotel cost", you can apply to Social Services for assistance. This will result in a full means test that takes into account the finances of an individual and their partner. As of January 2020, the legislation governing how adult children are called upon to contribute towards the cost of their parents' care home placement has been amended. Adult children are required to contribute towards the cost of their parents' care home placement only when their annual income is above Euro 100,000 (Stiegelmeier 2020).

Any medical services required by an older person living in a German care home are prescribed by their physician and provided by a relevant local professional in the same way as if they were at home. For example, a speech therapist, physiotherapist, or podiatrist will come to the care home once the prescription has been issued. There is no requirement for the therapist to contact the prescribing physician or any other healthcare professional involved in the provision of medical services. The professional will be paid by the health insurance company for completion of the prescribed treatment at the rate agreed upon between the insurance company and the organisation representing that specific professional group.

In reviewing how long-term care is funded in either country, it becomes clear that it is very much up to every citizen to take personal responsibility for their financial situation across the life-course if they want to maintain autonomy in later life. One obvious difference between Germany and England in how long-term care is funded is the role of the family and how in Germany the legal framework determines that adult children can be called upon to contribute towards their parent's care home costs.

The construction of the safety net for older people requiring support and guidance in their everyday lives is in place in both Germany and England. Differences do exist, however, in how these systems cover the actual cost of care, which impacts how care homes operate. These differences are a separate issue that would exceed the confines of this book chapter and would call for the contribution of a health economist. They do, however, impact on how care homes operate.

The care home sector

Whilst the approach across the world is to enable older people to stay at home until the end of their days, the reality is that there are situations where a move into a care home is unavoidable. This can simply be that the size or position of a bathroom makes it very difficult to undertake the vital activities of personal care that are required to start and end the day. It could also be that the medical condition is such that complex needs cannot be met in the home environment an older person has been living in for many years.

It is never an easy step to take, and balancing emotions with rational decision-making is a challenge for an older person and their family. This is why it is so important that care homes are able to meet expectations and provide the best possible services. Both the German and English governments have set a benchmark for how care homes are expected to operate to provide a good standard of service. These factors, in conjunction with how care is funded, are vital to the functioning of the care sector.

England

In England, the majority of care homes are in the ownership of for-profit organisations and constitute a "care market". This care market with 4566 thousand beds is distributed as follows: 3% are owned by Local Authorities, charitable organisations/foundations own 13%, and 84% of care home beds in 2019 were owned by "private players" (The Conversation 2021). Whilst there are many small to medium-sized businesses (SMB's) amongst the "private players", five leading operators dominate the market. In other words, while 16% of the market aims to break even, 84% are aiming to make a profit. This for-profit business model in the care market industry is reflected in the ratings of the homes undertaken by CQC following their mandatory inspection visits. Relating to CQC data, "The Conversation" (2021) points out that three out of five care homes in the private, for-profit sector are stated to "require improvement" or were considered "inadequate".

These factors are of great concern and link how care is funded in England to the service that is delivered, which is of considerable importance. Despite in-depth reviews, starting with the Royal Commission into Long-Term Care in 1999, it is an issue that has been consistently overlooked by successive governments of the country.

Germany

The structure of the care home market in Germany has changed since the introduction of the long-term care insurance system in 1995. One change has been the increase in the number of "for-profit" care homes in the country. A number of SMB's have been founded in urban areas, and these are often family-run businesses that are bolstered by private investment companies. The for-profit sector had a market share of 40.9% in 2015 (WHO 2020a).

Despite the strong growth of the for-profit sector, care services run by religious organisations such as the Protestant Lutheran Diakonie (Diakonie 2022) and the Catholic Caritas (German Caritas 2022) have a high profile. These two leading organisations have an extensive history in meeting the health and social care needs of the population and have a strong voice within local communities. Importantly, their care homes are integral to communities and provide a central point of long-term care services ranging from home care to end-of-life care. Many facilities that provide such a range of services also offer sheltered housing. An urban-based centre for senior citizens may well have 120 beds; in addition there could be 50 apartments offering sheltered housing. These facilities may also offer day care services that include the transport of the older person. If any medically related services are required, these are accessed externally and funded in the same way as they would be if the older person were living at home.

The ownership and size of care homes present a key difference between the countries in how long-term care services are structured and reflect how care services in each country have grown and developed to meet the needs of an ageing population. Importantly, in both countries, there is a highly skilled, undervalued care workforce doing their utmost to provide care to the best of their ability.

Education and training

The care home workforce in both countries daily faces the same tasks in providing services to residents of these homes. How well and effectively they provide care to an older person is dependent not only on their caregiving skills but also on their understanding of old age. Both are important factors determined by the education and continuing training they receive in their workplace.

England

The initial key element related to staffing care homes in England is the requirement for all healthcare professionals to be registered by the governing body of their profession. After gaining a qualification from university, the next step for a nurse, for example, is to register with the Nursing and Midwifery Council (www.nmc.org.uk). Any future employer, whether it is within the NHS or the independent sector, will check that registration. Someone with social work qualifications will register with the Social Work England organisation (www.socialworkengland.org.uk). To remain on these registers, it is important to prove continuing professional development (CPD).

Care assistants are not required to be on a register, but CQC will require an employer to provide Statutory Health and Safety training, and apprenticeships may be offered (Skills for Care 2022). It is also possible to gain a diploma in Health and Social Care while still in formal education and to build on the qualification. Care home operators are encouraged and supported to train all members of their workforce, and "Skills for Care" has an extensive programme of modules that facilitate educational building blocks for anyone wanting a career in the sector. This is especially valuable to people in mid-working life who also have family commitments that limit their ability to complete training in a set period. This system also offers opportunities to support the costs incurred by both employer and employee.

Germany

The traditional, well-established structure of occupational training in Germany is built on the apprenticeship system that almost goes back to the Middle Ages when guilds governing trade and industry were important. To this day, after leaving formal education after 13 years of schooling, most young people aim to gain an occupational qualification either through college or university. These educational institutions operate under the auspices of each of Germany's 16 Regional (Laender) governments. Specialist colleges focus on training healthcare professionals, whilst a university qualification is required for physicians, psychologists, and social workers.

Life-long learning has become part of this system and mature students wanting to gain healthcare qualifications are accommodated. Anyone undertaking a career change will be assessed and potentially financially supported by the Federal Department of Employment (Bundesanstalt fuer Arbeit). Many immigrants and refugees have benefited from this system and have been offered the option to gain an occupational qualification in health care, especially with a focus on the needs of older people.

In Germany, there is the stand-alone qualification in "Altenpflege" (Older Persons Carer) that until 2020 was provided in an apprenticeship style. As the training provided a balance between health and social care, it is not appropriate to describe this as geriatric care, which has a strong medical focus. After much debate, in 2020, a change in legislation governing all training in health care was implemented to professionalise the career through the introduction of specialist training during the last year of training (Bundesministerium für Gesundheit 2022d). The first cohort of students has yet to complete their training to become a "Health Care Specialist". Whether the student ultimately wants to focus on older adults, adults' or children, the first two years of the training program are the same. Specialisation then takes place in the third year. How this change will impact the care home sector remains to be evaluated.

There is an ongoing debate that has yet to be resolved around the creation of a register for qualified healthcare staff. At present, to be employed as a qualified Older Persons Carer, you need to present your diploma and references from all previous employers. Qualifications in adult or childcare are also acceptable to work as a qualified member of the German care home workforce. Further continuing professional development (CPD) post-qualification is encouraged and supported for both employers and their employees.

How training and education are provided is constantly under review in both England and Germany, especially in the light of the acute shortage of care staff across the board. There is a global shortage of healthcare workers whether it is in hospitals, care homes, or community-based home care. Workforce training is clearly a very vital factor in both countries which, when prioritised, acknowledges the high level of skill required to meet the complex care needs of older people. The tasks undertaken on a daily basis are similar in both countries where the importance of quality of life for an older person and their personal network is as important as that of the care workforce. It is essential that the profile of care work in long-term settings is improved, and that it is emphasised how important this highly skilled workforce is to the well-being of society.

Conclusion

As can be seen in Figure 12.1, the framework surrounding the provision of care is well structured, and each of the four sides is closely connected to one another. The final part, which strongly impacts the structure, goes directly from the government policy to the service provider. This cuts directly through the relationship between an older person and the caregiver and ultimately influences the provision of person-centred care.

One of the important elements in Germany and in England is how much direct contact time there is between care staff and an older person living in a care home. How much time is there for a care worker to actually offer choice or work with an older person to prepare themselves for the day or night ahead? Care staff are constantly juggling their time management and often need to cut corners out of necessity (Eyers 2007). Taking shortcuts more often than not means taking a strong task-oriented approach with little time to offer choice or to empower independence among those being cared for.

The delivery of actual hands-on care is strongly influenced by management style and the number of staff employed at a care home. The ratio of staff to older persons in care homes is determined by the available funding that supports the care service sector. This is especially highlighted by the funding system in Germany.

All care staff aim to provide care to the best of their ability. Their level of ability is dependent on the education and training they have had and the management support they receive. To empower both older people and care workers, there is also a need for governments to realistically address how care is funded. How funding is distributed must be addressed to ensure the provision of integrated care in long-term care homes.

Looking at both England and Germany, it could be argued that the historical systems of care delivery are standing in the way of progress. England urgently needs to address the future funding of long-term care and review the dominance of the for-profit sector. Germany urgently needs to address the task orientated delivery of service that hinders the delivery of integrated care.

Government policies are critical and must be realistic if we are to be successful in empowering healthy ageing whilst taking an integrated approach. In the process of developing long-term care policies, it is vital that the actual needs of the two key players at the centre of this framework are not overlooked.

References

Bourdieu, P. (1986). The Forms of Capital. In J.G. Richardson, *Handbook of Theory and Research for the Sociology of Education* (pp. 241–258). New York: Greenwood Press.

Bundesministerium für Gesundheit (2022a). *Finanzierung der Pflegeversicherung*. Retrieved March 19 2022 from https://www.bundesgesundheitsministerium.de/themen/pflege/online-ratgeber-pflege/die-pflegeversicherung/finanzierung.html

Bundesministerium für Gesundheit (2022b). *Pflege*. Retrieved March 7 2022 from https://www.bundesgesundheitsministerium.de/themen/pflege/

Bundesministerium für Gesundheit (2022c). *Kurzzeitpflege*. Retrieved March 20 2022 from https://www.bundesgesundheitsministerium.de/kurzzeitpflege.html

Bundesministerium für Gesundheit (2022d). *Pflegeberufsgesetz*. Retrieved March 18 2022 from https://www.bundesgesundheitsministerium.de/pflegeberufegesetz.html

Diakonie (2022). *Diakonie at a glance*. Retrieved March 18 2022 from https://www.diakonie.de/english

Eyers, I. (2007). Extracting the Essence of Formal Caregiving: A Comparative Study of Formal Care Givers in English and German Care Homes. In I. Paoletti (Ed.), *Family caregiving to older disabled people: relational and institutional issues* (pp. 273–294). Nova Science Publishers, New York, USA.

Eyers, I. & Backes, G. (2009). Gender and Ageing: The Role of Social Networks. In G. Naegele G. & A. Walker A. (Eds.), *Social Policy in Ageing Societies: Britain and Germany Compared* (pp. 106–124). London, Palgrave Macmillan.

German Caritas (2022). *About Us*. Retrieved March 18 2022 from https://www.caritas-germany.org/

GOV.UK (2020). Retrieved March 7 2022 from https://assets.publishing.service.gov.uk/government/uploads/system/uploads/attachment_data/file/897497/S0343_Care_Homes_Analysis.pdf

HelpAge International (2021). *HelpAge Voice Framework*. Retrieved March 18 2022 from https://www.helpage.org/what-we-do/society-for-all-ages/voice/

International Long Term Care Policy Network (2022). *LTC Responses to Covid 19*. Retrieved March 15 2022 from https://ltccovid.org/2022/02/22/international-data-on-deaths-attributed-to-covid-19-among-people-living-in-care-homes/

Kitwood, T. (1997a). *Dementia Reconsidered: The Person Comes First* (Vol. 20, pp. 7–8). Buckingham: Open University press.

Kitwood, T. (1997b). The Experience of Dementia. *Aging & Mental Health*, 1(1), 13–22.

Koren, M.J. (2010). Person-Centered Care for Nursing Home Residents: The Culture Change Movement. *Health Affairs*, 29(2). 1–6. doi: 10.1377/hlthaff.2009.0966

Legislation.gov.uk (2000). Retrieved March 7 2022 from https://www.legislation.gov.uk/ukpga/2000/14

Legislation.gov.uk (2012). *Health and Social Care Act 2012*. Retrieved March 18 2022 from https://www.legislation.gov.uk/ukpga/2012/7/contents/enacted

Legislation.gov.uk (2014). *Care Act*. Retrieved March 7 2022 from https://www.legislation.gov.uk/ukpga/2014/23/part/1/enacted

McCormack, B. (2003). A Conceptual Framework for Person-Centred Practice with Older People. *International Journal of Nursing Practice*, June, 202–209. https://doi.org/10.1046/j.1440-172X.2003.00423.x9

NHS (2018). *Carer's Assessments NHS*. Retrieved March 12 2022 from https://www.nhs.uk/conditions/social-care-and-support-guide/support-and-benefits-for-carers/carer-assessments/

NHS (2022). *Financial Assessment (Means Test) for Social Care*. Retrieved March 7 2022 from https://www.nhs.uk/conditions/social-care-and-support-guide/help-from-social-services-and-charities/financial-assessment-means-test/#:~:text=A%20financial%20assessment%20or%20means,the%20cost%20of%20your%20care.

Paparella, G. (2016). *Person-Centred Care in Europe: A Cross-Country Comparison of Health System Performance, Strategies and Structures Policy Briefing*: Picker Institute Europe, (February). Retrieved from www.pickereurope.orgwebsite: www.pickereurope.org

Stiegelmeier (2020). *Only a Number of Relatives Still to Contribute to Nursing Home Costs*. Retrieved March 11 2022 from https://www.stiegelmeyer-forum.com/en/articles-reports/only-a-few-relatives-still-to-contribute-to-nursing-home-costs.html

Skills for Care (2022). *Developing Your Workforce*. Retrieved from https://www.skillsforcare.org.uk/Developing-your-workforce/Developing-your-workforce.aspx

Ştefan, G. M (2015). European Welfare State in a Historical Perspective. A Critical Review. *European Journal of Interdisciplinary Studies*, 7(1), 25–38.

Sustain Consortium (2019). *Sustainable Tailored Integrated Care for Older People in Europe (SUSTAIN-project). Lessons Learned from Improving Integrated Care in Europe*. Retrieved from https://www.sustain-eu.org/wp-content/uploads/sites/4/2019/01/SUSTAIN-overarching-policy-report_final-version.pdf

The Conversation (2021). *Why Investment Firms Can Be Bad*. Retrieved March 10 2022 from https://theconversation.com/care-homes-why-investment-firms-can-be-bad-owners-158492

WHO Regional Office for Europe (2020a). *Germany, Country Case Study on the Integrated Delivery of Long-Term Care*. Copenhagen, WHO Regional Office.

WHO (2020b). *Decade of Healthy Ageing 2020–2030*. Retrieved March 18 2022 from https://www.who.int/docs/default-source/decade-of-healthy-ageing/final-decade-proposal/decade-proposal-final-apr2020-en.pdf

WHO (2021). *Framework for Countries to Achieve an Integrated Continuum of Long-Term Care*. Retrieved from https://www.who.int/publications/i/item/9789240038844

13
CANADIAN EXPERIENCE IN PROVIDING CARE IN LONG-TERM CARE HOMES

Suraj Laxman Gopinathbirla and Kanwal Shankardass

Introduction

Examining what defines long-term care is challenging due to the diversity in the services and niches it often occupies. The National Institute of Aging (NIA) (2019) definition succinctly captures the term by stating that long-term care is:

> A range of preventive and responsive care and supports, primarily for older adults, that may include assistance with Activities of Daily Living (ADLs) and Instrumental Activities of Daily Living (IADLs) provided by either not-for-profit and for-profit providers, or unpaid caregivers in settings that are not location specific and thus include designated buildings, or in home and community-based settings.
> *(National Institute on Ageing, 2019)*

Aging increases health heterogeneity as measured by various health metrics (Nguyen et al., 2020). In turn, the health heterogeneity of the elderly population translates to a spectrum of care needs that depends on the individual (Santoni et al., 2020; Vaupel et al., 1979). This population variability in health and care needs makes defining long-term care challenging. There is no single definition of long-term care that is accepted across Canada. For that matter, there is no single international definition of long-term care that is accepted widely, though organizations such as the Organization for Economic Co-Operation and Development (Francesca et al., 2011) and the World Health Organization (WHO) (World Report on Ageing and Health, 2015) have established their own definitions. What is important is the recognition and appreciation of a holistic approach to long-term care. Care is provided in various settings, whether it be at home or in designated facilities, and by various agents, from unpaid caregivers such as family and friends to healthcare professionals.

The focus of this chapter will be on the care of the elderly in congregate residential care settings. Within this category, the two main models in Canada are retirement homes and long-term care homes (Roblin et al., 2019). We will further narrow our focus in the chapter to long-term care homes. Retirement homes (RHs), also called assisted-living facilities elsewhere, are residential complexes that primarily house individuals over the age of 65 who prefer to live more independently but require some care services that are not fulfilled at home. Generally, residents of RHs tend to be more independent with a lesser burden of medical comorbidities. Therefore, retirement homes focus primarily on personal care, and medical care is limited to simple tasks such as assistance with taking medications. Unlike long-term care homes that are predominantly funded by the government, individuals seeking retirement homes must pay the full cost of housing and care.

Long-term care homes have various names across Canada, including nursing homes, residential care homes, and residential-based continuing care facilities. Though terms vary, they all provide an equivalent level of care across the country. These facilities provide 24-hour nursing care, meals, and assistance with activities of daily living and instrumental activities of daily living. Outside hospital facilities, LTCHs offer the highest level of institutional care for individuals. In contrast to the care in retirement homes, long-term care homes have specific requirements in the care provided as outlined under provincial legislation.

Resident profile

To understand and appreciate the level of care provided in LTCHs, it is imperative to analyze the resident profile. Census data from 2016 (Statistics Canada, 2017) showed that the overwhelming majority of residents in LTCHs were older adults; of the 168,205 individuals in LTCHs, 156,915 residents were age 65 or older. The average age of a resident in an LTCH is 83 years. Not only are individuals getting older, but they are also becoming more medically complex (Canadian Institute for Health Information, 2020b). Figure 13.1 provides a breakdown of some of the medical conditions present in the residents. About two in three individuals in LTCHs have dementia of some sort, and one in three of those residents have severe cognitive impairment. The increasingly complex resident populations of LTCHs directly relate to the residents' increasing level of care. Eighty-two percent of residents require extensive assistance with their Activities of Daily Living (ADL), and 21% of residents exhibit total dependence for their ADL.

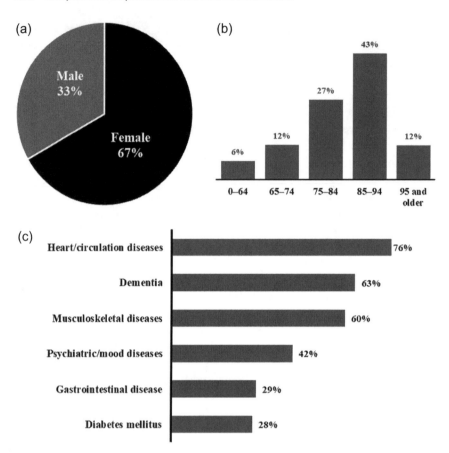

FIGURE 13.1 Resident profile of long-term care homes in Ontario A) shows the split of male to female residents, B) shows the age distribution of residents, and C) shows selected medical conditions present in residents.

Levels of governance

To fully understand the provision of long-term care homes in Canada, it is imperative to analyze and appreciate government legislation and policies that oversee long-term care homes. Here we will provide an overview of the pertinent governmental regulations aimed at long-term care homes and break down policies and legislation by the federal, provincial, and regional levels of governance. Given that the provincial and municipal levels of long-term care home governance are so varied across Canada, we will focus on the most populous province in the country, Ontario, and limit the regional examination to the Greater Hamilton Region, located in southwestern Ontario.

Federal

The federal jurisdiction of LTCHs falls under the *Canada Health Act* of 1984 (Canada Health Act, 1985). This landmark legislation enshrined universal healthcare in the country by establishing a single-payer public health insurance system funded by taxes. Through this, the risks are pooled, and the cost is shared with all Canadians to ensure that no one must suffer the financial burden of medical care.

The Act delineates healthcare services into insured health services and extended health services. Insured health services "are medically necessary hospital, physician and surgical-dental services provided to insured persons" (Health Canada, 2020). Extended health services are defined as "certain aspects of long-term residential care (nursing home, intermediate care and adult residential care services), and the health aspects of home care and ambulatory care services" (Health Canada, 2020). The designation of LTCHs under extended health services means that the provinces are not obligated by the federal government to provide them. By merit of the "extended health services" label, the tenets of insured health services, which include accessibility, comprehensiveness, public administration, portability, and universality, do not apply to long-term care homes. The exclusion of the LTCHs from insured health services has resulted in the federal government's essential exoneration in matters pertaining to the LTCHs. In addition to not being responsible for providing LTCHs to Canadians, there is no unifying national policy or vision for long-term care. This has pushed the responsibility onto provinces to provide long-term care.

Provincial

Dating back to Canada's confederation, under the Constitution Act of 1867, the provinces have been primarily responsible for administering health and welfare provisions—apart from special populations, such as Indigenous peoples. Along with the administration of federally co-financed and mandatory insured health services, the provinces provide extended health services as they deem necessary. Historically, each province has established some form of a long-term care program to ensure a proportion of the cost of long-term care homes is covered for its constituents. The diversity of policies and legislation between provinces makes meaningful discussion of the different approaches and their outcomes challenging, and therefore out of this work's scope. Thus, the provincial lens used in this section will be limited to Ontario. Ontario is Canada's most populous province, home to the nation's capital of Ottawa and an economic and cultural hub.

Before 2010 in Ontario, the regulation of LTCHs fell under the Charitable Institutions Act, the Homes for the Aged and Rest Homes Act, and the Nursing Homes Act. On July 1, 2010, the Long-Term Care Homes Act replaced the existing acts to ensure that one piece of legislation governed all LTCHs. The Long-Term Care Homes Act was designed to "ensure that residents of long-term care homes receive safe, consistent, high-quality, resident-centred care." Outlined in the Act are essential topics including, but not limited to, resident rights, service requirements, reporting mechanisms, compliance, and enforcement.

Whereas regulation and enforcement of LTCHs lie at the provincial level, the public, including residents, interacts with the system and accesses long-term care homes at a regional level through their Local Health Integration Networks.

Regional

Local Health Integration Networks (LHINs) are crown agencies established in 2006 by the province of Ontario. Under the *Local Health System Integration Act,* 2006 (Local Health System Integration Act, 2006), the province was demarcated into 14 distinct geographic regions, each with its own LHIN. The responsibility of the LHIN is to plan, coordinate, integrate, fund, and monitor health services in its respective region. The scope of the LHIN includes hospitals, mental health and addiction agencies, community support service agencies, community health centers, and long-term care homes (Local Health Integration Network, 2014).

The governing body for each LHIN is a decentralized board of directors that is responsible for their respective LHIN. Under the *Local Health System Integration Act,* 2006 (Local Health System Integration Act, 2006), no more than 12 (if needed 14) individuals are appointed by the province to serve on the board of directors. By making bylaws and passing resolutions regulating its proceedings, the board of directors conducts and manages its LHIN, which includes forming committees. Each LHIN may also appoint a chief executive officer to oversee the administration and management of the health network under the supervision and direction of the board of directors. As it pertains to long-term care homes, the public primarily interacts with Care Coordinators who are employed by the LHIN. Care Coordinators review the medical history of individuals who apply for LTCH placement to determine eligibility, discuss funding options, and assist in the transition to a care home.

In late 2019, the Government of Ontario restructured the 14 LHIN's into five regional geographic areas with a Transitional Lead in each area under the administration of Ontario Health. A new governance structure was executed in which a new Chief Executive Officer oversees the Transitional Leads, who in turn reports to the newly established Ontario Health Board. Most functions relating to long-term care will remain under the jurisdiction of the newly reimagined LHIN's.

Ownership and funding

Ownership of long-term care homes can be either privately owned or public. Within the private sector, homes can be owned by for-profit or not-for-profit organizations. In 2020, on average across Canada, 46% of homes were publicly owned, 28% were private, for-profit, and 23% were private not-for-profit homes (the remaining 3% were private without further breakdown) (Canadian Institute for Health Information, 2020a). The ownership of long-term care homes is a direct reflection of provincial legislation and policies (Daly, 2015). Examining the ownership split between for-profit and non-profit LTCHs in the two largest provinces, Ontario and Quebec, is sufficient to highlight the variations. In Ontario, only 16% of LTCHs were publicly owned, whereas in Quebec it was 86%. This is but one example of the diversity present in the LTCH sector across Canada.

The funding of LTCHs in Canada follows a mixed-model system in which some costs are covered by the government and some by the resident. In 2012, approximately 75% of the funding came from the government, with the rest contributed by residents through insurance or direct payments.

The funding scheme for care and services in long-term care homes is complex. Here we will use Ontario as the example again. Medical services such as physician fees, imaging, and laboratory investigations are funded through the Ontario Health Insurance Plan (OHIP), and most medications are covered by the Ontario Drug Benefit program. However, these programs are not limited to residents in LTCHs; these are universal programs that offer health care for all Ontario residents in the case of OHIP and medication coverage for individuals older than 65 in the case of the Ontario Drug Benefit.

With respect to the operating costs of the care home itself, the two major sources are the Ministry of Health and Long-Term Care (MOHLTC) and the residents themselves. The MOHLTC provides funding for care homes on a per diem basis that is bundled into different "envelopes." The ministry-defined envelopes are nursing and personal care, program and support services, raw food, and other accommodation. More information on the components of each envelope can be found in the LTCH Level-of-Care Per Diem Funding Policy (Ministry of Health and Long-Term Care, 2013). The funding designated for one envelope cannot be diverted into another, with the exception that surpluses can be diverted to the raw food envelope.

The private contribution to the cost of LTCHs either arises from insurance or direct payments by the resident. In general, the cost asked of the residents is the cost of accommodation. All provinces have policies in place to subsidize the cost of accommodation based on income levels. Once again, there is an inter-provincial diversity of co-payment requirements and subsidizations (Hirdes, 2001). The cost of accommodation also depends on the type of accommodation preferred by the resident. In Ontario, the maximum monthly rate for accommodation is $1,891.31 for a basic suite and increases to $2,701.61 for a private suite (Government of Ontario, 2018). The Long-Term Care Home Rate Reduction Program can subsidize up to $1,891.31 based on income level, which effectively guarantees no-cost LTCH for qualified individuals.

Example of long-term care home structure

To enrich the discussion of long-term care homes in Canada, it would be useful to describe a specific home and highlight pertinent structural and functional aspects of the facility. For the purposes of this illustration, we will use St. Peter's Residence at Chedoke as an example. LTCHs in Canada are diverse. Therefore, it is important to acknowledge that St. Peter's and its functioning, nor any other single facility, does not capture the diversity of LTCH operations across the country. Regardless, the examination of a specific facility in Canada could shed light on fundamental differences in care home structures across the world.

St. Peter's Residence at Chedoke is a not-for-profit, charitable home located in Hamilton, Ontario. The home opened in 2004, and since 2013, it has been operated by the Thrive Group. Thrive Group is a non-profit umbrella organization that is governed by a voluntary board of directors. Thrive Group provides back-office support such as finance, human resources, information technologies, and strategic planning. Like other LTCHs, it is common to have an external group provide management expertise for the LTCH.

The organization of residents within the building is divided into units. There are seven units, each housing 30 residents. One of the seven units is a secure (locked) facility that specifically cares for patients with dementia who are actively exit seeking. Most of the rooms are private accommodations, with some shared facilities in two of the seven units. Along with resident rooms that exceed current design standards established by the province, the building was designed with common areas for gathering, recreation, and dining. All meals are prepared in-house. Other amenities available for residents on-site include a hair salon, foot care, dentistry, and transportation using an accessible bus.

St. Peter's employs approximately 325 staff for the facility. Staff involved in the direct day-to-day care of the residents include registered nurses, registered practical nurses, and personal support workers. Along with direct care staff, there are a host of allied health workers involved in the residents' care to ensure care is holistic and resident-centered. These include recreationists, dieticians, occupational therapists, physiotherapists, pharmacists, and social workers. The staffing mix of direct care staff and other allied health staff of St. Peter's Residence is depicted in Table 13.1. Concerning pharmacy services, there is an on-call pharmacist available off-site for consultation.

TABLE 13.1 Direct care staffing mix within St. Peter's Residence

	Day	Evening	Night
Registered Nurse	2	2	2
Registered Practical Nurse	7	7	1
Personal Support Worker	28	21	9
Nurse Practitioner	1	-	-
Occupational Therapist	1	-	-
Physiotherapist	1	-	-
Physiotherapist Assistant	2	-	-
Social Worker	1	-	-
Recreation Therapist	4	2	-
Dietician	1	-	-

Medications are delivered to the home on a weekly basis and ad hoc as needed.

Family physicians (or general practitioners) provide medical services for the residents in long-term care homes (Lam et al., 2012). At St. Peter's Residence, there are two physicians taking care of the 221 residents within the facility. The physicians are required to visit each resident at least twice a month to provide medical services. By requirement, there is a physician available, either in-person or on-call, 24 hours a day. Though basic investigative services, such as x-rays, ultrasounds, and laboratory tests, are carried out within the building premises by mobile units, there is a limit to the extent of medical care that can be delivered. Specialty services are only available by external consultation or through admission to hospitals, and more complex medical care of residents, such as intravenous access, are not feasible.

We hope that a more in-depth discussion of a single LTCH within Canada serves as a reference when comparing facilities across the world.

Challenges

There are a multitude of challenges facing the care of the elderly in long-term care homes in Canada. Many of these are longstanding issues that numerous reports and advocacy groups have attempted to address, but to no avail (Estabrooks et al., 2020).

Currently, there is an unmet demand for long-term care homes in Canada. From 2015 to 2016, there were an estimated 430,000 Canadians with unmet home needs, and of them, more than 40,000 were on waitlists for LTCHs (Gilmour, 2018). A notable manifestation of the unmet demand is the number of alternate level of care (ALC) patients in hospitals. An ALC designation denotes a patient that occupies a hospital bed, though they do not require the intensity of hospital care. ALC rates across the country and between different regions depict a great deal of variability. For instance, in patient days in ALC (%), British Columbia had 13%, whereas Prince Edward Island had 21.5%. Of the patients designated ALC, those waiting for long-term care home placement comprise the largest group at 43%. It has been estimated that hospital-based ALC costs the government $2.3 billion annually (Simpson et al., 2015).

The unmet demand in LTCHs will be exacerbated by the demographic changes within Canada's population. Much like other industrialized countries, Canada's population is aging. A measure of population aging is the number of individuals over the age of 65 years. On July 1, 2020, Canada's total population was 38,005,238, and of that, 6,835,866 or 18% were seniors 65 years or older (Statistics Canada, 2020). By 2068, the proportion of the population that is 65 years or older will be 21.4% to 29.5% depending on the projection scenarios (Statistics Canada, 2019). Forecasting data shows that by 2035, Canada will need 454,000 LTCH beds, which is 199,000 more beds than were available in 2016 (Gibbard, 2017). This will continue to add pressure on a system that is already performing at capacity.

The staffing in care homes is another issue that is well known and understood but not addressed. Simply put, there is not enough staff to carry out the level of care needed for this complex patient population (Laucius, 2018). The trend in reducing regulated nursing staff in favor of unregulated healthcare aides (also known as personal support workers) has created a precarious situation. Healthcare aides often racialized women providing care as part-time employees must work in multiple homes to make a living wage. The wages in LTCHs tend to be lower than in hospitals and, coupled with the physically and mentally challenging work of providing care for LTCH residents, translate to negative consequences for care standards and worker well-being (Chamberlain et al., 2019). The demanding environment and work expected of these workers make it so that "dignified, humanistic care is nearly impossible" (Armstrong et al., 2009).

The physical environment of LTCHs has long been recognized as an issue. Many of the homes in Canada are old, built from 1950 to 1990. These old homes are large and outdated structures that tend to be for-profit homes (Stall et al., 2020). "They resemble hospitals, with communal bathrooms, rooms for 2–4 residents, narrower hallways, large communal dining areas, small crowded nursing stations and medication areas, and limited areas for staff and families away from resident rooms" (Estabrooks et al., 2020). Beyond ensuring there are an adequate number of beds in LTCHs for the growing demand, the design of these facilities must be up to par and future-proof.

The above-discussed challenges facing long-term care homes in Canada converge onto the final challenge, which is the presence of for-profit care homes. No longer are these for-profit homes "mom and pop" ventures; rather, they have become large international publicly traded companies.

There has been extensive research comparing for-profit versus non-profit establishments and notable differences in structure and deliverance of care (Comondore et al., 2009; McGregor et al., 2005; Ronald et al., 2016). For-profit homes have been shown to have less staffing, older infrastructure, and provide an inferior level of care when compared to not-for-profit homes. The for-profit homes in Canada have come under even greater scrutiny during the COVID-19 pandemic as the inferior care has manifested in a greater extent of COVID-19 outbreaks along with a higher number of resident deaths (Stall et al., 2020). To extract profit from a largely publicly funded system, for-profit homes operate in a manner that prioritizes shareholder equity rather than quality of care. There is a growing voice in Canada to increase regulations on for-profit care homes and even abolish the pursuit of profit in the care of the elderly in care homes (Jabbar, 2020).

Conclusion

The future of long-term care in Canada is presently in flux. The COVID-19 pandemic and the disproportionate impact on the elderly population—particularly those within long-term care homes—have brought the current state of LTCHs in Canada to the forefront of public discussion. The various foci of improvement, such as insufficient staffing, increasing demand for long-term care beds, older infrastructures in homes, and shortcomings of for-profit homes, cannot be viewed as separate entities. To address these issues in any meaningful way requires a rethinking of long-term care homes and a new vision of what care homes should be (Armstrong et al., 2020). Like universal health care, long-term care (including LTCHs) must be addressed at the federal level to ensure consistency across the country and universality of the changes.

Providing care for the elderly in an institutional setting, particularly in long-term care homes, is becoming a growing aspect of aging in Canada. However, providing good care in a home-like setting has been a challenge and will remain so for the foreseeable future if the issues plaguing the sector are not addressed. For almost all the residents of long-term care homes, this is their final destination. They deserve the care they need to live their final days with dignity, compassion, and respect. The COVID-19 pandemic has crystallized the shortcomings and provided us with a direction we now must take to ensure quality care for our frail elderly in long-term care homes.

References

Armstrong, P., Armstrong, H., Choiniere, J., Lowndes, R., & Struthers, J. (2020). *Re-imagining long-term residential care in the COVID-19 crisis*. Canadian Centre for Policy Alternatives.

Armstrong, P., Banerjee, A., Szebehely, M., Armstrong, H., Daly, T., & Lafrance, S. (2009). *They deserve better: The long-term care experience in Canada and Scandinavia*. Canadian Centre for Policy Alternatives.

Canada Health Act. (1985). In R.S.C., 1985, c. C-6 (Issue 2014, p. 18).

Canadian Institute for Health Information. (2020a). *Long-term care homes in Canada: How many and who owns them?* CIHI.

Canadian Institute for Health Information. (2020b). *Profile of residents in residential and hospital-based continuing care, 2019–2020*. Quick Stats.

Chamberlain, S. A., Hoben, M., Squires, J. E., Cummings, G. G., Norton, P., & Estabrooks, C. A. (2019). Who is (still) looking after mom and dad? Few improvements in care aides' quality-of-work life. *Canadian Journal on Aging*, 38(1), 35–50. https://doi.org/10.1017/S0714980818000338

Comondore, V. R., Devereaux, P. J., Zhou, Q., Stone, S. B., Busse, J. W., Ravindran, N. C., Burns, K. E., Haines, T., Stringer, B., Cook, D. J., Walter, S. D., Sullivan, T., Berwanger, O., Bhandari, M., Banglawala, S., Lavis, J. N., Petrisor, B., Schünemann, H., Walsh, K., ... Guyatt, G. H. (2009). Quality of care in for-profit and not-for-profit nursing homes: Systematic review and meta-analysis. *BMJ* (Online), 339(7717), 381–384. https://doi.org/10.1136/bmj.b2732

Daly, T. (2015). Dancing the two-step in Ontario's long-term care sector: Deterrence regulation = consolidation. *Studies in Political Economy*, 95(1), 29–58. https://doi.org/10.1080/19187033.2015.11674945

Estabrooks, C. A., Straus, S. E., Flood, C. M., Keefe, J., Armstrong, P., Donner, G. J., Boscart, V., Ducharme, F., Silvius, J. L., & Wolfson, M. C. (2020). Restoring trust: COVID-19 and the future of long-term care in Canada. *Facets*, 5(1), 651–691. https://doi.org/10.1139/FACETS-2020-0056

Francesca, C., Ana, L.-N., Jérôme, M., & Frits, T. (2011). *OECD health policy studies help wanted? Providing and paying for long-term care: providing and paying for long-term care* (Vol. 2011). OECD Publishing.

Gibbard, R. (2017). Sizing up the challenge: Meeting the demand for long-term care in Canada. The Conference Board of Canada, November, 1–48.

Gilmour, H. (2018). Unmet home care needs in Canada. *Health Reports*, 29(11), 3–11.

Government of Ontario. (2018). Long-term care accommodation costs and subsidy. https://www.ontario.ca/page/get-help-paying-long-term-care

Health Canada. (2020). Canada Health Act Annual Report 2018-2019. https://www.canada.ca/en/health-canada/services/publications/health-system-services/canada-health-act-annual-report-2018-2019.html

Hirdes, J. P. (2001). Long-term care funding in Canada: A policy mosaic. *Journal of Aging and Social Policy*, 13(2–3), 69–81. https://doi.org/10.1300/J031v13n02_06

Jabbar, A. (2020, May 6). *Let's keep profit out of long-term care*. The Toronto Star.

Lam, J. M., Anderson, G. M., Austin, P. C., & Bronskill, S. E. (2012). Family physicians providing regular care to residents in Ontario long-term care homes: characteristics and practice patterns. *Canadian Family Physician*, 58(11), 1241–1248.

Laucius, J. (2018, July 13). *"We are in crisis": Personal support workers are the backbone of home care in Ontario — and there aren't enough of them*. Ottawa Citizen.

Local Health Integration Network. (2014). Local Health Integration Network (LHIN). Queen's Printer for Ontario. http://www.lhins.on.ca/

Local Health System Integration Act, 2006 S.O. c4, E-Laws (2006).

McGregor, M. J., Cohen, M., McGrail, K., Broemeling, A. M., Adler, R. N., Schulzer, M., Ronald, L., Cvitkovich, Y., & Beck, M. (2005). Staffing levels in not-for-profit and for-profit long-term care facilities: Does type of ownership matter? *CMAJ*, 172(5), 645–649. https://doi.org/10.1503/cmaj.1040131

Ministry of Health and Long-Term Care. (2013). *Long-term care homes financial policy: LTCH level-of-care per diem funding policy*.

National Institute on Ageing. (2019). *Enabling the future provision of long-term care in Canada*. National Institute on Ageing White Paper.

Nguyen, Q. D., Moodie, E. M., Forget, M., Desmarais, P., Keezer, M. R., & Wolfson, C. (2020). Health heterogeneity in older adults: exploration in the Canadian longitudinal study on aging. *Journal of the American Geriatrics Society*, jgs.16919. https://doi.org/10.1111/jgs.16919

Roblin, B., Deber, R., Kuluski, K., & Silver, M. P. (2019). Ontario's retirement homes and long-term care homes: A comparison of care services and funding regimes. *Canadian Journal on Aging*, 38(2), 155–167. https://doi.org/10.1017/S0714980818000569

Ronald, L. A., McGregor, M. J., Harrington, C., Pollock, A., & Lexchin, J. (2016). Observational evidence of for-profit delivery and inferior nursing home care: When is there enough evidence for policy change? *PLOS Medicine*, 13(4), e1001995. https://doi.org/10.1371/journal.pmed.1001995

Santoni, G., Calderón-Larrañaga, A., Vetrano, D. L., Welmer, A.-K., Orsini, N., & Fratiglioni, L. (2020). Geriatric health charts for individual assessment and prediction of care needs: A population-based prospective study. *The Journals of Gerontology*: Series A, 75(1), 131–138. https://doi.org/10.1093/gerona/gly272

Simpson, C., Caissie, M., & Velji, K. (2015). Canada needs a national seniors' strategy. Toronto Star. https://www.thestar.com/opinion/commentary/2015/01/29/canada-needs-a-national-seniors-strategy.html

Stall, N. M., Jones, A., Brown, K. A., Rochon, P. A., & Costa, A. P. (2020). For-profit long-term care homes and the risk of COVID-19 outbreaks and resident deaths. *Canadian Medical Association Journal*, 192(33), E946–E955. https://doi.org/10.1503/cmaj.201197

Statistics Canada. (2017). 2016 census data tables – type of collective dwelling (16), age (20) and sex (3) for the population in collective dwellings of Canada, provinces and territories, 2016 census – 100% data. https://www12.statcan.gc.ca/census-recensement/2016/dp-pd/dt-td/Rp-eng.cfm?LANG=E&APATH=3&DETAIL=0&DIM=0&FL=A&FREE=0&GC=0&GID=0&GK=0&GRP=1&PID=109537&PRID=10&PTYPE=109445&S=0&SHOWALL=0&SUB=0&Temporal=2016&THEME=116&VID=0&VNAMEE=&VNAMEF=

Statistics Canada. (2019). Population projections for Canada (2018 to 2068), provinces and territories (2018 to 2043).

Statistics Canada. (2020). Canada's population estimates: Age and sex, July 1, 2020. The Daily. https://www150.statcan.gc.ca/n1/daily-quotidien/200929/dq200929b-eng.htm

Vaupel, J. W., Manton, K. G., & Stallard, E. (1979). The impact of heterogeneity in individual frailty on the dynamics of mortality. *Demography*, 16(3), 439–454. https://doi.org/10.2307/2061224

World Report on Ageing and Health. (2015). World Health Organization.

14

EXPANDING POLICIES FOR HIRING FOREIGN LONG-TERM CARE WORKERS IN JAPAN

Current status, challenges, and responses

Noriko Tsukada

Background of long-term care workers in Japan

Public LTC insurance program

The proportion of older adults among the total population was 29.1% on September 15th, 2022. Coupled with a continuously declining fertility rate, which was 1.3 in 2021 and was far below the population replacement level of 2.1, Japan has become the world's fastest and oldest aging society. Within such an aging society, long-term care (LTC) services are required to help support older citizens.

Japan began a public long-term care (LTC) insurance program in 2000, shifting a substantial portion of caregiving responsibility from family members, especially women (traditionally daughters-in-law), to society as a whole (called "Socialization of LTC"). The program was developed due to increased rates of women's labour force participation, the rising number of nuclear family households, and changing cultural values toward caregiving that resulted in a decline in the traditional source of care—female family members.

As our population ages, the number of persons certified as requiring LTC services under the LTC insurance program has been steadily increasing. According to the Ministry of Health, Labour and Welfare (2018b), in the year 2000, the number of persons certified as requiring LTC services under the public LTC insurance program was about 2,180,000, and the number has almost tripled by the year 2018, with about 6,440,000 persons certified as requiring LTC services. Moreover, as the number of persons certified as requiring LTC services increases, the number of actual LTC service users increases as well. It is also reported that the number of actual LTC service users has more than tripled from 1,490,000 in 2000 to 4,740,000 in 2018 (data include LTC preventive service users). Looking at the data more closely, the same data source revealed that in-home service users increased about 3.8 times in 18 years and facility service users increased 1.8 times. Thus, it is not surprising that the need for LTC workers also increased in accordance with the increase in LTC service users under the public LTC insurance program.

Current status of LTC workers in Japan

As our population ages, the number of working-age individuals decreases. Figure 14.1 shows the working-age population (15–64) and workforce, and the necessary number of LTC workers in 2007 and 2025. As shown in Figure 14.1, our working-age population, as well as the overall workforce, will shrink by 15% and by 5–13%, respectively. On the other hand, the necessary number of LTC workers is expected to increase by 80–117% by the year 2025 when all first-wave baby boomers (those who were born between 1947 and 1949) will reach the age of 75. Thus, we are facing a need for a dramatic increase in LTC workers now.

The number of training schools for Certified Care Workers,[1] however, has been decreasing. According to The Japan Association of Training Institutions for Certified Care Workers (2022), in 2022, the number of training schools

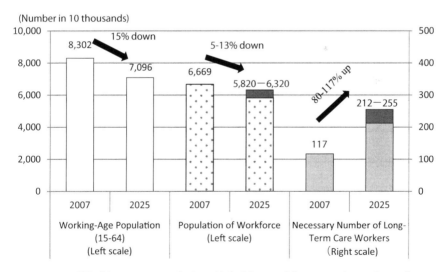

FIGURE 14.1 Working age population (15–64), workforce, and number of care workers needed, 2007 and 2025 (tentative calculation).

Source: Ministry of Health, Labour and Welfare (2010), "Workforce for 'Kaigo' (LTC) and future prospects of care workers," Reported by The 8th Committee for Future Directions of Training Care Workers, December 22, 2010, p.5. (translated by the author).

for Certified Care Workers was 314, which was a decrease of 131 training schools (about 29.5%) from 2008. Not only has the number of training schools been decreasing, but also student enrollment has been decreasing—from 71.8% in 2006 to 54.6% in 2022. Moreover, not all of the Certified Care Workers who do complete these programs end up taking care worker jobs. It is reported that the proportion of Certified Care Workers who are employed in those positions has been decreasing from about 61% in 2001 to about 54% in 2018. To make this situation worse, despite the trend in recent years toward stabilization of turnover rates of LTC workers, turnover rates of LTC workers remained a little higher, 14.3%, than the rate of 13.9% for all industries in 2021 (MHLW, 2022; Care Work Foundation, 2023).

Figure 14.2 presents many reasons why certified care workers changed their care worker jobs. As shown here, the most cited reason was "Human relationships at working place (34.9%)," followed by "Differences in missions of the corporation (33.3%)," "Low salary (29.8%)," and "Demanding job (24.4%)," and "Sexual and power harassment (23.4%)." The top and the fifth reasons turned out to be management issues. These should be solved to improve the working conditions for certified care workers and encourage continued employment in the field.

In summary, the figures introduced above suggest that the number of younger people who are able and willing to provide care to the frail and dependent older population has been decreasing, making the already existing

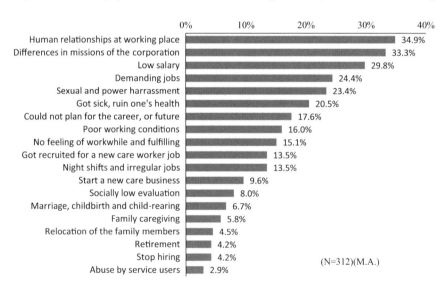

FIGURE 14.2 Reasons for why certified care workers experienced changing jobs.

Source: "Reasons for Why Certified Care Workers Experienced Changing Jobs," p.67, The 12th Research on Working Conditions and Awareness of Expertise among Certified Care Workers, The Japan Association of Certified Care Workers, March, 2017 (translated by the author).

manpower shortage issues more challenging. Given this, there is pessimism that without interventions, Japan will not be able to prepare enough LTC workers to match the LTC service needs generated through the public LTC insurance program. The Ministry of Health, Labour and Welfare (2015) officially estimated that by the year 2025, the demand for LTC workers will be 2,530,000 and the supply of LTC workers will be 2,152,000; as a result, Japan will be short about 377,000 LTC workers (definitive values) in the year 2025, which is coming soon.

Emergence of new era for foreign LTC workers in Japan

Basic principles for accepting foreign workers in Japan

Japan used to be a country where working-age individuals went to other countries seeking employment, including North and South America (the USA, Mexico, Brazil, etc.) until the beginning of the 1960s (Suzuki, 2006). It was only towards the end of the 1970s when foreigners started to come to Japan to work. This was mainly because of special labour demands caused by the Korean War and the lack of manpower related to Japan's high economic growth after World War II. The first Basic Plan for Employment Measures of 1967 the Japanese government issued, however, indicated that Japan would not accept foreign workers.

It is reported that there were discussions regarding foreign workers twice in Japan (Yorimitsu, 2005) after the Basic Plan was adopted. In the late 1970s, the numbers of Indochinese refugees and women from Southeast Asian countries who entered the Japanese entertainment industry started to increase. Additionally, the lack of workers in the fields of manufacturing and construction industries related to the "Bubble Economy" in the 1980s pushed to open labour markets to foreign countries. During this period, the first wave of national discussions occurred regarding foreign worker laws. It is reported that the policy document titled the 6th Basic Plan for Employment Measures of 1988 claimed that Japan promoted foreign workers in professional and technical fields as much as possible. As for unskilled/unprofessional workers, however, it is stated that it should be carefully considered whether or not to accept them, language that suggested that Japan would not accept unskilled workers. Although language added in the 7th Basic Plan for Employment Measures of 1992 included the phrase, "it is necessary to have a national consensus to accept unskilled workers," the general attitude toward accepting unskilled/unprofessional workers has not changed. Thus, admission of unskilled foreign workers into the Japanese workforce was not widely supported officially.

The discussion regarding foreign workers was reignited during the late 1990s, as Japan faced a shrinking workforce caused by ever-decreasing fertility rates. However, in the 9th Basic Plan for Employment Measures of 1999, Japan's general attitude regarding accepting foreign workers remained almost the same as in the past. The plan states that Japan promotes foreign workers in professional and technical fields as much as possible and that it is inevitable that accepting unskilled workers be very carefully considered based on national consensus.

Table 14.1 summarizes a list of status of residence categories, and there are 29 status of residence categories permitted in Japan as of March 2023, available for these individuals to enter Japan. Thus, Japan has maintained its attitude toward foreign workers being necessary to be professional and technical. Therefore, there remain no status of residence permits that allow unskilled workers to work in Japan.

TABLE 14.1 List of status of residence categories (as of March 2023)

Status of residence based on activities	
(1) Can work within a specified range	Diplomat, Official, Professor, Artist, Religious Activities, Journalist, Highly Skilled Professional, Business Manager, Legal /Accounting Services, Medical Services, Researcher, Instructor, Engineer/ Specialist in Humanities/International Services, Intra-company Transferee, Entertainer, Skilled Labor, **Technical Intern Training**,[*1] **Nursing Care (*kaigo*)**,[*2] **Specified Skilled Worker**[*3]
(2) Cannot work	Cultural Activities, Temporary Visitor, Student, Trainee, Dependent
(3) Whether or not people can work will depend on their approved activities	**Designated Activities** (e.g., EPA Certified Care Worker candidates)
Status of residence based on family relation	
(4) Can work with no limitation	Permanent Resident, Long-Term Resident, Spouse or Child of Permanent Resident, Spouse or Child of Japanese Nationals

Source: This table was summarized by the author based on the English translation of the Immigration Control and Refugee Recognition Act (Ministry of Justice, 2023).

[*1] This status of residence was started in 1993 and as of 2020, it included 82 job categories including 150 kinds of work, and a new "Nursing Care" (*kaigo*) job category was added to this status of residence and became effective on November 1, 2017.

[*2] The status of residence category, "Nursing Care" (*kaigo*) was newly created and became effective on September 1, 2017.

[*3] The status of residence category, "Specified Skilled Worker" was newly created and became effective on April 1, 2019.

Policies for accepting foreign LTC workers in Japan

Economic Partnership Agreement (EPA): The first policy for hiring foreign LTC workers

For the first time in its history, in August 2008, Japan officially opened its LTC labour market to foreign workers through an Economic Partnership Agreement (EPA) and started accepting Certified Care Worker candidates from Indonesia in 2008, from the Philippines in 2009, and from Vietnam in 2014. The purpose of this EPA, however, was to strengthen economic relationships between the two countries—not to cope with shortages of LTC workers. Therefore, the EPA limited the number of Certified Care Worker candidates accepted each year to 300 candidates per country.

Although each country in the EPA partnership has a different educational system, EPA-Certified Care Worker candidates who apply to the program are well-educated. For example, candidates from Indonesia are either graduates of higher educational institutions (more than 3 years) and are certified as nursing care workers by the Indonesian government or graduates of nursing schools, either stand-alone schools or schools that are part of a university. During their work experience, it is guaranteed that they are paid equally as Japanese LTC workers with the same qualifications. After 3 years of work experience in Japan as a care worker, EPA Certified Care Worker candidates take a national qualification examination for Certified Care Worker. Once they pass the exam and if they wish, the candidates can remain in Japan and work as a Certified Care Worker for an unlimited period of time by renewing their status of residence, "Designated Activities" shown in Table 14.1 in the previous section. Candidates who fail to pass the exam are supposed to leave Japan; however, those who satisfy certain conditions are given a second chance to take the exam.[2]

Table 14.2 shows results of national qualification exams for EPA Certified Care Worker candidates (Ministry of Health, Labour and Welfare, 2018a & 2023), which are released in every March. The pass rates of EPA-Certified Care Worker candidates range from 36% to 65%, and they are apparently doing a good job, knowing that all examinees' pass rate is about 58% to 84%.

New three policies for expanding the status of residence to hire foreign LTC workers

As previously mentioned, the main purpose of the EPA was not to address LTC workforce shortages. To cope with the shortage, the Japanese government enacted three new unprecedented policies to encompass foreign LTC workers from 2017 through 2019. The policies created a new status of

TABLE 14.2 Pass rates of national examination for EPA-Certified Care Worker candidates (%)

	2012	2013	2014	2015	2016	2017	2018	2019	2020	2021	2022	2023
All Examinees	63.9	64.4	64.6	61.0	57.9	72.1	70.8	73.7	69.9	71.0	72.3	84.3
EPA Candidates	37.9	39.8	36.3	44.8	50.9	49.8	50.7	46.0	44.5	46.2	36.9	65.4

Source: This table was summarized by the author based on the data from Ministry of Health, Labor and Welfare, 2018a & 2023

※*Candidates have mitigated exam conditions as follows:* (i) Inscription of all "Kanji" characters, (ii) English writings side by side for the names of the diseases, and (iii) 1.5 times expanded test time.

residence category, "Nursing Care" and added a "nursing care" job category option to an already existing status of residence—the "*Ginou-jissyu*" (Technical Intern Training) program in 2017, and created another status of residence, called "Specified Skilled Worker" in 2019.

As for the first new policy, this newly created status of residence allows foreigners to work as LTC workers in Japan if they hold a national qualification for Certified Care Workers. This policy became effective on September 1, 2017, and its transitional measures began on June 1, 2017. Prior to this, foreigners, even with a Japanese national qualification for Certified Care Worker, could not work in Japan. It is apparent that LTC jobs were not perceived to be professional or highly skilled jobs, even with a national qualification which was established in 1987.

Regarding the second new policy, the government added a "nursing care" job category to an existing status of residence called the "*Ginou-jissyu*" (Technical Intern Training) program, which originally began in 1993. The purpose of the Technical Intern Training program is human resource development in developing countries by transferring Japanese skills and technologies to future workers. Currently, the training program encompasses 82 job categories with 150 types of work. The program is not without problems (e.g., such exploitation of the human rights of trainees as unpaid wages, forcing trainees to work longer hours and/or in dangerous working conditions, passports being taken away by brokers, and a lot of debts before entering Japan), which have been pointed out and gained government attention (Iguchi, 2001; Japanese Bar Association, 2011; Miyajima & Suzuki, 2014; The Ministry of Internal Affairs and Communications, 2013; Japan Federation of National Service Employees, 2015; Ito, 2019; Koyama, 2019; Shimoyama & Ushida, 2020). Therefore, to ensure proper Technical Intern Training program and protection of Technical Intern Trainees in all job categories, the program newly established the Organization for Technical Intern Training (OTIT), which aims to promote international cooperation by transferring skills, technologies, or knowledge in Japanese industries to developing countries through human resource development (OTIT, 2017).

As for the "Nursing Care" trainees, this policy allows foreigners with Japanese Language Proficiency Test (JLPT)[3] level 4 (N4) to work in Japan to learn Japanese LTC skills and knowledge for the purpose of technology transfer with a maximum stay of 5 years. This language requirement was specifically added to the "Nursing Care" job category, knowing that "Nursing Care" is considered not to be the same as other trainings (e.g., working on the frontline of factories) and that "Nursing Care" requires communication skills. The "Nursing Care" trainees were expected to be at JLPT level 3 at the second year of training and to leave Japan if they won't meet the criteria.

However, the requirement was relaxed one year later. The policy change should have been contemplated thoroughly before its abolishment.

Moreover, the newly started policy in 2019 raised another issue. Originally, the purpose of the "*Ginou-jissyu*" (Technical Intern Training) Program is "technology transfer," and trainees go home after a maximum stay of 5 years; however, the latest policy that will be mentioned below enabled trainees to continue staying in Japan for an additional 5 years. As a result, trainees can stay working in Japan for a total of 10 years if they meet certain requirements, but without having their family members around.

The most recent policy regarding hiring foreign LTC workers is different than the polices we have reviewed so far. The government created a new status of residence, "Specified Skilled Worker" to make up for the labour shortages in 14 job categories, including "nursing care" in 2018 and became effective on April 1, 2019. This was the very first time the Japanese government stated that the purpose of the new policy was to make up for labour shortages. It is reported that Japan accepted about 5,000 LTC skilled workers for the first year and is supposed to hire up to 60,000 in 5 years. This new policy allows LTC skilled workers to stay in Japan for a maximum stay of 5 years. As mentioned above, "nursing care" trainees under the status of residence "*Ginou-jissyu*" (Technical Intern Training) can move to this new status of residence, "Specified Skilled Workers," without taking tests once they finish three years of training. Since trainees under "*Ginou-jissyu*" (Technical Intern Training) Program can stay and work up to 5 years under the program, in total, they can stay for a maximum of 10 years in Japan. Moreover, if they pass the national exam for the Certified Care Worker, then they can continue staying in Japan by renewing their status of residence forever. If this happens, it is noteworthy that the original purpose of "*Ginou-jissy*" (Technical Intern Training), "technology transfer," will have been lost and inconsistency occurs.

As of December 2022, it is reported that there were 130,915 foreigners under the status of residence, "Specified Skilled Worker." Among them, 16,081 foreigners (12.3%) are working in the LTC settings, and 5,958 (37%) came from Vietnam, followed by 3,286 (20.4%) from Indonesia and 2,049 (12.7%) from the Philippines (Ministry of Justice, 2022).

Nationwide survey—interview and mail surveys

Interview survey for LTC institutions for older adults that accepted EPA-Certified *Care Worker* candidates

The very first policy in Japan's history to accept foreign LTC workers was based on the EPA, where Certified Care Worker candidates came from Indonesia in 2008 first. Many Japanese people wondered how this policy worked and how those candidates lived and worked in Japan. During this time, news media coverage related to this LTC policy, service users' needs, and various issues related to this EPA policy (salary, job treatment, physical burden, "3K-job,"[4] etc.) were frequently reported.

At such a time, the following research was conducted to find out how administrators of LTC institutions for older adults, that accepted EPA-Certified Care Worker candidates, would perceive their institutional experience and to determine what sorts of problems they were encountering as employers. Interviews were conducted with either administrators and/or those who were in charge of EPA Certified Care Worker candidates.

Interview survey method

The interview survey was funded by the government[5] and was conducted during October 2009 through February 2010 (4 months) and during August 2010 through February 2011 (6 months). All nationwide LTC institutions that accepted EPA-Certified Care Worker candidates were contacted to see if they would agree to an interview. For the first year of research, 11 out of 53 LTC institutions that accepted the first team of Indonesian EPA-Certified Care Worker candidates agreed to participate in the interview, and the participation rate was 20.8%. For the second year, 20 out of 85 LTC institutions that accepted the second team of Indonesian EPA-Certified Care Worker candidates (the participation rate: 23.5%) as well as 26 out of 92 LTC institutions that accepted the first team of Philippine's EPA-Certified Care Worker candidates (the participation rate: 28.3%) agreed to participate in the interview survey.

During the first year, it took a long time to find institutions that agreed to participate in the interview; however, in the second year, hurdles for recruiting research participants went down tremendously, and more institutions agreed to participate in the interview within a much shorter period of time. As a result, a total of 57 LTC institutions throughout the country were interviewed, including Okinawa Prefecture in the south and Hokkaido in the north part of Japan. Out of 57 institutions, one interview was not conducted as scheduled at one institution on site, though lots of discussions were made. Moreover, interviews were not permitted to be recorded at two institutions, though interviews were actually conducted. Therefore, results of three institutions were omitted from the analyses. At the same time, two people responded to the interview questions respectively at three institutions; therefore, 57 responses in total were analyzed for this qualitative research.

Major interview questions to administrators

Major interview questions included the following eight questions: ① reasons for accepting "EPA Certified Care Worker candidates," ② whether or not administrators see the following four types of concerns: (i) candidates' ability to write Japanese, (ii) candidates' communication skills in Japanese with their Japanese co-workers, (iii) candidates' communication skills in Japanese with the clients and their family members, and (iv) candidates being prejudiced against by clients in the presence of foreigners. These four types of concerns were drawn from another survey of what administrators would worry most should they accept foreign LTC workers, and so they were verified in this interview, ③ kinds of preparations accepting institutions have made, ④ issues where they thought there might be a potential problem prior to the arrival of these workers but that turned out to be no problem related to those issues; also, experience in the course of working with this foreign worker program, in which something totally unexpected happened, ⑤ what interviewees would like to ask other facilities that have accepted these candidates from Indonesia or the Philippines, ⑥ the most difficult problem in relation to accepting EPA Certified Care Worker candidates and the most rewarding experience in the course of working with these future nursing care workers, ⑦ advice for those Japanese LTC facilities that are contemplating ways to participate in this EPA-Certified Care Worker program, and ⑧ suggestions for people in the community, local governments, the Japan International Corporations of Welfare Services (JICWELS), and Ministry of Health, Labour and Welfare regarding this EPA Certified Care Worker program.

Major research outcomes

This paper introduces outcomes gained from administrators regarding the second question: four types of concerns. Table 14.3 summarizes major responses to the four types of concerns. As shown in Table 14.3, before EPA Certified Care Worker candidates came to Japan, there were lots of concerns regarding cultural, religious, or food habits differences, etc. However, it turned out that these did not become major issues as previously expected. One of the reasons for this was that Japanese staff members, sometimes including clients' family members, learned about the countries, cultures, and religions of EPA-Certified Care Worker candidates and prepared for their arrival in advance.

Moreover, as for their nursing skills, the EPA-Certified Care Worker candidates provided quality care, and there were no problems that administrators identified. One of the reasons for this was that the EPA Certified Care Worker candidates were already trained and educated as nurses or a nursing care workers in their home countries. As a result, overall, they were

TABLE 14.3 Major responses to the four types of concerns

Concerns	Major responses (time passed after acceptance of EPA candidates)
(i) The ability to write case records and work diaries in Japanese	- We have not asked them to write case records or work diaries that are being handed from one shift to another (because they cannot write Japanese) (7 months). - We don't have them write case records and work diaries. They can read computer characters but not written characters (13 months).
(ii) The ability to communicate with their colleagues efficiently or to leave and receive instructions about case work at the time of shift changes	- There is no problem. They ask (Japanese staff members) again and study when they don't understand jargon. And Japanese staff members also try to speak slowly and use easier words to help them understand (8 months). - As for communication with Japanese staff members, there is no problem because they can ask again. Probably due to their refraining, we have often noticed that hearing "yes, we understand" did not necessarily mean that they really understood it (11months). - They don't understand deeply what Japanese staff members mean. Although there are mistakes with particles, we are impressed by their becoming to understand Japanese this much in such a short time. Their ability to understand is fast (11 months).
(iii) The ability to communicate efficiently with our nursing care clients in Japanese	- We had concerns about whether they can be accustomed to dialects, but they unexpectedly appear to enjoy using dialects during communications. They nicely communicate even with clients with dementia (9 months). - There is no problem at all in this regard. They communicate with clients using full body language, with charming faces full of smiles. They use their whole body to communicate because they know they are insufficient in language proficiency. By now, they are more popular among clients (than the Japanese staff members) (10 months).
(iv) Prejudice of our nursing care clients against foreigners	- No problems at all (Many interviewees responded so). - There were no prejudice and no problems among clients. Rather, they were welcomed (Many interviewees responded so). - Candidate were encouraged by clients because they made efforts to try to understand clients gently, with no bargaining to compensate for their language proficiency, and those attitudes were understood (Many interviewees responded so).

Source: Tsukada, N. (2012) "Casebook about LTC Institutions that Accepted EPA Certified Care Worker Candidates." (translated by the author).

well-liked in the Japanese LTC institutions for older adults and received many compliments about their work from their clients they were serving.

There were, of course, institutions that were having difficulties dealing with EPA Certified Care Worker candidates in the study. Typical difficulties identified included the following:

- "Candidates wouldn't study the Japanese language seriously."
- "Some candidates said, 'I am not smart, so I cannot understand Japanese. Will you let me work instead?'"
- "Candidates asked for longer vacation periods to go back home."
- "Candidates asked for higher salaries and bonuses."
- "Candidates sent lots of money to their home countries, leaving them with very little money to live on."

Despite these noted difficulties, research outcomes revealed that most administrators were unnecessarily worried. More importantly, many administrators indicated that they felt they had a lot to learn from EPA-Certified Care Worker candidates (e.g., smiles, sincere attitudes toward clients, the fundamentals of social welfare, a sense of humor, gentleness) once they began working at their institution. As a result, many administrators indicated that they would like to help the EPA-Certified Care Worker candidates with their studies toward the National Qualification Examinations for Certified Care Worker at the end of the 3 years of their work experience. As shown in Table 14.2, it turned out that the very first passing rate was not that bad at 37.9%, knowing the passing rate of all examinees was 63.9% in 2012.

Mail survey for perceptions of both administrators and Japanese LTC workers toward new policy options to accept foreign LTC workers

Given the fact that Japan has a relatively short history of working with foreign LTC workers, this mail survey was conducted to explore how administrators and LTC workers perceive new policy options that expand the status of residence categories to accept foreign LTC workers, including creating a new status of residence and adding a "Nursing Care" job category to the "*Ginou-jissyu*" (Technical Intern Training) program. This research was conducted before a new status of residence, "Specified Skilled Worker," was created, so this research did not include a question on "Specified Skilled Worker."

Mail survey method and major questions asked

The data used in this study were obtained from a nationwide mail survey of LTC institutions for older adults. This mail government-supported survey[6] was conducted during September to October of 2014, which was before the two new policy actions were actually enacted. A stratified random sampling method was used. Structured questionnaires were sent to a randomly selected 3,932 LTC institutions for older adults that were covered by public Long-Term Care Insurance. A total of 722 responses from administrators and 586 responses from LTC workers were obtained, and the response rates were 18.4% and 14.9%, respectively.

① Characteristics of the responding LTC institutions for older adults

Table 14.4 summarized characteristics of the responding LTC institutions obtained from administrators. The response rates of three kinds of institutions were almost the same as the actual proportions in Japan; however, the turnover rates of responding institutions appeared a bit lower than the national average of 17%. Nevertheless, about 50% of the respondents indicated that the number of LTC worker applicants to their institution falls below recruitment levels sometimes, always, or hardly. Moreover, about 70% of the institutions were not satisfied with the number of their LTC workers at their institution. Types and characteristics of the responding LTC institutions obtained from LTC workers were similar to those for administrators.

TABLE 14.4 Characteristics of responding institutions for the elderly (N=722)

Variables		n	(%)
Types of Institutions	LTC Facilities for the elderly	457	(63.3)
	LTC Health Facilities	203	(28.1)
	Recuperation Care Facilities for the elderly	55	(7.6)
Capacity of Institutions	1 ~ 50	181	(25.1)
	51 ~ 100	423	(58.6)
	101 ~ 150	82	(11.4)
	151 ~ 200	21	(2.9)
	201 or more	5	(0.7)
	No answer	10	(1.3)
Turnover Rates	Less than 5%	236	(32.7)
	5 ~ Less than 10%	221	(30.6)
	10 ~ Less than 15%	121	(16.8)
	15 ~ Less than 20%	60	(8.3)
	20 ~ Less than 25%	31	(4.3)
	25% or more	26	(3.6)
	No answer	27	(3.7)

(Continued)

TABLE 14.4 Continued

Variables		n	(%)
Recruitment Status of LTC Workers	Applicants are always more than recruitment levels	39	(5.4)
	Applicants are barely the same as recruitment levels	155	(21.5)
	Applicants sometimes fall below recruitment levels	143	(19.8)
	Applicants always fall below recruitment levels	180	(24.8)
	<u>Applicants hardly meet recruitment levels</u>	<u>182</u>	<u>(25.2)</u>
	No answer	23	(3.2)
Satisfaction Levels of Quality and Quantity of Care Workers	Satisfied with both quality and quantity	45	(6.2)
	Satisfied with quality but not with quantity	213	(29.5)
	Satisfied with quantity but not with quality	144	(19.9)
	<u>Not satisfied with quality or quantity</u>	<u>302</u>	<u>(41.9)</u>
	No answer	18	(2.5)
EPA Certified Care Worker Candidates	<u>Never accepted before</u>	<u>681</u>	<u>(94.3)</u>
	Have accepted before	41	(5.7)
Reasons for Accepting EPA's Certified Care Workers (M.A.) (n=41)	1. Accumulate know-how by accepting foreign LTC Workers in the future	<u>27</u>	<u>(65.9)</u>
	2. International Contribution	22	(53.7)
	3. Activation for workplace	16	(39.0)
	4. Facing a necessity of LTC workers	12	(29.3)
	5. Stimulation for Japanese LTC workers	11	(26.8)
	6. Because excellent foreign LTC workers are coming to Japan	8	(19.5)
	7. Candidates stay in the institution for at least 3 years	7	(17.1)
	8. Helpful for educating Japanese LTC workers	7	(17.1)

Source: Tsukada, N. (2018) "A Study of Factors that Affect Administrator's Views of Accepting Foreign Long-Term Care Workers: Analyses of a Nationwide Mail Survey," Japanese Journal of Social Welfare, 59(2), pp. 92–106, Table 1 on p. 96 (modified and translated by the author).
※Underlined parts in Table 4 are the highest value and proportion among the responses for each question.

② Characteristics of the respondents (administrators)

Table 14.5 shows the characteristics of the 722 administrators who responded. As shown here, the most frequently cited age range was 50 through 60 (35.2%), and about 75% were male. About 45% of the administrators had less than 5 years of experience as administrators. The most frequently indicated qualification (MA) was Care Manager (36.4%), followed by Social Welfare Officer (33.7%).

TABLE 14.5 Characteristics of the respondents (administrators) (N=722)

Variables		n	(%)
Age	Less than 30 years old	1	(0.1)
	30 ~ Less than 40	61	(8.4)
	40 ~ Less than 50	126	(17.5)
	<u>50 ~ Less than 60</u>	<u>254</u>	<u>(35.2)</u>
	60 ~ Less than 70	224	(31.0)
	70 ~ Less than 80	35	(4.8)
	80 years or more	7	(1.0)
	No answer	14	(2.0)
Sex	<u>Male</u>	<u>523</u>	<u>(74.9)</u>
	Female	175	(25.1)
Years of Experience as an Administrator	Less than 1 year	62	(8.6)
	<u>1 ~ Less than 5 years</u>	<u>260</u>	<u>(36.0)</u>
	5 ~ Less than 10 years	203	(28.1)
	10 ~ Less than 15 years	107	(14.8)
	15 ~ Less than 20 years	42	(5.8)
	More than 20 years	25	(3.5)
	No answer	23	(3.2)
Qualifications (M.A.)	Certificate of Administrators for Social Welfare Institutions	171	(23.7)
	Social Workers	114	(15.8)
	Certified Social Worker	1	(0.1)
	Certified Care Workers	132	(18.3)
	A Social Welfare Officer	243	(33.7)
	<u>Care Managers</u>	<u>263</u>	<u>(36.4)</u>
	Home Helpers	65	(9.0)
	Nurses	5	(6.5)
	Medical Doctors or Dentists	5	(6.5)
	No qualification	145	(20.1)
	Others	81	(11.2)
	No answer	18	(2.4)

Source: Tsukada, N. (2018) Ibid. Table 2 on p.98 (modified and translated by the author).
※Underlined parts in Table 5 are the highest value and proportion among the responses for each question.

③ Characteristics of the respondents (LTC workers)

Table 14.6 shows the characteristics of the 586 LTC workers who responded to this mail survey. As shown here, the most frequently cited age range was 30 through 40 (36.7%), and about 53% were female. The most frequently cited years of experience as an LTC worker was 10 through 15 years (34.1%); however, about one-third of the LTC workers had less than 10 years of LTC

TABLE 14.6 Characteristics of the respondents (LTC workers) (N=586)

Variables		n	(%)
Age	Less than 30 years old	33	(5.6)
	30 ~ Less than 40	<u>214</u>	<u>(36.5)</u>
	40 ~ Less than 50	161	(27.5)
	50 ~ Less than 60	141	(24.1)
	60 ~ Less than 70	30	(5.1)
	70 ~ Less than 80	2	(0.3)
	80 years or more	1	(0.2)
	No answer	4	(0.7)
Sex	Male	269	(45.9)
	Female	<u>313</u>	<u>(53.4)</u>
	No answer	4	(0.7)
Years of Experience as an LTC Worker	Less than 1 year	5	(0.9)
	1 ~ Less than 5 years	54	(9.2)
	5 ~ Less than 10 years	126	(21.5)
	<u>10 ~ Less than 15 years</u>	<u>200</u>	<u>(34.1)</u>
	15 ~ Less than 20 years	120	(20.5)
	More than 20 years	71	(12.1)
	No answer	10	(1.7)
Qualifications (M.A.)	Home Helpers	168	(28.7)
	Certified Social Worker	26	(4.4)
	Approved Certified Social Worker	4	(0.7)
	Care Managers	193	(32.9)
	A Social Welfare Officer	140	(23.9)
	<u>Certified Care Worker</u>	<u>478</u>	<u>(81.6)</u>
	Nurses	29	(4.9)
	Assistant Nurses	6	(1.0)
	Childcare Worker	29	(4.9)
	No qualifications	15	(2.6)
	Others	26	(4.4)

Source: This table was created by the author.

※Underlined parts in Table 6 are the highest value and proportion among the responses for each question.

worker experience. The most frequently indicated qualification (M.A.) among LTC workers was Certified Care Worker (81.6%), followed by Care Manager (22.9%).

Major research outcomes

Q1. Which levels of JLPT do you require for foreign LTC workers?

Figure 14.3 shows outcomes obtained from both administrators and LTC workers to Q1. As shown here, it is interesting to note that LTC workers

Expanding policies for hiring foreign LTC workers in Japan 247

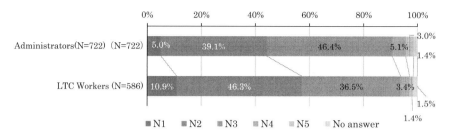

FIGURE 14.3 JLPT levels required by administrators and LTC workers.

Source: Tsukada, N. (2015a). "Nationwide survey on foreign LTC workers," Chiiki Caring (Regional Caring), 17(8), 75–81, Figure 2 on p.78. Permission for reuse of the original figure in Japanese was obtained from Chiiki Caring (translated by the author).

required higher JLPT levels than administrators. About 57% of the LTC workers felt at least JLPT level 2 or higher was necessary, as opposed to 44% of the administrators who felt so. Given that Japanese LTC workers are the ones who work with foreign LTC workers in daily practice, they may have a stronger sense of the level of Japanese proficiency needed to avoid unnecessary trouble communicating with foreign workers.

Q2. How do you feel about accepting foreign LTC workers?

Figure 14.4 shows outcomes for how respondents feel about accepting foreign LTC workers in Japan. As shown here, there was a difference between administrators and Japanese LTC workers. 59% of the administrators ("agree very much" + "agree") agreed to accept foreign LTC workers, but only about 49% of the Japanese LTC workers agreed.

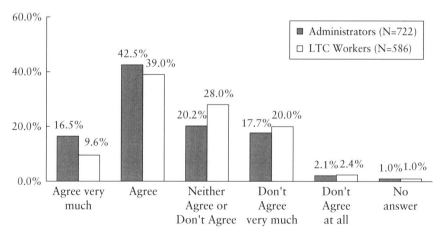

FIGURE 14.4 Perceptions to accept foreign LTC workers.

Source: Tsukada, N. (2015a). Ibid. Figure 1 in p.77. Permission for reuse of the original figure in Japanese was obtained from Chiiki Caring (translated by the author).

Q3. To what extent do you think the following factors are related to securing and retaining LTC workers in general?

Table 14.7 shows outcomes for this question where both administrators and LTC workers were asked to rate their perceptions of each factor. The numbers are averages of 5-point scaled scores. As shown here, there were differences in perceived scores for factors relating to securing and retaining rates of LTC workers between administrators and LTC workers, and the scores for LTC workers were higher than those for administrators for all factors but one (characteristics of location requirements for where LTC institutions are located).

TABLE 14.7 Averaged scores for factors relating to security and retention rates of LTC workers

Factors	Administrators (N=722)	LTC Workers (N=586)	t-test
Secure proper salary level that matches job description.	4.15	4.36	***
Qualifications, experience and duration of work experience can be reflected in the salary.	3.94	4.12	***
There are explicit goals and rules for career-up	3.54	3.64	n.s.
Opportunities to study and training systems for non-regular staff members as well.	3.25	3.41	**
Non-regular staff members can become regular employees.	3.58	3.88	***
Paid working environments for LTC and child-rearing are well established.	3.70	4.12	***
Multi-faceted personnel evaluation system is established.	3.27	3.48	***
Characteristics of location requirements for where LTC institutions are located (weather, population density, etc.).	3.53	3.37	**
Work-life balance (e.g., flexible time) is being promoted.	3.49	3.75	***
Public relations activities to promote awareness and understanding of LTC jobs are planned through work experience and media.	3.14	3.16	n.s.

(Continued)

Factors	Administrators (N=722)	LTC Workers (N=586)	t-test
Good communication in the workplace with colleagues and bosses.	4.12	4.28	**
LTC workers' competency, attitude, and pride toward their jobs	3.82	3.86	n.s.
Levels of social contributions and influence of professional organizations relating to LTC	3.12	3.21	n.s.
Various support systems including annual check-ups, back pain prevention devices, and mental health.	3.41	3.63	***
Promote its images of LTC workers.	3.70	3.76	n.s.
Promote social reputations and status.	3.90	3.97	n.s.
Promote management skills of administrators.	3.82	3.89	n.s.

Source: Tsukada, N. (2015a). Ibid. Table 1 on p.77, modified and added t-test results to the original table in Japanese. Permission for reuse of the original table was obtained from Chiiki Caring (translated by the author).

※5-point scale used in the study indicates 5 for the highest.

※**$p<0.01$; ***$p<0.001$; n.s.=not significant.

Although both groups indicated the highest scores for "secure proper salary level that matches job description," followed by "good communication in the workplace with colleagues and bosses," LTC workers also rated high for the factor of "qualification, experience and duration of work experience can be reflected to the salary" (4.12), and "paid working environment for LTC and child-rearing is well established" (4.12). Moreover, the biggest gap found between the two was 0.42 for "paid working environment for LTC and child-rearing is well established," followed by 0.3 for "Non-regular staff members can become regular employees," and 0.26 for "work-life balance (e.g. flexible time) is being promoted." Thus, it is very critical to increase salary levels to secure and retain LTC workers.

Q4. To what extent do you think these items are challenging when accepting EPA/foreign LTC workers?

Table 14.8 shows outcomes for this question where both administrators and LTC workers were asked to rate their perceptions for each item. As shown here, there were differences between the two, and LTC workers rated all items

TABLE 14.8 Averaged scores for challenges to accept EPA/foreign LTC workers

Factors	Administrators (N=722)	LTC Workers (N=586)	t-test
Can communicate with clients, their family members, and Japanese staff members	3.85	4.16	***
Can understand clients and build trust relationships with them	3.79	4.06	***
Prejudice and discomfort of clients and their family members	3.42	3.70	***
Prejudice and discomfort of Japanese staff members	3.03	3.26	***
Troubles caused by differences among cultures, customs, food habits, values, and religions	3.73	3.90	**
Human relationships with Japanese staff members become awkward	3.07	3.30	***
Cooperative environment may decrease once foreign LTC workers get together and speak their native language and do not interact Japanese staff members	3.08	3.37	***
Take time to have them get accustomed to work environment by providing psychological and language support	3.73	3.87	**
Various problems may occur out of office hours	3.29	3.37	n.s.
Problems relating to invitation of their family members	3.24	3.28	n.s.
Disappear suddenly from the workplace due to various reasons (e.g., marriages)	3.58	3.72	*
Cannot read or write Japanese fully	4.11	4.27	***
Strong self-assertion and/or dry reactions for extending working hours	3.53	3.78	***
Need to look for and/or provide with residence	3.29	3.31	n.s.
Hard to dismiss foreign LTC workers when violating contracts	3.42	3.36	n.s.

Factors	Administrators (N=722)	LTC Workers (N=586)	t-test
Troubles may occur due to Japanese staff members being unfamiliar with working with foreigners	3.08	3.28	**
Relationships do not work well or conflict with support groups for foreigners	3.28	3.35	n.s.
Foreign LTC workers may move to other institutions after passing the national exam.	3.43	3.39	n.s.
Clerical procedures to obtain visa may be cumbersome	3.39	N/A	N/A

Source: Tsukada, N. (2016). "A study on accepting foreign LTC workers," Chiiki Caring (Regional Caring), 18(6), 65–75, Table 1, p.69, modified and added t-test results to the original table in Japanese. Permission for reuse of the original table was obtained from Chiiki Caring (translated by the author).
※**$p<0.01$; n.s.=not significant.
※5-point scale used in the study indicates 5 for the highest.
※N/A= "Non-applicable."

higher than administrators except for two administrative items, including "Hard to dismiss foreign LTC workers when violating contracts" and "Foreign LTC workers may move to other institutions after passing the national exam."

Perceived challenges for both administrators and LTC workers were the same for the top three items, and the highest averaged score was obtained for the item, "Cannot read or write Japanese fully," followed by "Can communicate with clients, their family members and Japanese staff members" and "Can understand clients and build trust relationships with them." The biggest gap in average scores found between the two groups was 0.31 for the item "Can communicate with clients, their family members and Japanese staff members," and the second biggest gap was 0.29 for "Cooperative environment may decrease once foreign LTC workers get together and speak their native language and not interact Japanese staff members," followed by 0.28 for the item "Prejudice and discomfort of clients and their family members."

Q5. Do you agree with the three policy options, including increasing EPA Certified Care Worker candidates, creating a new status of residence, "Nursing Care," and adding a "Nursing Care" job category to "*Ginoujussyu*" (Technical Intern Training) program?

Figure 14.5 (a) through (c) shows outcomes for three policy options respectively. As shown in Figures, for all three policy options, administrators agreed more than LTC workers did, and among the three policy options,

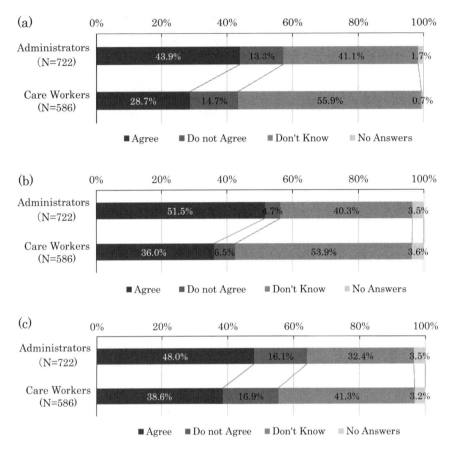

FIGURE 14.5 Perceptions toward three policy options (a). Increasing EPA Certified Care Worker Candidates. (b). Creating a New Status of Residence, "Nursing Care." (c). Adding a "Nursing Care" Job Category to the "*Ginou-jissyu*"(Technical Intern Training) Program.

Source: Tsukada, N. (2016). Ibid. Figures 3-5, p.70. Permission for reuse of 3 original figures in Japanese was obtained from Chiiki Caring (translated by the author).

administrators agreed most with creating a new status of residence "nursing care" at 51.5%, followed by adding a "nursing care" job category to the "*Ginou-jissyu*" (Technical Intern Training) program (48%), and increasing EPA Certified Care Worker candidates (43.9%). It is conceivable that administrators are more concerned with shortages of LTC workers as they need to manage their institutions, so they were more aggressive and tended to agree with any kinds of increase in the number of LTC workers more than LTC workers.

On the other hand, it was interesting that LTC workers agreed most with adding a "nursing care" job category to the "*Ginou-jissyu*" (Technical Intern Training) program at 38.6%, followed by creating a new status of residence (36%) and increasing EPA-Certified Care Worker candidates (28.7%). Thus, LTC workers were more passive in terms of accepting foreign LTC workers, and it is probable that they are the ones who communicate and work with foreign LTC workers in daily practice, so they may be hoping they don't want to avoid difficult and/or troublesome situations. Probably for the same reason, LTC workers are more likely than administrators not to agree with the three policy options.

Q6. Reasons for why respondents agreed or did not agree with the third policy option (M.A.).

Figure 14.6 shows reasons for why administrators and LTC workers agreed with the third policy option, adding a "Nursing Care" job category to the "*Ginou-jissyu*" (Technical Intern Training) program.

As shown in Figure 14.6, for both administrators and LTC workers, the most cited reason was "It's obvious that LTC workers are running out" (85.9% and 77.4%, respectively), followed by "Contributions to other aging countries through transferring LTC knowledge and skills" (55.6% and 50%) and "It's natural to accept foreign workers as a developed country" (48.1% and 43.8%, respectively). It should be noted that about 20% of LTC workers agreed with "*Ginou-jissyu*" for the reason, "securing manpower with relatively low costs."

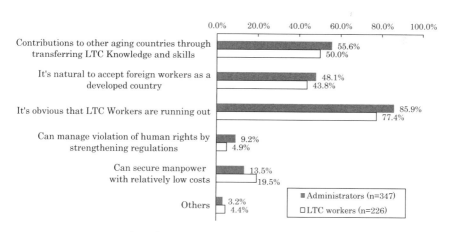

FIGURE 14.6 Reasons for why respondents agreed with adding a "Nursing Care" job category to the "*Ginou-Jissyu*" (Technical Intern Training) Program (MA).

Source: Tsukada, N. (2015a). Ibid. Figure 3, p. 78. Permission for reuse of the original figure in Japanese was obtained from Chiiki Caring (translated by the author).

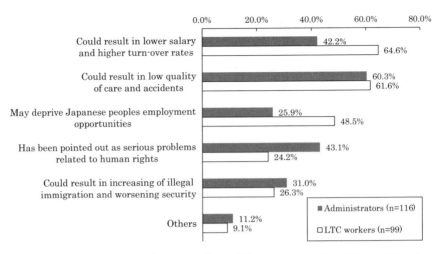

FIGURE 14.7 Reasons for why respondents did not agree with adding a "Nursing Care" job.

Source: Tsukada, N. (2015a). Ibid. Figure 4 on p.79. Permission for reuse of the original figure in Japanese was obtained from Chiiki Caring (translated by the author).

Next, Figure 14.7 shows reasons why administrators and LTC workers did not agree with the third policy option. As shown in Figure 14.7, there were some differences in responses between the two groups in the order of rated responses as well as their proportions for each reason. As for administrators, they did not agree with the reason "Could result in low quality of care and accidents" (60.3%) most, followed by "Has been pointed out as serious problems relating to human rights" (43.1%), and "Could result in lower salary and higher turn-over rates" (42.2%). On the other hand, as for LTC workers, the most cited reason was "Could result in lower salary and higher turn-over rates" (64.6%), followed by "Could result in low quality of care and accidents" (61.6%), and "May deprive Japanese people's employment opportunities" (48.5%). It can be inferred that by hiring LTC technical intern trainees, they were concerned with further lowering salaries, which is already low.

Challenges and future directions for long-term care workers in Japan

Before hiring foreign LTC workers: more management skills needed for administrators

Care Work Foundation (2020) in Japan reported survey outcomes on actual conditions of LTC labour. The report contains responses collected from 21,585 LTC workers working under public LTC insurance in 2019.

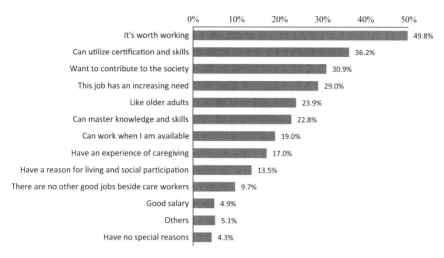

FIGURE 14.8 Reasons for why care workers chose their jobs (M.A.).

Source: Care Work Foundation (2020), "Surveys on Actual Conditions for LTC Labour," p.48 translated by the author).

Figure 14.8 shows reasons for why care workers chose their LTC worker jobs (M.A.). As shown in Figure 14.8, about 50% of LTC workers chose their jobs because they thought "It's worth working (49.8%)," followed by "Can utilize certifications and skills (36.2%)" and "Want to contribute to the society (30.9%)."

Figure 14.9 shows reasons for why care workers quit their previous care related jobs. As shown in Figure 14.9, the most cited reason was "Had problems with human relationships at the working place (27.5%)," followed by "Dissatisfaction with missions of the corporation (22.8%)," "Found better jobs/working places (19.0%)," and "Low salary (18.6%)." The top two reasons turned out to be management related issues.

It is a regrettable situation where LTC workers who like to be in the job field had to leave their jobs because of their dislike of the management practices where they work. Therefore, the working environment should be promptly improved for care workers. It is suggested that the management skills of the administrators should never be underestimated in coping with shortages of the LTC workforce (Kitaura, 2013).

Challenges for hiring foreign LTC workers in Japan

Major challenges that Japan has identified from hiring EPA-Certified Care Worker candidates are summarized in the following four points. First is the Japanese language issue. Even highly educated EPA-Certified Care Workers

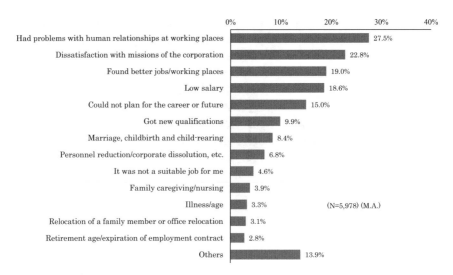

FIGURE 14.9 Reasons for why care workers quit their previous care-related jobs (M.A.).

Source: Care Work Foundation (2023), "Survey on Actual Conditions for LTC Labour," p.20 (translated by the author).

are having difficulties in communicating in Japanese, so it is questionable if new foreign care workers with even lower Japanese language proficiency levels than the EPA-Certified Care Worker candidates can adequately fulfill their job responsibilities. Second, not only do EPA-Certified Care Worker candidates go back to their home countries while working as candidates, but they also go home even after having passed the national exam for various reasons, including physical problems, marriages and childbirths, and changing jobs. Moreover, even if they want to stay and continue working in Japan, their spouses can work only for 28 hours per week because they do not hold a working visa. In addition, in order for their spouses to live and work in Japan, they need to learn and improve their Japanese proficiencies. However, such a learning environment has not been well developed. For the same reason, they may worry about education for their children.

To cope with the language problems among foreigners living in Japan, the Japanese government finally enacted a new law to promote a Japanese language education system for foreigners living in Japan on June 28, 2019. It is a big stride toward opening a multicultural society. Once foreign LTC workers leave their workplace, they will live in the same communities as Japanese people, so Japanese people living in the community may be required to adjust to living with foreigners. Accordingly, not only language education for foreigners but also multicultural education for Japanese people in the community will be needed to help foreigners integrate into Japanese society.

Unlike many other highly developed countries where immigration has been the norm for centuries, in Japan, foreigners account for only 1.7% of the total population, which is very low compared with other OECD countries (5.0% for Holland; 6.9% for France; 8.3% for Italy; 10.1% for Germany) (OECD, 2018).

Japan remains one of the world's most culturally homogeneous societies. Therefore, should we accept foreign LTC workers, it is critical to wisely learn from other nation's valuable experiences in employing foreign LTC workers, including Germany, the USA, and so forth (Tatara & Tsukada, 2004a, 2004b; Tsukada, 2010). Tsukada (2015b) conducted interview surveys on foreign LTC workers in Germany in 2014 and summarized recommendations for Japan. They include: (1) language (Japanese) competency should be highly required; (2) foreign LTC workers need to be paid equally as other Japanese LTC workers; (3) it is important that we should accept foreign LTC workers as "human beings" and that such prideful attitudes as pushing them in their work will not support the policy's success in the long term; and (4) we need to prepare for the development of a multicultural society where everyone coexists harmoniously. In addition, Japan needs to be very careful about incoming trainees under the "*Ginou-jissyu*" (Technical Intern Training) Program, knowing that long-lasting problems relating to human rights of the trainees are yet unsolved. The Japanese government has newly established a rigorous monitoring and supervising organization, the Organization for Technical Intern Training (OTIT), in January 2017 to address the issues; however, the establishment itself does not necessarily mean the problems will be solved properly and promptly. It should be remembered that without solving this issue, the "*Ginou-jissyu*" (Technical Intern Training) Program is merely treated as a tool for producing "a rotation of cheap LTC workers" (Honda, 2017). The Japanese government finally started discussing those issues of the "*Ginou-jissyu*" (Technical Intern Training) Program in December 2022, and according to the final report issued by the Immigration of Services Agency of Japan on November 30, 2023, the "*Ginou-jissyu*" (Technical Intern Training) Program and "Specified Skilled Worker" Program shall be reviewed with emphasis on the following three perspectives in order to gain international understanding and to make Japan the country of choice for foreign human resources; (1) protection of human rights of foreign nationals, (2) career advancement for foreign nationals, and (3) safe, secure, and cohesive society.[7]

In summary, the government of Japan clearly maintains that these policy changes are not related to immigration policies at all. However, this series of policy changes to broaden qualifications for residence appears very similar to Germany's creation of their guest worker program in the 1960s. The German guest worker program envisioned that foreign workers would eventually would return to their home countries, but most never did; instead, many not only stayed in Germany and made it their home, but some even brought over other family members and relatives from their home countries, raising major issues for social resources, social security, and so on. Regarding this situation, there is a famous insightful observation made by the Swiss playwright Max Frisch, that grew out of the European experience with recruiting foreign workers: "We wanted workers, but we got people instead" (Borjas, 2016, p.15). We must continuously seek better ways of (1) recruiting the workers needed to care for our burgeoning frail, older population; (2) establishing an ethical win-win relationship with these workers; and (3) learning how to live in an increasingly diverse (possibly unique) society. At the same time, we should not let an LTC job to be a job nobody wants to have. Why? After all, we are all the same people, and foreign LTC workers also leave such jobs once they become fluent in Japanese, looking for better jobs.

※ *This paper was prepared based on manuscripts already published by the author in Chiiki Caring (Tsukada, 2015a & 2016) and Japanese Journal of Social Welfare (Tsukada, 2018) (in Japanese), and in the book chapter in the edited book entitled "Coping With Rapid Population Ageing in Asia," by Komazawa, O. and Saito, Y., published by Jakarta ERIA (Economic Research Institute for ASEAN and East Asia) (Tsukada, 2021) (in English). Permission for reuse for all figures and tables used in this manuscript was obtained from the respective publishing companies.*

Notes

1 "Certified Care Worker" means "*Kaigo-fukushi-shi*" in Japanese. It is a national qualification delineated in the Certified Social Worker and Certified Care Worker Act that was enacted in 1987. In Japan, LTC workers can include the following five categories: (1) Approved Certified Care Workers, (2) Certified Care Workers, (3) Those who completed "Practitioner Training" that is equivalent to the former Home Helper 1, (4) Those who completed "Beginner's Training" that is equivalent to the former Home Helper 2, and (5) Those who do not have any qualifications or training. Currently, about 40% of the LTC workers have national qualifications and are "Certified Care Workers." Thus, the Certified Care Workers' job is a name monopoly, but not an occupational monopoly.
2 Conditions are such that candidates work under: (1) a contract with hiring institutions, (2) a declaration of their intention to work hard to pass the next exam, (3) an improved training plan provided by hiring institutions, (4) a declaration of intention by hiring institutions to secure a hiring environment and carry out their appropriate training plan, and (5) having exam scores on the first trial beyond a certain standard (Ministry of Health, Labour and Welfare, 2017).
3 N1 is the highest level among the five levels.
   N1: The ability to understand Japanese used in a variety of circumstances.
   One is able to read writings with logical complexity and/or abstract writings on a variety of topics, such as newspaper editorials and critiques, and comprehend both their structure and contents.

N2: The ability to understand Japanese used in everyday situations and in a variety of circumstances to a certain degree.

One is able to read materials written clearly on a variety of topics, such as articles and commentaries in newspapers and magazines, as well as simple critiques, and comprehend their contents.

N3: The ability to understand Japanese used in everyday situations to a certain degree.

One is able to read and understand written materials with specific content concerning everyday topics.

N4: The ability to understand basic Japanese.

One is able to read and understand passages on familiar daily topics written in basic vocabulary and kanji.

N5: The ability to understand some basic Japanese.

One is able to read and understand typical expressions and sentences written in hiragana, katakana, and basic kanji (Japanese Language Proficiency Test, 2017).

4 3K in the term "3K-job" means initials consisting of "*Kitsui* (physically demanding)," "*Kitanai* (dirty)," and "*Kyuryou ga yasui* (low payment)," and it has unfortunately been used to indicate LTC jobs.
5 This interview survey was funded by JSPS KAKENHI for 3 years (Grant #=21530609).
6 This mail survey was funded by JSPS KAKENHI for 3 years (Grant #=26380653).
7 On June 21, 2024, the "Act on Partial Revision of the Immigration Control and Refugee Recognition Act and the Act on Proper Technical Intern Training and Protection of Technical Intern Trainees" was promulgate. As a result, the "*Ginou-jissyu*" (Technical Intern Training) Program was fundamentally reviewed, and "Employment for Skill Development" program was established. The purpose of this program is to develop and secure human resources in industrial fields with labor shortages. This program will come into effect on a date to be specified by Cabinet Order within three years from June 21, 2024 (Ministry of Justice, 2024).

References

Borjas, J. G. (2016). *We wanted workers – Unraveling the immigration narrative*, New York: W.W. Norton & Company, Ltd.
Care Work Foundation (2020). Surveys on actual conditions for LTC labour in 2019. Retrieved from https://www.kaigo-center.or.jp/content/files/report/2020r02 _chousa_roudousha_chousahyou.pdf, 2024/6/30http://www.kaigo-center.or.jp/ report/2022r01_chousa_01.html, 2023/5/13
Care Work Foundation (2023). Surveys on actual conditions for LTC labour in 2022. Retrieved from https://www.kaigo-center.or.jp/content/files/report/2023r01 _chousa_gaiyou_0821.pdf, 2024/6/30
Honda, M. (2017). Current status and future challenges of foreign workers in LTC settings-with focus on EPA LTC worker candidate and Technical Intern Trainees, *Kokuminiryou*, 334, 63–69.
Iguchi, Y. (2001). *Foreign workers: New era*. Chikuma Shinsho, 288, Tokyo: Chikuma Shobo.
Immigration of Services Agency of Japan (2023). Interim report of expert meeting for ideal states for "*Ginou-jissyu*" (Technical Intern Training) Program and "Specified Skilled Worker" Program.
Ito, A. (2019). Issues for accepting foreign workers in LTC settings, *Journal of Science of Labour*, 74(4), 26–29.

Japan Federation of National Service Employees (2015). Review of *"Ginou-jissyu"* (Technical Intern Training) program, toward shifts of policies for foreign workers-ideal ways for *"Ginou-jissyu"* (Technical Intern Training) program (proposals), April 16, 2015. Retrieved from https://www.moj.go.jp/isa/content/001411530.pdf, 2024/6/30

Japanese Bar Association (2011). Proposals for abolishment of *"Ginou-jissyu"* (Technical Intern Training) program, April 15, 2011.

Japanese Language Proficiency Test (2017). N1-N5: Summary of linguistic competence required for each level. Retrieved from http://www.jlpt.jp/e/about/levelsummary.html, 2023/3/11

Kitaura, M. (2013). Policy issues for care workers: The securing and training of human resources in the care sector, *The Japanese Journal of Labour Studies*, 55(12), 61–72.

Koyama, M. (2019). Issues of g*inou-jissyu* program and labour movement, *Monthly Social Democracy*, 771, 48–51.

Ministry of Health, Labour and Welfare (2010). Workforce of *"Kaigo"* (LTC) and future prospects of care workers. Reported by the 8th Committee for Future Directions of Training Care Workers, December 22, 2010, p. 5 in Document 3. Retrieved from https://www.mhlw.go.jp/stf/shingi/2r9852000000zdft.html, 2024/6/30

Ministry of Health, Labour and Welfare (2015). Press release: Supply and demands of LTC workers toward 2015 (definitive numbers), June 24, 2015, p.1. Retrieved from http://www.mhlw.go.jp/stf/houdou/0000088998.html, 2024/6/30

Ministry of Health, Labour and Welfare (2017). Conditions for expanding the stay (Certified Care Worker candidates), March 28, 2017, Attachment 5. Retrieved from https://www.mhlw.go.jp/file/04-Houdouhappyou-12004000-Shakaiengokyoku-Shakai-Fukushikibanka/0000157135.pdf, 2023/3/11

Ministry of Health, Labour and Welfare (2018a). Results of the 30th national examination for certified care workers, Attachment 1. Retrieved from https://www.mhlw.go.jp/file/04-Houdouhappyou-12004000-Shakaiengokyoku-Shakai-Fukushikibanka/0000199589.pdf, 2024/6/30

Ministry of Health, Labour and Welfare (2018b). Current status and future roles of the public LTC insurance program. Retrieved from https://www.mhlw.go.jp/file/06-Seisakujouhou-12300000-Roukenkyoku/0000213177.pdf, 2024/6/30

Ministry of Health, Labour and Welfare (2022). Results of survey on employment structures in 2021, Results and Summary, Figure 1-1. Retrieved from https://www.mhlw.go.jp/toukei/itiran/roudou/koyou/doukou/22-2/dl/kekka_gaiyo-01.pdf, 2024/6/30

Ministry of Health, Labour and Welfare (2023). Results of the 35th national examination for certified care worker, Attachment 1. Retrieved from https://www.mhlw.go.jp/content/12004000/001075863.pdf, 2023/5/13

Ministry of Internal Affairs and Communications (2013). Report of outcomes for administrative evaluation and monitoring regarding policies for accepting foreigners: With focus on *"Ginou-jissyu"* (Technical Intern Training) program, April, 2013. Ministry of Internal Affairs and Communications, Administrative Evaluation Bureau.

Ministry of Justice (2022). Numbers of foreigners in Japan under status of residence, Specified Skilled Worker 1, December 2022, p.2, Immigration Services Agency of Japan. Retrieved from https://www.moj.go.jp/isa/content/001389884.pdf, 2023/3/11

Ministry of Justice (2023). Status of residence, Immigration Services Agency of Japan. Retrieved from https://www.moj.go.jp/isa/applications/guide/qaq5.html, 2024/6/30

Ministry of Justice (2024). Overview of Employment for Skill Development Program and Specified Skilled Worker System. Retrieved from https://www.moj.go.jp/isa/content/001421922.pdf, 2024/9/15

Miyajima, T. & Suzuki, E. (2014). *Questioning acceptance of foreign workers*. Iwanami Booklet, No.916. Tokyo: Iwanami Shoten.

OECD (2018). Immigration policies in the world, in *International Migration Outlook 2016*, translated by Tokunaga, Y., Tokyo: Akashi Publishing Company.

Organization for Technical Intern Training (OTIT) (2017). About OTIT (Organization for Technical Intern Training). Retrieved from https://www.otit.go.jp/about_en/, 2024/6/30

Shimoyama, H. & Ushida, A. (2020). Issues of policies for accepting foreign care workers in Japan, *Douhoufukushi*, 27, 45–61.

Suzuki, E. (2006). Policies for foreign workers in Japan. In Yoshida, Y. and Kono, S. (eds.), *New era for international population movement (Demography Library)* 4, 187–210. Tokyo: Hara Shobo.

Tatara, T. & Tsukada, N. (2004a). The study of foreign workers in the fields of nursing and medicine in Germany - Based on the fieldwork (1), *Gekkan Fukushi*, 87(2), 98–103.

Tatara, T. & Tsukada, N. (2004b). The study of foreign workers in the fields of nursing and medicine in Germany - Based on the fieldwork (2), *Gekkan Fukushi*, 87(3), 98–104.

The Japan Association of Certified Care Workers (2017). Reasons for why certified care workers experienced changing jobs, p.17, The 12th research on working conditions and awareness of expertise among certified care workers, Reported by The Japan Association of Certified Care Workers, March, 2017. Retrieved from https://www.jaccw.or.jp/kenkyu-H28_dokuji_hokoku.pdf, 2024/6/30

The Japan Association of Training Institutions for Certified Care Workers (2022). Trends in number of training schools and student enrollment. Retrieved from http://kaiyokyo.net/news/r2_teiin_juusoku.pdf, 2024/6/30

Tsukada, N. (2010). What we learn from other senior countries that accepted foreign workers, In Tsukada, N. (ed.), *Foreign LTC workers: How does LTC fields in Japan change?* 222–230. Tokyo: Akashi Shoten.

Tsukada, N. (2012). *Casebook about LTC institutions that accepted EPA LTC worker candidates*. Private printing.

Tsukada, N. (2015a). Nationwide survey on foreign LTC workers, *Chiiki Caring (Regional Caring)*, 17(8), 75–81.

Tsukada, N. (2015b). Latest information on foreign care workers in Germany, *HCR NEWS 2015 NO.2*, 2-5. International Home Care & Rehabilitation

Tsukada, N. (2016). A study on accepting foreign LTC workers, *Chiiki Caring (Regional Caring)*, 18(6), 65–75.

Tsukada, N. (2018). A study of factors that affect administrators' views of accepting foreign long-term care workers, *Japanese Journal of Social Welfare*, 59(2), 92–106.

Tsukada, N. (2021). A new era for policies for care workers in Japan: Current status and future directions, In Komazawa, O. & Saito, Y. (eds.), *Coping with Rapid Population Ageing in Asia*. 85–95. Jakarta: ERIA.

Yorimitsu. M. (2005). From foreign workers to, foreigners and immigrants. In Yorimitsu, M. (ed.), *Thinking about Japanese immigration policies*, 23–33. Tokyo: Akashi Shoten.

PART III
Dementia care

15

FORMAL COMMUNITY-BASED CARE

Older adults' experiences of home-based and day care services in South Africa

Maryna Rankin and Jaco R Hoffman

Introduction

Population ageing is a global process, and although sub-Saharan Africa (SSA) is the world's youngest region, its older population increases at an annual rate of 3.2%. This number is significant when compared to the global growth rate, which is 1% (Zimmer & Das, 2014). Of the sub-Saharan countries, South Africa has the second most rapidly ageing population with the absolute number of older people at 4.8 million in 2017. By the year 2050, the number of older South Africans will have almost tripled to around 11.6 million people (UN, 2017). With this dramatic growth of the older population, the demand for long-term care will increase at an equally dramatic pace (Jesmin et al., 2011). With a growing demand on the formal long-term care system in South Africa, policy advocates formal community-based care as a solution to the long-term care challenge. Research on this form of care in South Africa is limited, and no clear picture of the formal community-based long-term care situation exists. This chapter first aims to explore older adults' experiences of the current formal community-based care services in Sebokeng; second, it proposes to address the gap between the ideal of formal community care systems and its actual delivery; and effective implementation in practice as experienced by the older adults in need of such services.

Background review

Situational trends – Common trends that impact the growing need for long-term care (LTC) in SSA include migration, and the rise of non-communicable diseases, HIV/AIDS and changing family structures (Darkwa &

Mazibuko, 2002; Jesmin *et al.*, 2011; Schatz & Seeley, 2015; Zimmer & Das, 2014). Although South Africa's older population is experiencing the same trends, its long-term care management is unique to the rest of SSA. This is mainly determined by two drivers: its historical legacies of poverty, inequality and deprivation under apartheid and the HIV and AIDS epidemic (Tomita Burns, 2013).

South Africa's older population is uniquely characterised by their experience of apartheid (1948–1994). Apartheid saw the forcible removal of much of the black population to areas with inadequate educational resources, health services and a lack of career opportunities that would enable them to make provision for their old age (United Nations, 1963, in Kobayashi *et al.*, 2017; Aboderin *et al.*, 2016). The results of forced relocations are still experienced today as many older persons live in areas unsuitable for them and affording them very limited access to resources (Keating *et al.*, 2013).

Adding pressure to the formal long-term care systems in South Africa is the country's quadruple burden of diseases consisting of HIV and AIDS, TB, maternal and childhood diseases, non-communicable diseases, and violence and injuries (Naidoo, 2012). South Africa has the world's highest number of people living with HIV and AIDS (Nyirenda *et al.*, 2013). Few studies on HIV and AIDS have collected data on adults over the age of 54, but the literature available suggests substantial ageing with HIV and getting infected by HIV at older ages (Mojola *et al.*, 2015). It is estimated that South Africa will see a 50% increase in HIV infections among older adults over the next 15 years (Hontelez *et al*, 2011 in Mojola *et al.*, 2015). This is a perturbing statistic considering that the country's already overburdened long-term care system will have to keep up with this increase.

Older women, even those not at risk of infection, are among those mainly affected by the pandemic. They bear the brunt of caring for the sick and dying as they must care for their sick children and, often, for orphaned grandchildren (Ogunmefun *et al.*, 2011; Mutemwa & Adejumo, 2014; Lombard & Kruger, 2009). Caregiving is an economic burden on older adults, especially those already in the throes of poverty. They are at an age where their care needs should be met, but instead, they must provide emotional and physical care to their family members (Phethlu & Watson, 2014; in Mutemwa & Adejumo, 2014).

Apart from the HIV/AIDS epidemic, older adults, like in the rest of SSA, also suffer the burden of non-communicable diseases. High blood pressure, diabetes and arthritis are the most common medical conditions affecting older adults (Lloyd-Sherlock *et al.*, 2014; Statistics SA, 2015).

In addition, older adults make up one of South Africa's most vulnerable groups and are especially exposed to violence (Buthelezi *et al.*, 2017). Eldercide is a leading cause of non-natural death among older South Africans, with a rate of 25.2 per 100,000 of the older population (Matzopoulos *et al.*,

2015). Eldercide increases as the population ages and is therefore becoming more of a public health and social problem (Buthelezi *et al.*, 2017). As one of the factors of South Africa's quadruple burden of disease, increased violence towards its older population will have a negative impact on social and health-related LTC in South Africa.

Long-term care options

Against the backdrop of the above-discussed trends, there are two main options available to older adults in need of long-term care, namely informal care and formal long-term care.

Informal care is unpaid care provided to, in this study, older adults by someone with whom they have a social relationship, such as a family member, relative, neighbour or friend (Jesmin *et al.*, 2011). Traditionally, women are perceived as caregivers to those in need of care. Research has shown that this trend in informal caregiving is still the norm as most informal care activities are performed by female family members (Jesmin *et al.*, 2011; Yakubu & Schutte, 2018). Providing informal care involves helping with household chores, transport, social companionship, emotional support or arranging professional care (Jacobs *et al.*, 2014).

Most of the South African older population relies on informal long-term care due to a lack of resources and limited access to formal care (Bohman *et al.*, 2011). However, according to Aboderin (2018), informal care is increasingly unsustainable to address the long-term care challenge. There is inadequate availability of family care, ranging from the complete absence of a family carer to the temporary absence of a family carer. Care provided by family members lacks quality, as care is provided inconsistently, and family members do not respect the wishes of the older care recipient. Older adults receiving informal familial care experience loneliness, lack of access to health care, and abuse and neglect. Care provision is costly to families, as one family member has additional needs that have to be met, and whoever cares for the patient is unable to engage in gainful employment. It is also taxing on caregivers' mental and physical health. The financial burden of care is greater among the poor and those who have to care for sufferers of dementia or related conditions (Aboderin, 2018). Older adults are also increasingly being forced into the role of informal caregivers instead of receiving care due to limited resources, financial constraints and the HIV epidemic (Bohman *et al.*, 2009, Hoffman, 2016).

Formal long-term care is provided by paid professionals or carers (Cohen *et al.*, 2001). One form of formal long-term care is residential facilities. Residential facilities are institutions that provide accommodation and a 24-hour service to older adults (South Africa, 2005). Residential facilities, however, are inadequate in meeting the needs of South Africa's older population as they are mainly located in the former white areas, and most older adults are poor and live in rural areas (Lombard & Kruger, 2009; Statistics SA, 2015).

As an option for addressing the shortcomings of these two options of long-term care, the South African Policy for Older Persons (Department of Social Development, 2005) advocates formal community-based care as the best pathway to long-term care for older adults.

Community-based care is a form of formal long-term care that aims to promote and maintain the independent functioning of older persons in a community (South Africa, 2005). The aim of community-based care is achieved by enabling active and independent living and creating a supportive environment where older adults' care needs are met.

Formal community-based care consists of two types of services. Day care provides older adults with social, recreational and health-related activities in a formal community-based facility. Home-based care, on the other hand, aims at caring for frail, housebound adults. This includes basic nursing, housework, shopping, counselling and support to clients and their families (South Africa, 2005).

Theoretically, formal community-based care as set out by the policy seems promising. There are, however, concerns about the implementation and quality of community-based service programmes. The national audit of home and formal community-based care (Friedman *et al*, 2010) reported that community caregivers and managers lack adequate training and are mostly unprepared to meet the care demands of older adults. The quality of formal community-based care is also affected by limited human, material and infrastructure resources, and the absence of regulatory structures and oversight. Broadly, older adults are also underserved and experience a lack of access to good community care as a consequence of poor government coordination (WHO, 2017).

There is little discussion of the relative roles of informal, state and private sectors in meeting the care needs of older adults. Although there is awareness of the fact that informal care is increasingly inadequate in meeting care needs, it is still being promoted as the key strategy for providing for the increased need for long-term care. Formal community-based care is promoted by policy, but there is a lack of evidence of its implementation/ outcomes in the practical setting of long-term care for older adults.

Formal community-based care experiences of older persons

In a study conducted to explore older adults' experiences of current formal community-based care services in South Africa, it was found that older South Africans experience care on a continuum, with organised informal social care on the one end and organised home-based health care on the other.

Care setting – The research was conducted in the Sebokeng area, Gauteng. Sebokeng is Sesotho for "gathering place". By 2011, the national census indicated that the total population was 218,515, with 4.9% consisting of older adults. Of the population, 99.1% is black African, and 18.8% has no income (Statistics SA, 2015).

Ageing could potentially result in deteriorating health and physical strength, thus inducing a greater demand for long-term care (Phaswana-Mafuya et al., 2013). This is especially true for the oldest old (aged 75 years and older) (Nuscheler & Roeder, 2013). Participants were recruited by means of purposive sampling. The study recruited a minimum of ten participants using day care services and ten participants in need of home-based care. The aim was aimed to have an equal gender distribution in the participant group. The participants met the inclusion criteria of speaking Sesotho/Afrikaans/English and making use of day care and/or home-based care. Participants that suffered from dementia, Alzheimer's or any condition related to extreme forgetfulness or a diminished grasp on reality were excluded from the study.

Care responses – Across this continuum, their experiences of the care they currently receive can be categorised according to the following themes.

Older adults experience a lack of access to resources in their particular care situations

Lack of access and resources is experienced on three levels: organised 'informal'-familial social care, organised formal care, and day care. Where older adults are home-bound due to immobility, they need assistance with housework, bathing and other activities of daily living. These needs are mostly met by informal care, and no professional help is needed. There were, however, older adults who did not have any family members willing to provide them with this much-needed care and would benefit greatly from home-based community care. This is problematic as there are no formal home-based care services (as described and advocated by policy) in their immediate community. Community members provide home-based care for a fee, which makes it impossible for the older adults to obtain, as they do not have the means to pay for these services.

Even in contexts of limited resources, older adults make use of formal healthcare services for their short- and long-term health needs. Clinics provide home-based care to the extent of delivering chronic medication and, in some cases, monitoring blood pressure and sugar levels. This care is, however, mostly experienced as bad care in terms of access and perceived competence of caregivers. Access to life-sustaining medication is mostly unreliable, as the clinics often provide them with medication that makes them ill or only give them half the required dosages. In some cases, healthcare workers are regarded as unable to provide skilled medical care.

Older adults using the services of the day care centre all reported experiencing the care they received from the centre as good care. They did, however, feel that this care would improve greatly if they had access to financial resources and better infrastructure. All the older adults from the study are poor and reliant on a state pension. Often, they don't have money for transport and therefore cannot go to the centre. The centre requires a monthly contribution of R20 ($1.13) in order to provide them with food and sporting equipment, but this is insufficient, and oftentimes the centre manager personally provides them with meals. This is highly appreciated by the participants, as it shows her dedication to their care and well-being. The main factor influencing the experience of day care is the lack of funding and infrastructure. The centre consists of a single-room, corrugated iron structure and doesn't provide adequate shelter. They experience a dilemma in this regard as they do not have the financial means to obtain a proper building, and the law states that they cannot receive funding if they do not have a proper building that meets all the requirements as stated by law.

Good care is characterised by attentiveness and responsiveness

Care that pays attention to older adults' needs and responds to them in a way that is satisfactory to the participants is seen as good care. With attentive care, they do not have to point out their needs; the caregiver is interested in them, cares about them, and therefore pays attention to their wants and needs as individuals.

The older adults reported that they appreciate caregivers' response to unspoken needs, because this responsiveness implies the caregiver provides care not because he/she has to, but because he/she cares enough about the participants' well-being to *want* to provide care.

Most of the interviewees furthermore feel that providing good care means treating the care receiver with respect. Older adults want their caregivers to recognise them as being in control of their own care and treating them with patience and understanding. Participants want to feel dignified when receiving care. They have self-worth and expect to be treated in a patient way and not to be "shouted at".

Negotiating a configuration of informal and formal community-based care

Social care usually takes place in an individual's own home or care home, and aims to maintain the quality of life of individuals suffering from long-term health conditions or support the age-related needs of older adults (Willis *et al.*, 2016; Rand *et al.*, 2017). Where participants in this study receive informal care, they negotiate their social care in a configuration of informal and formal, long-term community-based care settings.

Informal social care – Informal social care spans across a wide care spectrum. The older adults' experiences of informal social care form a rather homogenous group, with companionship, financial support, instrumental help and physical care identified as the social care received to meet their everyday care needs. The majority reported that the informal social care they receive is more than adequate in meeting their needs and that they do not feel a need for "outsiders" to supplement the care received from their families.

This care in the private space is, however, complemented by external community-based care.

Community-based social care – Social care in the community is mainly provided by the church and the day care centre. The older adults receiving care from the church and the day care centre expressed their satisfaction and gratitude toward these two care providers. In some cases, the church provides food parcels or meals, and on special occasions (Mother's Day) older adults receive treats. The older adults from this study place a high value on the spiritual care the church provides and find great joy and peace in worshipping.

Care received from the day care centre participating in the study is experienced as good care. The three main themes that emerge from these experiences are companionship, sporting activities and the centre manager's regard for each older adult as an important individual. Meeting other older people and talking and playing games greatly relieve stress and feelings of depression. They also feel less lonely than before they started attending the centre. The sporting activities and games also contribute to their health and therefore improve their quality of life. The regard the older adults have for the manager was apparent in every interview. She cooks for them from her own pocket, shares her chronic medicine when the care workers didn't provide an adequate quantity, and treats them with dignity and respect.

The interviewees reported feeling lonely before they had access to the day care centre. Without these carers and other older adults to have conversations and share feelings and emotions with, they felt lonely. This loneliness caused them to feel depressed and physically ill. Especially day care users reported feeling happier and healthier since attending day care activities. Social care is most often associated with informal familial care. Modern times have, however, seen a decline in the ability of the family to provide care spanning across a vast continuum. For the majority of South Africa's older population, formal care is not a viable substitute as poverty makes it impossible to access these services. This situation has forced older adults to substitute their care by directing it using sources outside of the family and moving into the community.

Discussion

The options for families to assist their older members with health care are limited, and the only option for the older adults that participated in this research is the clinic in their area and the care workers bringing them medication. They indicated that, when they receive poor health care, they have nowhere to turn for additional help. They do, however, have options for additional care when it comes to social care provided by their families. When families provide inadequate social care, the older adults use community-based care from the church and day care centre to complement the care they do receive. South African policy advocates community-based day care and home-based care services in meeting the long-term care needs of older adults (South Africa, 2005). From the experiential narratives of the older adults, it is clear that, currently, this aim is not being successfully met. Home-based care is fragmented and consists only of providing basic chronic medication. Services aimed at instrumental care or supporting dignified living are non-existent.

Older adults enjoy going to the day care centre as it addresses loneliness and inactive living. The care received here, however, are inadequate in meeting all their care needs. Financial resources are required for transport, food and shelter, but they receive no government support. Being situated in a poverty-stricken area renders them unable to provide for their own financial needs. Older adults negotiate these shortcomings in the care they receive by organising social care from the church as well as informal care. Older adults' management of the division of tasks in their care networks is supported by the complementation model of care. According to this model, formal and informal caregivers have capabilities best suited to different tasks (Litwak, 1985). Providing care is not always predictable and some tasks require the caregiver to be in close proximity at certain times. Other tasks require professional skills that the informal caregiver cannot perform (Litwak, 1985). According to this model, instrumental care is most often provided by informal carers, whereas formal caregivers provide support with personal or self-care (Dwyer & Coward, 1991; Wolf et al., 1997).

Principles of good care

The following four interrelated care principles thus emerged from the experiential reflections of older adults in need of care, namely the importance of access to care, attentiveness and responsiveness. of carers, companionship as care, and dignity and choice through complementing care systems:

Access to care – Organisations lack buildings from which to provide community services; they also do not have access to water, electricity or computer equipment (Strydom, 2008; Friedman et al., 2010; Tshesebe & Strydom, 2016). Although infrastructure itself does not constitute good care, it has an impact on care and contributes to the care experience. Care does not meet needs if those in need cannot access it. Community-based care organisations are affected by high poverty rates and cannot provide good care for older adults in a situation where there are inadequate resources in terms of food, sanitation and accessibility of services (Strydom, 2008; Rosenberg *et al.*, 2005). Community caregivers – and in this case especially home-based healthcare workers – do not receive adequate skills training for providing long-term care to older adults. This means that community caregivers are largely unprepared for the demands of long-term care and, consequently, can't provide good-quality care (Friedman *et al.*, 2010)

Attentiveness and responsiveness of carers – A study conducted by Klaver and Baart (2016) identified nine types of attentiveness: relationship-based, meticulous, calculating, tolerating, settling, avoiding, process-oriented, hurried and disciplining. The type of attentiveness that stands out from the data gathered from the participants in this study is relationship-based. Relationship-based attentiveness is relational and attuned to the person receiving care. This type of attentiveness is characterised by using knowledge about the care receiver, sensing and keeping a broad view. This type of attentiveness in care is supported by an ethics of care approach, which is situational and relational (Leget, 2013)

Attentiveness is good care when the caregivers recognise unspoken needs and where the participants experience that the caregiver truly pays attention to them and their needs (Teka & Adamek, 2014). When considering Tronto's phases of care (1993), one can conclude that care starts with attentiveness and ends with attentiveness. The last phase of good care requires responsiveness from the older adult. The older adult expresses satisfaction with the care received or communicates dissatisfaction with the care services. This also requires attentiveness by the caregiver, as they must respond should the older adult feel that their needs were not met by the care received.

Companionship as care – Interviewees described companionship as good care, not only because they feel supported by it, but also because it provides them with enjoyable recreational opportunities. Rook (1990) identifies companionship as social involvement in shared recreational or non-recreational activities with the aim of enjoyment. According to Bromell and Cagney (2014), companionship is an indicator of loneliness and does not offer social support but provides pleasure (Bromell & Cagney, 2014). The participants did, however, indicate that they experience companionship as support given by informal care and the community-based day care. They enjoy taking part in conversation, sporting activities and games at the day care centre. It gives them pleasure to exercise, and they feel invigorated, and essentially "feel young" again. These enjoyable activities create distance between them and the loneliness and stressors they experience at home.

Dignity and choice through complementing care systems – According to Nordenfelt (2004), dignity can be conceptualised in four forms: dignity of merit, dignity of moral stature, dignity of identity and human dignity.

Dignity of merit is associated with prestige and can be bestowed upon people through some formal act or be achieved through deeds that deserve respect. *Dignity of moral stature* is associated with a special type of merit that is derived from behaviour that complies with moral standards. The third form, *dignity of identity*, is when we "attach to ourselves as integrated and autonomous persons, with a history and a future, with all our relationships to other human beings". Autonomy, independence, respect and privacy are included in this form of dignity. Dignity of identity has the most relevance in the context of older adults as it can be changed by external factors such as illness, injury or old age. *Human dignity* is present in all human beings and to the same degree. It is based on basic human rights and as long as we exist, this form of dignity persists.

Dignity is a fundamental need for all people, but it is especially important for older adults who face multiple losses that come with ageing (Black & Dobbs, 2014). Research suggests that dignity in ageing is complex and that personal perspectives and interpretation within a broader social context are both important in understanding this multifaceted concept (Black & Dobbs, 2014).

Research shows that dignity pertains to three domains: identity (self-respect, pride, integrity, trust); human rights (equality, choice, human entitlement to dignity); and autonomy (independence, self-determination, freedom of choice, control) (Calnan et al., 2006). Older adults configure their private (familial) and public (day care/church) care systems to negotiate their need for dignified care.

Ethics of care and the four principles of good care

The four principles of good care, as deduced from the study's data, are supported and strengthened by the ethics of care approach. Older adults regard care as good when they feel cared about, cared for, receive satisfactory care and have the opportunity to respond to the care received. The ethics of care supports paying close attention to the individual, recognising unspoken needs and listening to spoken ones (Tronto, 1998). The attentiveness of the caregiver means the older adult does not have to ask for care; needs are recognised even before they are expressed. Older adults experience good care when they feel cared for. The attentiveness of caregivers is especially relevant to the informal care older adults receive, i.e., family members providing personal care and financial support, and this care is appreciated as good care. Care receiving implies skilled competence (Tronto, 1998). Older adults want to know that healthcare workers are competent and knowledgeable so that they can trust the care they receive. Good care during the last phase is regarded as having the opportunity to respond to the care they receive. They give direction to their care by making their own choices, which are respected by the caregiver.

Implications of the study

Research on formal long-term community-based care in South Africa is limited. This study will add to the literature by sharing the experiences of those currently affected by the long-term care Options available to older adults and contribute to knowledge on how to provide them with care that they will experience as good care. The results showed that, although informal care might seem insufficient, it is still preferred by the majority of older adults, and families try to provide for their needs as best as possible.

Older adults are not passive receivers of care. They negotiate gaps in their care by directing it toward complementary care options. This self-direction should be facilitated as much as possible by providing information about and access to available alternative care options. This finding is supported by the identified care principles. In order to create good and effective guidelines, they should be based on lived experiences and be established by those receiving care. Older adults' care should be autonomous, starting with them stating how they want to be cared for.

Government should be made aware of the shortcomings in the implementation of legislation and policies. The government identified formal long-term community-based care as the answer to the current care shortcomings, but the lack of implementation means that there is no improvement in formal long-term care provision for older adults. Cooperation between government and communities is essential for making the vision of good long-term community-based care for older adults a reality.

Conclusion

This study had two aims: exploring and interpreting older adults' experiences of their current care situations and determining what they regard as good care. Results show that home-based health care does not meet the needs of older adults and that care workers should receive better training in being professional and providing care that meets the required standard.

Informal care is still the preferred way of care, with older adults expressing satisfaction with their informal care situation. When older adults feel that this care is inadequate, they try to obtain care from other available options, which in this case are community-based care provided by a day care centre and, to a lesser extent, the church.

Policy implementation is unsuccessful in establishing formal long-term care services or creating a supportive environment for community organisations that provide long-term care to older adults. The area in which this research was conducted has no social home-based care providers and no government day care centres. Funding is a major problem for unregistered non-profit organisations that aim to address the lack of formal long-term care. Registering in order to obtain government funding is tedious and complicated.

The findings of the research question of the study, "What is good care?", show that older adults want care that gives them access to resources and professional, competent care; shows the caregiver is attentive to their needs and willing to respond accordingly; provides companionship; and affords them dignity with choice. With these principles of care that speak to the four principles of good care postulated by the ethics of care, it is clear that using this approach as a framework when creating community-based care programmes will fulfil older adults' needs regarding good care.

Care is a complex concept that needs to be studied in its various forms and settings. With the lack of literature on formal long-term care provision to older South Africans, it is crucial that more comprehensive studies are conducted to get a better understanding of the true situation regarding long-term care in South Africa.

References

Aboderin, I. (2018). Optentia education workshop – Care economy. [http/www.optentia.co.za/education.php]

Aboderin, I., Mbaka, C., Egesa, C. & Owii, H.A. (2016). Human rights and residential care for older adults in sub-Saharan Africa: Case study of Kenya. In Meenan, H., Rees, N. and Doron, I. (Eds.) *Towards Human Rights in Residential Care for Older Persons: International perspectives*. New York: Routledge.

Black, K. & Dobbs, D. (2014). Community-dwelling older adults' perceptions of dignity: Core meanings, challenges, supports and opportunities. *Ageing & Society*, 34: 1292–1313. Doi: 10.1017/S0144686X13000020

Bohman, D.M., van Wyk, N.C. & Ekman, S.-L. (2009). Tradition in transition-intergenerational relations with focus on the aged and their family members in a South African context. *Scandinavian Journal of Caring Sciences*, 23: 446–455. Doi: 10.1111/j.1471-6712.2008.00640.x

Bohman, D.M., van Wyk, N.C. & Ekman, S.-L. (2011). South Africans' experiences of being old and of care and caring in a transitional period. *International Journal of Older People Nursing*, 6: 187–195. Doi: 10.1111/j.1748-3743.2010.00225.x

Braun, V. & Clarke, V. (2006). Using thematic analysis in psychology. *Qualitative Research in Psychology*, 3(2): 77–101.

Bromell, L. & Cagney, K.A. (2014). Companionship in the neighborhood context: Older adults' living arrangements and perceptions of social cohesion. *Research on Ageing*, 36(2): 228–243. Doi: 10.1177/0164027512475096

Buthelezi, S., Swart, L. & Seedat, M. (2017). The incidence and epidemiology of eldercide in the city of Johannesburg, South Africa. *Journal of Forensic and Legal Medicine*, 52: 82-88.

Calnan, M., Badcott, D. & Woolhead, G. (2006). Dignity under threat? A study of the experiences of older people in the United Kingdom. *International Journal of Health Services*, 36(2): 355–375.

Cohen, M.C., Miller, J. & Weinrobe, M. (2001). Patterns of informal and formal caregiving among elders with private long-term care insurance. *The Gerontologist*, 41(2): 180–187. Doi: https://doi.org/10.1093/geront/41.2.180

Darkwa, O.K. & Mazibuko, F.N.M. (2002). Population aging and its impact on elderly welfare in Africa. *International Journal of Aging and Human Development*, 54(2): 107–123. Retrieved from: http://journals.sagepub.com/doi/abs/10.2190/XTQG-6DXD-9XWE-9X85

Dwyer J.W. & Coward R.T. (1991) A multivariate comparison of the involvement of adult sons versus daughters in the care of impaired adults. *Journal of Gerontology: Social Sciences*, 46(5): S259–S269.

Friedman, I., Mothibe, N., Ogunmetun, C. & Mbatha, T. (2010). *A national audit of registered and unregistered home and community-based care (HCBC) organisations in South Africa*. Department of Social Development.

Hoffman, J.R. (2016). Negotiating care for older people in South Africa: between the ideal and the pragmatics. In Hoffman, J. (Ed). *Ageing in Sub-Saharan Africa. Spaces and practices of care*, 170–224. Great Britain: Policy Press.

Jacobs, M.T., Broese van Groenou, M.I., de Boer, A.H. & Deeg, D.J.H. (2014). Individual determinants of task division in older adults' mixed care networks. *Health and Social Care in the Community*, 22(1), 57–66. Doi: 10.1111/hsc.12061

Jesmin, S.S., Amin, I. & Ingman, S.R. (2011). Aging and caregiving crisis in the low and middle income societies. *Indian Journal of Gerontology*, 25(3): 309-328. Retrieved from: http://eds.a.ebscohost.com.nwulib.nwu.ac.za/eds/pdfviewer/pdfviewer?vid=3&sid=9d582078-2829-4552-96d4-c98cfe09f212%40sessionmgr4006&hid=4203

Keating, N., Eales, J. & Phillips, J.E. (2013). Age-friendly rural communities: Conceptualizing "Best-Fit". *Canadian Journal on Ageing*, 32(4): 319–322. Doi: 10.1017/S0174980813000408

Klaver, K. & Baart, A. (2016). Managing socio-institutional enclosure: A grounded theory of caregivers' attentiveness in hospital care. *European Journal of Oncology Nursing*, 22: 99–102. Doi: doi.org/10.1016/j.ejon.2016.04.002

Kobayashi, L.C., Glymour, M.M., Kahn, K., Payne, C.F., Wagner, R.G., Montana, L. ... Berkman, L. (2017). Childhood deprivation and later-life cognitive function in a population-based study of older rural South Africans. *Social Science & Medicine*, 190: 20–28. Doi: 10.1016/j.socscimed.2017.08.009

Leget, C. (2013). Analyzing dignity: A perspective from the ethics of care. *Medicine, Health Care and Philosophy*, 16: 945–952. Doi: 10.1007/s11019-012-9427-3

Litwak, E., 1985. Complementary roles for formal and informal support groups: A study of nursing homes and mortality rates. *The Journal of applied behavioural science*, 21 (4), pp. 407–425.

Lloyd-Sherlock, P., Beard, J., Minicuci, N., Ebrahim, S. & Chatterji, S. (2014). Hypertension among older adults in low- and middle-income countries: Prevalence, awareness and control. *International Journal of Epidemiology*, 43(1): 116–128. Doi: 10.1093/ije/dyt215

Lombard, A. & Kruger, E. (2009). Older persons: The case of South Africa. *Ageing International*, 34: 119–135. Doi: 10.1007/s12126-009-9044-5

Matzopoulos, R., Prinsloo, M., Pillay, M., van Wyk, V. et al. (2015). Injury-related mortality in South Africa: A retrospective descriptive study of post-mortem investigations. *Bull World Health Organ*, 93: 303–313.

Mojola, S.A., Williams, J., Angotti, N. & Gomez-Olive, F.X. (2015). HIV after 40 in rural South Africa: A life course approach to HIV vulnerability among middle aged and older adults. *Social Science & Medicine*, 143: 204–212. Doi.org/10.1016/j.socscimed.2015.08.023

Mutemwa, M. & Adejumo, O. (2014). Health challenges of elderly people caring for children orphaned by AIDS in a community setting in South Africa. *African Journal for Physical, Health Education, Recreation and Dance*, October (Supplement 1:2): 336–347. Retrieved from: https://repository.uwc.ac.za/handle/10566/1430

Naidoo, S. (2012). The South African national health insurance: A revolution in health-care delivery. *Journal of Public Health*, 34(1): 1149–1150. Doi.org/10.1093/pubmed/fds008

Nordenfelt, L. 2004. The varieties of dignity. *Health Care Analysis*, 12(2): 69–81.

Nuscheler, R. & Roeder, K. (2013). The political economy of long-term care. *European Economic Review*, 62: 154–173. Doi: 10.1016/j.euroecorev.2013.05.005

Nyirenda, M., Chatterji, S., Rochat, T., Mutevedzi, P. & Newell, M-L. (2013). Prevalence and correlates of depression among HIV-infected and – affected older people in rural South Africa. *Journal of Affective Disorders*, 151(1): 31–38. Doi: 10.1016/j.jad.2013.05.005

Ogunmefun, C., Gilbert, L. & Schatz E. (2011). Older female caregivers and HIV/AIDS-related secondary stigma in rural South Africa. *Journal of Cross-Cultural Gerontology*, 26: 85–102.

Phaswana-Mafuya, N., Peltzer, K., Ramlagan, S., Chirinda, W. & Kose, Z. (2013). Social and health determinants of gender differences in disability amongst older adults in South Africa. *Health SA Gesondheid (Online)*, 18(1): 1–9. Doi: 10.4102/hsag.v18i1.728

Rand, S., Caiels, J., Collins, G. & Forder, J. (2017). Developing a proxy version of the adult social care outcome toolkit (ASCOT). *Health and Quality of Life Outcomes*, 15: 108. Doi: 10.1186/s12955-017-0682-0

Rook, K. S. (1990). Social relationships as a source of companionship: Implications for older adults' psychological well-being. In Sarason, B.R., Sarason, I.G. & Pierce, G.R. (Eds.), *Wiley series on personality processes. Social support: An interactional view*, 219–250. Oxford, England: John Wiley & Sons.

Rosenberg, A., Mabude, Z., Hartwig, K., Rooholamini, S., Tetteth, D.O. & Merson, M. (2005). Improving home-based care in Southern Africa: An analysis of project evaluation. *South African Journal of HIV Medicine*, 19, 30–36.

Schatz, E. & Seeley, J. (2015). Gender, ageing and carework in East and Southern Africa: A review. *Global Public Health*, 10(10), 1185–1200. Doi: 10.1080/17441692.2015.1035664.

South Africa. (2005). South African Policy for Older Persons. Department of Social Development: Pretoria.

Statistics South Africa. (2015). *Statistical release P0302*. Mid-year population 2015.

Strydom, H. (2008). The Future of community-based services for older persons in South Africa. *Practice*, 20(2): 103–111. Doi: 10.1080/09503150802059002

Teka, A. & Adamek, M.A. (2014). "We prefer eating rather than greeting". Life in an elder care centre in Ethiopia. *Journal of Cross Cultural Gerontol*. 29: 389-404. Doi: 10.1007/s10823-014-9244-7

Tomita, A. & Burns, J.K. (2013). Depression, disability and functional status among community-dwelling older adults in South Africa: Evidence from the first South African National Income Dynamics Study. *International Journal of Geriatric Psychiatry*, 28: 1270–1279. Doi: 10.1002/gpp.3945

Tronto, J. (1993). Moral boundaries: A political argument for an ethic of care. In Lachman, V.D. 2012. Applying the ethics of care to your nursing practice. *MEDSURE Nursing*, 21(2): 112–116.

Tronto, J. (1998). An ethic of care. *Generations*, 22(3): 15–20.

Tshesebe, M. & Strydom, H. (2016). An evaluation of the community-based care and support services for older persons in a specific community. *Social Work/Maatskaplike Werk*, 52(1): 1–18 Doi: http://dx.doi.org/10.15270/52-1-476

United Nations, Department of Economic and Social Affairs, Population Division (2017). World Population Ageing 2017 (ST/ESA/SER.A/408).

Willis, R., Evandrou, M., Pathak, P. and Priya Khambhaita, P. (2016). Problems with measuring satisfaction with social care. *Health and Social Care in the Community*, 24(5): 587–559.

Wolf, D.A., Freedman, V. & Soldo, B.J. (1997). The division of family labor: Care for elderly parents. *The Journals of Gerontology*, 52B: 102–109.

World Health Organization (2017). *Toward long-term care systems in sub-Saharan Africa: WHO series on long-term care*. Geneva: World Health Organization.

Yakubu, Y.A., Schutte, D.W. Caregiver attributes and socio-demographic determinants of caregiving burden in selected low-income communities in Cape Town, South Africa. *J of Compassionate Health Care* 5, 3 (2018). https://doi.org/10.1186/s40639-018-0046-6

Zimmer, Z. & Das, S. (2014). The poorest of the poor: Composition and wealth of older person households in sub-Saharan Africa. *Research on Aging* 36(3): 271-296. Doi: 10.1177/0164027513484589

16
CARING FOR OLDER PEOPLE WITH DEMENTIA

A global perspective

Frances J. Morris

Introduction

There are many definitions of dementia, ranging from rather vague descriptions to those using very technical medical, neurological, psychological, or sociological terms which may or may not be understood by the various persons around the world seeking to learn more about this dastardly life changing disorder. The World Health Organization (WHO, 2018) definition is "a syndrome of cognitive impairment that affects memory, cognitive abilities and behaviour, and significantly interferes with a person's ability to perform daily activities." Alzheimer's disease is the most common form of dementia, accounting for approximately 60–70% of worldwide cases.

While the number of people with dementia (PwD) is reported by various international organizations as 50 million (Organization, 2018). The actual number eludes us because more than half of the PwD have yet to be diagnosed. This information is reported by the WHO as part of the 2018 Dementia Plan goals: to diagnose at least 50 percent of PwD (People with Dementia) in at least 50 percent of all countries by the year 2025. In order to best serve the needs of these PwD, we first we need to determine where they are living, why they remain undiagnosed, and establish both broad-based plans and more specific plans while respecting worldwide cultural differences. If we cannot provide a timely diagnosis, then how can we guide the PwD to begin the appropriate care pathway? With so many unknowns about the status of PwD, how can we as Global Caring Partners best assist the people who are not even aware of their need for us and our dementia care in the form of medical, psychological, social, and personal?

DOI: 10.4324/9781003528432-19

Status of timely diagnosis

The World Health Organization, in a September 2020 Fact Sheet on Caring in Dementia (WHO Media centre fact sheets: Dementia. Fact sheet N°362, n.d.), delineated its principal goals for dementia care:

- early diagnosis to promote early and optimal management
- optimizing physical health, cognition, activity, and well-being
- identifying and treating accompanying physical illnesses
- detecting and treating challenging behavioral and psychological symptoms
- providing information and long-term support to carers.

The first goal, "early diagnosis of dementia," while an admirable goal, is unfortunately fraught with obstacles on the pathway to achievement.

Impediments/roadblocks to timely diagnosis

Caregivers

In most cultures, the burden of caring for aging parents is felt to be the responsibility of the family. For some cultures, it is an honor to care for older parents. In others, the responsibility falls to the family because there are no other options. Even if there are care homes available, too often they are either too expensive or located in more populated, urban areas, far from the homes of the PwD. Because of the distance and/or cost, they are not considered by the family or, in many instances, there is no knowledge of the existence of these care homes.

The responsibility of caregiving generally falls to the women in the household. In predominantly Eastern cultures, the family unit encompasses the larger extended family. It is common for families to either live in one large domicile or in homes clustered close together. In these cultures, the women work together in caring for all the aged family members, including the PwD. In these cultures, the burden is spread over several people rather than just settling on the shoulders of one individual, due mostly to familism and filial piety having a large influence (Mccleary, Blair, 2013). Minority non-white caregivers are less likely to seek and utilize formal support services. At the same time, minority caregivers provide more direct care than their white counterparts (JR Pharr, 2014).

The caregiving role is delegated to female family members. This decision is based strictly on filial relationships. There is no consideration of whether the delegated caregiver(s) know(s) how to be a caregiver or wants to be a caregiver. Added to the burden of caregiving is the generally widespread notion among some cultures that the aging process naturally includes memory loss and aberrant behavioral issues; there is no recognition of the fact that the family member has dementia. Indeed, there is no knowledge of the existence of a disorder such as dementia. Family caregivers often are uneducated or undereducated. They do not question their role nor do they question the behavior exhibited by their older family members. The majority of "outside" caregivers hired to care for the PwD are generally also not educated about dementia (Robert, 2019). Caregivers in countries experiencing underdeveloped dementia support services have reported such scenarios as the PwD eating out of garbage, defecating all over the home, throwing bodily waste and other items from the home through the second-floor window onto the street, and the PwD physically harming the caregiver. They have also reported that, as often happens, the sole caregiver is the aged spouse of the PwD. They are no longer able to turn the PwD in the bed, and as a result, large bedsores have developed. Additionally, because of the lack of strength to move the spouse, cleaning after a bowel movement is incomplete and not all remnants of the stool are removed. The stool particles find their way into the bedsores and infection follows. The cost of paid caregivers who are younger and stronger is prohibitive for many families; younger family members living busy lives of their own are only sporadically available for assistance with caregiving. Because of the cost of medications, caregivers decide to administer only one of a plethora of necessary medications, the one they can afford. Would that this were the exception, but too often is a common finding (Wang, Xiao, 2013). The majority of PwD in the developing world are poor, uneducated, and do not have access to basic health care. PwD are usually undiagnosed and receive inadequate care from uneducated caregivers. The majority of people over 65 live in poverty and uncertainty. They have never heard the term "dementia," indeed, they do not know of its existence, but the manifestations of the disease, including memory loss and unusual behavioral issues, are considered caused by other disorders such as diabetes, high blood pressure, malaria, curses, or witchcraft. Some caregivers still seek help from traditional healers (Paddick, Mushi, Rongai, 2014).

In looking to the future of caregiving, the complexion of both the PwD and their informal caregivers will be changing as well as the increasing age of the caregivers. Ours is a global aging society due to the growth and development of treatment procedures for many diseases and the supportive public health domain. In the United States, the older population is not only growing older but is also becoming a more diverse group who will be living with some form of dementia. As early as 2030, 27 percent of the population of PwD will be members of the minority population. The reason for this increase in diversity is that older African Americans are almost twice as likely to develop dementia as older whites; Latinos are 150% more likely to develop one of the dementias than their older white counterparts. Additionally, changes in family structure are projected to result in fewer available informal family caregivers, with a change from 7:1 caregivers in 2010 to an estimated 4:1 by 2030. In general, the range of responsibilities for informal caregivers ranges from assisting with activities of daily living to coordinating, monitoring, and navigating health systems and delivering healthcare. As noted previously, the majority of informal caregivers are untrained and face financial strains in providing most levels of care (Dilworth-Anderson, Moon, Aranda, 2020) (Parker, 2020).

It would follow then that to encourage the goal of early diagnosis, the place to start is at the caregiver level. Caregivers must be educated. They must first understand what dementia is and that it is not part of the normal aging process. Unless they understand this concept, they will not seek out medical or psychiatric care, if available to them. For this education to provide a means to improve the quality of life of the PwD (Lok, Oncel, Ozer, Buldukoglu, 2017), it should be simple, easy to access, and understandable.

To this end, some measures have been taken. Education courses for caregivers have been made available at no cost on the World Wide Web. One example is Nottingham University, which is committed to providing a truly international format for education. Through the auspices of *Futurelearn* (http://.futurelearn.com/courses/comfortcare), they have developed MOOCs (Massive Online Courses) to be offered free on an international basis (Poole, Davis, Robinson, 2020). The purpose of the classes is to assist caregivers worldwide in gaining expert knowledge and skills to care for PwD. According to the syllabus for Foundations in Dementia, topics covered are causes and prevention of dementia; identification, diagnosis and ethical issues; communication skills; family and friends supporting PwD; living well with dementia; and end-of-life care. The Nottingham curriculum appears to be designed for more advanced learners than the family caregivers and some paid caregivers in developed countries. In considering those caregivers in families of PwD located in underdeveloped locations, as mentioned above, many of whom are uneducated or undereducated, this curriculum is inappropriate.

WHO has developed an excellent online educational program for caregivers, the i-Dementia Support Caregiver Training program, iSupport. It is a global online intervention developed for caregivers of people with dementia and is available on the World Wide Web to those who have access. It is an excellent program, situational and behavior based, reaching people of varying educational levels. WHO provides translation services to meet the needs of those desiring the program to be translated into their own cultural language. A generic version of the program is available at www.isupportfordementia.org.

Johns Hopkins University offers a MOOC (Massive Open Online Course) which is global in nature and written to be used by individual dementia caregivers around the world (https://learn.nursing.jhu.edu/online/mooc/elder-care.html).

At the university and college level, recognizing the need for education of dementia caregivers in an aging society, the University of Michigan (USA) College of Social Work offers a Certificate/Continuing Education program, Online Certificate in Advanced Clinical Dementia Practice (https://ssw.umich.edu/offices/continuing-education/certificate-courses/clinical-dementia).

Arizona State University's Edson College of Nursing & Health Innovation offers a series of free online classes related to dementia caregivers (https://nursingandhealth.asu.edu/programs/continuing-education/aging-elder-care).

Schoolcraft College and the Alzheimer's Association have launched a Dementia Care Certificate program that is offered as a virtual, online course (https://www.schoolcraft.edu/cepd/career-training/dementia-care).

In these sometimes efforts of epic proportions, there is the underlying assumption that the caregiver knows enough about dementia to seek out help in the form of more information. Unfortunately, as previously mentioned, many people across many cultures believe that dementia is a natural part of aging and that some people respond to the process of aging differently. To dispel this myth, it is imperative that we first educate caregivers on the care of aging populations. Within this education, we then teach them which behaviors are normal and for which they should reach out for additional medical help, e.g., dementia. By so doing, they can improve the QoL of the PwD (Robert, 2019).

With this basic background of information, it is assumed the caregiver will be more apt to reach out for professional care when needed. The physician can then diagnose the PwD. Unfortunately, in too many cultures, the education/training of caregivers is, at this time, but a "pipe dream." Indeed, there are yet societies where general practitioners do not know how to diagnose a person with dementia.

Stigma

Another major global stumbling block in the diagnosis and care of PwD is the stigma surrounding the diagnosis. The diagnosis of any incurable disease carries a stigma and, unfortunately, that includes dementia (Rosin, Blasco, Pilozzi, Huang, Yang, 2020). Stigma plays a pivotal role in defining the experience of the condition (Williamson, 2008). According to the World Health Organization, "stigma against older people with dementia...is widespread and its consequences far reaching" (Graham, Lindsay, Katona, Camus, Copeland, et al., 2003). Stigma accentuates and deepens the distress experienced by the person with dementia and unerringly adds to their existing disability (Thornicroft, 2006). Unfortunately, as Keating noted, it has been observed that all those "assigned a label of mental illness, take on an identity that is stigmatised" (Keating, 2006). Sadly, this appears to be a particularly powerful facet of dementia. It confers an almost "master status" on the person with dementia; "having dementia" not only becomes the most prominent aspect of the person's life but also sadly serves to subsume all their other good attributes and features into a single stigmatized identity (Goffman, 1963).

Cognitive decline and memory loss – and the negative responses to diagnosis and symptoms – profoundly undermine psycho-social well-being and quality of life. Loss of independence, roles and identity, and feelings of low self-esteem, value, and worth are widely noted in research with people with dementia (Husband, 1999). Research evidence further shows that receiving a dementia diagnosis allocates the older person to a new, lower-status social group and results in social dislocation, a function of both of the condition itself and responses to it (Katsuma, 2005; Lindesay, 2008). Relatives are not excluded from the consequences of secondary stigma, including isolation (Betts Adams, McClendon, 2006; Bowling, 2007). Add to this the fact that self-stigmatization, a process whereby stigma is absorbed by the individual, also plays a role. It encourages people with dementia to remain invisible and withdraw from social contact (Milne, 2008).

As if the burden of a dementia diagnosis and all the attendant memory loss and psycho-social issues isn't enough, the PwD, because of the stigma, even if they recognize their problems as dementia, some never seek help due to the fear of others knowing about the disease. For those who eventually seek help, it is often late in the disease process. Because of the stigma-induced delay in seeking help, often behavioral problems, which are sometimes aggressive, have already gotten to the point that the family caregivers can no longer handle them discreetly.

In 2016, the World Health Organization launched The Global Dementia Observatory, which included in the listing of global services, "The dementia plan supports dementia awareness, stigma reduction and dementia-friendly communities that are tailored to cultural contexts and the particular needs of a community, which can promote enhanced health and social outcomes that reflect the wishes and preferences of people with dementia, as well as improve their quality of life, that of their carers, and the broader community."

Education of general practitioners

In many cultures, the General Practitioner (GP) is the first person sought when a person feels ill, or a family member is having unusual symptoms, including those of a behavioral nature. In a global study (Jennings, Foley, Bradley, et al., 2018), GPs identified a need for more information on diagnosis, use of psychotropic drugs, as well as frustration at being placed in a situation where they are compelled to provide care beyond their expertise. Dementia is internationally under-diagnosed due to lack of knowledge about dementia among GPs. Global confidence and attitude increased following a dementia CME educational program (Mason, Annear, Lo, Tierney, Robinson, 2016).

The United Nations World Health Organization (WHO) Ministerial Conference on Global Action Against Dementia was held in Geneva in 2015. Ministers from around the world, as well as dementia experts and civil society representatives, were reminded that a new person was being diagnosed with dementia every 4 seconds. In 2020, that number has become one diagnosis every 3 seconds. And considering that so many people living with dementia are not diagnosed either due to a lack of diagnostic services or a lack of knowledge of dementia, this rate decreases even further.

Approximately 50 million people have dementia worldwide; this figure is expected to almost triple by 2050. Most people with dementia (approximately two-thirds) live in low- and middle-income countries (LMICs). This presents a significant challenge for such countries that often have limited financial resources and less well-developed health and social care systems. In the absence of a cure, reducing the future costs of dementia care and the burden of disease may be best achieved by a greater emphasis on (1) more timely diagnosis with earlier intervention to maintain functional independence and (2) undertaking "screening" in groups at high risk of developing dementia, case findings, and using brief cognitive assessment instruments. In clinical settings, a wide range of instruments for dementia screening and diagnosis are currently available; however, few cognitive assessment tools have been developed specifically for clinical use within LMIC settings. Screening for dementia and cognitive impairment in LMICs largely relies on tools adapted from high-income countries (HICs); these often lack validation in these settings, leading to education, literacy, and cultural biases. Research is urgently needed to develop cognitive assessment tools and dementia diagnostic approaches that are appropriate and feasible for clinical use in LMIC settings (Magklara, Stephan, Robinson, 2018).

It would seem that we have a conundrum of global import: dementia caregivers do not seek diagnosis and care for the aging subjects under their care because they are not educated to know the difference between normal aging behavior and aberrant behavior resulting from dementia. And if/when the caregivers are educated on a global scale to know enough to seek help, unless global efforts can reach and educate GPs in the diagnosis and care of dementia patients, the caregivers and their needy family members will remain undiagnosed and untreated.

Understanding that timely diagnosis and care management greatly improve the quality of life of those living with dementia, Australia has provided a CME course specifically designed to improve the dementia diagnostic skills of General Practitioners. Attesting to the need, over 3,000 GPs participated in the first offering of this program, with the result of increased awareness of dementia coupled with confidence in diagnosis (Casey, Islam, Shutze, Parkinon, Yen, et al., 2020). The Dementia Care Competency and Training Network (DCCTN) has developed an innovative web-based program that promotes improvement of the attitudes, knowledge, skills, behavior, and practice of clinicians, regardless of their work setting, in order to improve the quality of life for people living with dementia.

Dementia Care Pathways encompass the care of the PwD from the point of diagnosis to the end of life. These pathways are dependent on the knowledge base of PwD, their caregivers, and the GP or other people they approach for diagnosis and treatment. There is much information and answers to many questions about the various dementias and how to respond to various care needs available at no cost on the World Wide Web. However helpful this might be to those in their time of need who think to look it up on the internet, the fact is they need to know how to use a computer. In 2018, almost half of private households worldwide were estimated to have a computer at home. In developing countries, the PC penetration rate is lower, with around a third of households having a computer. In contrast, the share of households with a personal computer in developed countries exceeds 80 percent. In general, the share of households with a computer has steadily increased worldwide as computer usage and internet access become more prevalent around the world. The use of "smart phones" is, however, through the field of mHealth promising, global median ownership of smartphones (the primary technology for accessing mHealth) reaches only 59%. Older, less-educated, and lower-income individuals are more likely to lack smartphone and internet access. It is imperative to recognize and close this "digital divide" so that all patients have the opportunity to benefit from mHealth.

Herbal medicine interest

In recent years, interest in herbal medicine has increased, leading to greater scientific interest in the medicinal use of plants in treating disease and improving health, often without any significant side effects. Herbal medicines and natural products are the oldest remedies known to mankind. Medicinal plants have been used by all cultures throughout history. The demand for herbal products is growing exponentially throughout the world. Recent advances in the research, characteristics, and development of herbal medicines, because AD arises via multiple pathological or neurotoxic pathways, have the potential to be developed into optimum pharmaceuticals and nutraceuticals for AD because of their multi-function, multi-target characteristics (Kim, 2012).

Other treatment modalities

Mental disease in Africa is taboo and stigmatized, making it a challenge of a silent, even hidden epidemy (Pires, et al, 2019) Traditional Healers in rural

Uganda prepare herbs and salts for the treatment of PwD, both for ingestion and bathing. Special secret words are said over the potions by the healers before being administered to their "patient" (Owokuhaisa, Rukundo, Wakida, Obua, Buss, 2020). Informal caregivers are family members with no formal education. Many times, delusions of the PwD are seen as being spiritual in nature.

In Mali, none of the current anti-dementia drugs available in many countries are available for use. Rather, traditional animal slaughter, use of minerals, and other traditional medicines are used in the treatment of dementia by the traditional healers. There is little faith in Western/traditional medicine (Begagly, 2019).

In Sri Lanka, the occurrence of dementia has historically been seen as being possessed by an evil demon(s) and thus the PwD is taken to a traditional healer for the removal of the evil demons by the use of herbs (Ball, 2020). In Bangladesh, a small tropical Asian country, every part of various plants, from blossoms to leaves, roots, and seeds have been traditionally used in the treatment of Central Nervous System diseases, including Alzheimer's (Jossim Uddin, 2020). Today, their efficacy is being reviewed with greater emphasis on their actual efficacy for use in natural medicine.

The American West, the western states of the United States, has been home to many of the Native American Tribes for centuries. These tribe members have practiced herbal medicine, using various botanicals from their particular geographical areas. Many of these plant-based herbal remedies are now being studied by the Salk Institute and other groups, especially in the state of California, for their efficacy in the treatment of Alzheimer's (Mayer, Fischer, Liang, Sorian-Castelli, et al., 2020).

Thailand healers have, for many years, used the Kleeb Bua Daeng, a traditional Thai herb, as a means of treating the symptoms of dementia, albeit at the time they were not necessarily aware that the symptoms were derivative of a disease process/dementia. Today, this same herb is at the forefront of research for new medications for Alzheimer's/dementia (Chheng, Waiwut, Plekratoke, Chulikhit, et al, 2020).

Many of the plant-derived medications used by healers around the world are currently being studied by pharmaceutical companies as potential cures for the cure of Alzheimer's and other dementias. Preliminary studies of these medications, their chemical pathways, and the actions taken by some of the chemicals found within the medications look very promising (Fatma Tugce Guragac Dereli, 2021). Herbal medicines and the use of herbal compounds for memory disorders have their origins in ancient cultures, including those of the Egyptians, Indians, and Chinese. It involves the use of medicinal plants to treat AD and enhance general health and well-being. In fact, many pharmaceutical drugs are based on the synthesized adaptations of naturally occurring compounds found in plants (Akram, 2017).

In recent years, interest in herbal medicine has increased, leading to greater scientific interest in the medicinal use of plants in treating disease and improving health, often without any significant side effects. Herbal medicines and natural products are the oldest remedies known to mankind. Medicinal plants have been used by all cultures throughout history. The demand for herbal products is growing exponentially throughout the world. Recent advances in the research, characteristics, and development of herbal medicines, because AD arises via multiple pathological or neurotoxic pathways, have the potential to be developed into optimum pharmaceuticals and nutraceuticals for AD because of their multi-function, multi-target characteristics (Kim, 2012).

Quality of care available

The quality of care rendered to the PwD by both the primary care physician and the family/caregiver is at least partially contingent upon the quality of the initial assessment. The quality of the initial assessment of the PwD is dependent upon the experience and education of the primary care physician, for whom the lack of educational preparation for dealing with dementia patients has been discussed previously (Jennings, Foley, Bradley, et al., 2018). However, if a PwD receives the best available assessment, the follow-up by the caregiver(s) and the care plan developed for the PwD must also be a quality plan.

Unfortunately, one of the largest unmet needs reported by caregivers of PWD is the paucity of high-quality and available information, education, and support services to meet their unique needs, keeping in mind that each person responds differently to the dementia process because of the different causes, the mode and speed of the disease progress as well as comorbidities. Yet, when caregivers search for help, too often they only encounter "one size fits all" resources.

The Global Dementia Observatory

Recognition of these and other issues revolving around caregivers and PwD, the WHO launched The Global Dementia Observatory (GDO), a web-based platform to globally track progress on both the provision of services for PwD and their caregivers (http://who.int/mental_health/neurology/dementia/Global_Observatory/en/). Subdomain 1.1 of the GDO states,

> Dementia requires a broad public health approach involving the whole of government and multiple stakeholders, in order to develop a comprehensive response from the health and social care system (both public and private) and other government sectors. The development and coordination of policies, strategies, plans and integrated dementia programmes through a

multisectoral approach will support the recognition of the complex needs of people with dementia and address those needs within the context of each country. The inclusion of people with dementia and their carers with other relevant stakeholders and partners is crucial for the success and buy-in of this process.

International Consortium for Health Outcomes Measures

The International Consortium for Health Outcomes Measures (ICHOM) in 2017 brought together patient representatives, clinician leaders, and registry leaders from all over the world to identify a comprehensive set of outcomes and case-mix variables for all providers of services to PwD to be tracked. These standards are for all types and stages of dementia. If the assessment based on these guidelines is not completed in a quality manner according to these standards set forth by ICHOM, then it follows that a care plan based on a defective assessment will not be in the best interests of the PwD.

Person-centered care plans

Others, after research, have concurred that PwD care plans need to be Person-Centered (Molony, Kolanowski, Van Haitsma, Rooney, 2018). Person-Centered Care (PCC) is both a responsive and respectful approach to caring for a person. PCC contributes to the person's empowerment by involving them in decision-making and contributions to the total care plan. PCC looks at the PwD as a person, as an active partner in the treatment and care process to the best of their abilities. As early as the first medical school established by Hippocrates in 400 BC, PCC was at the forefront. His focus was not just on the empirical treatment of patients. His school also identified a moral and personal code of conduct that put the patient's needs first. Aristotle's principle of human flourishing described quality in the care of the patient as seeing them as a person, as a habit whereby a caregiver is able to both see and respond to the specific needs of the other person.

Assessments for PCC should include the following areas related to the PwD and their caregiver (Kales, Gitlin, Lyketsos, 2014):

- Neurocognitive function
- Decisional capacity
- Physical functioning, including both ADLs and IADLs
- Psychological, social, and spiritual activity and well-being
- Everyday routines and activities including personal care, exercise, recreational activity, and sleep
- Behavioral changes
- Comorbidities, both medical and psychiatric

- Health indicators, e.g., pain, nutritional status, oral health
- Medications, including both prescribed and over-the-counter, and supplements
- Safety and risk reduction

Assessment of the Caregiver should include these areas:

- Strengths/factors that support well-being, including experiences of at-homeness
- Challenges/unmet needs
- Living situation and care needs
- Advance planning and awareness of resources including education, support, and palliative care
- Health, unmet needs, stress
- Knowledge of diagnosis, care options, and community resources, e.g., Adult Dementia Day Care Facilities

PCC sources of information begin with interviewing the person, the PwD, as well as the caregiver/care partner (and/or healthcare proxy) (Molony, Kolanowski, Van Haitsma, Rooney, 2018). However, the perspective of the PwD should be prioritized as much as feasible in all situations (de Medeiros, Doyle, 2013).

The purpose of both the assessment and the care planning is to support the individual PwD and family to live the best possible life with dementia. In order to develop a person-centered care plan, the human rights of the PwD should be respected and acknowledged with all input in the planning stages as well as execution of the finalized plan. PwD should be included in the care planning process. They should have a voice/input into the planning for their own care to the extent they are able. It would follow then, that the sooner a diagnosis is made in the disease process and a care plan is developed, the more the PwD can actively and knowledgeably contribute to their own present and future plan of care. Letting their wishes be known for all care from the day of the plan's inception to end of life planning will give them ownership of their care, assuming the care plan thus developed is followed by all participants as closely as feasible. This process should likewise give the caregiver a feeling of being a true advocate for the PwD, and in some instances relieve their stress because a difficult decision has already been made by the PwD about their care, thus relieving the care giver of having to decide what the PwD would have wanted done in any given situation, including the very difficult ones (Tomaselli, Buttigieg, Rosano, Cassar, Grima, 2020).

Not surprisingly, the well-being of the caregiver/care partner strongly influences the wellbeing of the PwD. There is immense potential importance in the impact of the well-being of the caregiver on the well-being of the

PwD. Hence, tools have been developed to accommodate the assessment of the caregiver's well-being, self-efficacy, ability to perceive unmet needs, skills in caregiving, and motivation to provide needed care. Unfortunately, in most cases where the caregiver is an unpaid family member, they remain the caregiver regardless of abilities demonstrated during the assessment. And globally, there is a dearth of free, easily attainable caregiver education (Dilworth-Anderson, Heehyul Moon, Aranda, 2020).

Challenges to caregiving and unmet needs include home maintenance, food, daytime activity, socialization, psychological distress, vision/hearing, self-care, and accidental harm. Including these factors in the assessment may help to curtail certain issues. As with all assessments, unless the findings are heeded and the assessment is ongoing, the collection of data is at best futile and an egregious waste of time for all concerned.

Emerging trends

Dementia and human rights

The discussion of Person-Centered Care (PCC) must, of and in itself, include all aspects of the basic human rights of the PwD (Tomaselli, Buttigieg, Rosano, Cassar, Grima, 2020) or it is not and cannot be truly "Person Centered." At the WHO organized and sponsored Ministerial Conference on Global Action Against Dementia held in Geneva in 2015, one of the opening day speakers was Ms. Rosa Kornfield-Matte, a UN Independent Expert on the Enjoyment of All Human Rights by Older People. Matte noted, "The rights and needs of persons with dementia have been given low priority in the national and global agenda. In particular, with the progression of the disease, as their autonomy decreases, persons with dementia (PwD) tend to be isolated, excluded and subjected to abuse and violence." She went on to say how critical it is to "tackle" dementia using a human-rights-based perspective. She says this because PwD are "rights holders." She concluded her presentation on the opening day of the conference with this powerful statement:

> I call on all States and other stakeholders to adopt a human-rights approach when addressing dementia. Dementia is a public health issue, but also a human rights concern. Persons with dementia should be able to enjoy their rights and fundamental freedoms in any circumstances. Their dignity, beliefs, needs, and privacy must be respected at all stages of the disease.
>
> *(Kornfield-Matte, 2015)*

Since that conference and other appeals joining those of Kornfield-Matte, a slowly evolving rights-based focus on the dementia movement has begun to grow and, in turn, gain traction across the world. The Global Dementia Observatory was developed the following year in 2016 and contains the statement, "The development and coordination of policies, strategies, plans or frameworks through a comprehensive, multisectoral approach will support the recognition of people with dementia and address their complex needs and rights within the context of each country" (WHO, 2018). Further stated, "The dementia plan is sensitive to the needs, expectations, and human rights of people with dementia, consistent with the Convention on the Rights of Persons with Disabilities (CRPD) and other international and regional human rights instruments." This Dementia Rights movement has been able to grow due to the active work and support of the WHO, Alzheimer's Disease International (ADI), Alzheimer Europe, DAI, the Dementia Engagement & Empowerment Project (DEEP), the Scottish Dementia Working Group (SDWG), the Irish Dementia Working Group (IDWG), and several other regional and national dementia working groups (Cahill, 2018).

People with Dementia (PwD) have been shown by numerous authors to experience injustice, inequality, marginalization, discrimination, segregation, abuse, failure, social exclusion, and social exclusion as well as stigmatization (Jackson, Tolson, 2019); (Bioethics, 2009); (Molony, Kolanowski, Van Haitsma, Rooney, 2018); (Rosin, Blasco, Pilozzi, Huang, Yang,, 2020). Autonomy can be gained by adding opportunities to exercise choice and control in decisions related to their lives, which may be denied, such as those needed for PCC, as previously discussed (Tomaselli, Buttigieg, Rosano, Cassar, Grima, 2020).

There is a growing interest in dementia among international policymakers. The first meeting of the CRPD was in 2006. The impetus of the globally felt need to focus on Human Rights has grown since its 2006 roots to the point that it now meets twice a year. Twelve of the articles of the Convention are particularly relevant to dementia, those articles being Articles 3, 4, 5, 9, 12, 15, 19, 22, 25, 26, 30, and 33 (Cahill, 2018) Dementia and human rights are now regarded as a key challenge of the 21st century (Quaglio, Brand, Dario, 2016).

Facing down the modifiable risks of dementia

One-third of the cases of diagnosed people with dementia (PwD) can be prevented before 2045. The plan of prevention involves managing the modifiable or treatable risk factors for Alzheimer's and other dementias (Montero-Odasso, Ismail, Livingston, 2020). Some sources in the literature list nine risk factors for dementia (Man201): low level of education completion, midlife hearing loss, obesity, hypertension, late-life depression, smoking, physical inactivity, diabetes, and social isolation.

There are other modifiable or treatable risk factors that have been associated with impairment by other authors (Roberts, Zafonte, Speizer, Baggish, et al., 2020) (Montero-Odasso, Ishmail, Livingston, 2020) (Man, 201). These include sleep apnea, short sleep duration, obesity, hypertension, cardiovascular disease, chronic pain, depression, anxiety, smoking, physical impairment, and lack of physical activity. If mitigated, these potentially modifiable factors may reduce the risk of cognitive impairment even in persons with a history of head trauma or improve cognitive function among those already showing cognitive impairments.

The cost of total care can be exorbitant or even prohibitive to some. It has been estimated that the global annual costs to individuals and their families for pharmaceutical and other health and social care needs are approximately US$800 billion. Yet, the current care plans using secondary pharmacological means have failed. This failure has been attributed to the fact that our current understanding of the relationship and temporality between dementia pathology and impending cognitive impairment is incomplete at best. The fact that there are multiple pathways involved in the development of dementia further impedes clarity in understanding the processes of the disease. It has been recognized that some of the pathways include the modifiable factors mentioned above.

Based on the identification of these risks for Alzheimer's and other dementias that are modifiable, there has been a shift to primary prevention, and today, the focus is on treatment as prevention (Montero-Odasso, Ishmail, Livingston, 2020) found. It is acknowledged that to date no cure for any known dementias has been found. The next logical paradigm shift is to primary prevention. Today the focus is on treatment as prevention (Livingston, Sommerland, Oretega, et al, 2017). Interestingly, the Lancet Commission on Dementia Prevention, Intervention, and Care Report (Livingston, Sommerland, Oretega, et al, 2017) has suggested that if nine potentially reversible risk factors are tackled, as many as fully one-third of dementia cases may be preventable. At this point, there are still unanswered questions: How, at which stage, and for how long any lifestyle interventions would need to be undertaken.

Summary

We live in an aging global population, which brings with it the ever-present scourge of growing numbers of PwD, which is projected to triple by the year 2050, from 50 million to 152 million. Of the people developing dementia annually, 60 percent come from low- to middle-income countries. Many people who develop dementia are unaware that they have it due to poor recognition and education relating to dementia – what it is, its signs and symptoms, the stages, diagnosis, proper care of and for persons living with dementia.

Add to this that a large number of general practitioners who are on the front lines have not been educated in the diagnosis or treatment of this cognitive disorder. Efforts have begun globally to remedy these deficits through the development of proper educational programs. Global strides have been made in the determination and recognition of the fact that PwD are still the same persons they were prior to the diagnosis of dementia and, as such possess the same human rights' they had prior to the devasting diagnosis of dementia. A great boost in this much-needed transformation has been due to the work of the Convention on the Rights of Persons with Disabilities. These include the rights to continued dignity, respect, and the right to choose how they should live their own lives. Person-Centered Care Plans ensure that PwD has the right to participate in planning and be heard in terms of how they want to be cared for or treated in various situations related to the progression of the disease. With these strides toward human rights and justice, we are beginning to strip away the injustices, abuse, and neglect with which too many PwD have been met in the past.

For many years, international pharmaceutical companies, and university and biomedical researchers, have given hope to the awaiting public and PwD that we are just five years away from the "miracle" cure. After so many years of awaiting that prodigious promise, some researchers have begun to take a different route, a different approach to attempting to overcome the scourge of dementia and its attendant ravages of the PwD, their caregivers, care-partners, PwD of the future, and loved ones. This different approach will hopefully give surcease to many would-be PwD in the future. This new research is centered on stopping the onset of the disease process before it ever begins. The basis of the new paradigm is to modify the major factors that pose a risk for the development of dementia: low level of education completion, midlife hearing loss, obesity, hypertension, late-life depression, smoking, physical inactivity, diabetes, and social isolation. At this point in time, there is no research to validate this approach due to the timeframe of several years to assess the impact of the proposed modifications.

References

Akram, M. (2017). Effects of medicinal plants on Alzheimer's disease and memory deficits. *Neural Regeneration Research*, 12(4), 660–670.

Ball, D. (2020). *We died and were reborn: An anthropological study*. Lexington, KY: UKnowledge.

Begagly, M. (2019). Mali. In A. Burns (Ed.), *Dementia care: International perspectives*. Oxford: Oxford University Press, 9–14.

Betts Adams, K., & McClendon, M. (2006). Early-stage cognitive impairment: A social work practice and research agenda. *Families in Society*, 87(4), 590–600.

Bioethics, N. C. (2009). *Dementia: Ethical issues*. London: Nuffield Council on Bioethics.

Bowling, A. G. (2007). Lay theories of quality of life in older age. *Ageing and Society, 27*(6), 827–848.

Cahill, S. (2018). *Dementia and human rights*. Bristol: Policy Press.

Casey, C., Mofizul Islam, M., Schutze, H., Parkinson, A., Yen, L., & Shell, A. (2020). Australian education programs for general practitioners. *BMC Family Practice*, 1–16.

Chheng, C., Waiwut, P., Plekratoke, K., Chulikhit, Y., et al. (2020). Multitarget activities of kleeb bua daeng, a Thai traditional herbal formula, against Alzheimer's disease. *Frontiers in Pharmacology, 13*(5), 79. doi: 10.3390/ph13050079.

de Medieros, K., & Doyle, P. J. (2013). Remembering the person in person-centered residential dementia care. *Generations, 37*(3), 83–86.

Dereli, F. T. G. (2021). *Naturally occurring chemicals against Alzheimer's Disease*. Elsevier and Academic Press, USA.

Dilworth-Anderson, P., Moon, H., & Aranda, M. P. (2020). Dementia caregiving research: Expanding and reframing the lens of diversity, inclusivity, and intersectionality. *The Gerontologist, 60*(5), 797–805. doi: 10.1093/gerontologist/gnaa050.

Goffman, E. (1963). *Stigma: Notes on the management of spoiled identity*. London: Prentice-Hall.

Graham, A. J., & Tolson, D. (2019). *Textbook of dementia care an integrated approach*. New York: Routledge.

Graham, N., Lindsay, J., Katona, C., Camus, V., Copeland, J., et al. (2003). Reducing stigma and discrimination against older people with mental disorders: A technical consensus statement. *International Journal of Geriatric Psychiatry, 18*(8), 670–678.

Husband, H. (1999). The psychological consequences of learning a diagnosis of dementia: Three Case Examples. *Aging and Mental Health, 3*(2), 179–183.

Jennings, A. A., Foley, T., Bradley, C. P., et al. (2018). General practitioners' knowledge, attitudes, and experiences of managing behavioural & psychological symptoms of dementia: A mixed-methods systematic review. *Journal of Geriatric Psychology, 33*(9), 1163–1176.

Jossim Uddin, C. Z. (2020). Traditional herbal medicines against CNS disorders from Bangladesh. *Natural Products and BioProspecting, 10*, 377–410.

Kales, H. C,. Gitlin, L. N., & Lyketsos, C. G. (2014). Assessment and management of neuropsychiatric symptoms of dementia. *Journal of the American Geriatrics Society, 62*(4), 762–769.

Katsuno, T. (2005). Dementia from the inside: How people with early-stage dementia evaluate their quality of life. *Ageing and Society, 25*(2), 197–214.

Keating, F. (2006). *Breaking the spiral of oppression: Racism and race equality in the mental health services*. Pavillion Publishers.

Kim, G. (2012). Herbal medicines for the prevention and treatment of Alzheimer's disease. *Current Pharmaceutical Design, 18*(1), 57–75.

Kornfield-Matte, R. (2015). Dementia, a public health priority and human rights concern. Statement to the Ministerial Conference on Global Action Against Dementia World Health Organization (unpublished speech). Geneva.

Lindesay, J. (2008). *Memory clinics*. Oxford: Oxford University Press.

Livingston, G., Sommerland, A., Oretega, V., et al. (2017). Dementia prevention, intervention, and care. *Lancet*, 2673–2734.

Lok, N., Oncel, S., Ozer, Z., & Buldukoglu, K. (2017). Institutional services for dementia care. *Psikiyatride Guncel Yaklasmlar-Current Approaches to Pyschiatry, 9*(4), 464–473.

Mccleary, L., Blain, J. (2013). *Cultural values and family caregiving for persons with dementia*. Indian Journal of Gerontology, 27(1), 178–201.

Magklara, E., Stephan, B. C. M., Robinson, L. (2018). Current approaches to dementia screening and case finding in low-and middle-income countries: Research update and recommendations. *Geriatric Psychiatry, 34*(1), 3–7.

Mason, R., Annear, M., Lo, A., Tiernig, L., & Robinson, A. (2016). Development & preliminary psychometric properties of the General Practitioner Attitudes & Confidence Scale (GPACS-D) for Dementia. *BMC FamilyPractice, 17*, 1–8.

Mayer, P., Fischer, W., Liang, Z., Sorian-Castelli, D., et al. (2020, March 10). The value of herbarium collections to the discovery of novel treatments for Alzheimer's disease. *Frontiers in Pharmacology, 11*, 208.

Milne, A. P. (2008). *Challenges & resolutions to psycho-social well-being for people in receipt of a diagnosis of dementia: A literature review.* London: Mental Health Foundation & Alzheimer's Foundation.

Molony, S., Kolanowski, A., Van Haitsma, K., & Rooney,K. E. (2018). Person centered assessment and care planning. *Gerontologist, 58*, S32–S47.

Montero-Odasso, M., Ishmail, Z., & Livingston, G. (2020). One third of dementia cases can be prevented within the next 25 years by tackling risk factors. The case "for" and "against". *Alz Research Therapy, 12*, 1–5.

Organization, W. H. (2018). *Towards a dementia plan: A WHO guide.* Geneva: World Health Organization.

Owokuhaisa, J., Rukundo, G. Z., Wakida, E., Obua, C., & Buss, S. S. (2020). Community perceptions about dementia care in Southwest Uganda. *BMC Geriatrics, 20*, 135–147.

Paddick, S. M., Mushi, D., & Rongai, A. (2014). Social representation and practices related to dementia in Hai District of Tanzania. *BMC Public Health, 14*, 260–267.

Parker, M. (2020). Persistent barriers and facilitators to seeking help for a dementia diagnosis. A systematic review of 30 years of the perspectives of carers and people with dementia. *International Psychogeriatrics, 32*(5), 611–634.

Paulo Pires, et al. (2019). Mental health in Mozambique; A systematic review. *International Journal of Family & Community Medicine, 3*(4), 138–146.

Pharr, J. D., & Francis, C. D. (2014). Culture, caregiving and health: Exploring the influence of culture on caregiver experiences. *International Scholarly Research Notices*, 1–8.

Poole, M., Davis, N., & Robinson, L. (2020). Dementia care: Living well as dementia progresses: Meeting dementia career educational support needs. *Age & Ageing, 49*, 171–174.

Quaglio, G., Brand, H., & Dario, C. (2016). Fighting dementia in Europe. *The Lancet Neurology, 15*(5), 452–454. doi: 10.1016/S1474-4422(16)00079-X.

Robert, A. B. (2019). *Dementia care international perspectives.* New York City: Oxford University Press.

Roberts, A. L., Zafonte, R. D., Speizer, F. E., Baggish, A., et al. (2020). Modifiable risk factors for poor cognitive function in former American-style football players: Findings from the harvard football players health study. *Journal of Neurotrauma, 38*(2), 189–195.

Rosin, E. R., Blasco, D., Pilozzi, A. R., Huang, X., & Yang, L. H. (2020). A narrative review of Alzheimer's disease stigma. *Journal of Alzheimer's Disease, 78*(2), 515–528.

Thornicroft, G. (2006). *Actions speak louder...Tackling discrimination against people with mental illness.* London: Mental Health Foundation.

Tomaselli, G., Buttigieg, S. C., Rosano, A., Cassar, M., & Grima, G. (2020, March 06). Person-centered care from a relational ethics perspective for the delivery of high quality and safe healthcare: A scoping review. (B. U. Ulrich Laaser, Ed.) *Front Public Health.*

van der Lee, S. J., Tuenissen, C. E., & Pool, R. (2018). Circulating metabolites and general cognitive ability and dementia: Evidence from 11 cohort studies. *Alzheimer's Dementia, 14*(6), 707–722.

Wang, J., & Xiao, L. D. (2013). Family caregiver challenges in dementia care in a country with undeveloped dementia services. *Journal of Clinical Nursing, 70*(6), 1369–1380.

WHO. (2018). *Towards a dementia plan: A WHO guide.* Geneva: World Health Organization.

WHO Media centre fact sheets: Dementia. Fact sheet N°362. (n.d.). Retrieved 11 29, 2020, from http://www.who.int/mediacentre/factsheets/fs362/en/

Williamson, T. (2008). *Dementia: Out of the shadows.* London: Alzheimer's Society.

17
CARING FOR PEOPLE WITH DEMENTIA IN AUSTRALIA

Claire Morrisby and Barbara Blundell

Introduction

Dementia rates are increasing in Australia, with 70 percent of people experiencing this condition living in the community. People with dementia usually prefer to live and be cared for in the community (Gomes et al., 2013); as the condition progresses, people with dementia are increasingly reliant on informal and formal caregivers for support. However, admission to residential care has been associated with increases in behavioural symptoms for people with dementia and their carers experiencing guilt, depression, and feeling like failures (Sury et al., 2013). Challenges exist for the more than 215,517 informal carers in the community, including fatigue, interrupted sleep, and reduced social support, necessitating access to effective formal support services. This chapter outlines the current context of caregiving for people with dementia in Australia, drawing on a body of work the authors have been involved with (Ebert, 2019; Fowler, 2018; McGrath, 2019; Morrisby et al., 2019, 2020). It provides information about the caregiving context more broadly for both informal and formal caregivers, including family carers and paid careworkers. The interface between informal and formal care systems will be explored, highlighting issues for older people with dementia and their caregivers. These include the gendered and low-status nature of caregiving, service system gaps and recommendations, and relevant preliminary findings from the Australian Royal Commission into Aged Care Quality and Safety. It is proposed that caregiving is an important but undervalued role in Australian society. Changes in current systems are necessary to further support the well-being, dignity, and rights of older people with dementia.

DOI: 10.4324/9781003528432-20

Person- and family-centred care must be better supported, and tailored support is needed for the specific needs of spousal carers.

Ageing in Australia

Australia has an ageing population and it is projected that the proportion of people aged over 65 years will increase from 3.8 million (or 15 percent) in 2017 to 8.8 million (22 percent) by 2057 (Australian Institute of Health and Welfare [AIHW], 2018). There are more older females than males; non-Indigenous women have a higher average life expectancy of 83.4 years than non-Indigenous males at 80.2, though life expectancies for Aboriginal and Torres Strait Islander people are significantly lower, at 75.6 years for Indigenous women, and 71.6 for Indigenous men (AIHW, 2020a). Approximately 95.3 percent of Australian older people live in their own homes (Australian Bureau of Statistics [ABS], 2019), with the number of people receiving aged care services and supports increasing with age. Around 4.6 percent of older people live in "cared accommodation", which includes residential and other types of supported care accommodation (ABS, 2019), with 3 percent of older people receiving care services in their homes (AIHW, 2018). Chronic health issues and disability are not necessarily associated with ageing; however, the risk of developing these conditions does increase with age, with 80 percent of people aged 65 and over experiencing long-term health conditions (ABS, 2019; Royal Commission into Aged Care Quality and Safety, 2019). With increased age, the likelihood of developing dementia increases; 0.7 percent of Australians between the ages of 65–74 had a primary diagnosis of dementia, with this increasing to 12.6 percent in Australians aged 85 and over (ABS, 2019). Approximately 70 percent of people with dementia in Australia live in the community, with 30 percent living in supported accommodation, such as residential aged care (AIHW, 2012). It is estimated that 52 percent of people living in residential care have dementia (Brown & Hansnata, 2017).

Dementia

Dementia is a progressive degenerative condition characterised by declines in function and memory loss (Australian Institute of Health and Welfare, 2020b). Dementia is an umbrella term, rather than one specific disease, and it describes a collection of symptoms caused by one of over 100 different disorders that affect the brain (Dementia Australia, 2020c). The four most common types are Alzheimer's disease (approximately 50–75 percent), vascular dementia (20–30 percent), Frontotemporal dementia (5–10 percent), and dementia with Lewy bodies (up to 5 percent; AIHW, 2012). Some of the signs and symptoms of dementia include memory loss, difficulties with speech and language, changes in personality, mood, or behaviour, demonstrating poor judgement and lack of insight, difficulty completing everyday tasks (including self-care), loss of interest in activities once enjoyed, losing sense of time and place, problems with abstract thinking, and irregular sleep (Sclan & Reisberg, 1992). There is no current cure for dementia, though it is possible to slow its progression through both pharmacological and non-pharmacological interventions. Dementia is the second leading cause of death in Australia, with a proportional increase of 67 percent between 2010 and 2019 (Australian Bureau of Statistics, 2020).

Dementia can occur at any age but is most common after age 65. People who are diagnosed with dementia before the age of 65 are described as having younger onset dementia (YOD). It is estimated that 459,000 people in Australia are living with some form of dementia (Dementia Australia, 2020a), and this number is projected to rise to 1,100,890 by 2056 as the population both ages and increases (Brown & Hansnata, 2017). Individuals experience impairments in their performance of everyday tasks as dementia affects thinking and behaviour, which also interferes with social and working life (Dementia Australia, 2020c). As dementia progresses and the person's ability to care for themselves declines, support is needed to maintain the person in their own home or living in the community (van Exel et al., 2007). Most people with dementia and their caregivers prefer that they be cared for at home. This environment promotes independence and function due to familiarity and routine (van der Roest et al., 2009). Carers and people with dementia have described the importance of the home environment in allowing them to continue their daily activities. Remaining in their home improves the quality of life for people with dementia through opportunities to engage in meaningful roles such as gardening, cooking, cleaning, and caring for others, such as grandchildren (Morrisby et al., 2019). A shift towards de-institutionalising the care of older people (Egdell et al., 2010), along with "ageing in place" policies (Robinson et al., 2012) and the increasing cost of residential care (ABS, 2019; Low et al., 2011) has supported these preferences (Polacsek et al., 2020; van der Roest et al., 2009). Family caregivers commonly believe that people with dementia fare better in the home environment. This is underscored by a sense of familial responsibility and the belief that family carers are more able to support and anticipate the person with dementia's needs (AIHW, 2012).

In Australia, dementia is diagnosed in a range of clinical settings including general practitioner (GP) clinics, hospitals, memory clinics, specialists, community settings (such as the aged care assessment team), and residential care (Ng & Ward, 2019). GPs are frequently the first health professionals with whom memory concerns are raised; however, many GPs identify that their knowledge of dementia is insufficient to support effective diagnosis and care (Millard et al., 2011). People with dementia, carers, and health professionals have described either an apparent lack of care or a lack of up-to-date knowledge regarding non-pharmacological interventions to slow disease progression and improve quality of life (Morrisby et al., 2019, 2020). Diagnosis is usually completed by either a specialist or memory clinic; however, the quality of care received by people with dementia and carers is not consistent. For example, referrals to community support services are not routinely completed in all settings (Morrisby et al., 2019). Early access to multi-disciplinary memory clinics has the potential to reduce carer stress and improve psychosocial quality of life through enabling access to education and support (Logiudice et al., 1999). Australian Clinical Practice Guidelines (Guideline Adaptation Committee, 2016) recommend that assessment services and specialists provide a responsive service to support timely diagnosis, as well as organise comprehensive assessment, diagnostic, therapeutic, and rehabilitation services that accommodate the diverse needs of people with dementia and their carers and families. The Guidelines also suggest that referrals for health and aged care services be made directly by the memory assessment service or specialists involved.

Informal caregiving of people with dementia

Older people with dementia in Australia may be cared for by both informal (family and friends) and formal (paid) caregivers. Informal caregivers provide ongoing assistance and support to family members and friends who have a disability, health condition, or who are frail aged (ABS, 2019). It is estimated that 92 percent of people with dementia in the community receive support from one or more informal carers (AIHW, 2012). A survey conducted by the Australian Bureau of Statistics (2019) found that there were around 2.65 million informal caregivers in Australia, or 12 percent of the population, who provided unpaid care for older people and people with disabilities; 861,600 of these being primary carers who provide ongoing care for at least six months. Of this figure, around 420,700 were identified as primary carers of people over 65 years of age (ABS, 2019). In couples aged 65 years and older, spouses make up 57 percent of informal carers and are typically the first to provide care to their partner, despite often experiencing their own health issues (ABS, 2019). The next largest proportion of co-resident carers (i.e., those residing with the person with dementia) are children (36%). Caring is a gendered activity, with 72 percent of primary carers being female (Deloitte Access Economics, 2020). It has been reported that, while a significant number of men may care for an ill or frail partner (Thompson & Kramer, 2002), women generally undertake caring commitments more broadly across the lifespan in relation to children, partners, and parents (Schirmer, 2017).

Primary carers of older people and people with disabilities have been estimated to provide an average of 35.2 hours of care per week, with non-primary carers providing an estimated average of 10 hours per week (Deloitte Access Economics, 2020). Carers provide support in several areas, including help with housework, mobility, communication, medication management, providing personal care (i.e., showering and dressing), and social support (companionship, transport, and outings). They may also provide emotional and financial support (Carers Australia, 2024). Family caregivers may be motivated to provide care by factors such as love or reciprocity, a sense of duty, social pressures, guilt, spiritual fulfilment, and sometimes even greed (Eisdorfer, 1991). A recent Australian survey found that the three most common reasons primary caregivers provided for undertaking a caring role were: a sense of family responsibility (70.1%), emotional obligation (46.6%), and the ability to provide better care than anybody else (46.4%; ABS, 2019). Additionally, over one-third of those who were primary carers to someone over 65 years of age said that there were no other friends or family available to provide the care (ABS, 2019).

Spousal carers

Given co-resident carers are most commonly spouses or partners (AIHW, 2012), specifically considering the needs experienced by this group of carers is important. Wadham et al. (2016), Robinson et al. (2005) and Egilstrod et al. (2019) found that understanding the needs of spousal carers may contribute to developing more effective interventions to support community-dwelling people with dementia. In Australia, aged care policies and systems are dependent on informal carers, including spouses, to complete the majority of care and support for people with dementia. The role of caring for a person with dementia is highly intensive, particularly for spouses and partners (Cash et al., 2013). Spousal carers and people with dementia experience changes in intimacy, identity, and perceived value as they transition from the roles of "spouses" or "partners" to "carer and person with dementia" (Braun et al., 2009). In interviews with spousal dyads, both carers and people with dementia described the importance of working together and recognised that the transition to caring occurred within the context of many years of partnership (Morrisby et al., 2019). Spousal carers interviewed in this research were committed to supporting the person with dementia, and the key attitudes to maintaining the relationship were love, humour, patience, and tolerance.

Not all people with dementia are older. Carers of people with younger onset dementia (YOD) are most commonly spouses (Brown & Hansnata, 2017) and face unique challenges (Riedijk et al., 2006). Typically, YOD carers are in the workforce at the time of diagnosis, which gradually becomes impacted by their caring role, resulting in financial strain and reducing their subsequent ability to save for retirement (Harris & Keady, 2009). Due to the stigma associated with dementia and a lack of societal understanding about dementia in younger adults, families often describe a loss of social support following their diagnosis; this can contribute to carers feeling isolated and overwhelmed (Lockeridge & Simpson, 2013). As with carers of people with dementia, carers of those with YOD also find a lack of adequate and appropriate formal and informal support; this may result in early and inappropriate admission to residential aged care (Roach & Drummond, 2014). Therefore, appropriate supports and services are necessary to help alleviate the demand on carers and support the person with YOD to live at home.

Male caregivers

As mentioned previously, caregiving tends to be gendered in Australian society, with 72 percent of primary care being provided by females (Deloitte Access Economics, 2020). This may be due to the fact that it is often socially expected that women will take on a caring role (Revenson et al., 2016) and they are perceived to possess an innate nurturing ability based on their gender. A significant number of older males provide care to their spouse or partner, with the likelihood of providing care increasing with age for men to the point where, over the age of 75 years, more males are caring for female partners (56% male versus 44% female; Deloitte Access Economics, 2020, p. 10). Due to the gendered nature of caregiving, the needs of older male caregivers may be overlooked. This is despite a greater risk of negative health outcomes following their partner's entry to cared accommodation due to the combined effects of the emotional loss of their partner and reduced social support (Gaugler et al., 2010). For males caring for a partner, it has been found that this role is marked by considerable stress and burden, and when the care recipient's needs outweigh the caregiver's resources, the decision to move the recipient into full-time care is generally made (Ducharme et al., 2007; Fowler, 2018; Gaugler et al., 2010).

The costs of caregiving

Being an informal caregiver of a person with dementia is not without cost. While there are positive aspects, there are also high rates of what is termed "caregiver burden", which can have significant health, emotional, and financial impacts, including social isolation, physical ill-health, and financial hardship (Brodaty & Donkin, 2009). Many caregivers may reduce their working hours or give up employment entirely to provide care. Caregiving has been found to result in carer's fatigue, interrupted sleep, and reduced social support, which may result in a need for supplementary support from formal support services. Effective formal support services in the community have been found to delay the entry of the person into residential aged care (Alzheimer's Australia, 2011; Gaugler et al., 2005; Samus et al., 2014), by alleviating carer distress and giving carers additional capacity to manage their daily roles (Millenaar et al., 2016).

The replacement cost of informal care, or the estimated cost of purchasing an equivalent amount of paid care, has been calculated at AU$77.9 billion (Deloitte Access Economics, 2020). It is projected that the demand for informal carers will increase by around 23 percent over the next decade as the population continues to age (Deloitte Access Economics, 2020). Informal primary carers have access to several government payments to support them in their caring role. These include:

- Carer Payment: An income support payment for those unable to work in substantial paid employment because they provide full-time daily care to someone with a severe disability or medical condition, or to someone who is frail aged. This payment is income and asset tested. Payment rates depend on the family situation, and there are supplements that may be added.
- Carer Allowance: a fortnightly supplementary payment for parents or carers providing additional daily care to an adult or dependent child with a disability or medical condition, or to someone who is frail aged. This is an income-tested payment.
- Carer Supplement: An annual lump sum payment to help with care costs if you receive one of the above payments.

(Services Australia, 2020)

Carers have expressed that the cost of caregiving is not well compensated through the available government payments and allowances (Singh et al., 2015). Out-of-pocket expenses, including medical appointments and services, are significant, with one carer reporting, "He's at day clubs three times a week. If he was going to day club and I was on a package, one week would cost AU$360" (Morrisby et al., 2019, p. 40). In addition, accessing these payments has been found to be a challenge, with some carers identifying as barriers the complexity of access and time constraints in attending appointments at Centrelink (the government social security payments agency) to arrange access to payments. Informal care is often used to supplement paid care in the home or residential aged care. Formal (paid) care is largely funded by the government, with consumers contributing to costs based on their ability to do so. However, this has also been identified as a challenge for family carers, with those who are experiencing difficulties paying for the appropriate amount of support often not receiving fee reductions or waivers due to service provider inflexibility or a lack of awareness of this as an option (Morrisby et al., 2020; Singh et al., 2015).

Support for carers

Given the significant stress that may arise when caring for a person with dementia, informal carers should be supported to manage psychosocial aspects of caring alongside being provided with financial support. Psychosocial supports are most often in the form of education or information, carer support groups, and counselling. Education and counselling support services are funded in Australia through the National Dementia Support Program (Department of Health, 2020) and provided across Australia by Dementia Australia. To support people who are newly diagnosed with dementia in Australia, the Living with Dementia Program is available as a joint education programme for both the person with dementia and the carer (Dementia Australia, 2020b). This is often followed up with a referral to carer support groups or Memory Cafés (Dow et al., 2011), where the person with dementia and their carer attend a café-based support group, which provides a more social and less formal opportunity for joint support. Carers are also able to access individual or family counselling via telephone or in person. These services have been evaluated as effective; however, it is important to note that the majority of people diagnosed with dementia and their carers do not get referred to these services and supports, or do not access them (Dementia Australia, 2018).

Education and information

For carers to manage well in their role of supporting people with dementia to remain at home, education and information are critical. Dementia is not well understood in the general population; Alzheimer's Disease International (2019) conducted a survey which found over half of the Australian population believed people with dementia are impulsive or unpredictable, and 11 percent believe they are dangerous. This may impact on the help-seeking behaviours of carers and people with dementia themselves. Research into dementia attitudes and help-seeking intentions has found that 21.5 percent of respondents would delay seeking help for as long as possible for early signs of dementia, and 7.2 percent would not seek help at all (Phillipson et al., 2015). Once the initial barriers to a person with dementia receiving a diagnosis are addressed, carers often experience difficulties in knowing what the future will hold for them. A dementia specialist nurse stated:

> Probably the biggest thing is, is there a knowledge deficit about dementia. Because many people feel as though … 'Mum's doing this on purpose'. So, then I start thinking, well, we need to improve. If it was some exotic disease, we'd be on the internet, Googling, what is it about dementia?
> *(Morrisby et al., 2020, p. 8)*

The knowledge deficit extends beyond a lack of understanding of dementia to having little awareness of services and supports, and conversely, carers may become overwhelmed by the "maze of information out there" (Robinson et al., 2012, p. 205). A challenge reported by Australian service providers is providing the right information and education at the right time, within the confines of services that are funded (Morrisby et al., 2020). Service providers report that people with dementia enter residential care prematurely when the correct information is not available, such as how and when to access services.

Peer support for carers

Carer support groups are reported by most carers to be an important resource and an adaptive strategy and opportunity for socialisation, education, and peer support. Carer support groups and counselling have been shown to increase the uptake of services (Bauer et al., 2019). Given the lack of understanding of dementia in the general population and the time commitment involved in caring for a person with dementia, it is not surprising that carers may experience difficulties maintaining social connections. Studies with Australian carers (Morrisby et al., 2019; Nay et al., 2015) have reported the difficulty experienced in maintaining relationships with friends and that this can be managed in part through developing new social supports through memory cafés or other local support groups and networks. Recommendations from carers regarding support groups include effective group facilitation, the inclusion of information and some structured content, and the opportunity to develop social connections for carers and people with dementia (Morrisby et al., 2019). Carer choice in this is highly important, and some carers may not participate in carer support groups regardless of the available groups (Nay et al., 2015). However, it is important to note that a National Dementia Support Program (NDSP) evaluation identified that carer support groups may not meet the needs of specific populations, such as Indigenous Australians and carers from culturally and linguistically diverse backgrounds (Grenade et al., 2007). Research is currently being undertaken to investigate the efficacy of online and videoconference access to peer support (Parkinson et al., 2018). Challenges also arise from the current funding of carer support groups – when the person with dementia resides in the community, NDSP funding is accessible; however, once a person enters residential aged care or passes away, NDSP guidelines limit consistent access to support groups (Fowler, 2018; Jameson et al., 2020). This has a negative impact on the post-caring phase, reducing the ability of carers to transition back to previous roles (Jameson et al., 2020).

Support for spousal carers

Spousal carers benefit from holistic support to manage their role as a carer. Interviews with spousal carers and people with dementia identified that they experience needs for support around the social and physical environment, support services, and to engage in meaningful activities and maintain important supportive relationships with family and friends (Morrisby et al., 2019). Ongoing adaptation of daily activities and roles within the spousal relationship is necessary as dementia progresses; however, it is important to consider that this is accompanied by a complex process of loss (Robinson et al., 2005). Maintaining valuable roles, such as grand-parenting or helping the person with dementia to complete useful tasks around the home, is helpful to spousal carers as it can maintain their quality of life (Morrisby et al., 2019). Professional support provided by health professionals, such as occupational therapists, to tailor communication and adapt the environment to be more supportive, can assist carers of people with dementia to continue in important roles and occupations, but may increase caregiver burden (Vikström et al., 2005).

Other important strategies to support spousal carers include having time to relax and reflect on experiences of caring, developing strategies to cope, and receiving support from other carers of people with dementia (Morrisby et al., 2019). As carers, taking responsibility for looking after themselves by accessing education about dementia (via internet resources or community services), asking for help, and prioritising decisions that prioritise themselves are key. For example, the decision about when to access support services is often driven by the acceptance of the person with dementia; however, carers need to recognise that their own needs must also be met also. Carers who reflected on their previous experiences in caring felt more capable of making decisions regarding the future (Morrisby et al., 2019). Carers seek support from a range of social relationships – family, long-term friends, and new friendships with other carers; all of these connections have been identified as important (Morrisby et al., 2019).

Legislative changes have re-oriented community-based care towards consumer-directed aged care with the aim of providing greater flexibility and person-centredness (Low et al., 2011). However, for consumer-directed care places to be effective, carers face the challenge of choosing the "right" level of support for their husband or wife; this potentially creates conflict within spousal relationships (Cash et al., 2013). This can be a significant challenge when a person with dementia and their carer disagree about the level of support required. For example, Phillipson and Jones (2011) found that prior to the introduction of consumer-directed care, conflict between carers and people with dementia had the potential to limit access to support (Phillipson & Jones, 2011). The needs of people with dementia and their spouses need to be well understood to facilitate this important decision-making process.

Formal caregiving services and supports

Formal supports for people with dementia include aged and community care services, respite care, and residential aged care. Formal carers may be named differently depending on the organisation for whom they work, and roles include home care worker or staff, support worker, and community-based care worker (and many other combinations). These positions may be paid, volunteer, or an unpaid student placement. A wide range of government-funded home care services is available in Australia, organised into three key funding systems: the Commonwealth Home Support Programme (CHSP), Home Care Packages (HCP), and Veterans' Home Care (VHC; Productivity Commission, 2018). These systems provide funding for community services including domestic assistance, respite care, social support, assessment and information about service pathways and care strategies, residential respite, and the ongoing coordination of care for older adults, including those with dementia and their families (Productivity Commission, 2018). Care recipients may receive either a basic, low-level, intermediate, or high-level home care package to assist them at home, depending on their assessed needs (Australian Government, 2024).

People with dementia usually prefer living and being cared for at home (Gomes et al., 2013); therefore, it is important to understand the factors that support quality of life and maintain safety for people with dementia in the community. Australian research has shown that people who use care services in Australia live at home longer, with greater service use equating to better outcomes (Jorgensen et al., 2018). However, it has been argued that these care service systems are not currently working well (Day et al., 2017; Gill et al., 2018). For example, there are limited low-level, intermediate, and high-level care packages presently available, and it has been found that those eligible may wait over 12 months on average to access them (Department of Health, 2019). Reports indicate that in 2019, there were 62,942 people waiting for a package at their approved level, with another 49,295 offered a lower-level package to support their needs until one could become available (Department of Health, 2019). Many people have to access privately-funded community and in-home services to remain at home while waiting for government-supported services (Day et al., 2017). Though these Australian studies provide contextual knowledge about the benefits of and issues surrounding service use, the study samples did not specifically include people with dementia, though it is known that around 9 percent of people receiving these services have moderate to severe levels of cognitive impairment associated with dementia or similar conditions (AIHW, 2020b). In conjunction with systemic issues surrounding the availability and access to effective and appropriate home care services, the formal carers and health professionals who provide these supports have also been identified as an important variable in the path to supporting people with dementia and their family carers.

Access to formal support

In alignment with the interim report from the Royal Commission into Aged Care Quality and Safety, research with informal carers and service providers has identified that greater assistance is required from services in order for people with dementia to remain living at home longer. As dementia progresses, services are often prioritised around basic daily care needs, such as personal care and medication management. As these kinds of services increase, the opportunity for carers to receive respite, and for the person with dementia to access social supports, appears to decrease (Morrisby et al., 2020). An increased need for home support from a range of services and professions, including support workers and allied health professionals such as nurses, occupational therapists, or physiotherapists, has also been identified (McGrath, 2019). As previously described, the availability of services that provide the right level of care is critical in supporting people with dementia to remain at home. In one study, a care staff member reported, "they said it will be at least another six to 12 months before her home care package is released. And so basically, he [client's informal carer] had no option. He wasn't coping" (McGrath, 2019, p. 17).

Community-based services may be supplemented by access to residential respite care. Residential respite programmes are federally funded and provide up to 63 subsidised nights of care for a person with dementia in a residential care facility (My Aged Care, 2020). This support allows carers of people with dementia to have a longer break:

> It [residential respite care] helped me not have a mental breakdown. It helped me recuperate a little bit health-wise. So it helped. I guess it helped him [her father with dementia] as well because then he was getting the care that he needed. It was positive.
> *(McGrath, 2019, p. 19)*

However, challenges exist for carers seeking to use this support. Service providers have described that, while funding is available, there is no longer assistance for people to find and book suitable residential respite care (Morrisby et al., 2020). A further disincentive was the difficulty accessing residential respite care: "you just think, 'Oh, man. All I want is a break', and waiting four months, that's forever down the track" (McGrath, 2019, p. 17), and difficulties with the quality of care experienced as a result of understaffing.

Transition from home to residential care

As dementia is a progressive degenerative condition, there generally comes a time in the disease progression when the care needs of the person with dementia become too high for them to continue to be supported to live at home by informal and formal caregivers. Admission to residential care has been associated with an increased incidence of behavioural symptoms for people with dementia, and carers experiencing guilt, depression, and feeling like failures (Sury et al., 2013). The decision to move to residential care for people with dementia is influenced by a range of factors related to the person, their carer(s), health and community services, and the surrounding social, physical, and cultural environment (Afram et al., 2014; Toot et al., 2017). Over half, or 53 percent, of people living in residential aged care have a dementia diagnosis (Australian Institute of Health and Welfare, 2020b). Residential care for a person with dementia in Australia is associated with both financial and social costs. Annually, residential care costs approximately AU$88,000 for a person with dementia; this cost is split between the resident (or their family) and the Australian government (Gnanamanickam et al., 2018). People with dementia in residential care may experience difficult and distressing emotions, such as uncertainty, isolation, loss, fear, and a sense of worthlessness (Clare et al., 2008).

Additionally, residential aged care facilities are not designed to meet the specific and unique needs of people with YOD (Rimkeit & McIntosh, 2017); services are primarily designed around the interests and physical abilities of the majority of residents living in aged care facilities who are frail and older. Of the nearly 24,000 people with YOD in Australia in 2015, only 1,888, or less than 8 percent, resided in residential aged care facilities, indicating that the majority were being cared for at home (Brown & Hansnata, 2017).

As it is generally the preference of the person with dementia and their informal caregivers that they remain in the community setting as long as possible, research has investigated this "tipping point" to identify the factors influencing this transition in care (Ebert, 2019; McGrath, 2019). A number of individual, carer, and contextual factors have been identified that contribute to people with dementia moving into residential care. Individual factors included deterioration linked to worsening cognition, changed behaviours, a decline in the ability to perform activities of daily living, co-occurring health conditions, and safety concerns (McGrath, 2019). This transition was also sometimes linked to a sudden event or specific issue, such as the person with dementia having a serious fall and ending up in the hospital (McGrath, 2019). Brodaty et al. (2014) did not find a statistically significant association with caregiver burden or demographic variables, though living alone was viewed as likely to be associated with a person with dementia transitioning to residential care.

Carer factors have been investigated in relation to their impact on entry to residential care for people with dementia, and carers feeling unable to meet the care needs of people with dementia they care for have been linked to this transition. Family carers have identified that supporting a person with dementia may overwhelm the ability of the carer, leading to people with dementia being admitted to residential care. In a study by McGrath (2019), one carer reported that the demands of caring for her grandfather negatively impacted every part of her life, giving her no time to work or for her social life. Carer-related issues that have been identified include caregiver burden (Afram et al., 2014; Ducharme et al., 2007; Toot et al., 2017), the carer no longer being able to meet the person's care needs (Afram et al., 2014; McGrath, 2019), the level of dependency of the person being cared for (Afram et al., 2014), the impact of the support becoming too much for the carer (McGrath, 2019), a lack of family or social support, and needing greater assistance from services (McGrath, 2019).

A recent study explored the experiences of eight older male caregivers and their changing roles as primary caregivers when their partners entered full-time residential aged care (Fowler, 2018). The research found that this transition was a time of significant emotional turmoil, where male caregivers experienced emotions such as grief, loss, guilt, and regret about the decision to move their spouses into cared accommodation. However, these emotions were also intertwined with positive feelings of relief and reassurance that their partner's needs would be better supported. Although most still saw themselves as being caregivers after the move, they felt they could now go on to build a new life (Fowler, 2018). Male caregivers may need additional support, information, and possible case management after their partners move to cared accommodation to support them emotionally through this transition (Nikzad-Terhune et al., 2010). It has been found that older male caregivers may feel disassociated and confused after the transition, as their roles have unexpectedly changed from ones that provided central meaning to a different type of relationship, and they feel the loss of structure in their lives (Eriksson & Sandberg, 2008).

Many family carers perceive a lack of family or social support as a contributing factor for people with dementia transitioning to residential care (McGrath, 2019). A lack of family support can include family members inadequately assisting the person with dementia to ensure all care needs are met (Tatangelo et al., 2018). Where multiple family members are available, there is an expectation that the support is provided equitably, though this may not always be possible. Family support can provide significant benefits through sharing the caring load and providing alternative options to formal care and respite services (Morrisby et al., 2019; Tatangelo et al., 2018). Family support may be impacted by the geographical distance of family members. For instance, spousal carers have mentioned that when adult children or siblings live far from easy contact with the person with dementia, they tend to have less understanding of the impact dementia is having on function, and the need for high levels of support (Morrisby et al., 2019). Family support is also considered highly valuable in the process of accepting assistance from formal support services and organisations (Morrisby et al., 2019). In one study, spousal carers frequently reported that the key trigger for accepting services and supports that helped maintain the person with dementia living in the community was the recommendation and advice of adult children or friends: "Well, mostly you get pushed into it from the children, you know" (Morrisby et al., 2019, p. 4). This external but trusted validation of the need for support services from children, other family members, and friends means that people are provided with the right information at the right time (Peeters et al., 2010).

When gaps exist in family support, social support from friends or neighbours is perceived by spousal carers as critical. For example, carers described that neighbours are able to provide support to keep family members with dementia at home for longer through relatively small acts of support such as "keeping an eye out" for people (McGrath, 2019, p. 18). In order to maintain social support networks, a broader understanding of dementia and its impacts is required (Morrisby et al., 2019). Family carers have described how a lack of knowledge and education about dementia in their friends (and some family members) has been a barrier to support. Dementia still holds a stigma, as described by a carer: "She had friends in work, and we had quite a lot of friends, but when she was diagnosed with Alzheimer's ... her friends all went the other way. They thought it was something they could catch" (Morrisby et al., 2019, p. 4). In order to address this, greater education of the general public is needed as a key strategy for reducing the impact of stigma on social relationships (Morrisby et al., 2020; Werner et al., 2012). Given the importance of strong social supports, a continued focus on promoting public awareness of dementia and the role of social support is important (Alzheimer's Disease International, 2019).

In addition to family and social support, other factors that have been identified as assisting people with dementia to remain living at home longer are formal service assistance and dog ownership. While formal service assistance is self-explanatory, interestingly, dog ownership has been found to be beneficial and is proposed to support people with dementia to remain at home longer through orienting their thinking, due to having to provide care for the pet, as well as providing companionship and giving meaning to life (McGrath, 2019).

Services now, and recommendations for the future

Services designed to support people with dementia living in the community should focus on the person—not the task, have open communication, and be easily accessible (Grenade & Walker, 2005; Raivio et al., 2011; Ward-Griffin et al., 2012). Characteristics of high-quality dementia care services feature hours and availabilities that suit the carer and person with dementia, ensure continuity of services as dementia-related care needs increase, and are affordable (Phillipson & Jones, 2011; Raivio et al., 2011); these are generally determined by the funding model. In the aged care reforms of the past decade, it has been recognised that there is "a need for services that meet [carer and people with dementia] needs rather than the needs of the service providers" (Alzheimer's Australia, 2011, p. 8). Nine years later, the Royal Commission into Aged Care Quality and Safety (2019) has identified that the accessibility of Home Care Packages is limited, with national waitlists ranging from three to over twelve months to receive care at a level assessed as appropriate to meet the care recipients' needs. Within this, the My Aged Care system, an online portal designed to increase access to knowledge and choice for older Australians seeking home care or support, has not had a positive impact on the way people access services (Phillipson et al., 2019). In conjunction with issues surrounding the funding of adequate numbers of Home Care Packages, and easy access to reliable information, service providers and policymakers have been described as having "inconsiderate behaviours, especially taking into account that these caregivers are elderly, stressed, and unable to defend themselves" (Raivio et al., 2011, p. 6). While increasing the number of home care packages, or the number of Commonwealth Home Support Programme services, will go some way to addressing the shortfall of services, the broader issues experienced by people with dementia and their carers in Australia need to be addressed. Health professionals, the broader community, carers, and people with dementia require knowledge, support, and systems in place that will promote quality of life for those living with dementia.

Developing dementia-friendly communities

An issue commonly experienced by people with dementia and carers in Australia is difficulty maintaining social relationships and continuing to access their communities in meaningful ways (Ebert, 2019; McGrath, 2019; Morrisby et al., 2019). A lack of social support and community inaccessibility are factors that contribute to people with dementia entering care. Alzheimer's Disease International promotes social and health care that is continuous, integrated, and holistic in its approach to supporting people with dementia (Prince et al., 2016). Dementia-friendly communities are an initiative aimed at empowering people with dementia, carers, and communities by providing an inclusive and enabling environment that maximises the function of people with dementia and normalises their experiences (Rahman & Swaffer, 2018). Australian research by Courtney-Pratt et al. (2018) identified that developing dementia-friendly communities is potentially best led by grassroots initiatives that draw on the existing strengths and resources of communities. Recognising these assets is important to minimise the risk of motivating people and organisations to brand or label themselves or their business as "dementia-friendly" for benefits such as drawing in additional customers (Rahman & Swaffer, 2018). Another key factor identified in the literature is the impact of community education in reducing the stigma associated with dementia (Courtney-Pratt et al., 2018; Rahman & Swaffer, 2018). Education is needed not just for carers and people with dementia, but for the broader community as well. Reducing stigma through education may facilitate a reduction in the "otherness" of dementia (Bauer et al., 2019). This has been successfully achieved for other illnesses and disabilities such as cancer through policy changes, advocacy, and education (Courtney-Pratt et al., 2018) raising hope that dementia-friendly communities will be consistently achieved.

Supporting a positive early diagnosis

The experience of being diagnosed with dementia is not consistently positive in Australia, with variation in the timeliness and accuracy of diagnosis and advice or referrals that promote quality of life (Logiudice et al., 1999; Ng & Ward, 2019). Given the importance of appropriate diagnosis and the subsequent provision of education and support, understanding the factors that contribute to achieving a good outcome as people commence their journey with dementia is critical (Guideline Adaptation Committee, 2016). Comprehensive support is most commonly provided in memory clinics, and it is therefore recommended that all persons with suspected dementia be referred to this specialist service (Guideline Adaptation Committee, 2016; Ng et al., 2020).

In order to achieve this, a key strategy is to improve the dementia-related knowledge of Australian health professionals. Educational interventions such as the Understanding Dementia Massive Online Open Course (MOOC; Eccleston et al., 2019) and specific training for GPs (Mason et al., 2020) have demonstrated the effectiveness of training and education in improving health professionals' understanding of dementia. Training for GPs has been of high importance given the important role they play in providing primary care, as they are normally the first point of contact for people with memory and cognitive concerns (Mason et al., 2020; Tierney et al., 2019). Further research is needed to understand the long-term impacts of dementia-specific training and education on the quality of life and well-being of people with dementia and their carers.

A skilled workforce

The majority of Australian care workers are based in the community, are predominantly female (90%) and middle aged (45–54 years; Hodgkin et al.,

2016). There are low levels of permanency, and industry training requirements are poorly regulated (Elliott et al., 2012; Palesy et al., 2018). Most frequently, community-based support workers have completed a vocational training level course such as a Certificate III in Aged Care, and, in most instances, this type of training is too short and lacks adequate practical training to support sufficient development of skills, with many workers receiving "on-the-job training" (Palesy et al., 2018; Royal Commission into Aged Care Quality and Safety, 2019). There tends to be a high turnover of community-based support workers, which further impacts the quality of relationship-based care (Palesy et al., 2018). In the seven years since 2012–13, Australian aged care funding reports indicate that spending on workforce training has decreased by 62 percent. The ongoing training of community-based support workers has been significantly impacted by this lack of funding, due to both the decrease in opportunities to attend and the limited provision of high-quality development activities (Elliott et al., 2012; Elliott et al., 2013; Polacsek et al., 2020). Furthermore, the Royal Commission (2019) identified that, in combination with initial and ongoing training opportunities, low enablement levels (i.e., their sense of empowerment in their ability to undertake their roles) impact community-based support worker's ability to access ongoing education and remain in the workforce. In addition to support workers, nursing and allied health professionals such as occupational therapists and physiotherapists experience significant challenges in providing services and supports that meet the evidence-based recommendations of the Clinical Practice Guidelines for Dementia in Australia (Cations et al., 2019; Guideline Adaptation Committee, 2016).

To promote good quality care, workforce issues need to be carefully considered. Current recommendations are that, in conjunction with appropriate remuneration, the initial and ongoing training of paid or formal support workers be addressed. The Australian government has committed to fund Dementia Training Australia (DTA), which provides dementia-specific education and training to health professionals and support workers working in community, hospital, and residential care settings. Finally, the service contexts in which nurses and allied health practitioners provide post-diagnostic support to people with dementia and their carers may require changes to address time and funding constraints, which impact on the translation of best practices (Cations et al., 2019).

Conclusion

Providing care for people with dementia is an important but undervalued role in Australian society. It is necessary to support the well-being, dignity, and rights of older people, yet this caregiving work is not well recognised, compensated, or supported by the community and government. It is an often lonely and thankless occupation that can negatively impact negatively on the carer's own health, emotions, and financial situation. While it is important to recognise that carers often find intrinsic rewards in looking after their loved ones, some do this as they feel there is no one else who could provide quality care and support for the person. It is important to note also that the experiences of people with dementia and carers from Indigenous and culturally and linguistically diverse backgrounds are not thoroughly understood; however there is emerging research in these areas. As it seems clear that dementia rates will continue to increase until there is a medical breakthrough, we can expect increasing numbers of people with dementia and their carers in our community. Thus, it is important that we support people by providing adequate and tailored person- and family-centred care that recognises the unique needs of spousal caregivers, male caregivers, caregivers of people with younger onset dementia, and people from Indigenous and culturally and linguistically diverse backgrounds. Also necessary is a quality service system staffed by trained workers and professionals who can provide needed assistance in a timely manner. Dementia education for the community more broadly is critical in order to reduce isolation and improve the mental health of people with dementia and their caregivers, and to ensure our society is a more inclusive and accessible place for all.

References

Afram, B., Stephan, A., Verbeek, H., Bleijlevens, M. H. C., Suhonen, R., Sutcliffe, C., Raamat, K., Cabrera, E., Soto, M. E., Hallberg, I. R., Meyer, G., & Hamers, J. P. H. (2014). Reasons for institutionalization of people with dementia: Informal caregiver reports from 8 European countries. *Journal of the American Medical Directors Association, 15*(2), 108–116. https://doi.org/10.1016/j.jamda.2013.09.012

Alzheimer's Australia. (2011). *Consumer engagement in the aged care reform process*. Alzheimer's Australia. http://www.fightdementia.org.au/common/files/NAT/20120410_ConsumerEngagementAgedCareReformProcess.REPORT.pdf

Alzheimer's Disease International. (2019). *World Alzheimer report 2019: Attitudes to dementia*. https://www.alz.co.uk/research/WorldAlzheimerReport2019.pdf

Australian Bureau of Statistics. (2019, 24 October). *Disability, ageing and carers, Australia: summary of findings*. ABS. https://www.abs.gov.au/statistics/health/disability/disability-ageing-and-carers-australia-summary-findings/latest-release

Australian Bureau of Statistics. (2020, 23 October). *Causes of death, Australia, 2019*. ABS. https://www.abs.gov.au/statistics/health/causes-death/causes-death-australia/latest-release

Australian Government. (2024). Home Care Packages [webpage]. https://www.myagedcare.gov.au/help-at-home/home-care-packages

Australian Institute of Health and Welfare. (2012). *Dementia in Australia*. AIHW. Retrieved (Cat. no. AGE 70, from https://www.aihw.gov.au/reports/dementia/dementia-in-australia/contents/table-of-contents

Australian Institute of Health and Welfare. (2018, 10 September). *Older Australia at a glance* [webpage]. Australian Government. Retrieved 18 November 2020, from https://www.aihw.gov.au/reports/older-people/older-australia-at-a-glance

/contents/demographics-of-older-australians/australia-s-changing-age-and-gender-profile

Australian Institute of Health and Welfare. (2020a, 7 August). *Deaths in Australia*. Australian Government. Retrieved 26 November 2020, from https://www.aihw.gov.au/reports/life-expectancy-death/deaths-in-australia/contents/life-expectancy

Australian Institute of Health and Welfare. (2020b, 23 July). *Dementia*. Australian Government. Retrieved 26 November 2020, from https://www.aihw.gov.au/reports/australias-health/dementia

Bauer, M., Fetherstonhaugh, D., Blackberry, I., Farmer, J., & Wilding, C. (2019). Identifying support needs to improve rural dementia services for people with dementia and their carers: A consultation study in Victoria, Australia. *Australian Journal of Rural Health*, 27(1), 22–27. https://doi.org/10.1111/ajr.12444

Braun, M., Scholz, U., Bailey, B., Perren, S., Hornung, R., & Martin, M. (2009). Dementia caregiving in spousal relationships: A dyadic perspective. *Aging & Mental Health*, 13, 426–436. https://doi.org/10.1080/13607860902879441

Brodaty, H., & Donkin, M. (2009). Family caregivers of people with dementia. *Dialogues in Clinical Neuroscience*, 11, 217–228.

Brodaty, H., Connors, M. H., Xu, J., Woodward, M., Ames, D., & on behalf of the, P. s. g. (2014). Predictors of Institutionalization in Dementia: A Three Year Longitudinal Study. Journal of Alzheimer's Disease, 40, 221–226. https://doi.org/10.3233/JAD-131850

Brown, L., & Hansnata, E. (2017). *Economic cost of dementia in Australia 2016–2056*. National Centre for Social and Economic Modelling, Institute for Governance and Policy Analysis. https://www.dementia.org.au/files/NATIONAL/documents/The-economic-cost-of-dementia-in-Australia-2016-to-2056.pdf

Carers Australia. (2024). Who is a Carer? [webpage]. https://www.carersaustralia.com.au/about-carers/who-is-a-carer/

Cash, B., Hodgkin, S., & Warburton, J. (2013). Till death us do part? A critical analysis of obligation and choice for spousal caregivers. *Journal of Gerontological Social Work*, 56, 657–674. https://doi.org/10.1080/01634372.2013.823472

Cations, M., Radisic, G., de la Perrelle, L., Laver, K. E., Shepherd, K., Methorst, F., Baldwin, E., Maher-Norris, D., Gibson, J., Marsh, E., Brown, W., Palagyi, J., Arndt, P. M., Vladcoff, K.-A., Sabja, M. P., Caruana, E., Tung, J., Doljanin, J., Anderson, J., Brittain, J., Comerford, L., Wharley, A., McKenzie, E., Wong, S.-M., Seeliger, M., Delgado, V., Kaizik, C., Kuo, K., Millen, A., & The Agents of Change Collaborative Group. (2019). Post-diagnostic allied health interventions for people with dementia in Australia: A spotlight on current practice. *BMC Research Notes*, 12(1), 559. https://doi.org/10.1186/s13104-019-4588-2

Clare, L., Rowlands, J., Bruce, E., Surr, C., & Downs, M. (2008). The experience of living with dementia in residential care: An interpretative phenomenological analysis. *The Gerontologist*, 48(6), 711–720. https://doi.org/10.1093/geront/48.6.711

Courtney-Pratt, H., Mathison, K., & Doherty, K. (2018). Distilling authentic community-led strategies to support people with dementia to live well. *Community Development*, 49(4), 432–449. https://doi.org/10.1080/15575330.2018.1481443

Day, J., Taylor, A. C. T., Summons, P., Van Der Riet, P., Hunter, S., Maguire, J., Dilworth, S., Bellchambers, H., Jeong, S., Haydon, G., Harris, M., & Higgins, I. (2017). Home care packages: insights into the experiences of older people leading up to the introduction of consumer directed care in Australia. *Australian Journal of Primary Health*, 23(2), 162–169. https://doi.org/https://doi.org/10.1071/PY16022

Deloitte Access Economics. (2020). *The value of informal care in 2020.* https://www2.deloitte.com/au/en/pages/economics/articles/value-of-informal-care-2020.html

Dementia Australia. (2018). *Dementia Australia annual report 2017/18.* https://www.dementia.org.au/sites/default/files/annual-reports/DA-2017-18-Annual-Report.pdf

Dementia Australia. (2020a). *Dementia statistics.* Retrieved 9 December 2020, from https://www.dementia.org.au/statistics

Dementia Australia. (2020b). *Living with dementia program - for clients.* Retrieved 10 December 2020, from https://www.dementia.org.au/education/living-dementia-program-clients

Dementia Australia. (2020c). *What is dementia?* Retrieved 9 December 2020, from https://www.dementia.org.au/about-dementia/what-is-dementia

Department of Health. (2019). Home Care Packages Program: Data Report 1st Quarter 2019-2020. 1 July - 30 September 2019. https://www.gen-agedcaredata.gov.au/getmedia/18e55373-f4dd-4685-b42e-561ac6c27136/Home-Care-Data-Report-1st-qtr-2019-20.pdf

Department of Health. (2020). *National dementia support program.* https://www.health.gov.au/initiatives-and-programs/national-dementia-support-program-ndsp

Dow, B., Haralambous, B., Hempton, C., Hunt, S., & Calleja, D. (2011). Evaluation of Alzheimer's Australia Vic memory lane cafés. *International Psychogeriatrics,* 23(2), 246–255. https://doi.org/10.1017/S1041610210001560

Ducharme, F., Lévesque, L., Lachance, L., Gangbè, M., Zarit, S. H., Vézina, J., & Caron, C. D. (2007). Older husbands as caregivers: Factors associated with health and the intention to end home caregiving. *Research on Aging,* 29(1), 3–31. https://doi.org/10.1177/0164027506291749

Ebert, E. (2019). *'It can be a very daunting, lonely journey if you don't have that support': An Australian study on younger onset dementia and living at home* [Honours dissertation, Curtin University]. Perth, Western Australia.

Eccleston, C., Doherty, K., Bindoff, A., Robinson, A., Vickers, J., & McInerney, F. (2019). Building dementia knowledge globally through the understanding dementia Massive Open Online Course (MOOC). *NPJ Science of Learning,* 4(1), 3. https://doi.org/10.1038/s41539-019-0042-4

Egdell, V., Bond, J., Brittain, K., & Jarvis, H. (2010). Disparate routes through support: Negotiating the sites, stages and support of informal dementia care. *Health Place,* 16(1), 101–107. https://doi.org/10.1016/j.healthplace.2009.09.002

Egilstrod, B., Ravn, M. B., & Petersen, K. S. (2019). Living with a partner with dementia: A systematic review and thematic synthesis of spouses' lived experiences of changes in their everyday lives. *Aging & Mental Health,* 23(5), 541–550. https://doi.org/10.1080/13607863.2018.1433634

Eisdorfer, C. (1991). Caregiving: An emerging risk factor for emotional and physical pathology. *Bulletin of the Menninger Clinic,* 55(2), 238–247. https://pubmed.ncbi.nlm.nih.gov/2043900/

Elliott, K. E. J., Scott, J. L., Stirling, C., Martin, A. J., & Robinson, A. (2012). Building capacity and resilience in the dementia care workforce: A systematic review of interventions targeting worker and organizational outcomes. *International Psychogeriatrics,* 24(6), 882–894. https://doi.org/10.1017/S1041610211002651

Elliott, K. E. J., Stirling, C. M., Martin, A. J., Robinson, A. L., & Scott, J. L. (2013). Perspectives of the community-based dementia care workforce: "Occupational communion" a key finding from the work 4 dementia project. *International Psychogeriatrics,* 25(5), 765–774. https://doi.org/10.1017/S1041610212002323

Eriksson, H., & Sandberg, J. (2008). Transitions in men's caring identities: Experiences from home-based care to nursing home placement. *International Journal of Older People Nursing, 3*(2), 131–137. https://doi.org/10.1111/j.1748-3743.2007.00092.x

Fowler, J. (2018). *'You've got no support': The experiences of older male caregivers when their partner enters full-time care* [Honours dissertation, Curtin University]. Perth, Western Australia.

Gaugler, J. E., Kane, R. L., Kane, R. A., & Newcomer, R. (2005). Unmet care needs and key outcomes in dementia. *Journal of the American Geriatric Society, 53*(12), 2098–2105. https://doi.org/10.1111/j.1532-5415.2005.00495.x

Gaugler, J. E., Mittelman, M. S., Hepburn, K., & Newcomer, R. (2010). Clinically significant changes in burden and depression among dementia caregivers following nursing home admission. *BMC Medicine, 8*(1), 85. https://doi.org/10.1186/1741-7015-8-85

Gill, L., Bradley, S. L., Cameron, I. D., & Ratcliffe, J. (2018). How do clients in Australia experience Consumer Directed Care? BMC Geriatrics, 18(1), 148. https://doi.org/10.1186/s12877-018-0838-8

Gnanamanickam, E. S., Dyer, S. M., Milte, R., Harrison, S. L., Liu, E., Easton, T., Bradley, C., Bilton, R., Shulver, W., Ratcliffe, J., Whitehead, C., & Crotty, M. (2018). Direct health and residential care costs of people living with dementia in Australian residential aged care. *International Journal of Geriatric Psychiatry, 33*(7), 859–866. https://doi.org/10.1002/gps.4842

Gomes, B., Calanzani, N., Gysels, M., Hall, S., & Higginson, I. J. (2013). Heterogeneity and changes in preferences for dying at home: A systematic review. *BMC Palliative Care, 12*(1), 7. https://doi.org/10.1186/1472-684X-12-7

Grenade, L., & Walker, M. (2005). Caring for people with dementia through community aged care packages. *Geriaction, 23*(4), 5–13. http://search.ebscohost.com/login.aspx?direct=true&db=rzh&AN=2009118258&site=ehost-live

Grenade, L., Williams, P., Horner, B., & Carey, M. (2007). *Evaluation of the National Dementia Support Program (NDSP)*. https://www.dementia.org.au/sites/default/files/20120730_NAT_Final_Evaluation_Report15Feb07.pdf

Guideline Adaptation Committee. (2016). *Clinical practice guidelines and principles of care for people with dementia*. NHMRC. http://sydney.edu.au/medicine/cdpc/documents/resources/CDPC-Dementia-Guidelines_WEB.pdf

Harris, P. B., & Keady, J. (2009). Selfhood in younger onset dementia: Transitions and testimonies. *Aging & Mental Health, 13*(3), 437–444. https://doi.org/10.1080/13607860802534609

Hodgkin, S., Warburton, J., Savy, P., & Moore, M. (2016). Workforce crisis in residential aged care: Insights from rural, older workers. *Australian Journal of Public Administration, 76*(1), 93–105. https://agedcare.royalcommission.gov.au/system/files/2020-06/RCD.9999.0256.0017.pdf

Jameson, S., Parkinson, L., & Banbury, A. (2020). After the care journey: Exploring the experiences of family carers of people living with dementia. *Ageing and Society, 40*(11), 2429–2447. https://doi.org/10.1017/S0144686X19000667

Jorgensen, M., Siette, J., Georgiou, A., Warland, A., & Westbrook, J. (2018). Modeling the association between home care service use and entry into residential aged care: a cohort study using routinely collected data. *Journal of the American medical directors association, 19*(2), 117–121.

Lockeridge, S., & Simpson, J. (2013). The experience of caring for a partner with young onset dementia: How younger carers cope. *Dementia, 12*(5), 635–651. https://doi.org/10.1177/1471301212440873

Logiudice, D., Waltrowicz, W., Brown, K., Burrows, C., Ames, D., & Flicker, L. (1999). Do memory clinics improve the quality of life of carers? A randomized pilot trial. *International Journal of Geriatric Psychiatry, 14*(8), 626–632. https://doi.org/10.1002/(SICI)1099-1166(199908)14:8<626::AID-GPS990>3.0.CO;2-5

Low, L. F., Yap, M., & Brodaty, H. (2011). A systematic review of different models of home and community care services for older persons. *BMC Health Service Research, 11*, 93. https://doi.org/10.1186/1472-6963-11-93

Mason, R., Doherty, K., Eccleston, C., Winbolt, M., Long, M., & Robinson, A. (2020). Effect of a dementia education intervention on the confidence and attitudes of general practitioners in Australia: A pretest post-test study. *BMJ Open, 10*(1), e033218. https://doi.org/10.1136/bmjopen-2019-033218

McGrath, T. (2019). *The 'tipping point': Exploring the factors associated with entry into residential care for people with dementia* [Honours dissertation, Curtin University]. Perth, Western Australia.

Millard, F. B., Kennedy, R. L., & Baune, B. T. (2011). Dementia: Opportunities for risk reduction and early detection in general practice. *Australian Journal of Primary Health, 17*(1), 89–94. https://doi.org/10.1071/PY10037

Millenaar, J. K., Bakker, C., Koopmans, R. T. C. M., Verhey, F. R. J., Kurz, A., & de Vugt, M. E. (2016). The care needs and experiences with the use of services of people with young-onset dementia and their caregivers: A systematic review. *International Journal of Geriatric Psychiatry, 31*(12), 1261–1276. https://doi.org/10.1002/gps.4502

Morrisby, C., Ciccarelli, M., & Joosten, A. (2020). Mind the gap: Comparing perspectives of service providers to the needs of people with dementia living in the community. *Dementia*, 1–17. https://doi.org/10.1177/1471301220947837

Morrisby, C., Joosten, A., & Ciccarelli, M. (2019). Needs of people with dementia and their spousal carers: A study of those living in the community. *Australasian Journal on Ageing*. https://doi.org/10.1111/ajag.12609

My Aged Care. (2020). *Respite care*. Retrieved 10 December, from https://www.myagedcare.gov.au/short-term-care/respite-care

Nay, R., Bauer, M., Fetherstonhaugh, D., Moyle, W., Tarzia, L., & McAuliffe, L. (2015). Social participation and family carers of people living with dementia in Australia. *Health & Social Care in the Community, 23*(5), 550–558. https://doi.org/10.1111/hsc.12163

Ng, N., Ayton, D., Workman, B., & Ward, S. (2020). Understanding diagnostic settings and carer experiences for dementia diagnosis in Australia. *Internal Medicine Journal*. https://doi.org/10.1111/imj.14869

Ng, N. S. Q., & Ward, S. A. (2019). Diagnosis of dementia in Australia: A narrative review of services and models of care. *Australian Health Review, 43*(4), 415–424. https://doi.org/10.1071/AH17167

Nikzad-Terhune, K. A., Anderson, K. A., Newcomer, R., & Gaugler, J. E. (2010). Do trajectories of at-home dementia caregiving account for burden after nursing home placement? A growth curve analysis. *Social Work in Health Care, 49*(8), 734–752. https://doi.org/10.1080/00981381003635296

Palesy, D., Jakimowicz, S., Saunders, C., & Lewis, J. (2018). Home care in Australia: An integrative review. *Home Health Care Services Quarterly, 37*(2), 113–139. https://doi.org/10.1080/01621424.2018.1438952

Parkinson, L., Banbury, A., Livingstone, A., Gordon, S., Ray, B., Byrne, L., Nancarrow, S., Doran, C., McAllister, M., & Petersen, C. (2018). Caring for carers of people with dementia: a protocol for harnessing innovation through deploying leading edge technologies to enable virtual support groups and services. *Studies in Health Technology and Information, 246*, 29–41. https://doi.org/10.3233/978-1-61499-845-7-29

Peeters, J. M., Van Beek, A. P. A., Meerveld, J. H. C. M., Spreeuwenberg, P. M. M., & Francke, A. L. (2010). Informal caregivers of persons with dementia, their use of and needs for specific professional support: A survey of the National Dementia Programme. *BMC Nursing, 9*, 9–9. https://doi.org/10.1186/1472-6955-9-9

Phillipson, L., Johnson, K., Cridland, E., Hall, D., Neville, C., Fielding, E., & Hasan, H. (2019). Knowledge, help-seeking and efficacy to find respite services: An exploratory study in help-seeking carers of people with dementia in the context of aged care reforms. *BMC Geriatrics, 19*(1), 2. https://doi.org/10.1186/s12877-018-1009-7

Phillipson, L., & Jones, S. C. (2011). "Between the devil and the deep blue sea": The beliefs of caregivers of people with dementia regarding the use of in-home respite services. *Home Health Care Services Quarterly, 30*(2), 43–62. https://doi.org/10.1080/01621424.2011.569522

Phillipson, L., Magee, C., Jones, S., Reis, S., & Skaldzien, E. (2015). Dementia attitudes and help-seeking intentions: An investigation of responses to two scenarios of an experience of the early signs of dementia. *Aging & Mental Health, 19*(11), 968–977. https://doi.org/10.1080/13607863.2014.995588

Polacsek, M., Goh, A., Malta, S., Hallam, B., Gahan, L., Cooper, C., Low, L.-F., Livingston, G., Panayiotou, A., Loi, S., Omori, M., Savvas, S., Batchelor, F., Ames, D., Doyle, C., Scherer, S., & Dow, B. (2020). 'I know they are not trained in dementia': Addressing the need for specialist dementia training for home care workers. *Health & Social Care in the Community, 28*(2), 475–484. https://doi.org/10.1111/hsc.12880

Prince, M., Comas-Herrera, A., Knapp, M., Guerchet, M., & Karagiannidou, M. (2016). *World Alzheimer report 2016: Improving healthcare for people living with dementia: Coverage, quality and costs now and in the future.* https://www.alz.co.uk/research/WorldAlzheimerReport2016.pdf

Productivity Commission. (2018). *Report in government services 2018.* https://www.gen-agedcaredata.gov.au/Resources/Reports-and-publications/2018/January/Report-on-Government-Services-2018

Rahman, S., & Swaffer, K. (2018). Assets-based approaches and dementia-friendly communities. *Dementia, 17*(2), 131–137. https://doi.org/10.1177/1471301217751533

Raivio, M., Laakkonen, M. L., & Pitkala, K. H. (2011). Alzheimer's patients' spouses critiques of the support services. *ISRN Nurs, 2011*, 943059. https://doi.org/10.5402/2011/943059

Revenson, T. A., Griva, K., Luszczynska, A., Morrison, V., Panagopoulou, E., Vilchinsky, N., & Hagedoorn, M. (2016). Gender and caregiving: The costs of caregiving for women. In *Caregiving in the illness context* (pp. 48–63). Palgrave Macmillan UK. https://doi.org/10.1057/9781137558985_5

Riedijk, S. R., De Vugt, M. E., Duivenvoorden, H. J., Niermeijer, M. F., van Swieten, J. C., Verhey, F. R. J., & Tibben, A. (2006). Caregiver burden, health-related quality of life and coping in dementia caregivers: A comparison of frontotemporal dementia and Alzheimer's disease. *Dementia and Geriatric Cognitive Disorders, 22*(5–6), 405–412. https://doi.org/10.1159/000095750

Rimkeit, S., & McIntosh, J. (2017). The Voices of People with Younger Onset Dementia as They Face Aged Care. *International Journal of Health, Wellness & Society, 7*(3).

Roach, P., & Drummond, N. (2014). 'It's nice to have something to do': Early-onset dementia and maintaining purposeful activity. *Journal of Psychiatric and Mental Health Nursing, 21*(10), 889–895. https://doi.org/10.1111/jpm.12154

Robinson, A., Lea, E., Hemmings, L., Vosper, G., McCann, D., Weeding, F., & Rumble, R. (2012). Seeking respite: Issues around the use of day respite care for the carers of people with dementia. *Ageing and Society, 32*(02), 196–218. https://doi.org/10.1017/s0144686x11000195

Robinson, L., Clare, L., & Evans, K. (2005). Making sense of dementia and adjusting to loss: Psychological reactions to a diagnosis of dementia in couples. *Aging & Mental Health*, 9, 337–347. https://doi.org/10.1080/13607860500114555

Royal Commission into Aged Care Quality and Safety. (2019). *Interim report: Neglect.* https://agedcare.royalcommission.gov.au/publications/interim-report

Samus, Q. M., Johnston, D., Black, B. S., Hess, E., Lyman, C., Vavilikolanu, A., Pollutra, J., Leoutsakos, J.-M., Gitlin, L. N., Rabins, P. V., & Lyketsos, C. G. (2014). A multidimensional home-based care coordination intervention for elders with memory disorders: The Maximizing Independence at Home (MIND) pilot randomized trial. *The American Journal of Geriatric Psychiatry*, 22(4), 398–414. https://doi.org/10.1016/j.jagp.2013.12.175

Schirmer, J. (2017). *Carers in regional Australia: 2016 Regional wellbeing survey report.* Health Research Institute & Institute for Applied Ecology, University of Canberra. https://www.canberra.edu.au/research/institutes/health-research-institute/files/regional-wellbeing-survey/reports/2016-reports/Carers-report-ONLINE-10-July-2017.pdf

Sclan, S., G., & Reisberg, B. (1992). Functional Assessment Staging (FAST) in Alzheimer's disease: Reliability, validity, and ordinality. *International Psychogeriatrics*, 4(3), 55–69. https://doi.org/10.1017/S1041610292001157

Services Australia. (2020, 31 August). *Payments for carers.* Australian Government. https://www.servicesaustralia.gov.au/individuals/subjects/payments-carers

Singh, P., Hussain, R., Khan, A., Irwin, L., & Foskey, R. (2015). Carers' perspectives on sustainability of informal care for people with dementia. *SAGE Open*, 5(3), 1–11. https://doi.org/10.1177/2158244015607934

Sury, L., Burns, K., & Brodaty, H. (2013). Moving in: Adjustment of people living with dementia going into a nursing home and their families. *International Psychogeriatrics*, 25(6), 867–876. https://doi.org/10.1017/S1041610213000057

Tatangelo, G., McCabe, M., Macleod, A., & Konis, A. (2018). I just can't please them all and stay sane: Adult child caregivers' experiences of family dynamics in care-giving for a parent with dementia in Australia. *Health & Social Care in the Community*, 26(3), e370–e377. https://doi.org/10.1111/hsc.12534

Thompson, E. H., & Kramer, B. J. (2002). *Men as caregivers: Theory, research, and service implications.* Springer.

Tierney, L., Mason, R., Doherty, K., Winbolt, M., Long, M., & Robinson, A. (2019). Workshops on diagnosis and management of dementia for general practitioners: A pre–post intervention study of dementia knowledge. *BMJ Open*, 9(4), e027804. https://doi.org/10.1136/bmjopen-2018-027804

Toot, S., Swinson, T., Devine, M., Challis, D., & Orrell, M. (2017). Causes of nursing home placement for older people with dementia: A systematic review and meta-analysis. *International Psychogeriatrics*, 29(2), 195–208. https://doi.org/10.1017/S1041610216001654

van der Roest, H. G., Meiland, F. J. M., Comijs, H. C., Derksen, E., Jansen, A. P. D., Van Hout, H. P. J., Jonker, C., & Dröes, R. M. (2009). What do community-dwelling people with dementia need? A survey of those who are known to care and welfare services. *International Psychogeriatrics*, 21(5), 949–965. https://doi.org/10.1017/S1041610209990147

van Exel, J., de Graaf, G., & Brouwer, W. (2007). Care for a break? An investigation of informal caregivers' attitudes toward respite care using Q-methodology. *Health Policy*, 83(2–3), 332–342. https://doi.org/10.1016/j.healthpol.2007.02.002

Vikström, S., Borell, L., Stigsdotter-Neely, A., & Josephsson, S. (2005). Caregivers' self-initiated support toward their partners with dementia when performing an everyday occupation together at home. *OTJR*, 25, 149–159. http://search.proquest.com/docview/220299315?accountid=10382

Wadham, O., Simpson, J., Rust, J., & Murray, C. (2016). Couples' shared experiences of dementia: A meta-synthesis of the impact upon relationships and couplehood. *Aging & Mental Health, 20*(5), 463–473. https://doi.org/10.1080/13607863.2015.1023769

Ward-Griffin, C., Hall, J., DeForge, R., St-Amant, O., McWilliam, C., Oudshoorn, A., Forbes, D., & Klosek, M. (2012). Dementia home care resources: How are we managing? *Journal of Aging Research*, 11. http://search.ebscohost.com/

Werner, P., Mittelman, M. S., Goldstein, D., & Heinik, J. (2012). Family stigma and caregiver burden in Alzheimer's disease. *The Gerontologist, 52*, 89–97. https://doi.org/10.1093/geront/gnr117

18
CARE SERVICES FOR OLDER ADULTS WITH DEMENTIA IN TÜRKIYE

Isil Kalayci

Introduction

The demographic transformation in Türkiye has overall been triggered by reduced birth and mortality rates, improvements in healthcare services, emphasis on healthy lifestyles, adjustments in the conditions of working life, technological occupation in instrumental activities of daily living, and the increase in the standard of living and well-being (Kalaycı & Özkul, 2017, p. 91). In this transformation, Türkiye has witnessed a boosted older adult population despite maintaining its proportion of the young compared to countries such as Monaco, Japan, and Italy with an older age structure. Within the demographic structure, the population aged 65 and over was 6,651,503 in 2016 in Türkiye. The number of older adults increased by 24.0% in the last five years and reached 8,245,124 people in 2021. While the proportion of older adults in the total population was 8.3% in 2016, it increased to 9.7% in 2021 (Turkish Statistical Institute, 2022). The life expectancy is 78.6 years for Türkiye, and the remaining life expectancy of one aged 65 years is 18.0 years on average. While the life expectancy is 11.0 years at the age of 75, it is 6.0 years at the age of 85 (Turkish Statistical Institute, 2021).

The prolongation of life expectancy among older adults is likely to lead to an increase in their health problems. While aging, irreversible changes in phenotypic, physiological, and molecular signals occurring at the cellular level cause the emergence of chronic diseases (Guevara & Lawler, 2018, p. 257; Onder et al., 2020, p. 1175). In our country, the majority of older adults have at least one chronic disease affecting their circulatory, respiratory, digestive, nervous, and endocrine systems (General Directorate of

Services for Persons with Disabilities and the Elderly, 2022, p. 92; Kaya & Gamsızkan, 2022, p. 2).

Neurocognitive disorders have become prominent among the chronic diseases affecting older adults in our country (T.C. Sağlık Bakanlığı Türkiye Halk Sağlığı Kurumu, 2015, p. 8). Dementia is becoming a significant health problem with its increasing prevalence (General Directorate of Services for Persons with Disabilities and the Elderly, 2022, p. 93). It is a chronic and progressive syndrome characterized by a decrease in memory and intellectual capacity and impairment in at least two cognitive functions: speaking, perceiving, computing, reasoning, abstract thinking, and problem-solving (World Health Organization, 2021). Alzheimer's disease is the most prevalent cause of dementia and accounts for 60–70% of the cases. Other causes of dementia include vascular dementia (multi-infarction, white matter disease), alcoholism, Parkinson's disease, drug intoxications, vitamin deficiencies, endocrine and other organ failures, chronic infections, neoplastic diseases, psychiatric disorders, and degenerative diseases (Özbabalık & Hussein, 2017, p. 16). Despite affecting older adults prevalently, it is not an inevitable end of the aging process. Globally, more than 55 million people suffer from dementia, and each year witnesses 10 million new cases (World Health Organization, 2021). Considering the increasing proportion of older adults in every country, it is predicted that the number of patients with dementia will reach 78 million in 2030 and 139 million in 2050 (General Directorate of Services for Persons with Disabilities and the Elderly, 2022, p. 93).

Older people across the world are highly affected by dementia, considered among the major causes of disability and addiction. The countries with the highest incidence of the disease include Brazil (1,849,981), Germany (1,691,221), Italy (1,487,368), France (1,203,439), England (907,331), Spain (826,686), South Korea (671,288), and Poland (663,408) (GBD 2019 Dementia Forecasting Collaborators, 2022, p. 113). According to data from the Ministry of Health (MoH) in Türkiye, approximately 500,000 patients were diagnosed with Alzheimer's disease as of 2018. The disease accounted for 6% of the health problems of individuals aged 65 years and over in the last 12 months in 2019, according to the 2019 Health Statistics Yearbook. Dementia-related mortalities rank seventh among all diseases. In our country, 3% of deaths in 2019 were caused by Alzheimer's and dementia (General Directorate of Services for Persons with Disabilities and the Elderly, 2022, pp. 93–94). Contemporarily, the suppressive conditions and social isolation introduced by the pandemic have mediated an increase in depression (Başıbüyük et al., 2021, p. 300), which, in turn, makes an increase in the rate of dementia inevitable.

Older adults with dementia generally live with their families in Türkiye; therefore, families are primarily responsible for caring for older adults with dementia. Individuals caring for older adults often confront psychological, physiological, social, and economic problems, care burdens, and burnout (Kalınkara & Kalaycı, 2017, p. 30). Since caring for older adults may be demanding, caregiver family members seek ways to obtain help for the care of their older adult relatives, such as hiring paid caregivers, applying for home care services, and getting help from institutional care. On the other hand, even though qualified paid caregivers may not be found each time for older adults, family members tend to undertake their care, instead of quartering them into residential care centers, due to cultural and moral reasons or economic difficulties (Kalaycı et al., 2017, p. 644; Özkul & Kalaycı, 2018, p. 24).

Due to the physical, psychological, social, and financial impacts of dementia on older adults, their families, caregivers, and society, efficient care models may contribute to the quality of life of such patients. Care services for dementia patients are defined as professional support services provided at home or in an institution. Relevant ministries, local governments, non-governmental organizations (NGOs), educational institutions, and the informal care system have significant roles in planning these services.

Ministry-level services

The mission of the Ministry of Family and Social Services (MoFSS) is to generate and implement social work models for protecting, strengthening, and developing individual, family, and social values (Ministry of Family and Social Services, 2022). The Directorate of Services for the Disabled and Elderly, established within the ministry in 2011, bears responsibilities such as developing policies and strategies at the national level to ensure the participation of the disabled and older adults in social life, setting standards for social work activities, and ensuring cooperation and coordination between relevant public institutions and voluntary organizations (General Directorate of Services for Persons with Disabilities and the Elderly, 2011).

The directorate implements daycare services in elderly service centers, support services for home care, services at Hope Homes (Umut Evleri), and residential care and rehabilitation services. Daycare centers offer their services to increase the quality of life of older adults with dementia or Alzheimer's disease, to improve their social environment and relations, to ensure their safety, to alleviate their behavioral problems, to help them enjoy their leisure time, to meet their psychological and health needs, to provide counseling for them, to enhance their activities of daily living, to promote their physical activity, and to provide solidarity and sharing with their families (Özbabalık & Hussein, 2017, p. 16). Today, a total of 32 elderly daycare centers affiliated with the MoFSS serve approximately 300 older adults. Additionally, the number of residential institutions engaging in daycare services for their guests is 140 (General Directorate of Services for Persons with Disabilities and the Elderly, 2022, p. 98). Yet, the number of patients with dementia benefiting from such services is not shared publicly. A significant portion of families prefers to utilize daycare centers rather than residential institutions for the care of their older adult relatives (Nazlıer Keser, 2019a, p. 125). It is an advantage of such institutions that while older adults enjoy the services in these institutions, their family members have a chance to rest, attend to their personal affairs, and spare time for themselves (Alzheimer's Association, 2017).

Home care services came into force with the "Regulation on the Delivery of Home Care Services" and cover the provision of medical, social, and other services by an experienced caregiver to individuals with difficulties in meeting their self-care and maintaining their quality of life at home. Now, about 500,000 older adults benefit from home care services in Türkiye (General Directorate of Services for Persons with Disabilities and the Elderly, 2020). Indeed, home care services are the favored healthcare model for dementia patients. In this model, the care of dementia patients is ensured primarily in a home environment in contrast to residential care, which contributes to the social integration of both recipient older adults and their relatives and their quality of life (Türkiye Alzheimer Derneği, 2020).

Among the criteria for benefiting from home care services for dementia patients are being diagnosed with dementia, having poor mobility, nutrition, and continence, being bedridden, and having a decubitus ulcer due to limited mobilization, as well as legal approval by their relatives. Moreover, those who can limitedly perform their activities of daily living but live alone at home can also benefit from such services (Özbabalık & Hussein, 2017, p. 37).

In our country, units for home care services were deployed within healthcare institutions (public hospitals, training and research hospitals, family practice centers, community health centers, and oral and dental health centers) for all sorts of services for older adults, thanks to the "Directive on the Implementation Procedures and Principles of Home Health Services" coming into force in 2010 (Ministry of Health, 2016). At the same time, coordination centers came into service within the public health directorates (Özbabalık & Hussein, 2017, p. 37). In this way, it was primarily targeted to ensure the widespread procurement of relevant services. Besides, since the hospital environment may adversely affect the health of older adults and their relatives (Kalaycı & Özkul, 2019, p. 2260) and indirectly lead patients with dementia to skip a treatment phase (Nazlıer Keser, 2019a, pp. 123–124), home care services are rather helpful for such patients.

Another practice regarding home care services is a cash benefit for caregivers to promote the involvement of family members in the care of their older adult relatives. According to the Regulation on Detecting Disabled Persons in Need of Care and Care Service Principles, social assistance is provided for caregivers of older adults needing care and having a severe disability (at least 50%). In 2020, 140,111 (26.32%) of 532,337 people receiving cash benefits were over 60 years old (General Directorate of Services for Persons with Disabilities and The Elderly, 2022, p. 54). Dementia is a recognized disability for older adults to benefit from social assistance (Çabalar et al., 2011, p. 144). Thus, older adults with dementia who are not under institutional care can apply for a care pension as long as they satisfy the other necessary criteria. On the other hand, some family members may attempt to undertake the care of an older adult relative with dementia in order not to lose the cash benefit for home care; however, such individuals may not meet most of their care needs.

Hope Homes (Umut Evleri) may be a clear example of the institutional transformation into a community-based care service model. In this model, older adults and disabled individuals continue their lives in a home-style social service unit, are involved in inclusionary activities for social life, and receive care from professional care personnel (General Directorate of Services for Persons with Disabilities and the Elderly, 2022, p. 53). Moreover, individuals under institutional care but owning a house may petition the ministry to have their house designated as a Hope Home. If the request is deemed appropriate upon verification by the authorities, their houses are converted into Hope Homes. Community organizations, such as NGOs, volunteer organizations, universities, municipalities, and public institutions, may provide support for the opening and operation of such homes. Social, cultural, and occupational activities are organized for individuals in these homes (General Directorate of Services for Persons with Disabilities and the Elderly, 2008, p. 3). The first Hope Home came into service in Izmir in 2008, and the number of such homes reached 148 as of 2022 (General Directorate of Services for Persons with Disabilities and the Elderly, 2022, p. 53).

Residential care centers, or nursing homes, are public or private institutions where life-long care, rehabilitation, supervision, and counseling services are provided, and socialization opportunities are offered to older adults with difficulties maintaining their lives on their own. Approximately 36.3% of the nursing homes (452) are affiliated with the MoFSS, 4.4% with other public institutions, and 59.3% with private businesses. Besides, there are 104 rehabilitation centers affiliated with the MoFSS (General Directorate of Services for Persons with Disabilities and the Elderly, 2022, 52, pp. 97–98). Due to the insufficient number of residential care and rehabilitation centers in our country, older adults with dementia who should be under institutional care may have to stay with their families, leading these individuals and their families to have some care-related issues. Hence, the MoFSS offers older adults with Alzheimer's, whose economic and social deprivation is ensured through social investigations, free residence in residential care centers (Nazlıer Keser, 2019b, p. 97), and those in need of care can request a caregiver from the nearest nursing home (Özbabalık & Hussein, 2017, p. 14). In Türkiye, residential care centers provide spaces designed for dementia patients since the number of residential care centers only for Alzheimer's patients is quite inadequate, and older adults staying at such centers are at risk of developing dementia as they get older (Özbabalık & Hussein, 2017, p. 38).

Services offered by local governments

Local governments are obliged to provide home or institutional care for older people. The "Law on Metropolitan Municipalities" already defines the duties, authorities, and responsibilities of local governments regarding the long-term care of older people (Resmi Gazete, 2004). In this context, local governments are commissioned to implement and improve all kinds of social and cultural services for older adults through healthcare centers, hospitals, and mobile healthcare units and to cooperate with educational institutions, public institutions, and NGOs while carrying out these services. In Türkiye, municipalities undertake multiple roles such as offering care services, in-kind and cash aid, food support, and healthcare support for older adults—particularly those with low socioeconomic status and living alone—to maintain their lives without being isolated from society (Kalınkara & Arpacı, 2021, p. 728; İzmir Büyükşehir Belediyesi Alzheimer ve Demans Merkezi, 2022). Some Alzheimer's and Dementia Centers established by municipalities in our country carry out mental, psychological, social, and physical activities to improve the quality of life of patients, increase their social functionality, enrich their activities of daily living, and help delay the progression of the disease (Kadıköy Belediyesi Alzheimer Merkezi, 2020; İzmir Büyükşehir Belediyesi Alzheimer ve Demans Merkezi, 2022). The number of people who benefit from the elderly care services of Ankara Metropolitan Municipality is 453,362 (Nazlıer Keser, 2019b, p. 97), which is thought to be satisfyingly high.

Services offered by NGOs

Many NGOs offer practices for dementia patients and their relatives. Some of them are as follows:

The Turkish Alzheimer's Association was established in 1997 by the relatives of patients and medical doctors specializing in Alzheimer's disease. It performs its practices with its 11 branch offices across the country. The association primarily organizes seminars on public awareness and education on Alzheimer's disease and relevant care. Moreover, the association provides social and psychological support and implements educational activities to contribute to the quality of life of patients and their relatives. It carries out awareness-raising activities in cooperation with municipalities, other

NGOs, universities, and volunteers. In collaboration with local governments, the association offers elderly daycare and home care services and organizes "Professional Training on Elderly and Alzheimer's Patient Care." Moreover, the association provides nursing and patient care services free of charge to Alzheimer's patients at their homes (Türkiye Alzheimer Derneği, 2020). Another NGO operating on Alzheimer's disease is Alzheimer's Foundation, established in 2003. The foundation mainly aims to provide information and guidance on the scientific aspect of the disease and to plan and implement activities to facilitate patients' lives with the contributions of volunteers and patient relatives. It has held numerous scientific and social activities so far (Alzheimer Vakfı, 2021). The Dementia Friendly Community Association (2022) carries out its activities on a voluntary basis with those affected by the disease, their relatives, specialists, and professional groups. It provides consultancy services to patients and their relatives and supports them regarding their legal rights. The association holds training programs and activities to encourage social and political agents to take steps regarding disease-related practices. It also seeks international cooperation with European experts. Moreover, the association admits professionals for training in intercultural Alzheimer's care and dementia coaching.

Services offered by educational institutions

Relevant undergraduate and graduate programs in Türkiye raise gerontologists with the qualifications of a researcher, educator, practitioner, manager, and leader who can evaluate the aging needs of the country, provide gerontological services to individuals, families, and society, adopt interdisciplinary cooperation and teamwork, and act within their professional rights and responsibilities and ethical principles. Gerontologists graduating with advanced knowledge of dementia adopt a gerontological approach to preserve the competence, independence, and quality of life of older adults (Akıncı, 2020, p. 31; Suleyman Demirel University Department of Gerontology, 2021).

Students are admitted to the associate degree "Elderly Care Program" to be trained as professional staff to provide qualified and skilled care services to older adults in our country. The extensive coverage of dementia in the curriculum of these programs allows graduate students to provide quality care to target groups and meet their needs (Suleyman Demirel University Isparta Health Services Vocational School, 2019). Public education centers, affiliated with the General Directorate of Lifelong Learning within the Ministry of National Education (MoNE), are located in each city in Türkiye. These institutions organize various educational activities to improve the knowledge and skills of individuals of all ages (Ünal et al., 2006, p. 909). Moreover, such centers offer "Training for Those to Support the Self-Care of the Sick and Elderly" (160 hours) and "Training of Support Staff for Self-Care" (305 hours) courses. These courses aim to raise awareness, knowledge, and skills of those (e.g., family members, paid caregivers) who will engage in caring for patients and older people in need of care (Hayat Boyu Öğrenme Genel Müdürlüğü, 2021). Thanks to the extensive inquiry into dementia in the course content, those who successfully complete the course can provide quality care services to patients with dementia.

In Isparta, a drama course was offered at the Isparta Nursing Home and Care Center in cooperation with the Department of Gerontology at Suleyman Demirel University and the Isparta Public Education Center. The guests at the center were encouraged to show active participation in the course. The aim of offering such a course to older adults was to increase their cognitive and intellectual levels and, thus, reduce the possibility of dementia. Overall, it is aimed to disseminate this practice throughout Türkiye.

Informal services

Family members of older adults with dementia do not prefer residential care due to their cultural and moral values and economic conditions. Therefore, family members have to undertake all the responsibility for the care of their older adult relatives. The fact that the individuals caring for older adults are not well-educated on satisfying their physical and emotional needs, and the conditions and problems to be confronted in their care, may increase the care burden and cause caregivers to become distressed (Kalınkara & Kalaycı, 2017, p. 29; Özkul & Kalaycı, 2018, p. 17).

Carer family members experience the most difficulty in "poor self-care," "anxiety-restlessness distress," "continence," and "disruption in communication" among the symptoms and disorders arising from the nature of the disease. Moreover, "being dependent on home," "limited time for social life and themselves," "feeling tired," and "quick temper" are the most prevalent consequences of caregiving (Soner & Aykut, 2017, pp. 378–379). In the care of an Alzheimer's patient, carers need support most in the physical caring tasks such as bathing, eating, dressing, and undressing (Kaya Uygun & Taylan, 2018, p. 527). These situations often make caregivers tired, increase stress and tension, and feel frustrated. At the same time, the intense caregiving practices may ruin the family order (Say Şahin et al., 2019, p. 75; Fundinho et al., 2021, p. 372). Adverse conditions for care pose a risk for elder abuse (Kalaycı et al., 2016, p. 234; Kalaycı et al., 2020, p. 360).

Family members may sometimes have to work with paid and informal caregivers to care for their older adult relatives. Therefore, services oriented to elderly care are increasingly becoming an area of informal employment, bringing many problems among older adults, family members, and caregivers. Among the issues initiated by family members are offering low-wage and uninsured employment to caregivers, demanding long caregiving periods, not clarifying job descriptions, not providing the materials necessary for caregiving, and not assisting caregivers. On the other hand, the problems caused by caregivers may be not doing the job properly, being uneducated, interfering with the social life of older adults, resigning from the job without any notice, demanding high wages, etc. (Özkul & Kalaycı, 2018, pp. 13–15).

Conclusion

Türkiye is characterized by a social structure predominated by traditional relations. However, modernization and recent changes in the social structure have brought a transformation from the traditional family to the nuclear family. Moreover, the involvement of nuclear family members in working life and the participation of younger generations in formal and long education processes are likely to trigger problems in elderly care. In general, relatives of older adults undertake their care due to inherent cultural and social responsibility, emotional commitment, demands from older adults, or poor socioeconomic conditions. However, elderly care may bring significant problems to caregivers such as alienation from social life, exacerbated health problems, intense negative feelings (anxiety, helplessness, anger), failure in professional life, and financial inadequacies. This is the point when benefiting from other care services becomes helpful. It should be noted that families often do not prefer residential care for their older adult relatives under the influence of tight traditional bonds. Moreover, Turkish people generally describe older people staying in residential care centers as "orphans." Some rumors about such centers may also lead individuals needing residential care to change their preferences. Yet, Hope Homes have now become the preferred option since they allow individuals to live in a home environment. On the other hand, home care services are still utilized the most. The older people needing care stay at home, and their health and home-related needs are satisfied by professionals. Daycare institutions are also rapidly spreading in the country. Despite the delays in these institutions' coming into service due to the isolation measures against the pandemic, they appear as noteworthy service providers that support both older adults and their families. Across the country, ministries, local governments, public and educational institutions, NGOs, and volunteers work devotedly to improve the quality of life of older adults with dementia and their relatives.

References

Akıncı, A. Y. (2020). Antik Çağdan moderniteye gerontolojinin doğuşu. In D. Say Şahin (Ed.), *Etik Yönleriyle Yaşlılık ve Yaşlanma* (p. 132). Ekin Yayınevi (in Turkish).

Alzheimer's Association. (2017, July 20). *Alzheimer's disease facts and figures.* https://www.alz.org/media/HomeOffice/Facts%20and%20Figures/facts-and-figures.pdf

Alzheimer Vakfı. (2021). *Komitelerimiz.* https://alz.org.tr/komitelerimiz/ (in Turkish)

Çabalar, M., Demirtaş Tatlıdede, A., Yazar, T., Güveli,, B., & Yayla, V. (2011). Evaluation of the neurological disability rates in medical commission. *The Medical Journal of Bakırköy, 7*, 142–146. https://doi.org/10.5350/BTDMJB201107404

Demans Dostu Toplum Derneği. (2020). *Demans dostu toplum derneği.* https://demansdostu.com/sayfa/tr/3/biz-kimiz (in Turkish)

Fundinho, J. F., Pereira, D. C., & Ferreira-Alves, J. (2021). Theoretical approaches to elder abuse: a systematic review of the empirical evidence. *The Journal of Adult Protection, 23*(6), 370–383. https://doi.org/10.1108/JAP-04-2021-0014

GBD 2019 Dementia Forecasting Collaborators. (2022). Estimation of the global prevalence of dementia in 2019 and forecasted prevalence in 2050: An analysis for the Global Burden of Disease Study 2019. *Lancet Public Health, 7*, e105–125.

General Directorate of Services for Persons with Disabilities and The Elderly. (2008). *Umut homes directive for disabled individuals.* https://www.aile.gov.tr/uploads/eyhgm/uploads/pages/yonergeler/engelli-bireylere-yonelik-umut-evleri-yonergesi.pdf

General Directorate of Services for Persons with Disabilities and The Elderly. (2011). *Mission.* https://www.aile.gov.tr/eyhgm/kurumsal/misyon-ve-vizyonumuz/

General Directorate of Services for Persons with Disabilities and The Elderly. (2020). *Disabled and elderly statistics bulletin 2019 June.* https://www.ailevecalisma.gov.tr/media/52698/ebultenmart-nisan-2020-2.pdf

General Directorate of Services for Persons with Disabilities and The Elderly. (2022). *Disabled and elderly statistics bulletin (February 2022).* https://www.aile.gov.tr/media/102557/eyhgm_istatistik_bulteni_subat_2022.pdf

Guevara, E. E., & Lawler, R. R. (2018). Epigenetic clocks. *Evolutionary Anthropology: Issues, News, and Reviews, 26*(6), 256–260. https://doi.org/10.1002/evan.21745

Hayat Boyu Öğrenme Genel Müdürlüğü. (2021). *Kurs programları.* https://e-yaygin.meb.gov.tr/pagePrograms.aspx?rgKurslarChangePage=4_100 (in Turkish)

İzmir Büyükşehir Belediyesi Alzheimer ve Demans Merkezi. (2022). *İzmir büyükşehir belediyesi.* https://www.izmir.bel.tr/tr/AlzheimerVeDemansHastaVeAileleriBulusmaDanismaMerkezi/45/117 (in Turkish)

Kadıköy Belediyesi Alzheimer Merkezi. (2020). *Alzheimer merkezi yıllık eğitim ve destek programı.* https://alzheimermerkezi.kadikoy.bel.tr/anasayfa# (in Turkish)

Kalaycı, I., & Özkul, M. (2017). I wish I could protect my traditional position, be modern: Elderly experiences in modernization process. *SDU Visionary Journal, 8*(18), 90–110. https://doi.org/10.21076/vizyoner.308309

Kalaycı, I., & Özkul, M. (2019). The effect of hospital conditions on the care load and burnout level of the elderly releases. *Turkish Studies Social Sciences, 14*(5), 2249–2274. https://doi.org/10.29228/TurkishStudies.30284

Kalaycı, I., Özkul, M., & Oğuz, H. (2017). A type of work between compassion and commerce: emotional labor in elderly care services. *Süleyman Demirel Üniversitesi İktisadi ve İdari Bilimler Fakültesi Dergisi, 22*(3), 637–662.

Kalaycı, I., Özkul, M., Özbek Yazıcı, S., & Küpeli, A. (2016). Perceptions of the elderly on elderly abuse. *Turkish Journal of Geriatrics, 19*(4), 232–237.

Kalaycı, I., Tuna Uysal, M., & Özkul, M. (2020). Sözde saygın özde mağdur Türkiye'de ve Dünya'da yaşlı istismarı ve ihmali. In D. Say Şahin (Ed.), *Yaşlanmaya Sağlık Sosyolojisi Perspektifinden Multidisipliner Yaklaşımlar* (pp. 355–394). Ekin Yayınevi.

Kalınkara, V., & Arpacı, F. (2021). The research of burnout and life satisfaction of personnel that provides elderly care service within the scope of municipality services. *The Journal of Turkish Social Research*, 25(3), 727–742.

Kalınkara, V., & Kalaycı, I. (2017). Life satisfaction, care burden and burnout of the individuals who have a caregiver service to the elderly at home. *Elderly Issues Research Journal (EIRJ)*, 10(2), 19–39.

Kaya, A., & Gamsızkan, Z. (2022). The number of chronic diseases of elderly people and their visits to a family health centre: A single unit retrospective study. *Türk Aile Hekİmliği Dergisi*, 26(1), 1–5. https://doi.org/10.54308/tahd.2022.22932

Kaya Uygun, Ü., & Taylan, H. H. (2018). Factors affecting the care burden of family members providing primary caregiving to alzheimer patient. *International Journal of Social Science*, 71, 513–531. https://doi.org/10.9761/JASSS7819

Ministry of Family and Social Services. (2022). *Mission*. Aile ve sosyal hizmetler bakanlığı. https://www.aile.gov.tr/bakanlik/hakkinda/misyon-ve-vizyonumuz

Ministry of Health. (2016, February 19). *Evde sağlık hizmetlerinin uygulama usul ve esasları hakkında yönerge*. https://www.saglik.gov.tr/TR,11271/saglik-bakanliginca-sunulan-evde-saglik-hizmetlerinin-uygulama-usul-ve-esaslari-hakkinda-yonerge.html

Nazlıer Keser, E. N. (2019a). Social work interventions for alzheimer's patients. *Elderly Issues Research Journal (EIRJ)*, 12(2), 121–128.

Nazlıer Keser, E. N. (2019b). Social policies for alzheimer's patients and caregivers: Compare of Turkey and Germany. *Journal of Social Sciences and Humanities Researches*, 20(45), 93–118.

Onder, G., Rezza, G., & Brusaferro, S. (2020). Case-fatality rate and characteristics of patients dying in relation to COVID-19 in Italy. *Jama*, 323(18), 1775–1776. https://doi.org/10.1001/jama.2020.4683

Özbabalık, D., & Hussein, S. (2017). *Demans bakım modeli raporu*. Aile ve Sosyal Politikalar Bakanlığı Sosyal İçerme Politikaları Alanında Kurumsal Kapasitenin Artırılması Projesi. https://www.aile.gov.tr/media/9332/demans-bak%C4%B1m-modeli-proje-kitab%C4%B1.pdf (in Turkish).

Özgün Başıbüyük, G., Kaleli, I., Efe, M., Tiryaki, S., Ulus, F., Demirdaş, F. B., Dere, B., Özgür, Ö., Koç, Ö., & Tufan, İ. (2021). Depression tendency caused by social isolation: An assessment on older adults in Turkey. *Advances in Gerontology*, 3, 298–304. https://doi.org/10.1134/s2079057021030085

Özkul, M., & Kalaycı, I. (2018). Elderly care as an informal job and employment area: the problems between the relatives of the elder and caregiver. *Suleyman Demirel University Visionary Journal*, 9(20), 1–27. https://doi.org/10.21076/vizyoner.372115

Resmi Gazete. (2004, July 10). *Büyükşehir belediyesi kanunu*. https://www.mevzuat.gov.tr/MevzuatMetin/1.5.5216.pdf (in Turkish)

Say Şahin, D., Özer, Ö., & Yanardağ, M. Z. (2019). Perceived social support, quality of life and satisfaction with life in elderly people. *Educational Gerontology*, 45(1), 69–77. https://doi.org/10.1080/03601277.2019.1585065

Soner, S., & Aykut, S. (2017). Alzheimer's disease-processed caregiver family members difficulties and social work. *Ahi Evran University Institute of Social Sciences Journal*, 3(2), 375–387.

Suleyman Demirel University Department of Gerontology. (2021). *Department of gerontology*. https://saglik.sdu.edu.tr/gerontoloji

Suleyman Demirel University Isparta Health Services Vocational School. (2019). *Mission*. https://shmyo.sdu.edu.tr/tr/kurumsal/misyon-vizyon-11965s.html

T.C. Sağlık Bakanlığı Türkiye Halk Sağlığı Kurumu. (2015). *Türkiye sağlıklı yaşlanma eylem planı ve uygulama programı 2015-2020*. Anıl Reklam (in Turkish).

Turkish Statistical Institue. (2021, March 18). *Older adults with statistics, 2020* https://data.tuik.gov.tr/Bulten/Index?p=Istatistiklerle-Yaslilar-2020-37227

Turkish Statistical Institute. (2022, March 18). *Older adults with statistics, 2021.* https://data.tuik.gov.tr/Bulten/Index?p=Istatistiklerle-Yaslilar-2021-45636

Türkiye Alzheimer Derneği. (2020). *Biz Kimiz.* Türkiye alzheimer derneği faaliyet raporu kuruluş ve amaçlar. https://www.alzheimerdernegi.org.tr/biz-kimiz/ (in Turkish)

Ünal, F., Kalçık, C., & Saltuk, M. (2006). A review on the contributions of community education centres to the lifelong learning skills of female participants. *Turkish Studies, 11*(6), 905–930. https://doi.org/10.7827/TurkishStudies.9645

World Health Organization (WHO). (2021, September 2). *Dementia.* https://www.who.int/news-room/fact-sheets/detail/dementia

19
DEMENTIA CARE

Management and challenges in India

Esha Arora, Rhea Wason, and Ashish Goel

Dementia not only refers to the impairment of memory but also affects thinking and social abilities, which are severe enough to disrupt a person's daily life. Dementia can also cause a variety of more serious symptoms like hallucinations, paranoid delusions, and uninhibited behavior. Alzheimer's disease is the most common cause of dementia in older adults; however, it can be caused by a variety of other factors as well.

According to the World Health Organization, 50 million people are living with dementia worldwide, with 10 million new diagnoses every year. The prevalence of dementia in India is reported to be 2.7% (Ministry of Health and Family Welfare (MoHFW), National Institute of Health and Family Welfare (NIHFW), 2022) Prevalence of dementia increases with advancing age. With an improving healthcare system leading to an increased lifespan, the percentage of the older population is increasing in India, and so are the problems related to old age. The percentage of older people is expected to be 20% by 2050, with an expected dramatic increase in the prevalence of the disease (mint, 2015). The healthcare system in India needs to be better prepared to tackle the issues related to the geriatric population.

Risk factors of dementia

1. *Family history of dementia:* The diseases causing dementia, as well as some of the risk factors, can be linked to certain genes. Individuals of a family may also have a similar lifestyle that can again affect the probability of developing dementia. Thus, many times dementia may run in families (Cannon-Albright et al., 2019).

DOI: 10.4324/9781003528432-22

2. *Lifestyle:* Individuals with a healthy lifestyle are at a lesser risk of developing the disease. A well-balanced diet, regular exercise, and good sleep hygiene can reduce the lifetime risk (Dhana et al., 2020). Excessive alcohol use and smoking have been linked to early-onset dementia (Durazzo et al., 2014; Sabia et al., 2018).
3. *Existence of certain diseases:* Diseases like late-onset depression and Parkinson's disease are commonly associated with dementia (Szeto et al., 2020; Valkanova et al., 2017). Diabetes, hypertension, dyslipidemia, and obesity have also been linked to dementia (Biessels & Despa, 2018). As India moves toward an epidemic of these non-communicable diseases, an unprecedented number of people seem to be at risk of dementia. Medications prescribed for other diseases can also predispose individuals to dementia. Statins prescribed very commonly to lower blood cholesterol have been linked to memory problems (Schultz et al., 2018).
4. *Environmental factors:* A few studies have shown that air pollutants can hasten the degeneration of the nervous system, although more research needs to be done in this area (Peters et al., 2019).

Dementia: a disease or a symptom?

Contrary to the common misconception, dementia is not a disease but a symptom of diseases. Various diseases can have a loss of memory as their first presenting symptom. Being on the lookout for other associated symptoms is crucial to reaching a diagnosis and hence providing the appropriate support and treatment to the patient. Common diseases which can present with dementia are (National Health Service, 2021a):

1. *Alzheimer's disease:* For many people, dementia is synonymous with Alzheimer's disease. It is indeed the most common cause of dementia, beginning as benign forgetfulness and later progressing to serious cognitive disabilities. On the brighter side, it has a slow progression and hence has scope for early detection and intervention.
2. *Vascular dementia*: This is another common cause. The increased prevalence of atherosclerotic disease leading to multiple strokes can eventually lead to dementia.
3. *Alcoholism, drug, or medication intoxication:* Chronic intake of these toxins can decline nerve cell health. Moreover, malnutrition and the deficiency of vitamins seen in substance abusers can cause dementia in later life (Sabia et al., 2018).
4. *Other causes*: Various neuropsychiatric diseases can present with dementia. It can also be the neurological symptom of systemic diseases ranging from infections (AIDS, syphilis) to endocrine disorders (thyroid

and parathyroid disorders). Tumors and repeated head trauma are other rare causes.

Presentation

Dementia leads to progressive impairment of cognitive abilities. Although memory is the most commonly affected, other mental facilities like language, visuospatial ability, judgment, calculation, and problem-solving are also affected. It usually begins with benign forgetfulness and is initially dismissed by the patient and the family as insignificant. The disease then gradually progresses to a more serious problem that starts affecting the patient's day-to-day living. Understanding the implications of these symptoms on the patient, family, and the community is essential in order to provide effective supportive care.

Impairment of short-term memory leads to an inability to follow simple instructions, resulting in unemployment or difficulty managing the household. They might get lost when they go for walks and wander aimlessly. Orientation to time is gradually lost, and the patient might repetitively ask the time.

As the disease progresses, the language gets affected, leading to a communication gap between the caretaker and the doctor, which causes further problems. Gradually, the patient is unable to recognize their loved ones and even themselves in the mirror. This can lead to significant anxiety for the patient and their family. Motor abilities start getting affected, with difficulty walking progressing to an inability to dress, bathe, and feed themselves. In the later stages, the patient becomes bedridden with generalized muscle rigidity and incontinence. Death usually results from malnutrition and infections.

Some patients might not even be aware of their disease. Regardless of insight, the symptoms lead to significant distress for the patient. They might present to the clinic with depression and irritability (National Health Service, 2021b). The patient might become aggressive and exhibit violent and uninhibited behavior. Caretakers can oftentimes be frustrated by the patient, and elder abuse is not uncommon in such settings.

Management of the disease

A multifaceted approach is important for the effective management of a disease that affects so many aspects of a person and their family's life (Figure 19.1).

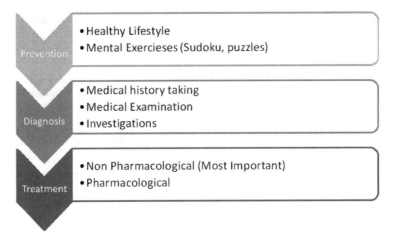

FIGURE 19.1   Management of dementia.

Medical history taking: a crucial tool for diagnosis

A thorough and detailed medical history stressing the onset and progression of the disease is very important to make the diagnosis and illustrate the cause of dementia. Alzheimer's disease has an insidious onset and slow progression. A history of stroke, hypertension, diabetes, and atrial fibrillation points toward vascular dementia. A history of acute or sub-acute onset points toward infections, metabolic derangements, or other reversible causes. History suggesting behavioral changes, delirium, hallucinations, and other associated symptoms should be taken. A history of any addictions, alcoholism, and thorough drug history needs to be taken. History of any infections like HIV, syphilis, etc. points toward infectious causes of dementia. A history of intravenous drug use or multiple sexual partners should raise a suspicion of central nervous system infections.

Medical examination: physical, neurological, and cognitive

A thorough examination is important to diagnose dementia and look for clues to find out the cause. A neurological examination illustrating hemiparesis suggests vascular dementia. Signs of systemic diseases and vitamin deficiencies should be looked for. An eye and ear examination should be done as visual or hearing impairment is common in the elderly. This can be disorienting in older adult and can be confused with dementia.

Mini-Mental State Examination (MMSE) is a good screening tool to diagnose cognitive impairment (Oxford Medical Education, 2015). It is a simple 30-point test of mental function that includes questions regarding orientation, registration, attention, calculation, recall, and language.

MMSE may be normal in many patients with Alzheimer's disease in the early stages of the disease. A more comprehensive neuropsychiatric examination is needed in such cases, which also focuses on functional assessment to determine the impact of the disease on day-to-day activities.

Investigations to be ordered

Laboratory tests to find out the reversible causes of dementia, such as vitamin deficiencies and endocrine disorders, should be ordered. Neuroimaging studies (CT or MRI) help to rule out tumors or vascular diseases. Specific patterns of brain involvement can point toward a specific cause of dementia. A lumbar puncture can be done to confirm the diagnosis of central nervous system infections.

Treatment

1) Non-pharmacological treatment: Important for prevention and cure

A healthy, well-balanced diet rich in antioxidants like vitamins A, C, and E, and carotenoids has a neuroprotective effect and is said to be protective against dementia. Regularly indulging in activities like solving sudoku and crossword puzzles delays onset. However, once dementia sets in, it has a progressive course. The progress can be slowed but not halted through various approaches.

Behavioral therapy has a pivotal role to play in its management. It can help relieve the accompanying psychiatric symptoms by helping the patient cope with the disease better. Dementia patients should be informed and explained early about their disease while they still understand the implications of their situation. This would prepare them in advance to make necessary arrangements for their care. This would also give them time to make their will, power of attorney, and end-of-life care arrangements.

Tender-loving care is important for these patients. They should be informed about their condition and reassured by the caretaker with a calm attitude. As these patients become unable to take care of themselves, attention needs to be given to their diet and hygiene. In the later stages of the disease, it might become important to shift the patient to an old-age home. This change in environment can be very difficult and confusing for a dementia patient. However, with constant support and care, they slowly settle in. Their room should be well-lit with large windows and should have photos of loved ones and other things that are meaningful to the patient. Their room should have a calendar with large print and a big wall clock, preferably digital. Frequent visits from loved ones should be encouraged. It is a good idea to form a support group involving the patients and their caregivers through an NGO.

Efforts should be made to maintain their routine. Patients should be encouraged to go for regular walks and engage in simple exercises and social activities. To make the patient's life easier, they should be given memory aids like lists, written schedules and medicine charts. Safety is also an important issue. It should be ensured that they have safe surroundings around the house. The bathroom should have railings in the shower area with anti-skid mats or tiles. The staircase should be well lit with railings. They should not be allowed to drive.

Regular assessment of hearing and vision and provision of adequate hearing and visual aids are important for rehabilitation.

2) Pharmacological treatment

Drugs, namely, Donepezil, Rivastigmine, Galantamine, and Memantine, have been approved for use in patients with Alzheimer's disease. Each of these drugs has low efficacy and limited action. Though they might help to slow down the progression, these drugs do not treat the disease.

Challenges to care

India has been a young nation with most of its population below the age of 60 years. Consequently, its healthcare system is not yet focused on the older population. However, with the declining birth rate and increasing lifespan, the geriatric population is on the rise. With the increasing geriatric population, the prevalence of chronic diseases and other diseases associated with old age, like dementia is going to increase. Thus, the healthcare system needs to buckle up to tackle the increase in the number of geriatric patients.

Our hospitals are ill-suited for the long-term care of dementia patients. India does not have a sufficient number of well-established old age homes or institutions dedicated to persons living with dementia. Doctors and nurses are not trained or sensitized in the care of the elderly, adding to the burden of morbidity. There are very few institutes in India that offer MD in Geriatric Medicine or other courses focusing on the care of older adults.

Forgetfulness is a common problem in older adults. Dementia is seen as a normal part of aging and thus symptoms are ignored in the early stages of the disease. Patients or their relatives do not seek consultation from the doctor early in the disease when the patient presents only with benign forgetfulness. This allows the disease to progress to more advanced stages where the management becomes difficult.

Dementia patients present with self-neglect, which leads to issues of hygiene and may result in various infections including skin and genitourinary infections. They are also unable to take care of their diet, leading to malnutrition. Infections and malnutrition are two important issues in the later stages of dementia and can also lead to death in these patients.

People with dementia are also prone to abuse. It could be physical abuse in the form assault or sexual abuse, or psychosocial abuse in the form of verbal abuse and neglect. Family members may become overwhelmed and vent their frustration on the patient. They are not involved in family discussions or important decisions, which may impact them mentally. Financial abuse occurs when the family or close ones misuse their money or property and make them a victim of fraud.

Abuse in dementia patients is different from abuse in normal adults as the disease prevents them from recognizing and reporting the problem. Also, they don't have the cognitive ability to remember it and even if they tell others about it, they might not be believed. Thus, it is very important for a healthcare provider to recognize the signs of abuse in a dementia patient and address them promptly.

Being neglected by their families, they are not cared for and not provided with a proper diet and medical care. These patients need a lot of help with day-to-day living and maintaining their hygiene. Family members not dedicated to the patient or busy with their own lives are unable to dedicate so much time and effort to these patients. Many families have financial constraints and thus cannot provide the patient with a staff dedicated to the care of the patient. Money is also an issue if the families want to provide the patients with institutional care, as India does not have many government-run old-age homes.

Many patients become totally dependent on their daily activities in the later stages of the disease. They do not recognize family members and sometimes become delusional, hostile, and violent. They might wander away from home. Later on, in the disease, they become bedridden and incontinent. It is very difficult for the family members to see their loved ones in such a condition and progress to worse conditions. Also, it is very difficult physically and mentally to provide care to such patients. Providing care to dementia patients takes a toll on the mental health of the caregiver and leads to their burnout. Thus, the caregivers also need constant support and counseling.

Addressing the challenges: the international perspectives

With the emerging idea of healthy aging becoming mainstream, all countries worldwide, including India, are focusing on the health and issues related to the health of older adults. The United Nations has declared 2021–2030 as the decade of healthy ageing.

In an era of digital aging, there are many tools available to improve the quality of life of dementia patients. Artificial intelligence can be used for diagnosis, assessment, and monitoring of dementia patients, as well as for the maintenance of function, leisure and activity, and caregiving and management (Astell et al., 2019). This would help reduce the caregiver burden.

Mobile phones are one such example that are widely available to everyone in India these days. One can set reminders on the mobile phone for taking medicines, going for walks, meetings, and various other activities. Lists can be saved on mobile phones for grocery shopping, etc.

Assistive technology devices in the form of wearable devices using global positioning systems (GPS) can help maintain outdoor mobility in dementia patients (Teipel et al., 2016). The idea is to help maintain the social life of dementia patients who fall victim to social isolation as they stop going out of the house in fear of getting lost. These devices can provide step-by-step guidance through a transition route or offer alternative routes.

Apart from integrating existing technology in geriatric healthcare, many countries are investing in the development of novel technology designed especially for the use of dementia patients (Active Assisted Living Programme Association, 2020). These technologies come with a promise to significantly improve the quality of life for people living with dementia.

Integrating lessons from other countries with the age-old practice of caring for and respecting older people can improve the quality of life several fold in India. In line with global developments, many initiatives have been taken to improve the health of older adults in India under the National Programme for Health Care of the Elderly.

National Programme for Health Care of Elderly: the milestone for geriatric care in India

The Ministry of Health and Family Welfare launched the National Programme for Health Care of Elderly in 2010–2011 with an objective to provide accessible, affordable, and high-quality long-term, dedicated, and comprehensive healthcare services to the aging population and to promote the concept of Active Ageing (Ministry of Health and Family Welfare, 2010).

The strategies to achieve the objectives of NPHCE are (Ministry of Health and Family Welfare, 2010):

1. Dedicated services at Primary Health Care centers and Community Health Centers, including domiciliary visits by trained healthcare workers.
2. Dedicated facilities at district hospitals with 10-bed wards, additional human resources, machinery and equipment, consumables and drugs, training, and IEC.

3. Strengthening eight regional medical institutes to provide dedicated tertiary-level medical facilities for the elderly, introducing PG courses in Geriatric Medicine, and training health personnel at all levels.
4. IEC uses mass media, folk media, and other communication channels to reach out to the target audience.
5. Promotion of public-private partnership in geriatric health care.
6. Mainstreaming AYUSH.
7. Reorienting medical education to support geriatric issues.

India and the world have a long way to go with respect to holistic care for older people, but the future seems promising. New policies and innovations need to go hand in hand in order to achieve our goal to improve the quality of life of the geriatric population.

References

Astell, J., Bouranis, N., Hoey, J., Lindauer, A., Mihailidis, A., Nugent, C., & Robillard, M. (2019). Technology and dementia: The future is now. *Dement Geriatr Cogn Disord*, 47(3): 131–139.

Biessels G. J., & Despa, F. (2018). Cognitive decline and dementia in diabetes mellitus: Mechanisms and clinical implications. *Nat Rev Endocrinol*, 14(10): 591–604.

Cannon-Albright, L. A., Foster, N. L., Schliep, K., Farnham, J. M., Teerlink, C. C., Kaddas, H., Tschanz, J., Corcoran, C., & Kauwe, J. S. K. (2019). Relative risk for Alzheimer disease based on complete family history. *Neurology*, 92(15): e1745–e1753.

Dhana, K., Evans, D. A., Rajan, K. B., Bennett, D. A., & Morris, M. C. (2020). Healthy lifestyle and the risk of Alzheimer dementia. *Neurology*, 95(4): e374.

Durazzo, T. C., Mattsson, N., & Weiner, M. W. (2014). Smoking and increased Alzheimer's disease risk: A review of potential mechanisms. *Alzheimer's & Dementia*, 10(3S): S122–S145.

Ministry of Health and Family Welfare. (2010). *National Programme for Health Care of the Elderly(NPHCE)*. https://main.mohfw.gov.in/major-programmes/Non-Communicable-Diseases/Non-Communicable-Diseases-1.

Ministry of Health and Family Welfare (MoHFW), National Institute of Health and Family Welfare (NIHFW). (2022, September 16). *Dementia*. https://www.nhp.gov.in/disease/neurological/dementia.

mint. (2015). *20% of Population to be Elderly by 2050: HelpAge India Report*. Internet. https://www.livemint.com/Politics/z6BacVOwf5SvmpD9P1BcaK/20-of-population-to-be-elderly-by-2050-HelpAge-India-repor.html.

National Health Service. (2021a). *Causes of Dementia*. @nhsuk. https://www.nhs.uk/conditions/dementia/causes/.

National Health Service. (2021b). *Coping with Dementia Behaviour Changes*. @nhsuk. https://www.nhs.uk/conditions/dementia/behaviour/.

Oxford Medical Education. (2015). *Mini-mental State Examination (MMSE)—Oxford Medical Education*. https://oxfordmedicaleducation.com/geriatrics/mini-mental-state-examination-mmse/.

Peters, R., Ee, N., Peters, J., Booth, A., Mudway, I., & Anstey, K. J. (2019). Air pollution and dementia: A systematic review. *J Alzheimers Dis*, 70(s1): S145–S163.

Sabia, S., Fayosse, A., Dumurgier, J., Dugravot, A., Akbaraly, T., Britton, A., Kivimäki, M., & Singh-Manoux, A. (2018). Alcohol consumption and risk of dementia: 23 year follow-up of Whitehall II cohort study. *BMJ*, 362: k2927.

Santacruz, K. S., & Swagert Active Assisted Living Programme Association. (2020, September 8). *5 Technologies that Help People Living with Dementia*. http://www.aal-europe.eu/5-technologies-that-help-people-living-with-dementia/.

Santacruz, K. S., & Swagerty, D. (2001). Early diagnosis of dementia. *Am Fam Physician*, 63(4): 703–713, 717–718.

Schultz, B. G., Patten, D. K., & Berlau, D. J. (2018). The role of statins in both cognitive impairment and protection against dementia: A tale of two mechanisms. *Transl Neurodegener*, 7(1). https://www.ncbi.nlm.nih.gov/pmc/articles/PMC5830056 %[2022-05-21T20:55:36.

Szeto, J. Y. Y., Walton, C. C., Rizos, A., Martinez-Martin, P., Halliday, G. M., Naismith, S. L., Chaudhuri, K. R., & Lewis, S. J. G. (2020). Dementia in long-term Parkinson's disease patients: A multicentre retrospective study. *NPJ Parkinson's Dis*, 6(1).

Teipel, S., Babiloni, C., Hoey, J., Kaye, J., Kirste, T., & Burmeister, O. K. (2016). Information and communication technology solutions for outdoor navigation in dementia. *Alzheimer's & Dementia*, 12(6): 695–707.

Valkanova, V., Ebmeier, K. P., & Allan, C. L. (2017). Depression is linked to dementia in older adults. *Practitioner*, 261(1800): 11–15.

20
THE SAN LAWRENZ DEMENTIA FRIENDLY COMMUNITY PILOT PROJECT

Pauline Refalo and Maria Aurora Fenech

Background

The Maltese Archipelago is an EU Member State with a number of islands, with Malta, the mainland, being the largest with 480,134 inhabitants; Gozo, the second in terms of size, has a population of 34,430 inhabitants; and Comino has a population of a mere 2 inhabitants (Regional Statistics Malta, 2021).

Between 2013 and 2019, the Maltese Archipelago registered the highest increases in the older person population cohort. Malta recorded the highest increases in older persons between 70 and 79 years (Figure 20.1); whilst Gozo and Comino accounted for the largest growth in those older persons aged 90 years and over (Figure 20.2) (Regional Statistics Malta, 2021).

With regard to the situation in Malta, the number of older persons living with dementia in 2019 was 6,552, and it was estimated that this would increase to 8,695 persons in 2025 and 14,117 persons in 2050 (Alzheimer Europe, 2019). Gozo and Comino accounted for 478 cases or 1.5% of older persons living with dementia. The Dementia in Europe Yearbook of 2019, Alzheimer Europe (2019) indicated a projected upward trend of older persons living with dementia in Malta for the period of 2018–2050 (Table 20.1).

This local increase in numbers merited a long-term care approach and the development of strategies and policies which met the needs and challenges of older persons living with dementia and informal carers. Both international and local consensus reiterated how informal carers of older persons living with dementia experienced stress and deteriorating health and social lives whilst caring for the latter (Banarjee, 2022; Refalo and Fenech, 2021; Greenwood and Smith, 2019; Zwaanswijk et al., 2013), with informal carers

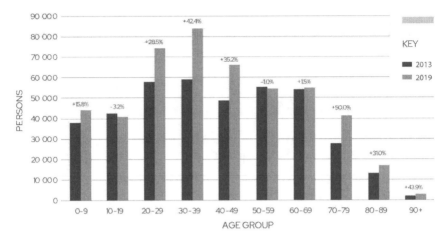

FIGURE 20.1 Changes in population structures in Malta by age groups and selected years (2013–2019).

Source: Malta Regional Statistics, 2021

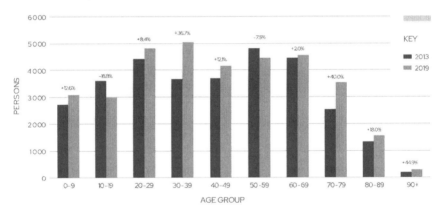

FIGURE 20.2 Changes in population structures in Gozo and Comino by age groups and selected years (2013–2019).

Source: Malta Regional Statistics, 2021

TABLE 20.1 Prevalence data of older persons living with dementia in Malta and Gozo

Year	Number of males	Number of females	% of the total population (males and females)
2018	2242	4309	1.38
2025	3078	5617	1.94
2050	5265	8852	3.31

Source: Alzheimer Europe, 2019

often requiring help for their physical and mental well-being. Informal carers, mostly female, often had to give up their paid jobs, putting further financial duress on the family and adding to the substantial economic costs related to dementia care (Banarjee, 2022; Refalo and Fenech, 2021; Greenwood and Smith, 2019).

Through the modelling of healthcare spending related to dementia care from 2000 to 2019 and evaluating the estimated future dementia spending from 2020 to 2050, Pedroza et al. (2022) revealed how health systems would experience increases in the challenges related to dementia care in the future. They estimated that global spending on dementia care increased by 4.5% annually from 2000 to 2019, reaching $263 billion, with healthcare spending on older persons living with dementia reaching $594 billion. They also projected that by 2050, dementia spending would reach $1.6 trillion or 11% of all expected health spending.

Several authors pointed to the physical, emotional, and financial hardships experienced by the informal carers of older persons living with dementia and argued how these were key contributors to pushing the former to seek relocation of their loved ones to a care home environment (Refalo and Fenech, 2021; Pace and Fenech, 2021; Saliba and Fenech, 2020; Milte et al., 2016; Williamson, 2016). Relocation to the care home, in turn, negatively impacted the older persons living with dementia through a general lack of privacy, independence, and freedom of movement at the facility, difficulty in complying with routines, and boredom and loneliness at no longer being able to participate in community life (Pace and Fenech, 2021; Saliba and Fenech, 2020; Mjorud et al., 2017).

Acknowledging the aforementioned harsh realities experienced by older persons living with dementia and their informal carers, the Maltese Central Government developed the first national dementia strategy covering the period 2015 to 2023 (Parliamentary Secretariat for Rights of Persons with Disability and Active Ageing, 2015). Adopting a dementia-friendly approach to improve the quality of life of older persons living with dementia and their informal carers, and ensuring they remained active contributors in and to society (Parliamentary Secretariat for Rights of Persons with Disability and Active Ageing, 2015), was an emerging, focal concept of this strategy.

In collaboration with the San Lawrenz Local Council, the Parliamentary Secretariat for the Rights of Persons with Disability embarked on a pilot project aimed at turning the small Gozitan town of San Lawrenz into a dementia-friendly community (Micallef, 2015).

Crampton et al. (2012) and later Blood (2017), reiterated how the inception of Dementia Friendly Communities was essential towards adopting a person-centred framework ensuring the re-integration of older persons living with dementia within their own communities and to be physically and socially friendly with these older persons, enhancing and encouraging the older persons' participation in their communities. Dementia Friendly Communities would essentially eliminate stigmatisation, preventing older persons living with dementia from becoming marginalised members of society, as well as supporting their informal carers (Refalo and Fenech, 2021; Blood, 2017; Crampton et al., 2012; Lin, 2017; Williamson, 2016). These arguments were based on the foundations laid earlier by Kitwood (1997), who called out the traditional medical approaches towards older persons living with dementia. which "demeaned and disregarded" these persons. Kitwood (1997) rather argued in favour of providing older persons living with dementia with a person-centred approach to care that focused on regarding them as members of equal status and rights within society, focusing rather on the person than on the disease and its associated comorbidities.

Kitwood's (1997) work on person-centred care and personhood for older persons living with dementia was central and pivotal to effective dementia care, with Blood (2017), aptly defining a Dementia Friendly Community as,

> In a 'Dementia Friendly Community', people with dementia are included and respected. Citizens, organisations and businesses work together to remove the barriers which stop people with dementia and their supporters from participating in community life.
>
> *(Blood, 2017, p.5)*

In conclusion, Dementia-Friendly Communities, in conjunction with educating the public on dementia-related matters (Refalo and Fenech, 2021; Topo, Kotilainen, and Eloniemi-Sulkava, 2012; Chung, Ellis-Hill and Coleman, 2017; Lin, 2017), should be the solid foundation towards nurturing approaches that assist these older persons to remain and interact with and within their communities, rather than remain isolated or confined to a care home setting.

Aims and methodology

The objective of this research project was mainly to analyse the impact of the "San Lawrenz Dementia Friendly Community Pilot Project", on the lives of older persons living with dementia as residents within the village and the informal carers supporting them. The researchers opted for a qualitative research methodology through interviews with the informal carers. The researchers were mainly interested in looking at the social implications of the pilot project and how the project *per se* was impinging on the informal carers' living experiences of caring for an older person living with dementia (Tuffour, 2017; Flick, 2018; Merriam, 2009). The researchers needed to understand the informal carer participants' lived experiences regarding the San Lawrenz Dementia Friendly Community Pilot Project that led them to feel or answer research questions the way they did (Flick, 2018). During the interviews with the informal carers, the researchers employed curiosity, open-mindedness, empathy, and flexibility in order to capture these experiences attentively (Denzin and Lincoln, 2017; Tuffour, 2017). Along these lines, this study specifically embarked on Interpretive Phenomenological Analysis (Smith, Flowers and Larkin, 2009), as the design *per se* allowed the researchers to interpret the informal carers' ensuing conversations within their own environments (Quest, 2014), revolving around their cultural, historical, and social factors (Eatough and Smith, 2006).

Interpretive Phenomenological Analysis was considered flexible and participant-oriented as its main objective was that of giving the opportunity to the informal caregivers to narrate their "lived experiences" freely (Alase, 2017; Tomkins, 2017; Smith, Flowers, and Larkin, 2009). This approach also enabled the researchers to closely engage with the carers and make sense of their worlds and experiences (Smith, Flowers, and Larkin,2009).

The three theoretical pillars underpinning Interpretive Phenomenological Analysis of heremeneutics, idiography, and phenomenology were employed (Smith and Osborn, 2003).

Hermeneutics is described as the "art and science of interpretation or meaning" (Tuffour, 2017, p. 3). The researchers used direct quotations from the conversations emerging from the informal carers. The fact that the San Lawrenz Dementia Friendly Community Pilot Project had not been evaluated prior to this research allowed the researchers to scrutinise the project in-depth and bring it to the fore through these same conversations. Through the double hermeneutic process (Smith, Flowers and Larkin, 2009), the informal carers made sense of their personal and social surroundings, and simultaneously, the researchers analysed this feedback (Smith, 2004). The researchers understood the importance of obtaining accurate results by accurately communicating accurately the informal carers' viewpoints (Finlay, 2011).

Idiography sought to provide a detailed and in-depth examination of how the informal caregivers in their unique setting made sense of the San Lawrenz Dementia Friendly Community Pilot Project. This was sought through an in-depth analysis of the participants' narratives, and their thoughts, beliefs, and attitudes about the pilot project. Each of the informal carers' emerging conversations was analysed thoroughly prior to moving to the next participant.

Phenomenology implied that the researchers sought to understand the meanings from the verbatim conversations with the respective carer participants by delving into the consciousness of each participant and retrieving their "inner life worlds" (Noon, 2018, p. 75). Phenomenology also involved bracketing the informal carers' knowledge and past experiences (Tuffor, 2017). Descriptive accounts from the experiential experiences of the informal carers, considered the experts, were therefore essential (Smith, Flowers and Larkin, 2009; Horrigan-Kelly, Millar and Dowling, 2016). The interpretations of the interviewees' experiences depended on their capability to express their realities in-depth and the researchers' abilities to dissect the collected data and understand its meaning by getting as close as possible to the participants' views and immersing themselves in their worlds (Larkin, Watts and Clifton, 2006; Noon, 2018).

Detailed information gathered through telephone interviews with 6 informal carers of older persons living with dementia within the community of San Lawrenz, Gozo, revealed their perspectives on the Dementia Friendly Community Pilot Project. Two observational tours of the village of San Lawrenz took place, one before the actual project to gauge a better understanding of the adaptations to the physical environment and a second visit to compare, contrast, and confirm the informal carers' experiences. Photos provided a graphical backdrop to the project.

Ethical clearance was sought and approved through the University of Malta's Faculty of Social Wellbeing's Research and Ethics Committee, ID number 3769 05.12.2019. The mayor of San Lawrenz acted as the gatekeeper as his invaluable knowledge and connection to the villagers were key to gaining access (Andoh-Arthur, 2019).

Information letters were distributed by the gatekeeper to all the informal carers of diagnosed older persons living with dementia, residents of San Lawrenz. All the informal carers were considered eligible based on their awareness of the adaptations around the village, even if they were not knowledgeable that these were carried out as part of the San Lawrenz Dementia Friendly Pilot Project. Interested parties were invited to contact the primary researcher through the provided contact numbers. The instrument was designed by the researchers and included questions on aspects of (1) physical accessibility, (2) the elimination of stigma, (3) raising awareness amongst the public about dementia, and (4) the involvement of community entities. The interview questions were provided in both the Maltese and English languages. Two interviews with informal carers were conducted and recorded as the pilot study. The rest of the interviews were conducted over the telephone due to the COVID-19 public health emergency declared in Malta on 1 April 2020 in accordance with the Public Health Act (Chapter 465 of the Laws of Malta). None of the informal carers took up the option of a virtual interview.

A purposive sample of six informal carers took part in the interviews. This non-probability sample fitted the small size of the population and the aim of the research (Crossman, 2020). Interpretive Phenomenological Analysis and purposive sampling worked hand-in-hand as the researchers' main aim was to scrutinise deeply the informal carers' experiences and phenomena under study (Smith, Flowers and Larkin, 2009). There were no specific right or wrong answers, and the detailed, rich, and compelling narratives were synonymous with the objectives of the research project; hence the small size (Noon, 2018). All the informal carer participants were female, akin to what Innes, Abela, and Scerri (2011) observed, that the majority of the informal caregivers in Malta are females.

The uneasiness created by the public health emergency rendered meeting up with the prospective participants impossible. Through mail post, all the participants consented to audio recording of the interviews. As Opdenakker (2006) had implied, telephone interviews still yielded a substantive amount of information. Notwithstanding, the researchers were attentive to non-verbal data such as hesitations, sighs, and intonations, emerging from the telephone interviews. All interviews were transcribed verbatim and subjected to thematic analysis (Figure 20.3).

In phase 1, the researchers became acquainted with the data corpus (data collection from all the collected data), initial codes were produced, and themes related to the research objectives were captured. The double hermeneutic process was applied during phase 2, where the researchers went through the transcripts a number of times for better acquaintance with the feedback from the informal carers taking care of older persons living with dementia within the Dementia Friendly Community of San Lawrenz. In phase 3, the researchers identified patterns which were expounded for interpretation and interpreted in relation to literature on older persons living with dementia, informal carers, dementia-friendly communities, San Lawrenz Dementia Friendly Community Pilot Project, and dementia care services. Phase 4 allowed the researchers to improve the themes and hence identify the themes and sub-themes.

Ethical requirements were ensured through (1) destroying all the data upon analysis and completion of the project, (2) respecting the informal carers' rights of autonomy, beneficence, and non-maleficence, and (3) providing a list of support services to the informal carers, including free of charge services on the Island of Gozo, at the end of the interviews.

Results

Prior to this project, the impact of the San Lawrenz Dementia Friendly Community Pilot Project had not been evaluated. The six informal carer participants provided a thorough narrative of their experiences caring for older persons living with dementia. The interviewees also provided a comprehensive outlook on how the San Lawrenz Dementia Friendly Community Pilot Project influenced the lives of their loved ones and themselves. It is important to clarify, at this early stage of the review, that five of the six informal carer participants were not aware of the local National Dementia Strategy and were also not aware of the Dementia Friendly Community Pilot Project within their same village. However, they were cognisant of the environmental modifications around the village.

354 Pauline Refalo and Maria Aurora Fenech

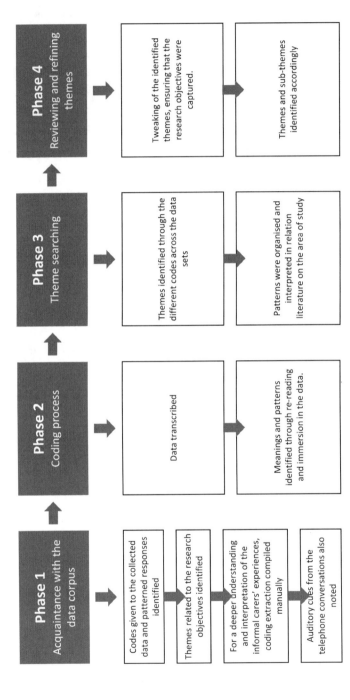

FIGURE 20.3 Thematic data analysis was employed (Braun and Clarke, 2006; Jeong and Othman, 2016; Smith, Flower and Larkin, 2009; Noon, 2018; Smith and Osborn, 2007).

Source: Authors

Table 20.2 provides a profile of the older persons living with dementia and informal carer participants. The informal carers' participant names are not their real names to protect their identities.

The impact from the COVID-19 pandemic was an emergent theme for all the interviewees, considering that the project was taking place in the midst of the pandemic. At the time, Malta and Gozo had registered their first cases, and mitigation measures had come into place. Interviews did not focus specifically on the pandemic; however, all the informal carers argued how the pandemic was adversely affecting their roles as well as those of the older persons living with dementia. An emotional carer had this to say on the matter,

> My brother is no longer visiting … since he's afraid of getting the COVID-19 and passing it on to my father. But the worst thing is my father's day is now empty … with nothing to do. And believe me, it has become a very serious problem … since it is affecting his behaviour. Sometimes I just want to cry because I don't know what to do with him. I mean we used to take him to Dar Padova (Dementia Activity Centre) regularly and he was very, very happy believe me … I mean he filled his day, it's like it improved his feelings … Because he felt useful at Dar Padova, engaging in activities like painting or tending the garden there. And then all of a sudden they closed it [Dar Padova] down. I know there's the pandemic, but can't they do something about it? Instead of just closing it down? Almost daily, he shouts, we shout at each other … he's going crazy and I'm going crazier … believe me.
> *(Petra)*

Three main themes were identified following the interviews with subsequent analysis of the informal carers' experiences, namely: (1) burden of care, (2) concern for the well-being of the older persons living with dementia, and (3) the impact and awareness of the dementia-friendly project and associated dementia-related services.

This review focuses entirely on the third emerging theme, that is, how the project impacted older persons and the informal carers, and whether the concept allowed for the integration of older persons living with dementia into their community, achieving their goals, and remain active in society.

The village of San Lawrenz, with a population of 772 persons (213 of these persons belong to the 65+ age category) (Regional Statistics Malta, 2021), made this a very positive and valuable feature for the informal carers. Participants agreed that the village's small population, geographic size, and lack of entertainment venues and amenities eased the burden of their caregiving role, as the risks for the older persons living with dementia associated with wandering and getting lost were diminished. The village community knew each other well and hence they all knew who the older persons living with dementia were. Nonetheless, none of the informal carer participants

TABLE 20.2 Profile characteristics of the older persons living with dementia and the informal carers (names are fictious)

Relation of Informal Carer to Older Person Living with Dementia	Older Persons Living with Dementia			Years as Informal Carer	Care Provision in 24-hours	Rotation of Care
	Age	Gender	Stage of Dementia			
Anne (sister-in-law)	86	F	Moderately Severe (Stage 6)	2	Alternate 24-hour care	Alternates care with the older person's sister
Martha (daughter)	80	F	Moderate (Stage 5)	2	12 hours	Help from Martha's brother
Ursola (sister)	85	F	Moderately Severe (Stage 6)	5	16	Help from Ursola's 2 older sisters
Janie (daughter)	80	F	Moderately Severe (Stage 6)	6	14 hours during the weekend; on weekdays daily after 3.30 pm	Help from Janie's brother and aunties
Petra (daughter)	85	M	Moderate (Stage 5)	5	18	Help through Skype from Petra's sister, residing in Australia
Klara (daughter)	83	F	Moderately Severe (Stage 6)	1	10	Help from Klara's brother

Source: Authors.

None of the informal carer participants were aware of the type of dementia the older person was living with, but were able to provide enough detail of the morbidity/co-morbidity of the older person living with dementia for the researchers to provide an approximate overview of the cognitive function of each of the older persons living with dementia on the Global Deterioration Scale, developed by Reisberg, et al. (1982). The Scale ranges from 1 to 7 with 7 being the most severe stage of dementia.

were comfortable with allowing the older persons living with dementia to go out unaccompanied, pointing to their moral obligations associated with protection, irrespective of the heavy burden associated with the care.

Public transport and accessibility through the village

None of the informal carers were keen for their loved ones to use the bus service, instead relying on personal means of transportation. They cited reasons associated with: (1) the lack of cognitive and physical capabilities of the older persons living with dementia to travel on their own; (2) buses not being dementia-friendly (steps to access the bus); (3) drivers being of foreign nationality and not able to converse in the Maltese language (and unless communication was affected, this older person cohort was conversant in the Maltese language only). Janie aptly captured this,

> I cannot imagine my mother using public transport alone ... I cannot even trust her alone in the streets, ... And then again the drivers are not Maltese speaking ... how can they help or talk with the older person? I would be truly insensitive if I let her use public transport alone.
>
> *(Janie)*

On the physical accessibility of the village, informal carers were quick to point out that the village Parish Church with its immediate vicinity as being a dementia-friendly refuge. The ramp adjacent to the Church made access easier for older persons, particularly for those using mobility aids. The priests' approaches were applauded by the informal carers, describing how the priests approached the older persons in their pews when giving Holy Communion. Informal carers were sure that had this not been the case, their loved ones would certainly not have managed to find their way back after receiving Communion. Janie recapped (Figure 20.4)

> The Church has always been friendly with the older persons. The ramp is very useful especially for persons like my mother, who is slow-moving. Also the priests know how to behave with the older persons ... they are very down to earth. They go straight to the person when giving Communion ... they approach the older persons themselves. The Church is the best place for my mother.
>
> *(Janie)*

Informal carers also referred to the road surfacing works around the village, which overall rendered accessibility easier. Ursola described how this was marred with objects randomly placed on pavements of some of the road walks, making it impossible for the older persons living with dementia to use (Figure 20.5).

FIGURE 20.4   The ramp leading up to the church of San Lawrenz. As can be observed, there is no pavement leading to the ramp, which is positive especially for persons with mobility issues. However, the gradient of the ramp stood at 15.5%. According to the Global Designing Cities Initiative (n.d.), pedestrian ramps should have a gradient of not more than 1:10 (10%) or ideally 1:12 (8%). The ramp leading to the Church was calculated as 1.4m:9m, leading to a gradient of 15.5%, affectively rendering the ramp to be steep.

Source: Authors

> The road works around the village did not always take into consideration the needs of the elderly or those who have problems walking like my sister ... I mean certain roadworks like the square for example are very friendly to walk onto because there are few obstacles ... but pavements, certain pavements around San Lawrenz are too high or for example have benches installed on them or are continuously interrupted by objects like garbage bags or flower pots. There are some roads which I purposely avoid when walking out with my sister because they are too dangerous because there are no pavements to walk on. We also avoid walking out at night ... large trucks for example or buses are especially dangerous because sometimes I think they won't even see you walking on the road ... let alone walking with someone like my sister.
>
> *(Ursola)*

Figures 20.6, 20.7, 20.8, 20.9, and 20.10, from the San Lawrenz Dementia Friendly Community Pilot Project, portray some of the project-related modifications within the village chore.

FIGURE 20.5   The Village Square with different shaded cobblestones, which potentially could have confused the older persons living with dementia when walking. There are no pavements, reducing the chances of falling incidents for older persons with mobility issues.

Source: Authors

FIGURE 20.6   Benches installed in the middle of the pavement, obstructing the sidewalk. Adequate height of the pavement which stood at 14 cm.

Source: Authors

FIGURE 20.7 Planters on the pavements.

Source: Authors

FIGURE 20.8 A discontinued pavement can be particularly dangerous considering the bend in this part of the road.

Source: Authors

FIGURE 20.9 A stone in the midst of the discontinued pavement. Vehicles are also parked against the wall, forcing pedestrians to walk straight on the road. Moreover, on the other side of the road, the pavement was discontinued through the installation of a ramp by a tenant with more planters on the other side of the pavement.

Source: Authors

The role played by San Lawrenz local entities

Informal carers praised the village's local entities, showing their appreciation for how the latter shared with the former the burden of caring for their loved ones. As indicated earlier, only one of the informal carer participants was at all mindful of the Dementia Friendly Community Pilot Project, with the other five carers not knowledgeable that the empathy, patience, and knowledge being shown by the village's core entities were due to the inception of the pilot project.

Informal carers particularly praised the untiring efforts of the village's Mayor, who was immersed and committed towards the older persons living with dementia. Informal participants described how the Mayor's empathic nature bred unity amongst the San Lawrenz community, reiterating how, together with the Parish Church, they brought the villagers and village entities on the same page. Together, they organised talks and invited the villagers

FIGURE 20.10 Another example from a part of the village where the pavement is non-existent. A temporary outer wall built in front of a construction site. Construction objects were placed against the outer side of the wall, serving as an obstruction for pedestrians walking on that side of the road.

Source: Authors

to capture the worlds of the older persons living with dementia. Informal carers also applauded the crucial roles played by the Church (as highlighted earlier) and the business community in giving the necessary attention and support to the carers and their relatives living with dementia. Six one-hour talks (1 presentation every 2 months), had taken place, providing general information regarding dementia and how carers could better support the older persons living with dementia. Klara, Janie, and Petra, gave succinct accounts of the roles played by the Local Council and the village's business community.

> My mother doesn't go out alone anymore…we need to be with her all the time … but luckily she can attend activities organized by the Local Council and the church. We initially were reluctant to take her to these activities, but then the Local Council assured us that they have the knowledge to be able to take care of her, so I won't have to go. It's a relief

really ... I now know what they are doing ... the Local Council is very, very, very dementia friendly and is of great help to us. The Local Council is on its own. The church and the Local Council ... I for one rely a lot on them.

(Klara)

We have only one grocery here in town ... until a few months ago, my mother was still doing the shopping herself ... and when she started forgetting and not able to find the things she wanted ... the shop owners were always available to help her. They showed patience ... I was grateful to them, believe me. Because patience is what you need with people like my mother. You need to be able to know how to interact with them.

(Janie)

I've always seen the shop owners at the talks. They show interest and engage in conversations surrounding this issue. Although my father doesn't do any shopping, I frequently engage in conversations with them about dementia. And I know that they know how to understand that a person has dementia. I appreciate that a lot because they show compassion and show interest.

(Petra)

Informal carers' awareness of the San Lawrenz Dementia Friendly Community Pilot Project and dementia-related services

The project's small sample size was hardly a representation of San Lawrenz's population. However, the participants' replies were a true indication that anyone who could have gained from the project was unaware of or not knowledgeable about it.

Anne and Marta were aware that the recent installation of signs, as well as the regular invites from the Local Council to talks on dementia and dementia-related matters were vaguely related to *some* initiative but were in the dark that the project was being implemented as part of the Maltese National Dementia Strategy. Meanwhile, some others associated the initiatives with the Government partnering with the village's care home with the scope of offering respite beds to their loved ones in order for them to take a deserved break.

I don't know what this project is ... I never heard of "dementia-friendly". I have attended meetings but the meetings, did not make much of a difference.

(Anne)

I heard the term "dementia-friendly" being spoken at the grocery but I never knew or asked what it refers to. Maybe the home for the elderly? ... now that you tell me what it is, yes I noticed signs around the village, especially around the town's square and I have attended some meetings as well about dementia ... but I don't know anything more than that.

(Marta)

As indicated earlier, through observational visits, the researchers looked at the signage within the village core. The installed signs have black font and yellow background and include pictures for the intended destination. In both Figures 20.11 and 20.12, the pole height distance from the pavement to the sign exceeds the 1.85 m mark. Arguably, the signage, which is placed quite high up, has small print, raising doubts as to the sensitivity towards the dementia-friendly concept. Moreover, it is not known whether an Occupational Therapist and/or a Physiotherapist were at all involved in the planning of the San Lawrenz Dementia Friendly Community Pilot Project (Refalo and Fenech, 2021), considering the noticeable environmental barriers (Figures 20.13 and 20.14).

Probing further on how the newly installed signage impacted the older persons living with dementia, Marta and Ursola expressed mixed notions on its effectiveness, praising the initiative while at the same time doubting how it would positively impact the older persons living with dementia,

"In my opinion, they did a good job by installing the signs so as to help older persons living with dementia to not get lost; but at the same time, they need to be able to notice the signs and read them."

(Marta)

They've installed a lot of signs on the streets. It's not that I don't agree with these signs because yes, it is a positive thing for the elderly, but not for who is mentally challenged. Tell me ... how can you read the sign if you are mentally impaired? In my opinion these signs will help the elderly but not the older persons living with dementia. And after all some of them are too high ... if you're walking on the other side of the road you would notice them but if you're walking on the same side of the road where the sign is located, I doubt if you'll be able to notice it because it is too high. Let alone for a person with dementia.

(Ursola)

Informal carers' feedback was particularly concerning in that they generally associated the project with talks and signage, revealing how limited their awareness of the San Lawrenz Dementia Friendly Community Pilot Project actually was.

FIGURE 20.11   Signage leading to the church of San Lawrenz. Signage is about 1.85 m from the pavement. The yellow colour of the sign blends with the stone colour of the houses in the background, possibly posing a challenge for older persons living with dementia to notice the sign. Signs should stand on their own on poles without other objects such as, in this case, mirrors. Mirrors can cause confusion to older persons living with dementia (Conners et al., 2014; Breen et al., 2001; Bartolotti et al., 2012). The planters on the pavement are obstructive to older persons living with dementia who might have mobility issues as well as visuospatial or depth perceptual issues.

Source: Authors

Recommendations and conclusion

The accounts of the informal carer participants in this project have been the first voices to offer an insight into how this pilot project has impacted on the lives of their loved ones living with dementia, as well as themselves as the informal carers. To date, the environmental modifications that took place in the village to bring it abreast with the direction of the Dementia Friendly Community Pilot Project remain as on the day of inception.

Data analysis revealed that the majority of the participants were not aware of the project, criticising the environmental barriers within the village. It is safe to assume that the pilot project had not at all influenced the ways in which the informal carer participants took care of the older persons living with dementia; nor had the Dementia Friendly Community Pilot Project in any way impacted the older persons' mobility outside their home environments. Informal carer participants were noticeably very protective of the older persons living with dementia, with carers revealing during the interviews that should they have been aware of the Dementia Friendly Community Pilot Project, they would have been ill at ease to "allow" the older persons living with dementia to roam around the village freely.

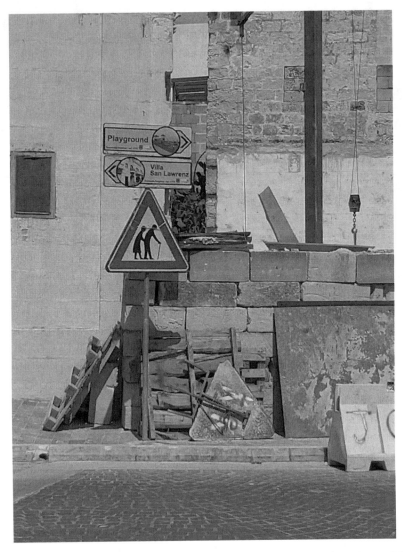

FIGURE 20.12 Signage with opposing directions to two separate locations within the village of San Lawrenz. The obstructive material on the pavement together with the building machinery, which the researchers noted at the time of the study.

Source: Authors

Considering the dearth of literature on dementia-friendly communities, both locally and internationally, it was not possible to compare and contrast the findings from this study. The COVID-19 pandemic had not influenced the informal carers' perception of the San Lawrenz Dementia Friendly Community Pilot Project, as the project had already been running for two

FIGURE 20.13 Sign at the entry of the village. The sign is too small to be noticed instantly, personifying the lack of awareness of the project amongst its own residents. A close-up image is provided in Figure 20.14.

Source: Authors

FIGURE 20.14 Close up of the entry sign to the village.

Source: Authors

years prior to the onset of the pandemic. Notwithstanding the informal carers' lack of awareness about the project, they were still keen to put forward recommendations, once through this research they were learning first-hand about the Dementia Friendly Community Pilot Project. This section will describe recommendations put forward by the informal carer participants;

the researchers will also include some other recommendations, which they believed would be beneficial in ascertaining the necessity of the San Lawrenz Dementia Friendly Community Pilot Project.

Intergenerational communication was particularly considered an asset in such initiatives, with the informal carers emphasising the importance that the community and families at large should have been engaged, and not merely the policymakers, Local Council, and the business community. They reiterated the importance of responsibilising one and all and not merely those parties with whom the policymakers were most comfortable. Moreover, they believed that as the primary stakeholders, both the older persons living with dementia (who retained the ability to voice their thoughts and opinions) and the informal carers should have been involved from the initial stages of this project. They believed that their experiences would have been insightful and crucial during the planning of such a project.

Activities that put social inclusion of older persons living with dementia at the centre were also considered paradigm by the informal carers, where they, together with the older persons living with dementia, would come together to socialise. This would bring together the major stakeholders and offer them the opportunity to share experiences and learn from each other. As the project also revealed how the informal carers were very much unaware of the services they could avail themselves of to assist them in caring for the older persons living with dementia, such an interaction is deemed beneficial. It is therefore imperative for informal carers who provide round-the-clock care for older persons living with dementia, that they are aware of the services they could avail themselves of, as this certainly would set the foundation for the success of this novel project. This project laid bare the reality that the informal carers, as indicated earlier, were largely unaware and not knowledgeable about the dementia care services they could avail themselves of.

The Local Council was adamant to make the project work but complained that following the inception of the project, they were largely left to fend for themselves, in that the challenges still present within the village, a case in point being cars and trucks speeding through the village square, were largely not addressed. Older persons living with dementia, as well as their informal carers, remained largely restricted within the confines of their homes, with some of the informal carers venturing out occasionally to attend dementia-related talks organised by the Local Council.

Informal carers expressed concern about the town's accessibility for older persons living with dementia, pointing to the narrow pavements and the installed signage, which were too high to be noticed. Such feedback conflicts directly with the objective of the Dementia Friendly Community Pilot Project, as its main objective was to facilitate the lives of older persons living with dementia. The authors suggest that 2 years down the line, the infrastructural works around the village should be revisited, where the authorities could possibly consider tapping into EU funds and issuing calls specifically for project proposals aimed at financing works. No specific priority axes under the current 2014–2020 structural funds, where projects about dementia would fit, were identified. Perhaps the closest one would be Priority Axis 2 of the 2014–2020 EU Operational Programme II (European Social Funds), which provides funding for projects aimed at promoting social inclusion amongst vulnerable groups, considering that older persons living with dementia are indeed vulnerable persons (Government of Malta, 2014). Nonetheless, this priority axis was aimed at improving employability amongst vulnerable groups, and therefore it was unclear whether projects about dementia would be approved under this priority axis. Therefore, it was paramount for the authorities to consider a priority axis in the operational programmes of the new funding period 2021–2027 aimed specifically at tackling dementia. Appropriate advice from Occupational Therapists and Physiotherapists, who have the right expertise and are better equipped to provide the right guidance in the design of such a project, would be crucial, as was another major suggestion put forward by the researchers.

It would also be appropriate for policymakers to explore alternative ideas to Dementia Friendly Communities, namely the idea of developing Age Friendly Communities instead. The researchers are proposing that both Age-Friendly Communities and Dementia-Friendly Communities could be placed on the same spectrum as they aim for the implementation of solutions that provide a positive difference in the lives of persons in need of assistance, namely older persons, even though the targeted vulnerable groups vary from one concept to the other (World Health Organization (WHO), n.d.; Blood, 2017; Buckner, et al., 2018; Turner and Cannon, 2018). While the dementia-friendly community concept is specifically aimed at older persons living with dementia and their informal caregivers, the World Health Organisation has actively pushed for the implementation of age-friendly policies in places around the world to facilitate the reintegration of older persons within communities. The World Health Organisation defined an Age-Friendly Community as a place that catered for and provided the necessary support to older persons to facilitate their inclusion in society and to stay healthy and active, with the result being the improvement of the quality of lives of older persons, irrespective of their health condition (World Health Organisation, n.d.). In fact, Turner and Morken, in 2016, outlined how the two concepts could be incorporated with one another. They identified eight domains that were related to the Age-Friendly Communities and ten sectors that fell under Dementia-Friendly Communities as follows:

(1) World Health Organisation Age-Friendly Domains that included, (a) outdoor spaces, (b) transportation, (c) housing, (d) social participation, (e) respect and social inclusion, (f) civic participation and employment,

(g) communication and information, and (h) community and health services.
(2) Dementia-friendly sectors that included (a) transportation, housing, and public spaces, (b) businesses, (c) legal and advance planning services, (d) banks and financial services, (e) neighbours and community members, (f) independent living, (g) communities of faith, (h) care throughout the continuum, (i) memory loss supports and services, and (j) emergency planning and first response.

The authors also called for the simultaneous development of the identified domains and sectors to save time and resources in the case of communities that were yet to start working to become a Dementia-Friendly Community or Age-Friendly Community. The report asserted that dementia-friendliness initiatives were mostly specifically focused on education, awareness, and elimination of stigma, whereas age-friendliness initiatives were mostly broadly designed to cater to the whole older person population. Thus, in the case of communities that were already Dementia-Friendly Communities, such as San Lawrenz, Turner and Morken (2016) suggested that these communities simply widen their work to pursue the 8 age-friendly domains, whereas already-established Age-Friendly Communities could utilise their resources and, if possible, partner with local NGOs to start targeting the elements that effectively render a community dementia-friendly concept.

In conclusion, it is unquestionable that this project, potentially coupled with Age-Friendly Communities, is of essence within our communities. Whilst the data emerging from the project did not offer an optimistic view of the project *per se*, the researchers believe that, notwithstanding, this would be a beacon towards improving and building on the existing Dementia Friendly Community Pilot Project, whilst engaging older persons living with dementia and informal carers as active team players in planning and decision making. Such projects cannot be incepted on the spur of the moment or because of the feel-good factor but rather require continuous planning, monitoring, and support of the services in place, together with crucial and focal input from older persons living with dementia. the informal carers, and the community at large.

References

Alase, A. (2017). The interpretative phenomenological analysis (IPA): A guide to a good qualitative research approach. *International Journal of Education & Literacy Studies*, 5(2), 9–19.

Alzheimer Europe. (2019). *Dementia in Europe yearbook 2019: Estimating the prevalence of Dementia in Europe*. Luxembourg: Alzheimer Europe.

Andoh-Arthur, J. (2019). Gatekeepers in qualitative research. In P. Atkinson, S. Delamont, A. Cernat, J. W. Sakshaug, & R. A. Williams (Eds.), *SAGE research methods foundations*. Thousand Oaks: Sage Publications Ltd.

Banarjee, S. (2022). So much done, so much to do, so much to gain by doing so. *Age and Ageing, 51,* 1–7.

Bortolotti, L., Cox, R., & Barnier, A. (2012). Can we recreate delusions in the laboratory? *Philosophical Psychology, 25*(1), 109–131.

Blood, I. (2017). *Technical report: Evidence review of dementia friendly communities*. European Union Joint Action on Dementia. Retrieved from https://c730156e-3528-4915-b393-4687f3ebead6.filesusr.com/ugd/775f77_d46a5d4647764177a5f90bb7c21c6428.pdf

Braun, V., & Clarke, V. (2006). Using thematic analysis in psychology. *Qualitative Research in Psychology, 3*(2). 77–101.

Breen, N., Caine, D., & Coltheart, M. (2001). Mirrored-self misidentification: Two cases of focal onset dementia. *Neurocase, 7*(3), 239–254.

Buckner, S., Mattocks, C., Rimmer, M., & Lafortune, L. (2018). An evaluation tool for age-friendly and dementia-friendly communities. *Working with Older People, 22*(1), 48–58

Chung, P., Ellis-Hill, C., & Coleman, P. (2017). Supporting activity engagement by family caregivers at home: maintenance of agency and personhood in dementia. *International Journal of Qualitative Studies on Health and Well-being, 12*(1), 1–14.

Connors, M. H., Barnier, A. J., Langdon, R., Cox, R. E., Polito, V., & Coltheart, M. (2014). Delusions in the hypnosis laboratory: Modelling different pathways to mirrored-self misidentification. *Psychology of Consciousness: Theory, Research, and Practice, 1*(2), 184–198.

Crampton, J., Dean, J., & Eley, R. (2012). *Creating a Dementia-friendly york*. Cambridge: Joseph Rowntree Foundation.

Crossman, A. (2020). Understanding purposive sampling: An overview of the method and its implications. Retrieved on May 18, 2020 from https://www.thoughtco.com/purposive-sampling-3026727

Denzin, N. K., & Lincoln, Y. S. (2017). The discipline and practice of qualitative research. In N. K. Denzin & Y. S. Lincoln (Eds.), *The SAGE handbook of qualitative research* (5th ed., pp. 1–26, 44). Texas: SAGE Publications, Inc.

Eatough, V., & Smith, J. (2006). I was like a wild wild person: Understanding feelings of anger using interpretive phenomenological analysis. *British Journal of Psychology, 97*(4), 483–498.

Finlay, L. (2011). *Phenomenology for psychotherapists: Researching the lived world*. West Sussex, UK: Wiley-Blackwell.

Flick, U. (2018). *An introduction to qualitative research* (6th ed.). London: SAGE Publications.

Global Designing Cities Initiative. (n.d.). *Universal accessibility*. Retrieved from https://globaldesigningcities.org/publication/global-street-design-guide/designing-streets-people/designing-for-pedestrians/universal-accessibility/

Government of Malta. (2014). *Operational programme under the 'Investment for Growth and Jobs' goal*. Retrieved from https://eufunds.gov.mt/en/Operational%20Programmes/Programming%20Period%202014%20-%202020/Operational%20Programme%202/Documents/OPII_Rev_Programme_2014MT05SFOP001_2_0_en%20(3).pdf

Greenwood, N., & Smith, R. (2019). Motivations for being informal caregivers of people living with dementia: A systematic review of qualitative literature. *BMC Geriatrics, 19*(169), 1–18.

Horrigan-Kelly, M., Millar, M., & Dowling, M. (2016). Understanding the key tenets of Heidegger's philosophy for interpretive phenomenological research. *International Journal of Qualitative Methods, 15*(1), 1–8.

Innes, A., Abela, S., & Scerri, C. (2011). The organization of dementia care by families in Malta: The experiences of family caregivers. *Dementia 10*(2), 165–184.

Jeong, H., & Othman, J. (2016). Using interpretative phenomenological analysis from a realist perspective. *The Qualitative Reports, 21*(3), 558–570.

Kitwood, T. M. (1997). *Dementia reconsidered: The person comes first*. Maidenhead and New York: Open University Press.

Larkin, M., Watts, S., & Clifton, E. (2006). Giving voice and making sense in interpretative phenomenological analysis. *Qualitative Research in Psychology, 3*(2), 102–120.

Lin, S. Y. (2017). Dementia-friendly communities and being dementia friendly in healthcare settings. *Current Opinion in Psychiatry, 30*(2), 145–150.

Merriam, S. (2009). *Qualitative research: A guide to design and implementation*. San Francisco, CA: Jossey-Bass.

Micallef, A. (2015, December 17). A dementia friendly village pilot project at San Lawrenz. *TVM News*. https://tvmnews.mt/en/news/a-dementia-friendly-village-pilot-project-at-san-lawrenz/

Milte, R., Shulver, W., Killington, M., Bradley, C., Ratcliffe, J., & Crotty, M. (2016). Quality in residential care from the perspective of people living with dementia: The importance of personhood. *Archives of Gerontology and Geriatrics, 63*, 9–17.

Mjorud, M., Engedal, K., Rosvik, J., & Kirkevold, M. (2017). Living with dementia in a nursing home, as described by persons with dementia: a phenomenological hermeneutic study. *BMC Health Services Research, 17*(93), 1–9.

Noon, E. J. (2018). Interpretive phenomenological analysis: An appropriate methodology for educational research? *Journal of Perspectives in Applied Academic Practice, 6*(1), 25–83.

Opdenakker, R. (2006). Advantages and disadvantages of four interview techniques in qualitative research. *Qualitative Social Research, 7*(4), Article 11. Retrieved from http://nbn-resolving.de/urn:nbn:de:0114-fqs0604118.

Pace, R., & Fenech, M. (2021). *The experience of friendship and social relations in older persons living in a residential care setting* [Dissertation]. Submitted to the University of Malta.

Parliamentary Secretariat for Rights of Persons with Disability and Active Ageing (PSRPDAA). (2015). *Empowering change: A national strategy for dementia in the Maltese Islands*. Retrieved from https://activeageing.gov.mt/en/Documents/book_english_book.pdf

Pedroza, P., Miller-Petrie, M., Chen, C., Chakrabarti, S., Chapin, A., Hay, S., Tsakalos, G., Wimo, A., & Dieleman, J. (2022). Global and regional spending on dementia care from 2000–2019 and expected future health spending scenarios from 2020–2050: An economic modelling exercise. *Clinical Medicine, 45*, 101337.

Quest, D. (2014). *Out of the way and out of place: An interpretive phenomenological analysis of the experiences of social interactions of bisexually attracted young people*. Portland, OR: Portland State University.

Refalo, P., & Fenech, M. (2021). *Towards advancing dementia friendly communities in the Maltese islands: The case of San Lawrenz dementia friendly pilot project* [Dissertation]. Submitted to the University of Malta. Retrieved from https://www.um.edu.mt/library/oar/handle/123456789/90119.

Regional Statistics Malta. (2021). Retrieved from https://nso.gov.mt/en/nso/Media/Salient-Points-of-Publications/Documents/2021/Regional 2021/Regional Statistics 2021_full publication.pdf

Reisberg, B., Ferris, S. H., de Leon, M. J., & Crook, T. (1982). The global deterioration scale for assessment of primary degenerative dementia. *American Journal of Psychiatry*, 139(9), 1136–1139.

Saliba, R., & Fenech, M. (2020). *Older person's relocation to a residential care setting: Reasons and decision-making processes* [Dissertation]. Submitted to the University of Malta.

Scerri, A., & Scerri, C. (2012). Dementia in Malta: New prevalence estimates and projected trends. *Malta Medical Journal*, 24(3), 21–24.

Smith, J. A. (2004). Reflecting on the Development of Interpretative Phenomenological Analysis and Its Contribution to Qualitative Research in Psychology. *Qualitative Research in Psychology*, 1, 39–54.

Smith, J. A., Flowers, P., & Larkin, M. (2009). *Interpretative phenomenological analysis: Theory, method and research* (1st ed.). London: Sage Publication.

Smith, J. A., & Osborn, M. (2003). Interpretative phenomenological analysis. In J. A. Smith (Ed.), *Qualitative psychology: A practical guide to research methods* (pp. 51–80). London: Sage Publications, Inc.

Smith, J. A., & Osborn, M. (2007). Pain as an assault on the self: An interpretative phenomenological analysis of the psychological impact of chronic back pain. *Psychology and Health*, 22(5), 517–534.

Tomkins, L. (2017). Using interpretative phenomenological psychology in organisational research with working caregivers. In J. Brook & N. King (Ed.), *Applied qualitative research in psychology* (pp. 86–100). London: Palgrave.

Topo, P., Kotilainen, H., & Eloniemi-Sulkava, U. (2012). Affordances of the care environment for people with dementia—An assessment study. *Health Environments Research & Design Journal*, 5(4), 118–138.

Tuffour, I. (2017). A critical overview of interpretative phenomenological analysis: A contemporary qualitative research approach. *Journal of Healthcare Communications*, 2(52). Retrieved from https://healthcare-communications.imedpub.com/a-critical-overview-of-interpretative-phenomenological-analysis-a-contemporary-qualitative-research-approach.php?aid=20787

Turner, N., & Cannon, S. (2018). Aligning age-friendly and dementia-friendly communities in the UK. *Working with Older People*, 22(1), 9–19.

Turner, N., and Morken, L. (2016). Better together: A comparative analysis of age-friendly and dementia-friendly communities.Washington: AARP International Affairs.

Williamson, T. (2016). *Mapping dementia-friendly communities across Europe*. Brussels: European Foundations' Initiative on Dementia.

World Health Organization. (n.d.). *Age-friendly cities and communities*. Retrieved from https://www.who.int/activities/creating-age-friendly-cities-and-communities

Zwaanswijk, M., Peeters, J. M., van Beek, A. P. A., Meerveld, J. H. C. M., & Francke, A. L. (2013). Informal caregivers of people with dementia: Problems, needs and support in the initial stage and in subsequent stages of dementia: A questionnaire survey. *The Open Nursing Journal*, 7, 6–13.

21
EPILOGUE ON CARE OF OLDER PERSONS
What the future holds

Mala Kapur Shankardass

Caring for older persons is a complex and multifaceted task that requires attention to their physical, mental, social, and financial well-being. The issue of care for older persons becomes even more critical as in the next three decades or so, the share of the global population over 60 will double from 1 billion to 2.1 billion, and that of those over 80s will triple to a remarkable figure of 426 million, according to recent WHO projections. With such drastic increases in the ageing population, with a share from almost all countries, the global concern for some innovative, sustainable, and cost-effective ways to take care of older persons is growing and needs to be urgently addressed. Many countries are experiencing a care crisis with rapidly increasing and expanding care needs of the ageing populations, notwithstanding the demands being made by demographic, socio-economic, and epidemiological transitions happening around the world. These transitions are having various kinds of impacts, some requiring prompt and immediate attention to address them. Though some concerns and responses reflect resilience and empowered dealings by older persons in taking care of themselves and a variety of practices providing favourable care are in place across the globe, our thinking on this front should evolve with reviews, analysing what works, what can be improved, what is going wrong, and what new measures are required to improve the quality of life of older persons. Thus, the question of how older people can be better cared for is pertinent in most countries. What kind of strategies and programmes are needed to support self-care and long-term care, and to bring in system responses from families, communities, or from the government to manage diverse situations related to their well-being, is becoming part of planning by both the public and private sector as well as by the wider international community. Developing a

DOI: 10.4324/9781003528432-24

care economy with adequate investments, provisions for appropriate healthcare services and training of care workers, protection of the rights of the carers and caregivers, along with an emphasis on quality-of-life issues, are all crucial aspects confronting ageing societies. Some aspects of these concerns have been dealt with in this book through various chapters that bring in perspectives from various experts and discussing some critical issues in different countries as well as highlighting practices in place for dealing with certain issues. However, more thought needs to go into developing different mechanisms for care by having multiple perspectives and sound approaches from different disciplinary backgrounds, which can be feasible for the heterogeneous ageing population nationwide and globally. As such, there is no end to thinking about what is appropriate care for older persons since technological developments, the expansion of knowledge, emerging needs, changes in relationships at different levels, available resources with families, communities, institutions, and society at large keep changing and shape up responses. For those working in this field and affected by these societal processes, care for older persons is clearly a dynamic concept, and its characteristics can't be captured and frozen. It must keep evolving, and we need to keep focusing on this. This book provides or rather touches on some aspects of the dynamic context of the care of older persons, which is reflected upon through 'met needs' and those 'unmet'. The former is a blessing and the latter a subject matter of developing gerontology by roping in views of cross-section stakeholders.

Researchers point out that there are many unmet needs for the care and support of older persons, which can be addressed through age-friendly policies, enabling environments, and changes in lifestyles. These individually and collectively can contribute towards reducing the burden of age care on societies. Raising awareness on age-related health and social issues, along with preparedness for later years, can facilitate the improvement of care mechanisms at the family and community levels. This is especially pertinent for older people living in low- and middle-income countries where illiteracy levels of the population are high and who are progressing towards ageing at a faster and shorter pace than higher-income nations. Demographic projections indicate that by 2050, these countries would comprise about 80 percent of the total world's population of older people. In addition, these countries, as per statistics reported in 2023, already have over 60 percent of those living with dementia globally. Dementia, which includes Alzheimer's disease, is the most dreaded health issue affecting older people, particularly as people live longer, having irreversible and progressive loss of memory and cognitive function. According to certain epidemiological estimates, 10 million additional cases of dementia are added each year, and this needs a strong plan to combat the problem since caring for dementia patients has serious consequences for families and society.

Old age also brings in various age-related ailments to deal with, for which many societies are gearing up as they come to terms with the ageing of their population. Though analysis and review of measures being taken indicate certain deficiencies in overall preparedness for countries in general. Of specific concern are issues related to providing long-term care, especially in managing chronic health problems, having a preventive care approach, facilities for end-of-life care, and dealing with crises/disasters. Besides, when the focus is paid to various dimensions related to the care of older persons, economic issues are also seen to play a role in the overall management of different aspects. The cost of care at individual, family, and national levels plays an important role in the way care is provided and used. Further, it is also observed that gender considerations and the availability of certain care benefits mould the way the care of older persons is structured, planned, and utilized. As the world is ageing, response to the care of older persons requires a different approach, taking into account many heterogeneous characteristics, such as people living longer with certain morbidities and disabilities, with differential economic status, in different residential areas, with families or spouses, or alone and if living in a community or in an institutional setup, etc.

Clearly, the future of caring for older persons presents both challenges and opportunities. Addressing the challenges in caring for older persons requires a holistic approach that can reduce inequalities in social, economic, health, environmental, and development issues which can then promote autonomy, community support, and quality social and health care. This is an important ingredient for promoting an ageing future where all parts of it can live a life of dignity and well-being. It is also an opportunity for the care economy to develop and for silver market products, processes, and needs of older persons to become a national and global agenda. Hopefully, the next few decades will focus on all these aspects.

INDEX

abuse 7, 14, 19, 28, 60, 129; forms 26
active ageing 96
adult daycare 3
advance care planning 22, 23
Africa 3, 111
age friendly 130
ageing population 3, 62, 67, 111, 130, 140, 141, 157, 173, 218, 265, 280, 299, 300, 325, 347, 374
ageing-in-place 12
ageism 29
age/senior care 3, 161; economic, legal, medical, social 170, 280
Asia Pacific 3, 6
assisted care 3, 160, 163, 167, 169, 219; technologies 7, 10
Australia 66, 299; demographics 300; Indigenous cultural backgrounds 317
autonomy 17; patients 18

beneficence principles 18, 26
British Columbia 32

Canada 3, 32, 218
care facilities 28, 60, 327
care homes 206, 210, 211, 265
care issues 3, 374; access 28; acute care 187; arrangements 140; assessment 291; burden 49, 55, 60, 76, 182, 281; care giving 59, 74; challenges 93, 173, 180, 225–226, 253, 270, 310, 342; costs 35; definition 59; dignified 12, 273–274; emotional 7, 126; end of life 3, 22–24, 26, 44; geriatrics 7 (nursing 8; social workers 8); good care 124, 270, 272; health care 3, 21, 61, 75, 94, 95; high quality 17; home care 3, 7, 26, 62, 66, 68, 124, 161, 163, 183, 265, 309, 328; hospice care 3, 169; hospital care 3, 7, 11; integrated 10, 96, 219; medical aspects 3, 7; mental health care 11, 51; palliative 44, 169; person centered 14, 204, 290, 349–350; residential 11, 59, 60, 66, 68, 187; respite care 310; services 3, 66 (community 3, 26, 28, 166; family 3, 26, 165; institutional 3, 190); social care 3; unmet needs 375
care settings 27, 328
care standards 206, 291, 328
carers 7, 281, 303; care givers 7, 49, 64, 73, 161, 281; competencies 76–78; funding 9; paid 7, 9; role 75, 302–303; support 73, 313; training 7, 48, 49, 54, 73–75, 78
China 53, 67
clinical governance 103
cognitive decline 18, 19
community care/services 28, 60, 111, 124, 163, 176, 191, 265, 268, 270, 302, 310, 329
community psychology 114, 132

Index

COVID 19 pandemic 3, 6, 11, 19, 27–29, 202, 227
cultural diversity 27

day care centers 123, 271, 328
death & dying 22, 45
Decade of Healthy Ageing 202
decision making 18–20, 22
deinstitutionalization 12
delivery 6, 187, 195, 215; by government 14, 65, 187, 222–223, 227, 330; by private sector 14, 65, 222–223, 227, 330
dementia 3, 5, 6, 21, 22, 75, 280, 281, 299, 325, 337, 347; burden 286, 299, 306, 327; care giver training 283, 284, 306; care giving 299, 302, 342; carers support 307–308; cost 282, 286, 294, 304–305; demographics 286; diagnosis 281, 300–301, 315, 338, 340; friendly communities 314–315, 357, 368; global dementia observatory 289; health outcome measures 290; management 339; modifiable risks 293; patients with dementia 282, 342; practitioners training 285; quality care 289, 299, 314, 316; residential care 299; risk factors 337; spousal carers 303; stigma 284, 315; treatments 287, 288, 341
digital means 29
disability 157

England 201, 206, 208
ethical care 17, 39; challenges 22; dilemmas 19, 21, 24, 29; questions 26, 28, 273–274, 353
Europe 3, 140, 159
euthanasia 26

family support 26, 60, 62, 73, 74, 129, 161, 300, 312, 326
foreign domestic workers 19
formal care 74, 265, 266, 299, 309, 310
frailty 3, 7, 11, 99, 100

gender 3, 9, 51, 129, 158, 220, 230, 299, 304, 312
generational relationships 125–127, 162, 180, 300
Germany 201, 205, 207, 210
gerontological nursing 104

health care systems 203, 210–212, 314, 327, 342
health condition/status 157, 159, 218, 266, 300, 325, 376
health insurance 201, 207, 210
healthcare costs 35, 182, 281, 305, 349
healthcare manpower/ professionals 22, 23, 230; providers 24; foreign workers 233–234
health/medical financing/insurance 181, 182, 207, 208, 210, 230, 328
healthy ageing 95, 96, 104

India 46, 49, 63, 67, 98, 102, 337
informal care 9, 73, 124, 192, 267, 271, 299, 302, 332, 355, 363
informed Consent 19
institutional care 3, 60, 163; nursing care/homes 3, 26, 28, 101, 188, 190, 237, 329; residential 3, 61, 64, 219, 299, 311, 329; senior care/homes 7, 62, 160, 163, 209, 219, 224; facilities 7
interdependence 132
Interpretive Phenomenological Analysis 351
intrinsic capacity 97, 99

Japan 53, 62, 230
justice 19, 26

legislations 112, 125, 128, 159, 179–181, 203, 205–207, 220–222, 308
long-term care 3, 11, 95, 97, 98, 111, 112, 159, 160, 165, 187, 201, 207, 218, 230, 265–267

Malta 347
models of care 161, 209, 211, 327

neglect 26, 129
Netherlands 140, 141; care needs 143, 147; demographics 142; disabilities 146; health indicators 145; social health insurance 146
New Zealand 67
non-maleficence principle 18, 26
nurses 104; role 106

older adults/persons 3, 25, 28, 32, 45, 60, 70, 106, 125, 140, 209, 269, 326, 347; immgrants 36, 37; living alone 36; women 36

pain management 25
pain relief 26
patients 20; confidentiality 20; wellbeing 22
person centered care 201, 204
perspectives 3, 160, 327; administrative 3, 219–220, 244, 327, 349; Asian 44, 49; care givers 3 (moral responsibility 20); care receivers 3; equity 3, 19; ethical 3, 10, 17, 39, 41 (principles 17, 22; responsibility 21, 22); ideological 3; legal 3; medical 3, 209; nursing 3, 237; policy making 3, 12, 38, 54, 140, 209, 220–222, 238, 300, 368; practitioners 3; social justice 19, 32, 37, 38
physician-assisted death 26
Poland 157; senior care 161
policy frameworks/planning 6, 13, 14, 54, 115, 131, 140, 159, 177, 202, 212, 213, 220, 230, 235, 267, 293, 303, 327, 342, 368
preventive health 197, 294, 340
private pensions 33
professional care 64; standards 12, 24; work conditions 232
public health 3; approach 3, 207, 213, 215, 219, 220, 230, 349; system 35, 230, 327
public pensions 33, 182, 329

quality & safety 102, 316

rights 17, 27, 128, 292, 349

SEARO 99
senior's poverty 32, 128

sense of belonging 112–114; intersectoral inclusion 127, 128, 131, 134
services by NGOs/CSOs 330, 331; by educational institutions 331
Singapore 54, 173; center-based services 192; demographics 173–176; health care manpower 179; housing 183–186
skilled workforce 316
social assistance 33, 159, 160, 162, 166
social care 202, 203
social relationships 115
social work 160, 327
South Africa 112, 114, 129, 130, 265
South Korea 54
strategies 24, 94, 140, 159, 193, 215, 220, 315
successful ageing 39

technology 10, 29, 125, 287
Thailand 54
training 3, 22, 47, 49, 65, 74; models 83–89, 213–214, 231
Turkiye 325; demographics 325–326; health issues 326

United Nations Madrid International Plan of Action on Ageing 17, 62
United States of America 3, 17, 22, 23, 26

Vancouver 34
Voluntary welfare organizations 194
vulnerability 25

wellbeing 128
World Health Organization (WHO) 96, 104, 129, 280, 283

Printed in the United States
by Baker & Taylor Publisher Services